AN INTRODUCTION TO
POLITICAL THOUGHT

AN INTRODUCTION TO
Political Thought

Key Writings from the Major Political Thinkers

M. J. RENDELL

SIDGWICK & JACKSON
LONDON

First published in Great Britain in 1978
by Sidgwick and Jackson Ltd

Copyright © M. J. Rendell 1978

ISBN 0 283 98141 5

Set by Malvern Typesetting Services and
Printed in Great Britain by
Biddles Ltd of Guildford, Surrey
for Sidgwick and Jackson Limited
1 Tavistock Chambers, Bloomsbury Way
London WC1A 2SG

TO MY FAMILY

Acknowledgements

Acknowledgements and thanks for the use of the excerpts in this book are due to the following publishers and owners of copyright:

The Clarendon Press, Oxford, for extracts from *The Dialogues of Plato*, trans. B. Jowett, 4th ed., 1953; *The Republic of Plato*, trans. with introduction and notes by F. M. Cornford, 1941; Aristotle: *The Politics*, trans. B. Jowett, 1905; *The Institutes of Gaius*, ed. and trans. by F. de Zulueta, 1946; *The Institutes of Justinian*, ed. and trans. by J. B. Moyle, 5th ed., 1913; Francisco Suarez: *Tractatus de Legibus ac Deo Legislatore* (*On Laws and God the Lawgiver*), trans. G. Williams, A. Brown and J. Waldron, 1944; Richard Hooker: *Works*, 1890; Hugo Grotius: *On the Law of War and Peace*, trans. F. W. Kelsey, 1925; Samuel Pufendorf: *De Jure Naturae et Gentium* (*On the Law of Nature and Nations*), trans. C. H. and W. A. Oldfather, 1934; Benedict de Spinoza: *The Political Works*, ed. and trans. A. G. Wernham, 1958.

J. M. Dent & Sons Ltd, and E. P. Dutton & Co Inc, New York, for the following extracts from the Everyman's Library series: Thucydides: *The History of the Peloponnesian War*, trans. R. Crawley, 1910; Niccolo Machiavelli: *The Prince*, trans. W. K. Marriott, 1908; J. Milton: *Prose Writings*, 1958; Jean-Jacques Rousseau: *The Social Contract*, trans. G. D. H. Cole, 1913; Thomas Paine: *The Rights of Man*, 1915; J. S. Mill: *Utilitarianism, Liberty and Representative Government*, 1910.

Macmillan International Ltd, for extracts from Polybius: *Histories*, trans. E. S. Schuckburgh, 1889; Dante: *De Monarchia*, trans. F. C. Church, in R. W. Church: *Dante: An Essay*, 1878.

The Loeb Classical Library (Harvard University Press, William Heinemann) for extracts from Cicero: *De Officiis*, trans. W. Miller, 1913; Cicero: *De Republica* and *De Legibus*, trans. C. W. Keyes, 1928.

Harvard University Press, Cambridge, Mass., for extracts from James I: *Political Works*, ed. C. H. McIlwain, 1918.

G. Bell & Sons Ltd for extracts from Diogenes Laertius: *Lives of the Philosophers*, trans. C. D. Yonge, 1891; Marcus Aurelius: *Meditations*, trans. G. Long, 1891; Junius Brutus: *Vindiciae Contra Tyrannos*, trans. H. J. Laski, 1924; Montesquieu: *The Spirit of Laws*, trans. T. Nugent, rev. by J. V. Prichard, 1914.

Penguin Books Ltd for extracts from Seneca: *Letters from a Stoic*, trans. R. Campbell, Penguin Classics, 1969. Copyright © Robin Alexander Campbell, 1969.

The Shrine of Wisdom, Fintry, Surrey, for an extract from Dionysius the Areopagite: *Celestial Hierarchies*, 1965.

T. & T. Clark, Edinburgh, for extracts from Irenaeus: *Against Heresies*, in *The Ante-Nicene Christian Library*, Vol. IX, 1869; St Augustine: *The City of God*, trans. M. Dods, 1872.

Wm B. Eerdmans Publishing Co, Grand Rapids, Mich., for extracts from *A Select Library of Nicene and Post-Nicene Fathers*, Second series, Vol. XII, 1956.

Oxford University Press for extracts from *Documents of the Christian Church*, selected and edited by Henry Bettenson, published by Oxford University Press, 1967; Edmund Burke: *Reflections on the Revolution in France*, 1907.

Basil Blackwell, Oxford, for extracts from B. Pullan: *Sources for the History of Medieval Europe*, 1966; St Thomas Aquinas: *Selected Political Writings*, ed. A. P. d'Entreves, trans. J. G. Dawson, 1959; Jean Bodin: *Six Books of the Commonwealth*, trans. M. J. Tooley, 1955; Thomas Hobbes: *Leviathan*, ed. M. Oakeshott, 1946; Sir Robert Filmer: *Patriarcha*, ed. P. Laslett, 1949; John Locke: *Second Treatise of Civil Government*, ed. J. W. Gough, 1949; Jeremy Bentham: *A Fragment on Government* and *Introduction to the Principles of Morals and Legislation*, ed. W. Harrison, 1948.

Columbia University Press, New York, for extracts from *The Correspondence of Pope Gregory VII*, trans. E. Emerton, 1932; Marsilius of Padua: *Defensor Pacis*, trans. A. Gewirth, in A. Gewirth: *Marsilius of Padua*, Vol. II, 1956; Pierre Dubois: *The Recovery of the Holy Land*, trans. W. I. Brandt, 1956.

Routledge & Kegan Paul Ltd for extracts from E. Lewis: *Medieval Political Ideas*, 1954; James Harrington: *Oceana*, Morley's Universal Library, 1887.

Alfred A. Knopf, Inc, New York, for extracts from *Medieval Political Ideas* by Ewart Lewis. Published 1954 by Alfred A. Knopf, Inc. Reprinted by permission of the publisher.

Fortress Press, Philadelphia, for extracts from *The Works of Martin Luther*, 1930.

The Classics Club (Walter J. Black, Inc) for extracts from Francis Bacon: *Essays and New Atlantis*, ed. G. S. Haight, 1942.

Frank Cass & Co Ltd for an extract from *Leveller Manifestoes of the Puritan Revolution*, ed. D. M. Wolfe, published by Frank Cass & Co Ltd, London, 1967.

Macmillan Publishing Co Inc, New York, for extracts from *From Absolutism to Revolution, 1648-1848*, ed. H. H. Rowen, (©) Copyright, The Macmillan Company, 1968.

Longman Group Ltd for extracts from T. H. Green: *Lectures on the Principles of Political Obligation*, 1941.

Lawrence & Wishart Ltd for extracts from *Marx and Engels: Selected Works*, 1968.

Progress Publishers, Moscow, for extracts from V. I. Lenin: *The State and Revolution*.

University of Illinois Press, Urbana, for extracts from G. Gentile: *Genesis and Structure of Society*, trans. H. S. Harris, 1960.

George Allen & Unwin Ltd, for extracts from K. Marx: *Capital*, trans. S. Moore and E. Aveling, 13th ed., 1909.

Cambridge University Press for extracts from B. Mussolini: *The Doctrine of Fascism*, trans. M. Oakeshott in M. Oakeshott: *The Social and Political Doctrines of Contemporary Europe*, 1939.

Jonathan Cape Ltd and Harper & Row, New York, for extracts from *The Selected Writings of Alfred Rosenberg*, edited and introduced by R. Pois, 1970.

Hutchinson Publishing Group Ltd and Houghton Mifflin & Co, Boston, for extracts from A. Hitler: *Mein Kampf*, trans. R. Manheim, 1969.

Eyre & Spottiswoode Ltd, and Beacon Press, Boston, for extracts from J. Althusius: *The Politics*, trans. F. S. Carney, 1964. Copyright (©) 1964 by Frederick S. Carney. Reprinted by permission of Beacon Press.

Preface

Ideally, the study of political thought should concern itself primarily with the writings of the political philosophers themselves and only secondarily with the interpretations of commentators. Too often, however, the contact which the student has with the original writer is tenuous or even non-existent, since the ideas which are the subject of scrutiny are encountered only at second-hand after they have been analysed and paraphrased.

The aim of this book is to redress the balance by emphasizing the original texts and documents, thereby departing from the conventional practice of providing descriptive and analytical comment alone. To that end, the book contains a large number of extracts from the most important political texts ranging over the whole period of European thought, together with an explanatory and linking commentary.

Normally, there can be no perfect substitute for reading the great works of political philosophy in their entirety, but in some cases, for example where the original is tedious or repetitive, or where the political content forms a small proportion of the total output of a writer, the presentation of extracts is fully justified. Moreover, even when, for reasons of space, the extract can only be a relatively short illustration of a writer's political argument, a case for its inclusion can be made on the ground that even a brief acquaintance with an important theory is better than no acquaintance at all. One may hope that the reader's appetite will be so whetted by his first taste of, say, Plato's *Republic*, that he will be encouraged to consume the remainder of that masterpiece.

The commentary which precedes each set of extracts is designed to perform two essential functions. First, it attempts to set the political thinkers in their historical and theoretical contexts and to point out, where appropriate, the ideological links between them. Secondly, it tries to explain as plainly as possible, but I hope without over-simplifying, the essence of each theory and its contribution to the main currents of political thought.

In compiling this book I have kept in mind the needs of two groups of potential readers. One group comprises students in sixth forms, in colleges and in universities, who are pursuing a course in political thought and who require a book which is introductory in the important sense that it introduces them to the original works of the philosophers that they are studying. The second group at which this book is aimed, is composed of general readers who, while not academically engaged, are nevertheless interested in the intellectual antecedents of the concepts of political philosophy such as 'justice', 'rights', 'democracy', and so on, which are used so often without any real understanding. I hope that both of these groups will find in this book, if not 'truth' in the sense of the Platonic Forms, at least sufficient material for them to make rational evaluations about the current problems of political philosophy.

M. J. Rendell
Bournemouth

Contents

PART ONE

Greek and Roman Political Ideas

CHAPTER 1

The Greek City State

Western political theory, at least in its written form, began in the city state or *polis* of the ancient Greeks. Speculation about the nature of law and justice, the best type of government and political constitution, and, indeed, about almost every conceivable political subject was stimulated by the Greek political experience of life in the *polis*. In order, therefore, to understand the origins of political thought we must look closely at the Greek city, and, in particular, at Athens which, during its democratic period of the fifth and fourth centuries B.C., best exhibited the political ideals of most free men.

Development of the *Polis*

About two thousand years before Christ, the territory we now know as Greece was invaded and conquered by semi-nomadic tribesmen from the Balkans. These were the Ionian Greeks and they were followed some centuries later by further waves of invaders, the Achaeans and the Aeolians. The basic political unit of the settlers was the patriarchal clan (*genos*) whose members were all descendants of the same ancestor. Clans would combine into wider fraternities (*phratries*) which, in time, would tend to group together into tribes tied by the bond of a common religion. Such tribes would, in turn, become the members of a quite extensive subject population recognizing the authority of a single ruler, such as the king of Mycenae.

At the close of the twelfth century B.C. another invasion took place, this time by the barbarian Dorian Greeks. The result was the destruction of the brilliant Mycenaean civilization and the enslavement of the ruling Achaeans. The Greek dark ages began, during which period not only were the arts of civilization (including writing) lost, but political development was set back. The primitive clan system became once more predominant, except in the Ionian cities of the Aegean islands and the coast of Asia Minor which, being unaffected by the Dorian invasion, were able to continue the development of their political institutions.

However, even in mainland Greece, once the turmoil caused by the

Dorian invasion had passed, political evolution began again. Whereas in Mycenaean times the political unit had been the relatively large kingdom, the new development was towards small city states with each claiming complete independence. Geographically Greece lends itself naturally to the city state system. Its territory is split into small areas physically demarcated from each other by sea and mountains. The inhabitants of a valley separated from those of other valleys would naturally tend to develop their own separate political association. This tendency would be reinforced by the insecurity felt by people who had no strong central power able to protect them, and who would therefore make their own defensive arrangements. It would be true to say that by 800 B.C. the *polis* system had become established in Greece.

Development of Athenian Democracy

All the Greek cities originally seem to have been monarchies. The king's authority stemmed from his supposedly divine origin, although his power was limited by the existence of a council composed of the most powerful nobles. Monarchy was invariably succeeded by aristocracy, in most cases not from violent overthrow, but from a gradual transference of the royal functions by stages to the nobles. Very often, as at Athens, even when the government had become aristocratic a link with the monarchy was retained by electing annually a magistrate with the title of 'king' who had solely religious functions.

The Athenian aristocracy was governed by three magistrates called *archons* who were elected each year. Retired *archons* formed the Council of the *Areopagus* which was responsible for administration and for the supervision of the magistrates. A popular assembly (*ecclesia*) existed but its only significant function was to nominate the magistrates from among those aristocratically qualified.

Three factors during the seventh century eventually led to the ending of the Athenian aristocracy. First, many non-aristocratic citizens became wealthy through trade and industry and began to claim a share of political authority. Secondly, there was a growing discontent with the partial and arbitrary laws and judgements of the aristocracy. Thirdly, the economic gap between landowners and small peasants was widening, with the latter often falling into debt and enslavement. The result of these factors was to establish a potentially revolutionary situation in Athens by the latter part of the century. In other cities such situations had produced tyranny; in Athens this stage was postponed by giving first to Draco (621 B.C.) and then to Solon (594 B.C.) the responsibility for providing a new written code of laws to reduce the tension.

Solon's reforms to some extent laid the foundation for the future Athenian democracy. Among many measures which bettered the life of the Athenian peasants, he abolished imprisonment for debt and restored the land to those who had been forced to sell it to the great landowners. Among his constitutional reforms was his division of the citizens into four classes graduated according to income derived from land. The higher political and military offices were confined to the higher classes, whereas all citizens had the right to attend the assembly and to sit in the *heliaea*—the popular tribunal established to review the decisions of the magistrates. In addition, Solon was responsible for creating the *boule*—a council of four hundred members with the function of preparing the agenda for the *ecclesia*.

For a great part of the sixth century Athens was governed by the tyrant Pisistratus who, paradoxically, strengthened the foundation of the future democracy by his policy of land redistribution. The constitution of Athens was finally made democratic by Cleisthenes who by 500 B.C. had completed his work of constructing Athenian political institutions on a decimal basis.

Democratic Athens

By the middle of the fifth century the democratic constitutional structure of Athens, under the leadership of Pericles, had assumed its most developed form, which it was to retain until the independence of the Greek cities was destroyed by Macedonia. Athenian society was rigidly divided between slaves, resident foreigners and citizens, and it is therefore enlightening to look fairly closely at each of these groups.

Slaves

Although estimates of the number of Athenian slaves vary widely, it is likely that slaves formed almost half of the Athenian population of about 300,000. Since the reforms of Solon, no citizen could be enslaved, hence the most important source of slaves was the merchant who imported and sold non-Greek 'barbarians' for work in households, workshops and on the land. The number of slaves owned by an individual tended to be small since the absence of large-scale industry and agriculture made uneconomic the employment of large work forces.

Large numbers of slaves were owned by the *polis* itself; many would be employed, for example, as assistants to the magistrates. The greatest single group, however, was consigned to the silver mines at Laurium where working conditions were so wretched that the only slave revolt of the fifth century took place there. Elsewhere Athenian slaves seem to have been generally well treated, and even possessed certain legal rights. Manumission was possible, perhaps as a reward for some service, but the position of freed slaves always remained inferior to that of citizens.

The institution of slavery was, paradoxically, one of the main supports of Athenian democracy. Slaves allowed the citizen to take time off from his work to spend in public service, and state revenue from the silver mines provided the payment which made possible the participation of the poorer citizens in the Courts and in the assembly.

Resident Foreigners (Metics)

There were perhaps 50,000 metics living in Athens in the latter part of the fifth century. They were foreigners who had come to Athens from other cities, attracted by Athenian culture or commerce. Some were very wealthy, especially those engaged in banking and transport. Many were prominent in art and medicine and particularly in philosophy. Most of the sophists, for example, were born outside Athens. Metics were excluded from political rights and could not own land or houses, although they were allowed to participate in the ceremonies of the city. They were subject to a special war tax (from which citizens were exempt) and were eligible for military service, serving as armoured infantry (hoplites) and as sailors.

Citizens

The famed Athenian democracy was, of course, a democracy of the male adult citizens only, who, together with their women and children, constituted only about one third of the population. Citizenship was based on descent, so that admission to the citizen body was impossible for anyone not born of free Athenian parents.

The citizen's attitude to politics can be summed up as the identification of self with community. Aristotle in the Politics represented the views of most Athenian citizens when he wrote: 'Man who is unable or who has no need to live in society must be either a beast or a god.'

It was generally felt that participation in the political, cultural and religious affairs of the polis gave to man his essentially human characteristics. The material and moral 'good life', it was believed, could only be achieved with the help of the wider community. The modern concept of individual natural rights which cannot be legitimately infringed by the state was quite alien to the Greek attitude to citizenship.

Athenian political institutions reflected two fundamental political ideas: the supremacy of the will of the community and the equality of citizens, politically, legally and socially. Equality was expressed in the terms: isonomia, or equality before the law, and isegoria, equal right of speech. It was manifested not only in the political institutions but also in social customs; for example, the abolition of titles of nobility and family names generally.

The institution through which the popular will was expressed was the assembly or *ecclesia* which all qualified citizens were eligible to attend. Its functions were to vote on questions of policy and to make minor decrees. Major legislation was unlikely because most Athenians considered that since the time of Solon no more laws were necessary. The only record of a division in the *ecclesia* shows a total attendance of only 3,600, a very small proportion of the eligible citizens. It was because of the difficulty in securing a satisfactory attendance in the period at the end of the Peloponnesian war that payment was introduced for participation in the Assembly.

The *ecclesia* could not discuss any matter until it had been put on the agenda by the Council of Five Hundred or *boule*. This body functioned as a general purposes committee and sat daily to transact business between assemblies. The *boule* was divided on a tribal basis, into ten sub-committees, and each served for one tenth of the year. The councillors were chosen by lot from candidates elected from the *demes* (the local areas). Each day one councillor was chosen by lot to be president, a post which allowed him to be the official head of state for the day.

The administration of the city was performed by amateur boards of magistrates who were chosen, mainly by lot, from lists of selected candidates. Each magistrate after his year of service was subjected to a public scrutiny when any citizen with cause could charge him with misconduct. Magistrates who, because of the nature of their work, needed special qualifications were elected by the *ecclesia* on a show of hands. The most important group of these was the board of ten generals (*strategoi*) who, in practice, tended to exert great influence over the *ecclesia* and the other institutions. Unlike the other magistrates, the generals could be re-elected annually.

The popular courts (*heliaea*) were each composed of more than two hundred citizens over the age of thirty. Six thousand candidates were elected by the *demes* from those willing to serve. Each day the jurymen needed for the courts would be selected by lot from that number. The courts had the functions of trying cases, fixing penalties, examining magistrates after their yearly term, and deciding constitutional questions.

Apart from the fact that every citizen was theoretically able to participate in all these institutions, political equality depended in practice upon two devices: selection by lot and payment for attendance. Athenians, generally, considered the lot to be the only democratic method of selecting public servants. Elections were considered oligarchic since they meant that men with the advantages of wealth, connections and fluency in speech would be preferred to others, perhaps more worthy but without such advantages. Payment for the services of jurymen, councillors and magistrates prevented the exclusion of any citizen on the grounds of poverty, although the wage was too low to act as an important incentive to political participation.

Pericles (457-429 B.C.)

'Athens, though still in name a democracy, was in fact ruled by her greatest citizen,' wrote Thucydides of Pericles. This great democratic leader ruled Athens for nearly thirty years and for most of that time was consistently elected to the board of *strategoi*. His authority was based on nothing more than his standing as a military leader, his eloquence, and his dominating personality, but nevertheless under his guidance Athens reached its cultural and political apogee.

The classical statement of Athenian democratic ideals was composed by the historian Thucydides in the funeral oration which he attributed to Pericles (Extract 1). Although Pericles never delivered this exact speech, there is little doubt that he had heard Pericles utter similar sentiments in probably much the same language.

Plato (428-347 B.C.)

Plato, perhaps the most illustrious of all Athenians, was born of aristocratic parents and grew up during the years of the Peloponnesian war. As a young man he came under the influence of Socrates whom he revered as the wisest and most righteous of men.

His aristocratic background and upbringing, the poor showing of the Athenian democracy in the war against Sparta, and the trial and execution of Socrates in 399 B.C., all disposed him to a fierce dislike of democratic government. His anti-democratic views are most forcibly expressed in Book VIII of the *Republic* where with withering sarcasm he shows the consequences of extreme democracy (Extract 2). It seems very likely that this passage is meant, at least in part, to be a parody of the Periclean funeral oration.

FURTHER READING

Texts
Thucydides: *History of the Peloponnesian Wars*
Plato: *The Republic*

Commentaries
V. Ehrenburg: *The Greek State* (Methuen 1969)
G. Glotz: *The Greek City and its Institutions* (Routledge and Kegan Paul 1965)
H. Lloyd Jones (ed.): *The Greeks* (Watts 1962)
H. D. F. Kitto: *The Greeks* (Penguin 1957)
A. Zimmern: *The Greek Commonwealth* (Oxford 1961)

1 PERICLES: THE FUNERAL ORATION

Our constitution does not copy the laws of neighbouring states; we are rather a pattern to others than imitators ourselves. Its administration favours the many instead of the few; this is why it is called a democracy. It we look to the laws, they afford equal justice to all in their private differences; if no social standing, advancement in public life falls to reputation for capacity, class considerations not being allowed to interfere with merit; nor again does poverty bar the way, if a man is able to serve the state, he is not hindered by the obscurity of his condition. The freedom which we enjoy in our government extends also to our ordinary life. There, far from exercising a jealous surveillance over each other, we do not feel called upon to be angry with our neighbour for doing what he likes, or even to indulge in those injurious looks which cannot fail to be offensive, although they inflict no positive penalty. But all this ease in our private relations does not make us lawless as citizens. Against this fear is our chief safeguard, teaching us to obey the magistrates and the laws, particularly such as regard the protection of the injured, whether they are actually on the statute book, or belong to that code which, although unwritten, yet cannot be broken without acknowledged disgrace.

Further, we provide plenty of means for the mind to refresh itself from business. We celebrate games and sacrifices all the year round, and the elegance of our private establishments forms a daily source of pleasure and helps to banish the spleen; while the magnitude of our city draws the produce of the world into our harbour, so that to the Athenian the fruits of other countries are as familiar a luxury as those of his own.

If we turn to our military policy, there also we differ from our antagonists. We throw open our city to the world, and never by alien acts exclude foreigners from any opportunity of learning or observing, although the eyes of an enemy may occasionally profit by our liberality; trusting less in system and policy than to the native spirit of our citizens; while in education, where our rivals from their very cradles by a painful discipline seek after manliness, at Athens we live exactly as we please, and yet are just as ready to encounter every legitimate danger. In proof of this it may be noticed that the Lacedaemonians do not invade our country alone, but bring with them all their confederates; while we Athenians advance unsupported into the territory of a neighbour, and fighting upon a foreign soil usually vanquish with ease men who are defending their homes. Our united force was never yet encountered by any enemy, because we have at once to attend to our marine and to dispatch our citizens by land upon a hundred different services; so that, wherever they engage with some such fraction of our strength, a success against a detachment is magnified into a victory over the nation, and a defeat into a reverse suffered at the hands of our entire people. And yet if with habits not of labour but of ease, and courage not of art but of nature, we are still willing to encounter danger, we have the double advantage of escaping the experience of hardships in anticipation and of facing them in the hour of need as fearlessly as those who are never free from them.

Nor are these the only points in which our city is worthy of admiration. We cultivate refinement without extravagance and knowledge without effeminacy;

wealth we employ more for use than for show, and place the real disgrace of poverty not in owning to the fact but in declining the struggle against it. Our public men have, besides politics, their private affairs to attend to, and our ordinary citizens, though occupied with the pursuits of industry, are still fair judges of public matters; for, unlike any other nation, regarding him who takes no part in these duties not as unambitious but as useless, we Athenians are able to judge at all events if we cannot originate, and instead of looking on discussion as a stumbling-block in the way of action, we think it an indispensable preliminary to any wise action at all. Again, in our enterprises we present the singular spectacle of daring and deliberation, each carried to its highest point, and both united in the same persons; although usually decision is the fruit of ignorance, hesitation of reflection. But the palm of courage will surely be adjudged most justly to those, who best know the difference between hardship and pleasure and yet are never tempted to shrink from danger. In generosity we are equally singular, acquiring our friends by conferring, not by receiving, favours. Yet, of course, the doer of the favour is the firmer friend of the two, in order by continued kindness to keep the recipient in his debt; while the debtor feels less keenly from the very consciousness that the return he makes will be a payment, not a free gift. And it is only the Athenians who, fearless of consequences, confer their benefits not from calculations of expediency, but in the confidence of liberality.

In short, I say that as a city we are the school of Hellas; while I doubt if the world can produce a man, who where he has only himself to depend upon, is equal to so many emergencies, and graced by so happy a versatility, as the Athenian.

(Thucydides, *The History of the Peloponnesian War*, tr. R. Crawley, Bk II, pp. 93–5, Everyman Library Edition, Dent, London and E. P. Dutton, New York, 1910.)

2 PLATO: DEMOCRACY

Now what is the character of this new [democratic] régime? Obviously the way they govern themselves will throw light on the democratic type of man.

No doubt.

First of all, they are free. Liberty and free speech are rife everywhere; anyone is allowed to do what he likes.

Yes, so we are told.

That being so, every man will arrange his own manner of life to suit his pleasure. The result will be a greater variety of individuals than under any other constitution. So it may be the finest of all, with its variegated pattern of all sorts of characters. Many people may think it the best, just as women and children might admire a mixture of colours of every shade in the pattern of a dress. Any any rate if we are in search of a constitution, here is a good place to look for one. A democracy is so free that it contains a sample of every kind; and perhaps anyone who intends to found a state, as we have been doing, ought first to visit this emporium of constitutions and choose the model he likes best.

He will find plenty to choose from.

Here, too, you are not obliged to be in authority, however competent you may be, or to submit to authority, if you do not like it; you need not fight when your fellow citizens are at war, nor remain at peace when they do, unless you want peace; and though you may have no legal right to hold office or sit on juries, you will do so all the same if the fancy takes you. A wonderfully pleasant life, surely, for the moment.

For the moment, no doubt.

There is a charm, too, in the forgiving spirit shown by some who have been sentenced by the courts. In a democracy you must have seen how men condemned to death or exile stay on and go about in public, and no one takes any more notice than he would of a spirit that walked invisible. There is so much tolerance and superiority to petty considerations; such a contempt for all those fine principles we laid down in founding our commonwealth, as when we said that only a very exceptional nature could turn out a good man, if he had not played as a child among things of beauty and given himself only to creditable pursuits. A democracy tramples all such notions under foot; with a magnificent indifference to the sort of life a man has led before he enters politics, it will promote to honour anyone who merely calls himself the people's friend . . .

These then, and such as these, are the features of a democracy, an agreeable form of anarchy with plenty of variety and an equality of a peculiar kind for equals and unequals alike . . .

Oligarchy was established by men with a certain aim in life: the good they sought was wealth, and it was the insatiable appetite for money-making to the neglect of everything else that proved its undoing. Is democracy likewise ruined by greed for what it conceives to be the supreme good?

What good do you mean?

Liberty. In a democratic country you will be told that liberty is its noblest possession, which makes it the only fit place for a free spirit to live in.

True; that is often said.

Well then, as I was saying, perhaps the insatiable desire for this good to the neglect of everything else may transform a democracy and lead to a demand for despotism. A democratic state may fall under the influence of unprincipled leaders, ready to minister to its thirst for liberty with too deep draughts of this heady wine; and then, if its rulers are not complaisant enough to give it unstinted freedom, they will be arraigned as accursed oligarchs and punished. Law-abiding citizens will be insulted as nonentities who hug their chains; and all praise and honour will be bestowed, both publicly and in private, on rulers who behave like subjects and subjects who behave like rulers. In such a state the spirit of liberty is bound to go to all lengths.

Inevitably.

It will make its way into the home, until at last the very animals catch the infection of anarchy. The parent falls into the habit of behaving like the child, and the child like the parent: the father is afraid of his sons, and they show no fear or respect for their parents, in order to assert their freedom. Citizens, resident aliens, and strangers from abroad are all on an equal footing. To descend to smaller matters, the schoolmaster timidly flatters his pupils, and the pupils make light of their masters as well as of their attendants. Generally speaking, the young copy their elders, argue with them, and will not do as they are told; while the old, anxious not to be thought disagreeable tyrants, imitate the young and condescend to enter into their jokes and amusements. The full measure of popular liberty is reached when the slaves of both sexes are quite as free as the owners who paid for them; and I had almost forgotten to mention the spirit of freedom and equality in the mutual relations of men and women.

Well, to quote Aeschylus, we may as well speak 'the word that rises to our lips'.

Certainly; so I will. No one who had not seen it would believe how much more freedom the domestic animals enjoy in a democracy than elsewhere. The very dogs behave as if the proverb 'like mistress, like maid' applied to them; and the horses and donkeys catch the habit of walking down the street with all the dignity of freemen, running into anyone they meet who does not get out of their way. The whole place is simply bursting with the spirit of liberty.

No need to tell me that. I have often suffered from it on my way out of the town.

Putting all these items together, you can see the result: the citizens become so sensitive that they resent the slightest application of control as intolerable tyranny, and in their resolve to have no master they end by disregarding even the law, written or unwritten.

(*The Republic of Plato*, tr. F. M. Cornford, Bk 8, pp. 276-7, 282-3, Clarendon Press, Oxford 1941.)

CHAPTER 2

Pre-Platonic Political Thought

In order to understand the political ideas of the thinkers who lived before Plato it is necessary to examine the origins and development of some of the concepts that they used. In fact, Greek political thought can be understood only if it is realized that concepts such as justice, law, and nature meant to the Greeks something substantially different from what they mean to us today. The Greek words which most closely corresponded to our term 'justice' were *themis* and *dikè*.

Themis

Themis appears in Homeric literature as a goddess (the wife of Zeus) who personifies divine justice. This code was confined to the clans of the ancient monarchies and aristocracies and was presented in the form of *themistes*, or infallible decrees, revealed to men upon the request of a qualified person, normally the clan priest, to whom would be transmitted through dreams or oracles the advice of the gods. Examples of *themis* in Homeric society were the duty to entertain strangers and to propitiate the gods.

As monarchy was displaced by aristocracy, and as in turn the clan élitism of aristocracy declined and gave way to democracy, so the notion of *themis* grew weaker and justice came to be regarded as a code governing the relationships of all men. This was *dikè*.

Dikè

Dikè also appears in Homer, but not as a goddess. Although generally it referred to the actions of gods, kings and nobles, originally it seems to have applied to physical things also. The *dikè* of a group of persons was often no more than the traditional conduct of that group, although even as early as Homer the idea appears that *dikè* is the 'right' or 'straight' thing to do. In the poems of Hesiod, where *dikè* is personified as the goddess daughter of Zeus and Themis, the moral nature of the concept is consistently emphasized, particularly as a restraint upon the conduct of the aristocratic élite.

In time *dikè* acquired a more concrete meaning as the justice dispensed by the courts (*dikasterion*). Hence, in their judgements, the popular courts at Athens expressed the people's view of the 'straight' or equitable way.

Nomos

This word is best translated as law, although not in the sense of contemporary legislation. Whereas *dikè* was concerned with indicating the right way in particular cases, *nomos* was the general rule whose origin was either immemorial custom or the written formulation of an allwise legislator of the past such as Solon. Unlike *themis* and *dikè*, *nomos* was invariably referred to in connection with the *polis*; citizens considered their laws as their guarantee of freedom and therefore worth fighting for.

The Ionian Physicists

The beginnings of Greek scientific and philosophical thought occur in the sixth century B.C. with the founding of the Milesian School of Cosmology by Thales. For the first time in western thought (Egypt and Babylon probably preceded the west in this respect) attempts were made to explain the operation of the physical universe in terms other than myth and magic. These scientific speculations invariably involved the search for some single 'key' which would explain the mysteries of cosmic phenomena. The Ionian philosophers referred to this key or principle as *physis* or 'nature' and early theories of what constituted the natural principle seem to us extremely naive. For instance, Thales saw water as the essential natural substance, whereas Anaximenes considered it to be air.

Of these early philosophers, at least two, Pythagoras and Heraclitus, found that their enquiries into the physical world necessarily involved them in speculations about the moral and political world of man.

Pythagoras

Pythagoras of Samos settled in Croton in southern Italy in 532 B.C. where he founded a philosophical school whose influence was to last for centuries. He and his disciples lived a communal life devoted to philosophy and in time they became the ruling power in the city.

Pythagorean doctrine was based essentially upon the concept of 'number'. Pythagoras discovered the mathematical relationship existing between the pitch of a musical note and the length of the string which produced the note when plucked. The fact that the phenomenon of sound could be reduced to a numerical measure was such an exciting discovery that the Pythagoreans were led to dismiss as misconceived the earlier physicists' attempt to explain the world by a material principle, and they substituted abstract number as the universal key.

The principle of mathematics was applied by the Pythagoreans to the moral as well as to the material world. For example, eight, the number associated with the harmony of the octave, was identified with love, and justice was seen as a square number. As a square number is perfectly harmonious in that the number of parts is equal to the value of each part, so the just and harmonious city is one which possesses a social and economic equality. We find here the seeds of the later theories of justice expressed by both Plato and Aristotle.

Several other ideas indicate the indebtedness of Plato to the Pythagoreans. The importance of mathematics, particularly geometry, in philosophy is emphasized by Plato in his scheme of education. The Pythagorean division of men into the lovers of wisdom, honour and gain is reflected in the Platonic theory of the tripartite soul. The mode of life followed by the Pythagorean community—music for the purification of the soul, and diet for the purification of the body—is paralleled by Plato's scheme of primary education. Finally, the doctrine of the transmigration and purification of souls after death is the core of the myth of Er described in the last pages of the *Republic*.

Heraclitus

Although Heraclitus wrote in about 500 B.C. his speculations seem to be much closer in spirit to the early physicists of the sixth century than to Pythagoras. Like Thales and Anaximenes, he too chose one of the elements as the natural universal principle; in this case, fire. He was led to this conclusion by his theory of 'flux' or change. Whereas the philosophers of the sixth century had viewed the world as essentially material and static, Heraclitus considered it to be in a state of continuous change. He is reputed to have said: 'You cannot step twice into the same river.' The idea of flux led him to believe that material things were like flames: they were processes rather than static realities, and everything was merely a transformation of fire.

The process by which change takes place in the material world is governed by an immutable law of reason similar to the law which governs men in the state. In all cases departure from *dikè* is punished by the Furies or by fire itself because: 'all human laws are sustained by the one divine law.'

The Sophists

The intellectual climate of Athens in the mid and late fifth century B.C. was such that the teachings of the Sophists simply crystallized ideas that already existed in the minds of many. Before the fifth century men had tended to accept their own laws and customs (*nomos*) as unalterable and probably of divine origin. The Ionian physicists had reinforced this view by their naive parallel between the laws of men and the natural laws underlying physical phenomena.

However, in the course of the fifth century, this widespread belief in the absolute nature of human laws was being replaced by a more critical attitude. The anthropological writings of Herodotus describing the variety of human customs, even relating to such significant matters as marriage and burial, led many Athenians to wonder whether their own customs were indeed rooted in the unchangeable nature of things. The creation of laws by men, particularly in the new colonies, stimulated speculation into the possibility that all laws and customs were man-made and reflected chance historical development rather than immutable principle.

The reaction against the rigidity of the Ionian philosophy was spearheaded by the Sophists who were active in Athens in the second half of the fifth century B.C. These men, nearly all of foreign origin, were professional peripatetic teachers who came to Athens because it was the intellectual and cultural centre of Greece. They did not form a philosophical school; they were willing to teach whatever was in demand, and hence it is not surprising that their most common characteristic was versatility. Hippias of Elis, for example, was a teacher of poetry, art, music, mathematics, morals, history and politics.

The most frequently taught subject was rhetoric, or fluency in argument, this being regarded by the pupils of the Sophists as a useful preparation for public life. Such an education was considered particularly relevant by the wealthy and oligarchically inclined, since it would help them to use the democratic methods of participation and debate for their own anti-democratic ends. Although the word 'sophist' stems from the Greek word for wisdom, the Sophists were less interested in acquiring truth than in teaching the ability to argue any case. In that lies the reason why many of the Sophists came to acquire a certain disrepute and partly why they came under such a heavy attack from Plato in the *Republic*.

Intellectually, what the Sophists held in common was the distinction that they made between nature (*physis*) and law (*nomos*). The first man to make this distinction was not a Sophist but a physicist: Archelaus of Athens, a disciple of the Ionian philosopher Anaxagoras. The supposed antithesis of nature and law rested primarily upon an assumption made by nearly all Sophists, that man is naturally egoistic and law, by definition, imposes a social morality on him. For many Sophists it followed that the law of the *polis* was tyrannical, forcing men to act against their natural selfish interests.

Protagoras of Abdera (c. 500–c. 430 B.C.)

The earliest of the Sophists, Protagoras, was a teacher of rhetoric but also a moral and political philosopher of great importance. Little, if anything, exists of his own writings and thus, as with most of the other Sophists, we must rely on the Platonic dialogues for his political views. In Plato's *Theaetetus* his theory of knowledge is stated in the words: 'man is the measure of all things' (Ex. 3a). This is a direct attack on the old-fashioned notion that the laws and morality of states are absolute. Protagoras substitutes instead the humanist thesis that man is responsible for erecting his own scale of values, although he argues that the morality of the *polis*, being based upon the consensus of common-sense opinion in the community expresses, what is expedient and therefore should be obeyed.

The second extract, which is from Plato's *Protagoras*, illustrates his attempt to justify the democratic principle that all persons are qualified to give advice on matters of public policy (Ex. 3b). His argument is presented in the form of a myth about the origins of human society. According to the myth, men, after their creation, lacking the necessary political wisdom to form communities, lived a naturally selfish existence. In time, however, the need for self-preservation drove them to set up cities but, because of their lack of political virtue, they injured one another and society was destroyed. Fearing the destruction of the entire human race, Zeus sent Hermes to take to men the gifts of justice and reverence. Human society once more developed, but now it was permanent because it was grounded upon each man's possession of the political virtues.

Protagoras's solution to the problem of the antithesis of *physis* and *nomos* was therefore that man should follow *nomos*, since the life of conventional justice was seen as immeasurably superior to the savage and miserable life of nature.

Antiphon of Athens

Antiphon was an Athenian Sophist of the late fifth century B.C., and is unique in that a considerable fragment of his written work survives. His book *On Truth* was probably written as a reply to the theory of Protagoras (Ex. 4). Where Protagoras is conservative in advocating the following of *nomos* rather than *physis*, Antiphon is radical in that he conceives of nature as the truth which should be followed wherever possible. The basic law of nature is the egoistic principle that each man should follow his own self-interest. The laws of the state, on the other hand, are based merely on convention, and work contrary to nature and to the best interests of the individual. It therefore follows that the *nomos* should be obeyed only when it is expedient to do so, and at other times it should be disobeyed.

In common with certain other Sophists such as Hippias, Antiphon considers that the natural equality of mankind can be deduced from its common human characteristics. Nature is seen by Antiphon as the physical process of life and development, and in this there is no distinction between Greek and Barbarian.

Callicles

All that is known about Callicles is derived from a passage in Plato's *Gorgias*. Although it is possible that he was an actual person given a pseudonym by Plato, he may have been an imaginary character created by Plato for the express purpose of expounding the most extreme Sophist doctrine: might is right. Callicles enters the dialogue at the point where Polus has shown himself inadvertently to be an exponent of conventional morality by agreeing that wickedness is dishonourable (Ex. 5). According to Callicles, conventional morality is merely the law made by the many weak in society to subjugate the few strong. Hence the *nomoi* of the state although conventionally just are, in reality, totally unjust since they frustrate the natural right of the strong man to rule his inferiors.

True justice would, therefore, give free reign to nature and allow the strong and superior man to gratify his desires to the full. Inequality is the natural rule; equality is merely the conventional rule of man.

Thrasymachus of Chalcedon

Thrasymachus was a Sophist of relatively minor importance who taught rhetoric in late fifth-century Athens. He appears, however, as an important character in the first book of Plato's *Republic*, although it is difficult to determine whether Plato is accurately representing his political ideas.

Following the discussion between Socrates and Polemarchus on the nature of justice, Thrasymachus intervenes with his definition: 'justice is nothing else than the interest of the stronger' (Ex. 6). Superficially this seems to have a close affinity with the Calliclean view that might confers right, but the 'justice' referred to by Thrasymachus is the conventional rather than the natural kind. He argues that in every state the laws are made by the ruler (the stronger power) in his own interest. Justice is simply obedience to these laws. It follows that injustice is superior to justice since the unjust man looks after his own good, whereas the just man in obeying the laws considers only the good of the law-maker.

Glaucon

Plato's brother Glaucon appears in the *Republic* as a character whose main function is to express agreement with the arguments of Socrates. At the beginning of the second book (which follows the dialogue with Thrasymachus), Glaucon complains that the Thrasymachean theory of justice has not been properly refuted and demands that Socrates prove that justice is good in itself, regardless of possible rewards. In order to elicit such a proof Glaucon states the case for injustice as forcibly as he can, drawing upon views preached by contemporary radical Sophists (Ex. 7).

Men say that to do wrong to others is desirable but to suffer wrong is not, and the disadvantages of the latter outweigh the advantages of the former. Therefore men compromise by making a pact with each other to refrain from mutual injury. This pact is the foundation of justice since, in order to maintain it, laws are enforced which prevent wrongdoing. Justice is therefore a compromise based upon convention rather than nature, and stemming from fear. If the fear of punishment for disobeying the law were to be removed, only an insane person would behave justly. Glaucon illustrates his account by the story of Gyges' ring which, by allowing its wearer to become invisible at will, enables a man to lead a life of wickedness and yet to evade the consequences. In such a situation no person would pursue a just life.

The remainder of the *Republic* can be regarded as an attempt by Socrates to refute this commonly held view by showing that only a life of justice is in accordance with the true nature of man.

FURTHER READING

Texts
Plato: *Theaetetus*
Plato: *Protagoras*
Antiphon: *On Truth*, in E. Barker: *Greek Political Theory* (Methuen 1960)
Plato: *Gorgias*
Plato: *Republic*

Commentaries
E. Barker: *Greek Political Theory* (Methuen 1960)
J. Burnet: *Greek Philosophy* (Macmillan 1968)
T. Gomperz (tr. L. Magnus): *The Greek Thinkers*, vol. 1 (John Murray 1901)
W. K. C. Guthrie: *The Sophists* (Cambridge University Press 1971)
T. A. Sinclair: *A History of Greek Political Thought* (Routledge & Kegan Paul 1951)

3a PROTAGORAS (PLATO: THEAETETUS)

Soc. Well, you have delivered yourself of a very important doctrine about knowledge; it is indeed the opinion of Protagoras, although he has another way of expressing the same view. 'Man', he says, 'is the measure of all things, of the existence of things that are, and of the non-existence of things that are not':—You have read him?

Theaet. O yes, again and again.

Soc. Does he not say [or mean] that things are to you such as they appear to you, and to me such as they appear to me, and that you and I are men? . . .

And is there not most likely to be firm ground in the distinction which we were indicating on behalf of Protagoras, viz. that most sensations, such as hot, dry, sweet, and all others of that class, are only such as they appear; if, however, superiority of opinion is to be allowed at all, surely we must allow it in respect of health or disease? for every woman, child, or living creature has not such a knowledge of what conduces to health as to enable them to cure themselves.

Theod. I quite agree.

Soc. Or again, in politics, while affirming that just and unjust, honourable and disgraceful, holy and unholy, are in reality to each state such as the state thinks and makes lawful, and that in determining these matters no individual or state is wiser than another, still the followers of Protagoras will not deny that in determining what is or is not *expedient* for the community one state is wiser and one counsellor better than another—they will scarcely venture to maintain, that what a city enacts in the belief that it is expedient will always be really expedient. But in the other case, I mean when they speak of justice and injustice, piety and impiety, they are confident that in nature these have no existence or essence of their own—the truth is that which is agreed on at the time of the agreement, and as long as the agreement lasts; and this is the philosophy of many who do not altogether go along with Protagoras.

(Plato, *Theaetetus*, in *The Dialogues of Plato*, tr. B. Jowett, 4th edn, vol. 3, pp. 246-7, 270-1, Clarendon Press, Oxford 1953.)

3b PROTAGORAS (PLATO: PROTAGORAS)

Once upon a time there were gods only, and no mortal creatures. But when the appointed time came that these also should be created, the gods fashioned them out of earth, and fire and various mixtures of both elements in the interior of the earth; and when they were about to bring them into the light of day, they ordered Prometheus and Epimetheus to equip them, and to distribute to them severally their proper qualities. Epimetheus said to Prometheus: 'Let me distribute, and do you inspect.' This was agreed, and Epimetheus made the distribution. There were some to whom he gave strength without swiftness, while he equipped the weaker with swiftness; some he armed, and others he left unarmed; and devised for the latter some other means of preservation. Upon those whom he clothed in diminutive bodies, he bestowed winged flight or subterranean habitation: those which he aggrandized with magnitude, he protected by their very size: and similarly with the rest of his distribution, always compensating. These devices he used as precautions that no race should be destroyed. And when he had provided against their destruction by one another, he contrived also a means of protecting them against the seasons of heaven; clothing them with close hair and thick skins sufficient to defend them against the winter cold, yet able to resist the summer heat, and serving also as a natural bed of their own when they wanted to rest; also he furnished them with hoofs and hair and hard and callous skins under their feet. Then he gave them varieties of food,—herbs of the soil to some, to others fruits of trees, and to others roots, and to some again he gave other animals as food. And some he made to have few young ones, while those who were their prey were very prolific; and in this manner the race was preserved. Thus did Epimetheus, who, not being very wise, forgot that he had distributed among the brute animals all the qualities which he had to give,—and when he came to man, who was still unprovided, he was terribly perplexed. Now while he was in this perplexity, Prometheus came to inspect the distribution, and he found that the other animals were quite suitably furnished, but that man was naked and shoeless, and had neither bed nor arms of defence. The appointed hour was approaching when man in his turn was to emerge from earth into the light of day; and Prometheus, not knowing how he could devise his salvation, stole the mechanical arts of Hephaestus and Athene, and fire with them (they could neither have been acquired nor used without fire), and gave them to man. Thus man had the wisdom necessary to the support of life, but political wisdom he had not; for that was in the keeping of Zeus, and the power of Prometheus no longer extended to entering into the citadel of heaven, where Zeus dwelt, who moreover had terrible sentinels; but he did enter by stealth into the common workshop of Athene and Hephaestus, in which they used to practise their favourite arts, and carried off Hephaestus' art of working by fire, and also the art of Athene, and gave them to man. And in this way man was supplied with the means of life. But Prometheus is said to have been afterwards prosecuted for theft, owing to the blunder of Epimetheus.

Now man, having a share of the divine attributes, was at first the only one of the animals who had any gods, because he alone was of their kindred; and he would raise altars and images of them. He was not long in inventing articulate speech and names; and he also constructed houses and clothes and shoes and beds, and drew sustenance from the earth. Thus provided, mankind at first lived dispersed, and there were no cities. But the consequence was that they were destroyed by the wild beasts, for they were utterly weak in comparison of them, and their practical attainments were only sufficient to provide them with the means of life, and did not enable them to carry on war against the animals: food they had, but not as yet the art of government, of which the art of war is a part. After a while the desire of self-preservation gathered them into cities; but when they were gathered together, having no art of government, they evil entreated one another, and were again in process of dispersion and destruction. Zeus feared that the entire race would be exterminated, and so he sent Hermes to them, bearing reverence and justice to be the ordering principles of cities and the bonds of friendship and conciliation. Hermes asked Zeus how he should impart justice and reverence among men:—Should he distribute them as the arts are distributed; that is to say, to a favoured few only, one skilled individual having enough of medicine or of any other art for many unskilled ones? 'Shall this be the manner in which I am to distribute justice and reverence among men, or shall I give them to all?' 'To all,' said Zeus; 'I should like them all to have a share; for cities cannot exist, if a few only share in the virtues, as in the arts. And further, make a law by my order, that he who has no part in reverence and justice shall be put to death, for he is a plague of the state.'

And this is the reason, Socrates, why the Athenians and mankind in general, when the question relates to carpentering or any other mechanical art, allow but a few to share in their deliberations; and when anyone else interferes, then, as you say, they object, if he be not of the favoured few; which, as I reply, is very natural. But when they meet to deliberate about political virtue, which proceeds only by way of justice and wisdom, they are patient enough of any man who speaks of them, as is also natural, because they think that every man ought to share in this sort of virtue, and that states could not exist if this were otherwise. Such ,Socrates, is the reason of this phenomenon.

(Plato, *Protagoras*, in *The Dialogues of Plato*, tr. B. Jowett, 4th edn, vol. 1, pp. 145-8, Clarendon Press, Oxford 1953.)

4 ANTIPHON

I

Justice [in the ordinary view] consists in not transgressing [or rather, is not being known to transgress] any of the legal rules of the State in which one lives as a citizen. A man, therefore, would practise justice in the way most advantageous to himself if, in the presence of witnesses, he held the laws in high esteem, but, in the absence of witnesses, and when he was by himself, he held in high esteem the rules of nature. The reason is that the rules of the laws are adventitious, while the rules of nature are inevitable [and innate]; and again that the rules of the laws are created by covenant and not produced by nature, while the rules of nature are exactly the reverse. A man, therefore, who transgresses legal rules, is free from shame and punishment whenever he is unobserved by those who made the covenant, and is subject to shame and punishment only when he is observed. It is otherwise with transgression of the rules which are innate in nature. If a man strains any of these rules beyond what it can bear, the evil consequences are none the less, if he is entirely unobserved, and none the greater, if he is seen of all men; and this is because the injury which he incurs is not due to men's opinion, but to the facts of the case.

The question with which we are here concerned arises from every point of view. Most of the things which are legally just are [none the less] in the position of being inimical to nature. By law it has been laid down for the eyes what they should see and what they should not see; for the ears what they should hear, and what they should not hear; for the tongue what it should speak, and what it should not speak; for the hands what they should do, and what they should not do; for the feet whither they should go, and whither they should not go; and for the mind what it should desire, and what it should not desire. Now the things from which the laws seek to turn men away are no more

[? less] agreeable or akin to nature than the things which the laws seek to turn men towards. [This may be proved as follows.] To nature belong both life and death. Men draw life from the things that are advantageous to them: they incur death from the things that are disadvantageous to them. But the things which are established as advantageous in the view of the law are restraints on nature [i.e. they prevent men from drawing life, which belongs to nature, from the things that are really advantageous to them], whereas the things established by nature as advantageous are free [i.e. they leave men free to draw life from the things that are really advantageous to them; for they are identical with those things]. Therefore things which cause pain [and so are akin to death] do not, on a right view, benefit nature more [on the contrary, they benefit nature less] than things which cause pleasure [and so are akin to life]; and therefore, again, things which cause suffering would not be more advantageous [on the contrary, they would be less advantageous] than things which cause happiness—for things which are really advantageous ought not to cause detriment, but gain . . . [Take the case of those] who retaliate only after suffering injury, and are never themselves the aggressors; or those who behave well to their parents, though their parents behave badly to them; or those, again, who allow others to prefer charges [against them] on oath, and bring no such charges themselves. Of the actions here mentioned one would find many to be inimical to nature. They involve more suffering when less is possible, less pleasure when more is possible, and injury when freedom from injury is possible.

II

[Those who are born of a great house] we revere and venerate: those who are born of a humble house we neither revere nor venerate. On this point we are [not civilized, but] barbarized in our behaviour to one another. Our natural endowment is the same for us all, on all points, whether we are Greeks or barbarians. We may observe the characteristics of any of the powers which by nature are necessary to all men . . . None of us is set apart [by any peculiarity of such natural powers] either as a Greek or as a barbarian. We all breathe the air through our mouth and nostrils.

(Antiphon, *Two Fragments on Truth*, in E. Barker, *Greek Political Theory*, 5th edn, pp. 95-8, Methuen, London 1960.)

5 CALLICLES (PLATO: GORGIAS)

The truth is, Socrates, that you, who pretend to be engaged in the pursuit of truth, are appealing now to the popular and vulgar notions of right, which are admirable by convention, not by nature. Convention and nature are generally at variance with one another: and hence, if a person is too modest and timid to say what he thinks, he is compelled to contradict himself. Perceiving this subtlety, you play fast and loose in your arguing; when a speaker is stating his case on the basis of convention, you insinuate a question based on the rule of nature; and if he is talking of the rule of nature, you slip away to convention:

as, for instance, you did in this very discussion about doing and suffering injustice. When Polus was speaking of the conventionally disgraceful, you kept on pursuing the argument from the point of view of nature; for by the rule of nature, to suffer injustice is the greater disgrace because the greater evil; but conventionally, to do evil is the more disgraceful. For the suffering of injustice is not the part of a man, but of a slave, who indeed had better die than live; since when he is wronged and trampled upon, he is unable to help himself, or any other about whom he cares. The reason, as I conceive, is that the makers of laws are the majority who are weak; and they make laws and distribute praises and censures with a view to themselves and to their own interests; and they terrify the stronger sort of men, and those who are able to get the better of them, in order that they may not get the better of them; and they say that self-interested ambition is shameful and unjust, meaning, by the word injustice, the desire of a man to have more than his neighbours; for knowing their own inferiority, I suspect that they are only too glad of equality. And therefore the endeavour to have more than the many is conventionally said to be shameful and unjust, and is called injustice, whereas nature herself intimates that it is just for the better to have more than the worse, the more powerful than the weaker; and in many ways she shows, among men as well as among animals, and indeed among whole cities and races, that justice consists in the superior ruling over and having more than the inferior. For on what principle of justice did Xerxes invade Hellas, or his father the Scythians? (not to speak of numberless other examples). Nay, but these men, I suggest, act in this way according to the nature of justice; yes, by Heaven, and according to the law of nature, though not, perhaps, according to that law which we enact; we take the best and strongest of our fellows from their youth upwards, and tame them like young lions,—enslaving them with spells and incantations, and saying to them that with equality they must be content, and that the equal is the honourable and the just. But if there were a man born with enough ability, he would shake off and break through, and escape from all this; he would trample under foot all our formulas and spells and charms, and all our laws which are against nature: the slave would rise in rebellion and be lord over us, and the light of natural justice would shine forth. And Pindar, I think, confirms what I say in the poem where he refers to

'Law the king of all, of mortals as well as of immortals';

this, as he says,

'Makes might to be right, doing violence with highest hand; as I infer from the deeds of Heracles, for without buying them—'

this is something like what he says—I do not know the poem by heart; the meaning is, that without buying them, and without their being given to him, he drove away the oxen of Geryon, it being the law of natural right that the oxen and all the possessions of the weaker and inferior properly belong to the stronger and superior. How can a man be happy who is the servant of anything? On the contrary, I plainly assert that he who would truly live ought to allow his desires to wax to the uttermost, and not to chastise them; but when they have grown to their greatest he should have courage and intelligence to minister to them and to satisfy all his longings. And this I affirm to be natural justice and nobility. To this, however, the many cannot attain; and they blame the strong man because they are ashamed of their own weakness, which they desire to conceal, and hence they say that intemperance is base. As I have remarked already, they enslave the nobler natures, and being unable to attain full satisfaction of their pleasures, they praise temperance and justice out of their own cowardice. For if a man had been originally the son of a king, or had a nature capable of acquiring an empire or a tyranny or sovereignty, what could be more truly base or evil'than temperance and justice—to a man like him, I say, who might freely be enjoying every good, and has no one to stand in his way, and yet has himself admitted convention and reason and the disapproval of other men to be lords over him?—must not these fine conceits of justice and temperance have brought him to a miserable plight, when he cannot favour his own friends above his enemies even though he be a ruler in his city? Nay, Socrates, you profess to be a votary of the truth, and the truth is this:—that luxury and intemperance and licence, if they be provided with means, are virtue and happiness—all the rest is a mere bauble, agreements contrary to nature, foolish talk of men, nothing worth.

(Plato, *Gorgias*, in *The Dialogues of Plato*, tr. B. Jowett, 4th edn, vol. 2, pp. 576-8, 586, Clarendon Press, Oxford 1953.)

6 THRASYMACHUS (PLATO: THE REPUBLIC)

Listen then, Thrasymachus began. What I say is that 'just' or 'right' means nothing but what is to the interest of the stronger party. Well, where is your applause? You don't mean to give it me.

I will, as soon as I understand, I said. I don't see yet what you mean by right being the interest of the stronger party. For instance, Polydamas, the athlete, is stronger than we are, and it is to his interest to eat beef for the sake of his muscles; but surely you don't mean that the same diet would be good for weaker men and therefore be right for us?

You are trying to be funny, Socrates. It's a low trick to take my words in the sense you think will be most damaging.

No, no, I protested; but you must explain.

Don't you know, then, that a state may be ruled by a despot, or a democracy, or an aristocracy?

Of course.

And that the ruling element is always the strongest?

Yes.

Well then, in every case the laws are made by the ruling party in its own interest; a democracy makes democratic laws, a despot autocratic ones, and so on. By making these laws they define as 'right' for their subjects whatever is for their own interest, and they call anyone who breaks them a 'wrongdoer' and punish him accordingly. That is what I mean: in all states alike 'right' has the same meaning, namely what is for the interest of the party established in power, and that is the strongest. So the sound conclusion is that what is 'right' is the same everywhere: the interest of the stronger party . . .

Now, Thrasymachus, tell me, was that what you intended to say—that right means what the stronger thinks is to his interest, whether it really is so or not?

Most certainly not, he replied. Do you suppose I should speak of a man as 'stronger' or 'superior' at the very moment when he is making a mistake?

I did think you said as much when you admitted that rulers are not always infallible.

That is because you are a quibbler, Socrates. Would you say a man deserves to be called a physician at the moment when he makes a mistake in treating his patient and just in respect of that mistake; or a mathematician, when he does a sum wrong and just in so far as he gets a wrong result? Of course we do commonly speak of a physician or a mathematician or a scholar having made a mistake; but really none of these, I should say, is ever mistaken, in so far as he is worthy of the name we give him. So strictly speaking—and you are all for being precise—no one who practises a craft makes mistakes. A man is mistaken when his knowledge fails him; and at that moment he is no craftsman. And what is true of craftsmanship or any sort of skill is true of the ruler: he is never mistaken so long as he is acting as a ruler; though anyone might speak of a ruler making a mistake, just as he might of a physician. You must understand that I was talking in that loose way when I answered your question just now; but the precise statement is this. The ruler, in so far as he is acting as a ruler, makes no mistakes and consequently enjoins what is best for himself; and that is what the subject is to do. So, as I said at first, 'right' means doing what is to the interest of the stronger . . .

At this point, when everyone could see that Thrasymachus' definition of justice had been turned inside out, instead of making any reply, he said:

Socrates, have you a nurse?

Why do you ask such a question as that? I said. Wouldn't it be better to answer mine?

Because she lets you go about sniffling like a child whose nose wants wiping. She hasn't even taught you to know a shepherd when you see one, or his sheep either.

What makes you say that?

Why, you imagine that a herdsman studies the interests of his flocks or cattle, tending and fattening them up with some other end in view than his master's profit or his own; and so you don't see that, in politics, the genuine ruler regards his subjects exactly like sheep, and thinks of nothing else, night and day, but the good he can get out of them for himself. You are so far out in your notions of right and wrong, justice and injustice, as not to know that 'right' actually means what is good for someone else, and to be 'just' means serving the interest of the stronger who rules, at the cost of the subject who obeys; whereas injustice is just the reverse, asserting its authority over those innocents who are called just, so that they minister solely to their master's advantage and happiness, and not in the least degree to their own. Innocent as you are yourself, Socrates, you must see that a just man always has the worst of it. Take a private business: when a partnership is wound up, you will never find that the more honest of two partners comes off with the larger share; and in their relations to the state, when there are taxes to be paid, the honest man will pay more than the other on the same amount of property; or if there is money to be distributed, the dishonest will get it all. When either of them holds some public office, even if the just man loses in no other way, his private affairs at any rate will suffer from neglect, while his principles will not allow him to help himself from the public funds; not to mention the offence he will give to his friends and relations by refusing to sacrifice those principles to do them a good turn. Injustice has all the opposite advantages. I am speaking of the type I described just now, the man who can get the better of other people on a large scale: you must fix your eye on him, if you want to judge how much it is to one's own interest not to be just. You can see that best in the most consummate form of injustice, which rewards wrongdoing with supreme welfare and happiness and reduces its victims, if they won't retaliate in kind, to misery. That form is despotism, which uses force or fraud to plunder the goods of others, public or private, sacred or profane, and to do it in a whole-sale way. If you are caught committing any one of these crimes on a small scale, you are punished and disgraced; they call it sacrilege, kidnapping, burglary, theft and brigandage. But if, besides taking their property, you turn all your countrymen into slaves, you will hear no more of those ugly names; your countrymen themselves will call you the happiest of men and bless your name, and so will everyone who hears of such a complete triumph of injustice; for when people denounce injustice, it is because they are afraid of suffering wrong, not of doing it. So true is it, Socrates, that injustice, on a grand enough scale, is superior to justice in strength and freedom and autocratic power; and 'right', as I said at first, means simply what serves the interest of the stronger party; 'wrong' means what is for the interest and profit of oneself.

(*The Republic of Plato*, tr. F. M. Cornford, Bk 1, pp. 17-18, 20, 24-5, Clarendon Press, Oxford 1941.)

7 GLAUCON (PLATO: THE REPUBLIC)

What people say is that to do wrong is, in itself, a desirable thing; on the other hand, it is not at all desirable to suffer wrong, and the harm to the sufferer outweighs the advantage to the doer. Consequently, when men have had a taste of both, those who have not the power to seize the advantage and escape the harm decide that they would be better off if they made a compact neither to do wrong nor to suffer it. Hence they began to make laws and covenants with one another; and whatever the law prescribed they called lawful and right. That is what right or justice is and how it came into existence; it stands half-way between the best thing of all—to do wrong with impunity—and the worst, which is to suffer wrong without the power to retaliate. So justice is accepted as a compromise, and valued, not as good in itself, but for lack of power to do wrong; no man worthy of the name, who had that power, would ever enter into such a compact with anyone; he would be mad if he did. That, Socrates, is the nature of justice according to this account, and such the circumstances in which it arose.

The next point is that men practise it against the grain, for lack of power to do wrong. How true that is, we shall best see if we imagine two men, one just, the other unjust, given full licence to do whatever they like, and then follow them to observe where each will be led by his desires. We shall catch the just man taking the same road as the unjust, he will be moved by self-interest, the end which it is natural to every creature to pursue as good, until forcibly turned aside by law and custom to respect the principle of equality.

Now, the easiest way to give them that complete liberty of action would be to imagine them possessed of the talisman found by Gyges, the ancestor of the famous Lydian. The story tells how he was a shepherd in the King's service. One day there was a great storm, and the ground where his flock was feeding was rent by an earthquake. Astonished at the sight, he went down into the chasm and saw, among other wonders of which the story tells, a brazen horse, hollow, with windows in its sides. Peering in, he saw a dead body, which seemed to be of more than human size. It was naked save for a gold ring, which he took from the finger and made his way out. When the shepherds met, as they did every month, to send an account to the King of the state of his flocks, Gyges came wearing the ring. As he was sitting with the others, he happened to turn the bezel of the ring inside his hand. At once he became invisible, and his companions, to his surprise, began to speak of him as if he had left them. Then, as he was fingering the ring, he turned the bezel outwards and became visible again. With that, he set about testing the ring to see if it really had this power, and always with the same result: according as he turned the bezel inside or out he vanished and reappeared. After this discovery he contrived to be one of the messengers sent to the court. There he seduced the Queen, and with her help murdered the King and seized the throne.

Now suppose there were two such magic rings, and one were given to the just man, the other to the unjust. No one, it is commonly believed, would have such iron strength of mind as to stand fast in doing right or keep his hands off other men's goods, when he could go to the market-place and fearlessly help himself to anything he wanted, enter houses and sleep with any women he chose, set prisoners free and kill men at his pleasure, and in a word go about among men with the powers of a god. He would behave no better than the other; both would take the same course. Surely this would be strong proof that men do right only under compulsion; no individual thinks of it as good for him personally, since he does wrong whenever he finds he has the power. Every man believes that wrongdoing pays him personally much better, and, according to this theory, that is the truth. Granted full licence to do as he liked, people would think him a miserable fool if they found him refusing to wrong his neighbours or to touch their belongings, though in public they would keep up a pretence of praising his conduct, for fear of being wronged themselves. So much for that.

Finally, if we are really to judge between the two lives, the only way is to contrast the extremes of justice and injustice. We can best do that by imagining our two men to be perfect types, and crediting both to the full with the qualities they need for their respective ways of life. To begin with the unjust man: he must be like any consummate master of a craft, a physician or a captain, who, knowing just what his art can do, never tries to do more, and can always retrieve a false step. The unjust man, if he is to reach perfection, must be equally discreet in his criminal attempts, and he must not be found out, or we shall think him a bungler; for the highest pitch of injustice is to seem just when you are not. So we must endow our man with the full complement of injustice; we must allow him to have secured a spotless reputation for virtue while committing the blackest crimes; he must be able to retrieve any mistake, to defend himself with convincing eloquence if his misdeeds are denounced, and, when force is required, to bear down all opposition by his courage and strength and by his command of friends and money.

Now set beside this paragon the just man in his simplicity and nobleness, one who, in Aeschylus' words, 'would be, not seem, the best'. There must, indeed, be no such seeming; for if his character were apparent, his reputation would bring him honours and rewards, and then we should not know whether it was for their sake that he was just or for justice's sake alone. He must be stripped of everything but justice and denied every advantage the other enjoyed. Doing no wrong, he must have the worst reputation for wrong-doing, to test whether his virtue is proof against all that comes of having a bad name; and under this life-long imputation of wickedness, let him hold on his course of justice unwavering to the point of death. And so, when the two men have carried their justice and injustice to the last extreme, we may judge which is the happier.

(*The Republic of Plato*, Bk 2, pp. 42-5.)

CHAPTER 3

Plato (428–347 B.C.)

The *Republic* of Plato is arguably the greatest single work in the history of political philosophy. Written when Plato was in his fifties, it reflects his profound disillusionment with Athenian politics and politicians, and his contempt for the egoistic philosophy of the Sophists. As with all Plato's philosophical writing it is in the form of a dialogue, with Socrates, the main speaker, representing Plato's own views.

As a young man Plato was a close associate of Socrates and must often have seen him in disputation with the Sophists. Such public debates often took the form of *eristic* duels in which, by the method of question and answer, one of the parties would be eventually defeated by being driven into an *elenchus*—a position inconsistent with his original thesis. Many of these debates were used by the Sophists to show their own skill in argument rather than as a means for discovering truth. Socrates, however, used the occasions for serious philosophical enquiry in pursuance of his mission to convince men of their ignorance. The term 'dialectic' was used by Plato to describe this intellectually serious type of argument and it is the dialectical style that Plato incorporates into his writings.

The *Republic* is ostensibly an enquiry into the nature of justice, although it is also incidentally a treatise on education, metaphysics, epistemology, the arts and politics. In the previous chapter it was shown that Book I and the first part of Book II of the *Republic* contain some representative Sophist theories about justice. In response to the request made by Glaucon and Adeimantus that he enquire into the real nature of justice, Socrates begins by making an analogy between the individual and the state, suggesting that justice can more easily be discerned on a large scale in the city than on a small scale in the individual (Ex. 8a). The parallel between individual and state implies that the state is an 'organism'; a conception that imputes to the political association a life and personality of its own.

The Origin of the State
The perfectly just *polis* is constructed in four stages. The first stage is

that of the austere city which comes into existence to provide for man's material needs, consisting of just enough people to provide for these needs utilizing a simple division of labour.

Glaucon interrupts Socrates's description of the simple but enjoyable life of the citizens to demand the addition of everyday luxuries. Socrates agrees to the request and shows how the austere *polis* will grow into a luxurious *polis* if people demand a way of life beyond that of material subsistence (Ex. 8b). This 'swollen' state will include many new trades to cater for the non-necessary desires; the population will grow and more territory will be required to support it. In order to acquire more land and to defend what the city already possesses, armed force becomes necessary. On the same principle of specialization, skilled professional soldiers or 'guardians' provide this force, but because of the potential danger of military tyranny, the guardians must be trained to be gentle and rational as well as courageous.

Education and the Class Structure

The third stage in the development of the ideally just state is the purification of the 'swollen', luxurious *polis*. This is effected by educating the guardians to be wise, courageous and temperate, and by eliminating from the city all potential causes of discord. In his scheme of primary education Plato relies heavily upon the contemporary Athenian curriculum of 'music' and 'gymnastic'—the former consisting of reading, writing and the arts, and the latter including everything to do with the care of the body. In order that the guardians should grow up with the 'right' characteristics and morality, literature and music are to be censored. Everything that is irreligious, immoral and intemperate is to be expurgated.

The primary education of the guardians is completed by two years or so of military training, and at the age of twenty those who have passed successfully through a variety of tests are selected to be future rulers and to continue their education for a further stage. The remainder stay as 'auxiliaries'—soldiers and minor administrators (Ex. 8c).

The city is thus divided into three classes: rulers, auxiliaries and producers. The centre of interest henceforward is the guardian group of rulers and auxiliaries; we hear little more about the producer class. Each person is to be taught to accept his place in the class structure by a myth which, it is hoped, will ultimately be believed by everyone in the state (Ex. 8d). The myth tells how each person has metal mixed in his soul by the gods. Rulers have golden souls, auxiliaries have silver souls, and the souls of the producers contain iron and brass. Parents normally produce children of a similar type to themselves, but occasionally a child of different metallic composition will be born. If this should happen, the child must be transferred to the class for which his nature best fits him.

Social Organization

Perhaps the most interesting, and certainly the most well-known parts of the *Republic* are those which deal with the way of life of the upper classes. In order to guarantee their unselfishness, the guardians are to live a communal life of great austerity (Ex. 8e). They are not to possess property of any kind; their wages come in the form of food and clothes supplied by the class of producers. Thus they will have no inducement to neglect the common good.

The most radical proposals are those concerned with the breeding arrangements for the guardians (Ex. 8f). The family in its conventional form is to be abolished because it exists as a rival focus of loyalty to that of the state. On the same principles by which animals are selectively bred, the guardians are to be paired off and mated to produce the best offspring, allowing those of superior qualities to mate more frequently than the rest. To prevent the identifying of offspring by their natural parents, the children born of such unions are to be taken from their mothers after birth and brought up in state nurseries. In such a way the traditional family will be ultimately replaced by a family unit that is co-extensive with the whole community.

Justice

Having outlined the 'good' state, Socrates is now able to discern in it the four cardinal virtues of wisdom, courage, temperance and justice (Ex. 8g). Wisdom is found in the knowledge possessed by the rulers. Courage is the quality of the military class. Temperance or 'harmony' is a quality possessed by all classes and refers to the acceptance of the rule of the superior elements in the state. Justice, the remaining virtue, must therefore be that quality which secures the maintenance of the former three. It is, in fact, the principle of specialization itself: 'that one man should practise one thing only'.

The object of the Socratic enquiry being primarily justice in the person rather than in the city, attention is now directed to the human soul. Three distinct parts of the soul are identified: the rational, the spirited and the appetitive. Each of the parts is seen to correspond with one of the classes in the state, thereby indicating a close parallel between the state and the human soul. It is therefore valid to argue that the virtues in the state are also parallels of the virtues in the soul (Ex. 8h). Thus justice in the individual must mean, by analogy with justice in the state, that the three parts of the soul are each performing their proper function; that is that reason rules appetite with the aid of spirit.

The Philosopher-Kings

The fourth and final stage in the construction of the ideal city is concerned with the development of 'true knowledge' (*episteme*) within the souls of the rulers. Knowledge of the eternal 'Forms'—the permanent principles of reality which lie behind the semi-real world of the senses—is the distinguishing quality of the true philosopher, and Plato conceives of his perfect state as one ruled by philosophers (Ex. 8i). The prospective philosopher-rulers are to spend ten years studying the mathematical sciences which will train them in the processes of abstract reasoning. At the age of thirty those who are capable of further progress complete their formal education with five years' study of dialectic.

In this period those who possess the true philosophic qualities come to understand the Forms and in particular the 'Form of the Good', which is the ultimate principle of rational order in the light of which the other Forms possess reality (Ex. 8j). Those who graduate at the age of thirty-five are qualified to rule, but for a period of fifteen years they must serve the state in an administrative capacity to acquire experience and to have continual tests put on their zeal and unselfishness. Finally, at the age of fifty, those who have survived all the tests will become philosopher-kings spending their lives meditating on the Form of the Good and occasionally participating in the onerous duty of making political decisions.

There is no doubt that Plato's *Republic* has had a remarkable influence on later political thought. Indeed it may be said to have initiated the tradition of regarding politics as a branch of some more exact study, such as mathematics or theology, and political problems as deviations from a 'correct' political order. Thus, St Augustine, Calvin, Rousseau and the numerous devisers of ideal utopian communities in their very different ways all represent the Platonic principle that the perfect political solution exists, may be known, and can be imposed upon imperfect political societies.

FURTHER READING

Text
Plato: *The Republic.*

Commentaries
E. Barker: *Greek Political Theory* (Methuen 1960)
R. C. Cross and A. D. Woozley: *Plato's Republic: a Philosophical Commentary* (Macmillan 1966)
G. C. Field: *The Philosophy of Plato* (Oxford University Press 1969)
R. E. Nettleship: *Lectures on the Republic of Plato* (Macmillan 1962)

K. Popper: *The Open Society and its Enemies* vol. I (Routledge & Kegan Paul 1962)

8a PLATO: THE ORIGIN OF THE STATE

We think of justice as a quality that may exist in a whole community as well as in an individual, and the community is the bigger of the two. Possibly, then, we may find justice there in larger proportions, easier to make out. So I suggest that we should begin by inquiring what justice means in a state. Then we can go on to look for its counterpart on a smaller scale in the individual . . .

Suppose we imagine a state coming into being before our eyes. We might then be able to watch the growth of justice or of injustice within it. When that is done, we may hope it will be easier to find what we are looking for . . .

A state comes into existence because no individual is self-sufficing; we all have many needs . . .

So, having all these needs, we call in one another's help to satisfy our various requirements; and when we have collected a number of helpers and associates to live together in one place, we call that settlement a state.

So if one man gives another what he has to give in exchange for what he can get, it is because each finds that to do so is for his own advantage . . .

Now let us build up our imaginary state from the beginning. Apparently, it will owe its existence to our needs, the first and greatest need being the provision of food to keep us alive. Next we shall want a house; and thirdly, such things as clothing.

How will our state be able to supply all these demands? we shall need at least one man to be a farmer, another a builder, and a third a weaver. Will that do, or shall we add a shoemaker and one or two more to provide for our personal wants?

By all means.

The minimum state, then, will consist of four or five men.

Apparently.

Now here is a further point. Is each one of them to bring the product of his work into a common stock? Should our one farmer, for example, provide food enough for four people and spend the whole of his working time in producing corn, so as to share with the rest; or should he take no notice of them and spend only a quarter of his time on growing just enough corn for himself, and divide the other three-quarters between building his house, weaving his clothes, and making his shoes, so as to save the trouble of sharing with others and attend himself to all his own concerns?

The first plan might be the easier, replied Adeimantus.

That may very well be so, said I; for, as you spoke, it occurred to me, for one thing, that no two people are born exactly alike. There are innate differences which fit them for different occupations.

And will a man do better working at many trades, or keeping to one only.

Keeping to one.

And there is another point: obviously work may be ruined, if you let the right time go by. The workman must wait upon the work; it will not wait upon his leisure and allow itself to be done in a spare moment. So the conclusion is that more things will be produced and the work be more easily and better done, when every man is set free from all other occupations to do, at the right time, the one thing for which he is naturally fitted.

We shall need more than four citizens, then, to supply all those necessaries we mentioned. You see, Adeimantus, if the farmer is to have a good plough and spade and other tools, he will not make them himself. No more will the builder and weaver and shoemaker make all the many implements they need. So quite a number of carpenters and smiths and other craftsmen must be enlisted. Our miniature state is beginning to grow.

(*The Republic of Plato*, tr. F. M. Cornford, Bk 2, pp. 54-6, Clarendon Press, Oxford 1941.)

8b PLATO: THE LUXURIOUS STATE

Then we must once more enlarge our community. The healthy one will not be big enough now; it must be swollen up with a whole multitude of callings not ministering to any bare necessity: hunters and fishermen, for instance; artists in sculpture, painting, and music; poets with their attendant train of professional reciters, actors, dancers, producers; and makers of all sorts of household gear, including everything for women's adornment. . . .

And with this manner of life physicians will be in much greater request . . .

The country, too, which was large enough to support the original inhabitants, will now be too small. If we are to have enough pasture and plough land, we shall have to cut off a slice of our neighbours' territory; and if they are not content with necessaries, but give themselves up to getting unlimited wealth, they will want a slice of ours . . .

So the next thing will be, Glaucon, that we shall be at war.

No doubt.

We need not say yet whether war does good or harm, but only that we have discovered its origin in desires which are the most fruitful source of evils both to individuals and to states . . .

This will mean a considerable addition to our community—a whole army, to go out to battle with any invader, in defence of all this property and of the citizens we have been describing.

Why so? Can't they defend themselves?

Not if the principle was right, which we all accepted in framing our society. You remember we agreed that no one man can practise many trades or arts satisfactorily.

True.

Well, is not the conduct of war an art, quite as important as shoemaking?

Yes.

But we would not allow our shoemaker to try to be also a farmer or weaver or builder, because we wanted our shoes well made. We gave each man one trade, for which he was naturally fitted; he would do good work if he confined himself to that all his life, never letting the right moment slip by. Now in no form of work is efficiency so important as in war; and fighting is not so easy a business that a man can follow another trade, such as farming or shoemaking, and also be an efficient soldier. Why, even a game like draughts or dice must be studied from childhood; no one can become a fine player in his spare moments. Just taking up a shield or other weapon will not make a man capable of fighting that very day in any sort of warfare, any more than taking up a tool or implement of some kind will make a man a craftsman or an athlete, if he does not understand its use and has never been properly trained to handle it.

No; if that were so, tools would indeed be worth having.

These guardians of our state, then, inasmuch as their work is the most important of all, will need the most complete freedom from other occupations and the greatest amount of skill and practice.

I quite agree.

And also a native aptitude for their calling.

Certainly.

So it is our business to define, if we can, the natural gifts that fit men to be guardians of a commonwealth, and to select them accordingly.

(*The Republic of Plato*, Bk 2, pp. 60-1.)

8c   PLATO: THE GUARDIANS

As I said just now, then, we must find out who are the best guardians of this inward conviction that they must always do what they believe to be best for the commonwealth. We shall have to watch them from earliest childhood and set them tasks in which they would be most likely to forget or to be beguiled out of this duty. We shall then choose only those whose memory holds firm and who are proof against delusion.

We must also subject them to ordeals of toil and pain and watch for the same qualities there. And we must observe them when exposed to the test of yet a third kind of bewitchment. As people lead colts up to alarming noises to see whether they are timid, so these young men must be brought into terrifying situations and then into scenes of pleasure, which will put them to severer proof than gold tried in the furnace. If we find one bearing himself well in all these trials and resisting every enchantment, a true guardian of himself, preserving always that perfect rhythm and harmony of being which he has acquired from his training in music and poetry, such a one will be of the greatest service to the commonwealth as well as to himself. Whenever we find one who has come unscathed through every test in childhood, youth, and manhood, we shall set him as a Ruler to watch over the commonwealth; he will be honoured in life, and after death receive the highest tribute of funeral rites and other memorials. All who do not reach this standard we must reject. And that, I think, my dear Glaucon, may be taken as an outline of the way in which we shall select Guardians to be set in authority as Rulers.

I am very much of your mind.

These, then, may properly be called Guardians in the fullest sense, who will ensure that neither foes without shall have the power, nor friends within the wish, to do harm. Those young men whom up to now we have been speaking of as Guardians, will be better described as Auxiliaries, who will enforce the decisions of the Rulers.

(*The Republic of Plato*, Bk 3, pp. 102-3.)

8d   PLATO: THE MYTH OF THE METALS

Now, said I, can we devise something in the way of those convenient fictions we spoke of earlier, a single bold flight of invention, which we may induce the community in general, and if possible the Rulers themselves, to accept?

What kind of fiction? . . .

I shall try to convince, first the Rulers and the soldiers, and then the whole community, that all that nurture and education which we gave them was only something they seemed to experience as it were in a dream. In reality they were the whole time down inside the earth, being moulded and fostered while their arms and all their equipment were being fashioned also; and at last, when they were complete, the earth sent them up from her womb into the light of day. So now they must think of the land they dwell in as a mother and nurse, whom they must take thought for and defend against any attack, and of their fellow citizens as brothers born of the same soil . . .

It is true, we shall tell our people in this fable, that all of you in this land are brothers; but the god who fashioned you mixed gold in the composition of those among you who are fit to rule, so that they are of the most precious quality; and he put silver in the Auxiliaries, and iron and brass in the farmers and craftsmen. Now, since you are all of one stock, although your children will generally be like their parents, sometimes a golden parent may have a silver child or a silver parent a golden one, and so on with all the other combinations. So the first and chief injunction laid by heaven upon the Rulers is that, among all the things of which they must show themselves good guardians, there is none that needs to be so carefully watched as the mixture of metals in the souls of the children. If a child of their own is born with an alloy of iron or brass, they must, without the smallest pity, assign him the station proper to his nature and thrust him out among the craftsmen or the farmers. If, on the contrary, these classes produce a child with gold or silver in his composition, they will promote him, according to his value, to be a Guardian or an Auxiliary. They will appeal to a prophecy that ruin will come upon the state when it passes into the keeping of a man of iron or brass. Such is the story; can you think of any device to make them believe it?

Not in the first generation; but their sons and descendants might believe it, and finally the rest of mankind.

Well, said I, even so it might have a good effect in making them care more for the commonwealth and for one another; for I think I see what you mean.

(*The Republic of Plato*, Bk 3, pp. 103-5.)

8e PLATO: THE ABOLITION OF PROPERTY

Besides education, it is only common sense to say that the dwellings and other belongings provided for them must be such as will neither make them less perfect Guardians nor encourage them to maltreat their fellow citizens.

With that end in view, let us consider how they should live and be housed. First, none of them must possess any private property beyond the barest necessaries. Next, no one is to have any dwelling or store-house that is not open for all to enter at will. Their food, in the quantities required by men of temperance and courage who are in training for war, they will receive from the other citizens as the wages of their guardianship, fixed so that there shall be just enough for the year with nothing over; and they will have meals in common and all live together like soldiers in a camp. Gold and silver, we shall tell them, they will not need, having the divine counterparts of those metals always in their souls as a god-given possession, whose purity it is not lawful to sully by the acquisition of that mortal dross, current among mankind, which has been the occasion of so many unholy deeds. They alone of all the citizens are forbidden to touch and handle silver or gold, or to come under the same roof with them, or wear them as ornaments, or drink from vessels made of them. This manner of life will be their salvation and make them the saviours of the commonwealth. If ever they should come to possess land of their own and houses and money, they will give up their guardianship for the management of their farms and households and become tyrants at enmity with their fellow citizens instead of allies.

(*The Republic of Plato*, Bk 3, p. 106.)

8f PLATO: THE BREEDING ARRANGEMENTS

It follows from what we have just said that, if we are to keep our flock at the highest pitch of excellence, there should be as many unions of the best of both sexes, and as few of the inferior, as possible, and that only the offspring of the better unions should be kept. And again, no one but the Rulers must know how all this is being effected; otherwise our herd of Guardians may become rebellious . . .

We must, then, institute certain festivals at which we shall bring together the brides and the bridegrooms. There will be sacrifices, and our poets will write songs befitting the occasion. The number of marriages we shall leave to the Rulers' discretion. They will aim at keeping the number of the citizens as constant as possible, having regard to losses caused by war, epidemics, and so on; and they must do their best to see that our state does not become either great or small . . .

I think they will have to invent some ingenious system of drawing lots, so that, at each pairing off, the inferior candidate may blame his luck rather than the Rulers . . .

Moreover, young men who acquit themselves well in war and other duties, should be given, among other rewards and privileges, more liberal opportunities to sleep with a wife, for the further purpose that, with good excuse, as many as possible of the children may be begotten of such fathers . . .

As soon as children are born, they will be taken in charge by officers appointed for the purpose, who may be men or women or both, since offices are to be shared by both sexes. The children of the better parents they will carry to the crèche to be reared in the care of nurses living apart in a certain quarter of the city. Those of the inferior parents and any children of the rest that are born defective will be hidden away, in some appropriate manner that must be kept secret.

They must be, if the breed of our Guardians is to be kept pure.

These officers will also superintend the nursing of the children. They will bring the mothers to the crèche when their breasts are full, while taking every precaution that no mother shall know her own child; and if the mothers have not enough milk, they will provide wet-nurses. They will limit the time during which the mothers will suckle their children, and hand over all the hard work and sitting up at night to nurses and attendants.

That will make child-bearing an easy business for the Guardians' wives.

So it should be. To go on with our scheme: we said that children should be born from parents in the prime of life. Do you agree that this lasts about twenty years for a woman, and thirty for a man? A woman should bear children for the commonwealth from her twentieth to her fortieth year; a man should begin to beget them when he has passed 'the racer's prime in swiftness', and continue till he is fifty-five.

Those are certainly the years in which both the bodily and the mental powers of man and woman are at their best.

If a man either above or below this age meddles with the begetting of children for the commonwealth, we shall hold it an offence against divine and human law. He will be begetting for his country a child conceived in darkness and dire incontinence, whose birth, if it escape detection, will not have been sanctioned by the sacrifices and prayers offered at each marriage festival, when priests and priestesses join with the whole community in praying that the children to be born may be even better and more useful citizens than their parents.

You are right.

The same law will apply to any man within the prescribed limits who touches a woman also of marriageable age when the Ruler has not paired them. We shall say that he is foisting on the commonwealth a bastard, unsanctioned by law or by religion.

As soon, however, as the men and the women have passed the age prescribed for producing children, we shall leave them free to form a connexion with whom they will, except that a man shall not take his daughter or daughter's daughter or mother or mother's mother, nor a woman her son or father or her son's son or father's father; and all this only after we have exhorted them to see that no child, if any be conceived, shall be brought to light, or, if they cannot prevent its birth, to dispose of it on the understanding that no such child can be reared.

That too is reasonable. But how are they to distinguish fathers and daughters and those other relations you mentioned?

They will not, said I. But, reckoning from the day when he becomes a bride-groom, a man will call all children born in the tenth or the seventh month sons and daughters, and they will call him father. Their children again he will call grandchildren, and they will call his group grandfathers and grandmothers; and all who are born within the period during which their mothers and fathers were having children will be called brothers and sisters. This will provide for those restrictions on unions that we mentioned; but the law will allow brothers and sisters to live together, if the lot so falls out and the Delphic oracle also approves.

(*The Republic of Plato*, Bk 5, pp. 155-8.)

8g PLATO: THE VIRTUES IN THE STATE

I take it that our state, having been founded and built up on the right lines, is good in the complete sense of the word.

It must be.

Obviously, then, it is wise, brave, temperate, and just.

Obviously.

Then if we find some of these qualities in it, the remainder will be the one we have not found. It is as if we were looking somewhere for one of any four things: if we detected that one immediately, we should be satisfied; whereas if we recognized the other three first, that would be enough to indicate the thing we wanted; it could only be the remaining one. So here we have four qualities. Had we not better follow that method in looking for the one we want?

Surely.

To begin then: the first quality to come into view in our state seems to be its wisdom . . .

I think the state we have described really has wisdom; for it will be prudent in counsel, won't it?

Yes.

And prudence in counsel is clearly a form of knowledge; good counsel can-not be due to ignorance and stupidity.

Clearly . . .

Well then, is there any form of knowledge, possessed by some among the citizens of our new-founded commonwealth, which will enable it to take thought, not for some particular interest, but for the best possible conduct of the state as a whole in its internal and external relations?

Yes, there is.

What is it, and where does it reside?

It is precisely that art of guardianship which resides in those Rulers whom we just now called Guardians in the full sense.

And what would you call the state on the strength of that knowledge?

Prudent and truly wise . . .

So, if a state is constituted on natural principles, the wisdom it possesses as a whole will be due to the knowledge residing in the smallest part, the one which takes the lead and governs the rest. Such knowledge is the only kind that deserves the name of wisdom, and it appears to be ordained by nature that the class privileged to possess it should be the smallest of all . . .

Next there is courage. It is not hard to discern that quality or the part of the community in which it resides so as to entitle the whole to be called brave.

Why do you say so?

Because anyone who speaks of a state as either brave or cowardly can only be thinking of that part of it which takes the field and fights in its defence; the reason being, I imagine, that the character of the state is not determined by the bravery or cowardice of the other parts.

No.

Courage, then, is another quality which a community owes to a certain part of itself. And its being brave will mean that, in this part, it possesses the power of preserving, in all circumstances, a conviction about the sort of things that it is right to be afraid of—the conviction implanted by the education which the law-giver has established. Is not that what you mean by courage? . . .

Two qualities, I went on, still remain to be made out in our state, temperance and the object of our whole inquiry, justice. . . .

At first sight, temperance seems more like some sort of concord or harmony than the other qualities did.

How so?

Temperance surely means a kind of orderliness, a control of certain pleasures and appetites. People use the expression, 'master of oneself', whatever that means, and various other phrases that point the same way. . . .

I think, however, that the phrase means that within the man himself, in his soul, there is a better part and a worse; and that he is his own master when the part which is better by nature has the worse under its control. ⁻. . .

Do you see that this state of things will exist in your commonwealth, where the desires of the inferior multitude will be controlled by the desires and wisdom of the superior few? Hence, if any society can be called master of itself and in control of pleasures and desires, it will be ours.

Quite so.

On all these grounds, then, we may describe it as temperate. Furthermore, in our state, if anywhere, the governors and the governed will share the same conviction on the question who ought to rule. Don't you think so?

I am quite sure of it.

Then, if that is their state of mind, in which of the two classes of citizens will temperance reside—in the governors or in the governed?

In both, I suppose.

So we were not wrong in divining a resemblance between temperance and some kind of harmony. Temperance is not like courage and wisdom, which made the state wise and brave by residing each in one particular part. Temperance works in a different way; it extends throughout the whole gamut of the state, producing a consonance of all its elements from the weakest to the strongest as measured by any standard you like to take—wisdom, bodily strength, numbers, or wealth. So we are entirely justified in identifying with temperance this unanimity or harmonious agreement between the naturally superior and inferior elements on the question which of the two should govern, whether in the state or in the individual.

I fully agree.

Good, said I. We have discovered in our commonwealth three out of our four qualities, to the best of our present judgement. What is the remaining one, required to make up its full complement of goodness? For clearly this will be justice.

Clearly. . . .

You remember how, when we first began to establish our commonwealth and several times since, we have laid down, as a universal principle, that everyone ought to perform the one function in the community for which his nature best suited him. Well, I believe that that principle, or some form of it, is justice.

We certainly laid that down.

Yes, and surely we have often heard people say that justice means minding one's own business and not meddling with other men's concerns; and we have often said so ourselves.

We have.

Well, my friend, it may be that this minding of one's own business, when it takes a certain form, is actually the same thing as justice. Do you know what makes me think so?

No, tell me.

I think that this quality which makes it possible for the three we have already considered, wisdom, courage, and temperance, to take their place in the commonwealth, and so long as it remains present secures their continuance, must be the remaining one. And we said that, when three of the four were found, the one left over would be justice.

It must be so.

Well now, if we had to decide which of these qualities will contribute most to the excellence of our commonwealth, it would be hard to say whether it was the unanimity of rulers and subjects, or the soldier's fidelity to the established conviction about what is, or is not, to be feared, or the watchful intelligence of the Rulers; or whether its excellence were not above all due to the observance by everyone, child or woman, slave or freeman or artisan, ruler or ruled, of this principle that each one should do his own proper work without interfering with others.

It would be hard to decide, no doubt.

It seems, then, that this principle can at any rate claim to rival wisdom, temperance, and courage as conducing to the excellence of a state. And would you not say that the only possible competitor of these qualities must be justice? . . .

Most certainly.

Where there are three orders, then, any plurality of functions or shifting from one order to another is not merely utterly harmful to the community, but one might fairly call it the extreme of wrongdoing. And you will agree that to do the greatest of wrongs to one's own community is injustice.

Surely.

This, then, is injustice. And, conversely, let us repeat that when each order—tradesman, Auxiliary, Guardian—keeps to its own proper business in the commonwealth and does its own work, that is justice and what makes a just society.

(*The Republic of Plato*, Bk 4, pp. 118-26.)

8h PLATO: THE VIRTUES IN THE INDIVIDUAL

We are fairly agreed that the same three elements exist alike in the state and in the individual soul.

That is so.

Does it not follow at once that state and individual will be wise or brave by virtue of the same element in each and in the same way? Both will possess in the same manner any quality that makes for excellence.

That must be true.

Then it applies to justice: we shall conclude that a man is just in the same way that a state was just. And we have surely not forgotten that justice in the state meant that each of the three orders in it was doing its own proper work. So we may henceforth bear in mind that each one of us likewise will be a just person, fulfilling his proper function, only if the several parts of our nature fulfil theirs.

Certainly.

And it will be the business of reason to rule with wisdom and forethought on behalf of the entire soul; while the spirited element ought to act as its subordinate and ally. The two will be brought into accord, as we said earlier, by that combination of mental and bodily training which will tune up one string of the instrument and relax the other, nourishing the reasoning part on the study of noble literature and allaying the other's wildness by harmony and rhythm. When both have been thus nurtured and trained to know their own true functions, they must be set in command over the appetites, which form the greater part of each man's soul and are by nature insatiably covetous. They must keep watch lest this part, by battening on the pleasures that are called bodily, should grow so great and powerful that it will no longer keep to its own work, but will try to enslave the others and usurp a dominion to which it has no right, thus turning the whole of life upside down. At the same time, those two together will be the best of guardians for the entire soul and for the body against all enemies from without: the one will take counsel, while the other will do battle, following its ruler's commands and by its own bravery giving effect to the ruler's designs.

Yes, that is all true.

And so we call an individual brave in virtue of this spirited part of his nature, when, in spite of pain or pleasure, it holds fast to the injunctions of reason about what he ought or ought not to be afraid of.

True.

And wise in virtue of that small part which rules and issues these injunctions, possessing as it does the knowledge of what is good for each of the three elements and for all of them in common.

Certainly.

And, again, temperate by reason of the unanimity and concord of all three, when there is no internal conflict between the ruling element and its two subjects, but all are agreed that reason should be ruler.

Yes, that is an exact account of temperance, whether in the state or in the individual.

Finally, a man will be just by observing the principle we have so often stated.

Necessarily.

Now is there any indistinctness in our vision of justice, that might make it seem somehow different from what we found it to be in the state?

I don't think so. . . .

And so our dream has come true—I mean the inkling we had that, by some happy chance, we had lighted upon a rudimentary form of justice from the very moment when we set about founding our commonwealth. Our principle that the born shoemaker or carpenter had better stick to his trade turns out to have been an adumbration of justice; and that is why it has helped us. But in reality justice, though evidently analogous to this principle, is not a matter of external behaviour, but of the inward self and of attending to all that is, in the fullest sense, a man's proper concern. The just man does not allow the several elements in his soul to usurp one another's functions; he is indeed one who sets his house in order, by self-mastery and discipline coming to be at peace with himself, and bringing into tune those three parts, like the terms in the proportion of a musical scale, the highest and lowest notes and the mean between them, with all the intermediate intervals. Only when he has linked these parts together in well-tempered harmony and has made himself one man instead of many, will he be ready to go about whatever he may have to do, whether it be making money and satisfying bodily wants, or business transactions, or the affairs of state. In all these fields when he speaks of just and honourable conduct, he will mean the behaviour that helps to produce and to preserve this habit of mind; and by wisdom he will mean the knowledge which presides over such conduct. Any action which tends to break down this habit will be for him unjust; and the notions governing it he will call ignorance and folly.

(*The Republic of Plato*, Bk 4, pp. 136-9.)

8i PLATO: PHILOSOPHER KINGS

Well, there is one change which, as I believe we can show, would bring about this revolution—not a small change, certainly, nor an easy one, but possible.

What is it? . . .

Unless either philosophers become kings in their countries or those who are now called kings and rulers come to be sufficiently inspired with a genuine desire for wisdom; unless, that is to say, political power and philosophy meet together, while the many natures who now go their several ways in the one or the other direction are forcibly debarred from doing so, there can be no rest from troubles, my dear Glaucon, for states, nor yet, as I believe, for all mankind; nor can this commonwealth which we have imagined ever till then see the light of day and grow to its full stature.

(*The Republic of Plato*, Bk 5, pp. 174-5.)

8j PLATO: DIALECTIC

No one will maintain against us that there is any other method of inquiry which systematically attempts in every case to grasp the nature of each thing as it is in itself. The other arts are nearly all concerned with human opinions and desires, or with the production of natural and artificial things, or with the care of them when produced. There remain geometry and those other allied studies which, as we said, do in some measure apprehend reality; but we observe that they cannot yield anything clearer than a dream-like vision of the real so long as they leave the assumptions they employ unquestioned and can give no account of them. If your premiss is something you do not really know and your conclusion and the intermediate steps are a tissue of things you do not really know, your reasoning may be consistent with itself, but how can it ever amount to knowledge?

It cannot.

So, said I, the method of dialectic is the only one which takes this course, doing away with assumptions and travelling up to the first principle of all, so as to make sure of confirmation there. When the eye of the soul is sunk in a veritable slough of barbarous ignorance, this method gently draws it forth and guides it upwards, assisted in this work of conversion by the arts we have enumerated. From force of habit we have several times spoken of these as branches of knowledge; but they need some other name implying something less clear than knowledge, though not so dim as the apprehension of appearances. 'Thinking', I believe, was the term we fixed on earlier; but in considering matters of such high importance we shall not quarrel about a name.

Certainly not.

We shall be satisfied, then, with the names we gave earlier to our four divisions: first, knowledge; second, thinking; third, belief; and fourth, imagining. The last two taken together constitute the apprehension of appearances in the world of Becoming; the first two, intelligence concerned with true Being. Finally, as Being is to Becoming, so is intelligence to the apprehension of appearances; and in the same relation again stand knowledge to belief, and thinking to imagining. . . .

Well, I certainly agree on those other points, so far as I can follow you.

And by a master of dialectic do you also mean one who demands an account of the essence of each thing? And would you not say that, in so far as he can render no such account to himself or to others, his intelligence is at fault?

I should.

And does not this apply to the Good? He must be able to distinguish the essential nature of Goodness, isolating it from all other Forms; he must fight his way through all criticisms, determined to examine every step by the standard, not of appearances and opinions, but of reality and truth, and win through to the end without sustaining a fall. If he cannot do this, he will know neither Goodness itself nor any good thing; if he does lay hold upon some semblance of good, it will be only a matter of belief, not of knowledge; and he will dream away his life here in a sleep which has no awakening on this side of that world of Death where he will sleep at last for ever.

I do most earnestly agree with you.

(*The Republic of Plato*, Bk 7, pp. 248–9.)

CHAPTER 4

Aristotle (384–322 B.C.)

Aristotle was born at Stagira in northern Greece, and was the son of the court physician to the Macedonian king. It is quite likely that his early contact with medicine and biology was partly responsible for his later passionate interest in science. At the age of seventeen he entered Plato's Academy, staying there as student and teacher until the death of Plato twenty years later. Aristotle seems to have found life at the Academy stimulating and congenial, and the philosophy of Plato always remained the dominant intellectual influence on him, notwithstanding his divergence from many Platonic principles.

A quarrel with Plato's successor at the Academy led Aristotle to leave Athens and in 342 B.C. he took up an appointment as tutor to Alexander, the young heir to the Macedonian throne. The association between Aristotle and Alexander seems to have produced little lasting influence on the minds of either one, although they remained friends. Even when, in later years, Alexander's conquests were fundamentally changing territorial boundaries, Aristotle never wavered from his conviction that the *polis* was the normal and most advanced form of political association.

In 335 when Alexander succeeded Philip to the throne of Macedonia, Aristotle returned to Athens where he established his own school, the Lyceum. Here he remained for twelve years, teaching, conducting scientific experiments and writing his most important works. Aristotle's intellectual activity was phenomenal. He wrote on almost every branch of human knowledge including logic, metaphysics, ethics, politics, aesthetics, psychology, biology and physics. His contributions to most of these subjects are still regarded as worthy of serious study.

Metaphysics

Although we are primarily interested in his political ideas, it is first necessary to explain how Aristotle's metaphysical philosophy differed from that of Plato. As has been shown in the previous chapter, Plato conceived of the Forms as being the permanent objects of real knowledge apprehended by reason, as opposed to the semi-real material world perceived by the senses. Things possess true reality only through their participation in the Forms. Aristotle, on the other hand, considered that the Platonic Forms are so remote from the material world that they cannot possibly be known and cannot be the cause of individual material entities. Instead, Aristotle emphasized that the material thing contains a latent form. It is the form which confers actuality upon the potentiality of matter. In other words, forms do exist but only as characteristics of individual things, not as entities separate from the material world. It follows that for Aristotle, unlike Plato, the objects of sense perception are the primary reality, and the material world may therefore be the object of knowledge.

The Politics

The two books in which Aristotle considered the moral and social conduct of man are the *Nicomachean Ethics* and the *Politics*; the former being perhaps the better book, but the latter more specifically relevant to political thought. The *Politics* is a curious and untidy work; it does not appear to have been written as a single treatise with a unifying theme. Rather, it seems to be a collection of essays on political subjects which cannot be compiled in any logical order. Of the eight books which make up the *Politics*, the first three deal with the nature and theory of the state, Books IV, V, and VI examine actual constitutions, and Books VII and VIII are concerned with the depiction of an ideal state. One theory is that the *Politics* is, in reality, three sets of lectures given by Aristotle at the Lyceum. The text is therefore either Aristotle's own lecture notes—perhaps written up after the lecture—or the notes of a student who attended the courses. Evidence for this is supplied by the written style of the book, which is often formless and laboured.

The Nature of the State

In the opening chapters of the book Aristotle discusses the *polis* and conceives of it as the natural culmination of the social development of mankind (Ex. 9a). Men and women first come together in households and villages in order to improve their material lives. However, they have a natural impulse towards further combination and this impulse is satisfied only with the formation of the state. It is the state alone which provides the conditions necessary for the 'good life'—the full development of man's faculties. Only in such conditions can man be truly happy, although the degree of happiness attained will depend upon the goodness of the *polis* which is formed.

Aristotle's theory of natural development implies the organic analogy; the state is seen as a parallel to a living creature whose true nature is realized in its final stage of development. Thus, man as an isolated individual is incomplete. His essential humanity is observed only when he is participating with others in the common affairs of the city. A man, in fact, can be defined only by reference to the state of which he forms a part; 'the state is prior to the individual.'

Slavery

Aristotle is possibly the most notable exponent of the discredited theory of racial inequality (Ex. 9b). Nature, he tells us, is characterized by the relationship between rule and subordination. Among men we find some who are as inferior to others as beasts are to men. Such inferior individuals are natural slaves; what makes them inferior is their lack of reason which fits them to be the property of their rational masters. Unlike Sophists such as Antiphon and Hippias who thought that all men possessed a common human nature, Aristotle considers that Greeks are by nature superior to Barbarians (non-Greeks) who are naturally slaves. By pursuing this argument Aristotle is led to reject the enslavement of Greeks which, being based only upon convention, is against nature and therefore wrong.

Citizenship

Obviously Aristotle could not conceive of slaves being citizens in any *polis*. In Book III he examines the nature of citizenship and concludes that a citizen is one 'who has the power to take part in the deliberative or judicial administration of a state' (Ex. 9c). He is then led to the important question of whether the virtue of the good citizen and the virtue of the good man are the same kinds of virtue. The good citizen will express his goodness in promoting the good of his *polis*, but as the constitutions of cities vary, it must follow that this goodness is not uniform but relative to the ethos of the *polis*. On the other hand, the good man possesses an absolute goodness which does not vary. Clearly the two forms of goodness are not necessarily the same. Although the remainder of this argument is not entirely clear, Aristotle seems to conclude that the good citizen and the good man are identical only in the good *polis* where the citizens possess a latent capacity for ruling as well as for being ruled.

If this is the case, then, argues Aristotle, not only slaves and foreigners, but manual labourers also cannot be regarded as citizens in a good *polis* (Ex. 9d). Manual work, although necessary for the maintenance of the state, is such a degrading occupation that the worker cannot possibly acquire the requisite virtues for citizenship.

Classification of Constitutions

The distinction that Aristotle has made between good and bad states is later developed in a formal six-fold classification of constitutions

(Ex. 9e). There are three 'right' constitutions which consider the common interest: monarchy (the rule of one), aristocracy (the rule of a few), and polity (the rule of a large number of the moderately wealthy). Corresponding to each of these types there is a 'perversion' where the rulers consider exclusively their own interest: tyranny (aiming at the good of the tyrant), oligarchy (aiming only at the good of the wealthy few), and democracy (aiming at the good of the poor masses). In order of preference, monarchy is the best form, aristocracy the second best, and polity the least good of the lawful constitutions. However, as the perversion of the best leads to the worst, the preferential order of the corrupt constitutions is reversed, with democracy being the least bad and tyranny the worst of the perverted types of government.

The Polity

In practice most constitutions tend to be either oligarchic or democratic. The 'polity' or 'constitutional democracy'—'the best constitution for most states, and the best life for most men'—is a mean between the two extremes. It draws upon the principles of both democracy and oligarchy keeping the good elements and rejecting the selfish (Ex. 9f). From democracy come the claims of freedom and equality, and from oligarchy the claims of wealth, education, and social position. In accordance with its basic principle of the mean or the middle way, polity gives sovereign power to a large, moderately wealthy, middle class which is likely to rule more justly in the interests of the whole community than either the very rich or the very poor.

Aristotle and Plato

If we compare the political thought of Aristotle with that of Plato, it is clear that there are many superficial similarities. Both are dominated by the *polis*; they are unable to conceive of any superior type of political association. Both see the state as the agency for the good life: both are anti-democratic (although Aristotle is less so than Plato), and both accept the organic view of the state. But it is the dissimilarities between the two that are more striking. Plato is the archetypal 'ivory-tower' philosopher, remote from every-day reality, preferring theories to facts, and deducing fascinating, if sometimes rather absurd, conclusions from decidedly shaky general axioms. Aristotle, on the other hand, is the down-to-earth inductive political scientist, whose conclusions are generally based upon factual material. Of the two, Plato may be preferred as the greater artist and perhaps the more profound thinker, but it is Aristotle who has more relevance to the empirical methods of modern political science.

FURTHER READING

Texts
Aristotle: *The Politics*

Commentaries
E. Barker: *The Political Thought of Plato and Aristotle* (Dover Publications 1959)
T. Gomperz (tr. G. Berry): *The Greek Thinkers*, vol. 4, (John Murray, 1912)
W. F. R. Hardie: *Aristotle's Ethical Theory* (Clarendon Press 1968)
W. Jaeger: *Aristotle. Fundamentals of his Development* (Oxford University Press 1967)
E. Voegelin: *Order and History*, vol. 3 (Louisiana State University Press 1957)

9a   ARISTOTLE: ORIGIN AND DEVELOPMENT OF THE STATE

Every state is a community of some kind, and every community is established with a view to some good; for mankind always act in order to obtain that which they think good. But, if all communities aim at some good, the state or political community, which is the highest of all, and which embraces all the rest, aims, and in a greater degree than any other, at the highest good.

Now there is an erroneous opinion that a statesman, king, householder, and master are the same, and that they differ, not in kind, but only in the number of their subjects. . . .

But all this is a mistake; for governments differ in kind, as will be evident to any one who considers the matter according to the method which has hitherto guided us. As in other departments of science, so in politics, the compound should always be resolved into the simple elements or least parts of the whole. We must therefore look at the elements of which the state is composed, in order that we may see in what they differ from one another, and whether any scientific distinction can be drawn between the different kinds of rule.

He who thus considers things in their first growth and origin, whether a state or anything else, will obtain the clearest view of them. In the first place (1) there must be a union of those who cannot exist without each other; for example, of male and female, that the race may continue; and this is a union which is formed, not of deliberate purpose, but because, in common with other animals and with plants, mankind have a natural desire to leave behind them an image of themselves. And (2) there must be a union of natural ruler and subject, that both may be preserved. For he who can foresee with his mind is by nature intended to be lord and master, and he who can work with his body is a subject, and by nature a slave; hence master and slave have the same interest. Nature, however, has distinguished between the female and the slave. For she is not niggardly, like the smith who fashions the Delphian knife for many uses; she makes each thing for a single use, and every instrument is best made when intended for one and not for many uses. But among barbarians no distinction is made between women and slaves, because there is no natural ruler among them: they are a community of slaves, male and female. Wherefore the poets say,—

'It is meet that Hellenes should rule over barbarians;'

as if they thought that the barbarian and the slave were by nature one.

Out of these two relationships between man and woman, master and slave, the family first arises, and Hesiod is right when he says,—

'First house and wife and an ox for the plough,'

for the ox is the poor man's slave. The family is the association established by nature for the supply of men's every day wants, and the members of it are called by Charondas 'companions of the cupboard' and by Epimenides the Cretan, 'companions of the manger'. But when several families are united, and the association aims at something more than the supply of daily needs, then comes into existence the village. . . .

When several villages are united in a single community, perfect and large enough to be nearly or quite self-sufficing, the state comes into existence, originating in the bare needs of life, and continuing in existence for the sake of a good life. And therefore, if the earlier forms of society are natural, so is the state, for it is the end of them, and the [completed] nature is the end. For what each thing is when fully developed, we call its nature, whether we are speaking of a man, a horse, or a family. Besides, the final cause and end of a thing is the best, and to be self-sufficing is the end and the best.

Hence it is evident that the state is a creation of nature, and that man is by nature a political animal. And he who by nature and not by mere accident is without a state, is either above humanity, or below it; he is the

'Tribeless, lawless, heartless one,'

whom Homer denounces—the outcast who is a lover of war; he may be compared to a bird which flies alone.

Now the reason why man is more of a political animal than bees or any other gregarious animals is evident. Nature, as we often say, makes nothing in vain, and man is the only animal whom she has endowed with the gift of speech. And whereas mere sound is but an indication of pleasure or pain, and is therefore found in other animals (for their nature attains to the perception of pleasure and pain and the intimation of them to one another, and no further), the power of speech is intended to set forth the expedient and inexpedient, and likewise the just and the unjust. And it is a characteristic of man that he alone has any sense of good and evil, of just and unjust, and the association of living beings who have this sense makes a family and a state.

Thus the state is by nature clearly prior to the family and to the individual, since the whole is of necessity prior to the part; for example, if the whole body be destroyed, there will be no foot or hand, except in an equivocal sense, as we might speak of a stone hand; for when destroyed the hand will be no better. But things are defined by their working and power; and we ought not to say that they are the same when they are no longer the same, but only that they have the same name. The proof that the state is a creation of nature and prior to the individual is that the individual, when isolated, is not self-sufficing; and therefore he is like a part in relation to the whole. But he who is unable to live in society, or who has no need because he is sufficient for himself, must be either a beast or a god: he is no part of a state. A social instinct is implanted in all men by nature, and yet he who first founded the state was the greatest of benefactors. For man, when perfected, is the best of animals, but, when separated from law and justice, he is the worst of all; since armed injustice is the more dangerous, and he is equipped at birth with the arms of intelligence and with moral qualities which he may use for the worst ends. Wherefore, if he have not virtue, he is the most unholy and the most savage of animals, and the most full of lust and gluttony. But justice is the bond of men in states, and the administration of justice, which is the determination of what is just, is the principle of order in political society.

(Aristotle, *The Politics*, tr. B. Jowett, Bk 1, pp. 1-5, Clarendon Press, Oxford 1905.)

9b   ARISTOTLE: SLAVERY

Let us first speak of master and slave, looking to the needs of practical life and also seeking to attain some better theory of their relation than exists at present. For some are of opinion that the rule of a master is a science, and that the management of a household, and the mastership of slaves, and the political and royal rule, as I was saying at the outset, are all the same. Others affirm that the rule of a master over slaves is contrary to nature, and that the distinction between slave and freeman exists by law only, and not by nature; and being an interference with nature is therefore unjust.

Property is a part of the household, and therefore the art of acquiring property is a part of the art of managing the household; for no man can live well, or indeed live at all, unless he be provided with necessaries. And as in the arts which have a definite sphere the workers must have their own proper instruments for the accomplishment of their work, so it is in the management of a household. Now, instruments are of various sorts; some are living, others lifeless; in the rudder, the pilot of a ship has a lifeless, in the look-out man, a living instrument; for in the arts the servant is a kind of instrument. Thus, too, a possession is an instrument for maintaining life. And so, in the arrangement of the family, a slave is a living possession, and property a number of such instruments; and the servant is himself an instrument, which takes precedence of all other instruments. . . . The master is only the master of the slave; he does not belong to him, whereas the slave is not only the slave of his master, but wholly belongs to him. Hence we see what is the nature and office of a slave; he who is by nature not his own but another's and yet a man, is by nature a slave; and he may be said to belong to another who, being a human being, is also a possession. And a possession may be defined as an instrument of action, separable from the possessor.

But is there any one thus intended by nature to be a slave, and for whom such a condition is expedient and right, or rather is not all slavery a violation of nature? . . .

First then we may observe in living creatures both a despotical and a constitutional rule; for the soul rules the body with a despotical rule, whereas the intellect rules the appetites with a constitutional and royal rule. And it is clear that the rule of the soul over the body, and of the mind and the rational element over the passionate is natural and expedient; whereas the equality of the two or the rule of the inferior is always hurtful. The same holds good of animals as well as of men; for tame animals have a better nature than wild, and all tame animals are better off when they are ruled by man; for then they are preserved. Again, the male is by nature superior, and the female inferior; and the one rules, and the other is ruled; this principle, of necessity, extends to all mankind. Where then there is such a difference as that between soul and body, or between men and animals (as in the case of those whose business is to use their body, and who can do nothing better), the lower sort are by nature slaves, and it is better for them as for all inferiors that they should be under the rule of a master. For he who can be, and therefore is another's, and he who participates in reason enough to apprehend, but not to have, reason, is a slave by nature. Whereas the lower animals cannot even apprehend reason; they obey their instincts. And indeed the use made of slaves and of tame animals is not very different; for both with their bodies minister to the needs of life. Nature would like to distinguish between the bodies of freemen and slaves, making the one strong for servile labour, the other upright, and although useless for such services, useful for political life in the arts both of war and peace. But this does not hold universally: for some slaves have the souls and others have the bodies of freemen. And doubtless if men differed from one another in the mere forms of their bodies as much as the statues of the Gods do from men, all would acknowledge that the inferior class should be slaves of the superior. And if there is a difference in the body, how much more in the soul? but the beauty of the body is seen, whereas the beauty of the soul is not seen. It is clear, then, that some men are by nature free, and others slaves, and that for these latter slavery is both expedient and right.

(Aristotle, op. cit., Bk 1, pp. 5-9.)

9c ARISTOTLE: THE NATURE OF THE CITIZEN

He who would enquire into the nature and various kinds of government must first of all determine 'What is a state?' At present this is a disputed question. Some say that the state has done a certain act; others, no, not the state, but the oligarchy or the tyrant. And the legislator or statesman is concerned entirely with the state; a constitution or government being an arrangement of the inhabitants of a state. But a state is composite, and, like any other whole, made up of many parts;—these are the citizens, who compose it. It is evident, therefore, that we must begin by asking, Who is the citizen, and what is the meaning of the term? For here again there may be a difference of opinion. He who is a citizen in a democracy will often not be a citizen in an oligarchy. Leaving out of consideration those who have been made citizens, or who have obtained the name of citizen in any other accidental manner, we may say, first, that a citizen is not a citizen because he lives in a certain place, for resident aliens and slaves share in the place; nor is he a citizen who has no legal right except that of suing and being sued; for this right may be enjoyed under the provisions of a treaty. Even resident aliens in many places possess such rights, although in an imperfect form; for they are obliged to have a patron. Hence they do but imperfectly participate in citizenship, and we call them citizens only in a qualified sense, as we might apply the term to children who are too young to be on the register, or to old men who have been relieved from state duties. . . . But the citizen, whom we are seeking to define, is a citizen in the strictest sense, against whom no such exception can be taken, and his special characteristic is that he shares in the administration of justice, and in offices.

There is a point nearly allied to the preceding: Whether the virtue of a good man and a good citizen is the same or not. But, before entering on this discussion, we must first obtain some general notion of the virtue of the citizen. Like the sailor, the citizen is a member of a community. Now, sailors have different functions, for one of them is a rower, another a pilot, and a third a look-out-man, a fourth is described by some similar term; and while the precise definition of each individual's virtue applies exclusively to him, there is, at the same time, a common definition applicable to them all. For they have all of them a common object, which is safety in navigation. Similarly, one citizen differs from another, but the salvation of the community is the common business of them all. This community is the state; the virtue of the citizen must therefore be relative to the constitution of which he is a member. If then, there are many forms of government, it is evident that the virtue of the good citizen cannot be the one perfect virtue. But we say that the good man is he who has perfect virtue. Hence it is evident that the good citizen need not of necessity possess the virtue which makes a good man.

The same question may also be approached by another road, from a consideration of the perfect state. If the state cannot be entirely composed of good men, and each citizen is expected to do his own business well, and must therefore have virtue, inasmuch as all the citizens cannot be alike, the virtue of the citizen and of the good man cannot coincide. All must have the virtue of the good citizen—thus, and thus only, can the state be perfect; but they will not have the virtue of a good man, unless we assume that in the good state all the citizens must be good.

But will there then be no case in which the virtue of the good citizen and the virtue of the good man coincide? To this we answer [not that the good citizen, but] that the good ruler is a good and wise man, and that he who would be a statesman must be a wise man. And some persons say that even the education of the ruler should be of a special kind; for are not the children of kings instructed in riding and military exercises? As Euripides says:

'No subtle arts for me, but what the state requires.'

As though there were a special education needed by a ruler. If then the virtue of a good ruler is the same as that of a good man, and we assume further that the subject is a citizen as well as the ruler, the virtue of the good citizen and the virtue of the good man cannot be always the same, although in some cases [i.e.

in the perfect state] they may; for the virtue of a ruler differs from that of a citizen.

(Aristotle, op. cit., Bk 3, pp. 67-73.)

9d ARISTOTLE: ARTISANS

There still remains one more question about the citizen: Is he only a true citizen who has a share of office, or is the mechanic to be included? If they who hold no office are to be deemed citizens, not every citizen can have this virtue of ruling and obeying which makes a citizen. And if none of the lower class are citizens, in which part of the state are they to be placed? For they are not resident aliens, and they are not foreigners. To this objection may we not reply, that there is no more absurdity in excluding them than in excluding slaves and freedmen from any of the above-mentioned classes? It must be admitted that we cannot consider all those to be citizens who are necessary to the existence of the state; for example, children are not citizens equally with grown up men, who are citizens absolutely, but children, not being grown up, are only citizens in a qualified sense. Doubtless in ancient times, and among some nations, the artisan class were slaves or foreigners, and therefore the majority of them are so now. The best form of state will not admit them to citizenship; but if they are admitted, then our definition of the virtue of a citizen will apply to some citizens and freemen only, and not to those who work for their living. The latter class, to whom toil is a necessity, are either slaves who minister to the wants of individuals, or mechanics and labourers who are the servants of the community. These reflections carried a little further will explain their position; and indeed what has been said already is of itself explanation enough.

Since there are many forms of government there must be many varieties of citizens, and especially of citizens who are subjects; so that under some governments the mechanic and the labourer will be citizens, but not in others, as, for example, in aristocracy or the so-called government of the best (if there be such an one), in which honours are given according to virtue and merit; for no man can practise virtue who is living the life of a mechanic or labourer.

(Aristotle, op. cit., Bk 3, pp. 75-6.)

9e ARISTOTLE: CLASSIFICATION OF CONSTITUTIONS

The conclusion is evident: that governments, which have a regard to the common interest, are constituted in accordance with strict principles of justice, and are therefore true forms; but those which regard only the interest of the rulers are all defective and perverted forms, for they are despotic, whereas a state is a community of freemen.

Having determined these points, we have next to consider how many forms of government there are, and what they are; and in the first place what are the true forms, for when they are determined the perversions of them will at once be apparent. The words constitution and government have the same meaning, and the government, which is the supreme authority in states, must be in the hands of one, or of a few, or of many. The true forms of government, therefore, are those in which the one, or the few, or the many, govern with a view to the common interest; but governments which rule with a view to the private interest, whether of the one, or of the few, or of the many, are perversions. For citizens, if they are truly citizens, ought to participate in the advantages of a state. Of forms of government in which one rules, we call that which regards the common interests, kingship or royalty; that in which more than one, but not many, rule, aristocracy [the rule of the best]; and it is so called, either because the rulers are the best men, or because they have at heart the best interests of the state and of the citizens. But when the citizens at large administer the state for the common interest, the government is called by the generic name,—a constitution. And there is a reason for this use of language. One man or a few may excel in virtue; but of virtue there are many kinds: and as the number increases it becomes more difficult for them to attain perfection in every kind, though they may in military virtue, for this is found in the masses. Hence, in a constitutional government the fighting-men have the supreme power, and those who possess arms are the citizens.

Of the above-mentioned forms, the perversions are as follows:—of royalty, tyranny; of aristocracy, oligarchy; of constitutional government, democracy. For tyranny is a kind of monarchy which has in view the interest of the monarch only; oligarchy has in view the interest of the wealthy; democracy, of the needy: none of them the common good of all.

(Aristotle, op. cit., Bk 3, pp. 79-80.)

9f   ARISTOTLE: THE MIDDLE-CLASS POLITY

Next we have to consider how by the side of oligarchy and democracy the so-called polity or constitutional government springs up, and how it should be organized. The nature of it will be at once understood from a comparison of oligarchy and democracy; we must ascertain their different characteristics, and taking a portion from each, put the two together, like the parts of an indenture. Now there are three modes in which fusions of government may be effected. The nature of the fusion will be made intelligible by an example of the manner in which different governments legislate, say concerning the administration of justice. In oligarchies they impose a fine on the rich if they do not serve as judges, and to the poor they give no pay; but in democracies they give pay to the poor and do not fine the rich. Now (1) the union of these two modes is a common or middle term between them, and is therefore characteristic of a constitutional government, for it is a combination of both. This is one mode of uniting the two elements. Or (2) a mean may be taken between the enactments of the two: thus democracies require no property qualification, or only a small one, from members of the assembly, oligarchies a high one; here neither of these is the common term, but a mean between them. (3) There is a third mode, in which something is borrowed from the oligarchical and something from the democratical principle. For example, the appointment of magistrates by lot is democratical, and the election of them oligarchical; democratical again when there is no property qualification, oligarchical when there is. In the aristocratical or constitutional state, one element will be taken from each—from oligarchy the mode of electing to offices, from democracy the disregard of qualification. Such are the various modes of combination. . . .

We have now to enquire what is the best constitution for most states, and the best life for most men, neither assuming a standard of virtue which is above ordinary persons, nor an education which is exceptionally favoured by nature and circumstances, nor yet an ideal state which is an aspiration only, but having regard to the life in which the majority are able to share, and to the form of government which states in general can attain. As to those aristocracies, as they are called, of which we were just now speaking, they either lie beyond the possibilities of the greater number of states, or they approximate to the so-called constitutional government, and therefore need no separate discussion. And in fact the conclusion at which we arrive respecting all these forms rests upon the same grounds. For if it has been truly said in the Ethics that the happy life is the life according to unimpeded virtue, and that virtue is a mean, then the life which is in a mean, and in a mean attainable by every one, must be the best. And the same principles of virtue and vice are characteristic of cities and of constitutions; for the constitution is in a figure the life of the city.

Now in all states there are three elements; one class is very rich, another very poor, and a third in a mean. It is admitted that moderation and the mean are best, and therefore it will clearly be best to possess the gifts of fortune in moderation; for in that condition of life men are most ready to listen to reason. But he who greatly excels in beauty, strength, birth or wealth, or on the other hand who is very poor, or very weak, or very much disgraced, finds it difficult to follow reason. Of these two the one sort grow into violent and great criminals, the others into rogues and petty rascals. And two sorts of offences correspond to them, the one committed from violence, the other from roguery. The petty rogues are disinclined to hold office, whether military or civil, and their aversion to these two duties is as great an injury to the state as their tendency to crime. Again, those who have too much of the goods of fortune, strength, wealth, friends, and the like, are neither willing nor able to submit to authority. The evil begins at home: for when they are boys, by reason of the luxury in which they are brought up, they never learn, even at school, the habit of obedience. On the other hand, the very poor, who are in the opposite extreme, are too degraded. So that the one class cannot obey, and can only rule despotically; the other knows not how to command and must be ruled like slaves. Thus arises a city, not of freemen, but of masters and slaves, the one despising, the other envying; and nothing can be more fatal to friendship and good fellowship in states than this: for good fellowship tends to friendship; when men are at enmity with one another, they would rather not even share the same path. But a city ought to be composed, as far as possible, of equals and similars; and these are generally the middle classes. Wherefore the city which is composed of middle-class citizens is necessarily best governed;

they are, as we say, the natural elements of a state. And this is the class of citizens which is most secure in a state, for they do not, like the poor, covet their neighbours' goods; nor do others covet theirs, as the poor covet the goods of the rich; and as they neither plot against others, nor are themselves plotted against, they pass through life safely. Wisely then did Phocylides pray,—

'Many things are best in the mean; I desire to be of a middle condition in my city.'

Thus it is manifest that the best political community is formed by citizens of the middle class, and that those states are likely to be well-administered, in which the middle class is large, and larger if possible than both the other classes, or at any rate than either singly; for the addition of the middle class turns the scale, and prevents either of the extremes from being dominant. Great then is the good fortune of a state in which the citizens have a moderate and sufficient property; for where some possess much, and the others nothing, there may arise an extreme democracy, or a pure oligarchy; or a tyranny may grow out of either extreme,—either out of the most rampant democracy, or out of an oligarchy; but it is not so likely to arise out of a middle and nearly equal condition. I will explain the reason of this hereafter, when I speak of the revolutions of states. The mean condition of states is clearly best, for no other is free from faction; and where the middle class is large, there are least likely to be factions and dissensions. For a similar reason large states are less liable to faction than small ones, because in them the middle class is large; whereas in small states it is easy to divide all the citizens into two classes who are either rich or poor, and to leave nothing in the middle. And democracies are safer and more permanent then oligarchies, because they have a middle class which is more numerous and has a greater share in the government; for when there is no middle class, and the poor greatly exceed in number, troubles arise, and the state soon comes to an end. A proof of the superiority of the middle class is that the best legislators have been of a middle condition; for example, Solon, as his own verses testify; and Lycurgus, for he was not a king; and Charondas, and almost all legislators. . . .

The legislator should always include the middle class in his government; if he makes his laws oligarchical, to the middle class let him look; if he makes them democratical, he should equally by his laws try to attach this class to the state. There only can the government ever be stable where the middle class exceeds one or both of the others, and in that case there will be no fear that the rich will unite with the poor against the rulers. For neither of them will ever be willing to serve the other, and if they look for some form of government more suitable to both, they will find none better than this, for the rich and the poor will never consent to rule in turn, because they mistrust one another. The arbiter is always the one trusted, and he who is in the middle is an arbiter. The more perfect the admixture of the political elements, the more lasting will be the state.

(Aristotle, op. cit., Bk 4, pp. 123-31.)

CHAPTER 5

The Hellenistic Schools

The 'Hellenistic' age, as distinguished from the 'classical' age of Greece, was the period when Greek culture became widespread in the eastern part of the ancient world. This was the age of the Macedonian domination, first under Philip (359-336 B.C.), and then under Alexander (336-324 B.C.). The Schools of philosophy referred to as 'Hellenistic' flourished during this period and afterwards, and were a response to the collapse of the city state and the widespread rejection of the city-state ethos.

The Decline of the Polis
The conquests of Alexander the Great had the effect of breaking down the actual independence of the Greek cities, although they did manage to retain a formal independence until their submergence in the Roman Empire. Furthermore, the traditional community spirit of the *polis* was being undermined by an increasing economic gulf between the rich and the poor. New wealth from the Alexandrian conquests in Persia led to a galloping inflation in which the already wealthy landowners and merchants became richer and the labouring classes poorer. In addition the mingling of Greeks with Macedonians (whom many Greeks had regarded as semi-barbaric and hence inferior to themselves) and the mingling of both with Persians and other non-Greeks, tended to cause the old distinctions between Greeks and foreigners to crumble.

All of these social changes had highly significant consequences. Whereas the *polis* dweller had relied upon his community, his participation in public life, and his supposed superiority to other men to give him self-esteem, he was now partially isolated and insecure. The cocoon of the city was no longer strong enough to provide him with a comfortable feeling of invulnerability. Consequently, many people looked for a new philosophy which would provide a substitute for the security which they now lacked.

The Schools
The Hellenistic schools of philosophy all claimed to supply for their

adherents the sense of tranquillity that would cushion them against the insecurities of human life. These new philosophies were all 'individualist' in the sense that the human being was seen to be the complete master of himself. His virtue lay in his own actions, not as formerly in his participation in a larger organic whole. In this the Hellenistic schools differed profoundly from the city-state philosophies of Plato and Aristotle, but they possessed certain similarities with Sophist individualism, although the crude egoism of the latter was hardly comparable to the Hellenistic ideas of virtue.

The three most important schools of Hellenistic philosophy were Cynicism, Stoicism and Epicureanism. Chronologically, the Cynics pre-dated the school of Epicurus, but the latter will be discussed first since it had relatively little later influence, whereas the Cynics and Stoics were essentially connected and were influential in the later Roman world.

Epicureanism

The founder of the school, Epicurus (341-270 B.C.), was born in Samos and came to Athens where he set up his school, the 'Garden', in about 307 B.C. Little of his writings has survived, although from what is still available it is quite possible to gain a considerable amount of information about his philosophy. Later writers, such as Lucretius and Diogenes Laertius, supplement the writings of Epicurus himself.

Epicurus was a highly original thinker; the only important influence on him is said to have been the materialism of the Ionian atomists. He sought individual tranquillity and found it in the pursuance of a life of pleasure. Such pleasure, however, is not indulgence, but simply freedom from pain, so that the wise man is he who lives temperately, avoiding all actions which are likely to upset his equilibrium (Ex. 10a). Thus, involvement in public life is normally to be avoided by the wise man, since such activity will probably lead to trouble and anxiety. His theory of religion is consistent with his emphasis upon the avoidance of pain. The gods are known to exist but they do not concern themselves with human affairs, and therefore there is no reason for men to fear the possibility of divine punishment after death.

Epicurus's emphasis upon the importance of pleasure and pain led him to a view of morality and the state not unlike that of Hobbes, the materialist philosopher of the seventeenth century, and distinctly similar to some Sophist theories of the fifth century B.C. Laws are just or otherwise according to whether they provide for man's pleasure. There are no absolute moral rules; man is basically dominated by self-interest and justice is therefore a convention which men have agreed to obey in order to protect themselves (Ex. 10b). Even the foundation of the state itself rests upon a contract. There is an obvious similarity here to the views represented by Glaucon in the second book of Plato's *Republic*.

Cynicism

The Cynics are notable largely because of the debt owed to them by the Stoics, although as advocates of a certain way of life rather than as an intellectual school their influence continued into the early Christian era. As Epicureanism was not at all 'epicurean' in the modern meaning of the term, so the Cynics were not 'cynical'. The word, in fact, is derived from the Greek word for 'dog' which expresses the kind of life followed by members of the school.

Antisthenes, a contemporary and disciple of Socrates, was the founder of Cynicism, although Diogenes, his successor, is most closely associated with the school. Unfortunately there are no extant Cynic writings; we must be content with the description of Diogenes and his philosophy given by Diogenes Laertius in his *Lives of the Philosophers* (Ex. 11).

The chief doctrine of Cynicism was that nothing mattered except 'virtue'. A man can be happy only by being virtuous, and virtue consists in following a life of nature. Such a life involves a repudiation of all the conventions and institutions of civilization. The wise and self-sufficient man, inwardly fortified against the misfortunes of life, is he who lives, eats and dresses in the simplest possible way, renouncing worldliness and culture. The city state itself would, of course, be one of the institutions repudiated by the Cynics. Diogenes is reputed to have said: 'the only true commonwealth is that which is as wide as the universe.' It seems unlikely that Diogenes was arguing for an actual world state or 'cosmopolis'; it is probable that he meant simply that the *polis*, like the family and the coinage, was one of the evil institutions that the wise man would have nothing to do with.

The asceticism of the Cynics, despite its superficial similarity to that of the Epicureans, was in fact based upon a fundamentally different premise. Epicurean poverty was expedient because it led to the happiest life for men; Cynic poverty was according to nature and hence virtuous. The Cynics were thorough-going critics of every aspect of civilization. Even the traditional sexual taboos of the Greeks —especially that of incest—were despised and flouted. It was perhaps the very fact that nothing was sacred to them which prevented them from becoming an important threat to contemporary society, since they preached withdrawal from the world rather than active resistance to its evils. Paradoxically Cynicism, at least in retrospect, became a quite respectable doctrine and the great Stoic sages, even including the Roman emperor Marcus Aurelius, were not ashamed to admit their debt to Diogenes and his followers.

Stoicism

Stoicism was by far the most important of the Hellenistic philosophies; for about six centuries it was the predominant system of thought throughout the Mediterranean world. The school was founded by Zeno of Citium (336–264 B.C.) who settled in Athens in about 317 B.C. At first he studied Cynic doctrines as expounded by Crates, the successor of Diogenes; and his book, the *Republic*, written at this time contained little that differed in essentials from Cynicism. By 300 B.C. Zeno was himself teaching in a public *'stoa'* or porch (from which the word 'stoic' is derived) and attracting a considerable following.

The philosophy of Stoicism passed through three main phases of development. The early *stoa*, with which is associated Zeno and his successors Cleanthes and Chrysippus, all of whom lived in the third century B.C.; the middle *stoa* of the second and first centuries B.C. when the doctrine was introduced to the Roman world by Panaetius and Posidonius; and the later *stoa* whose main exponents were the Romans, Seneca and Marcus Aurelius, in the first and second centuries A.D. In this chapter we will be concerned only with the first *stoa* and defer a consideration of Roman Stoicism to Chapter 6.

Zeno's philosophy (and in all essentials it was adhered to by his successors of the early *stoa*) was yet one more attempt to answer the question: how may a man be happy? As we might expect from a man with his Cynic background, Zeno's answer was virtue. The happiest man is he who is able to know the good in a passionless way and to act accordingly. Man is enabled to know the good by his possession of reason which is a part of the divine reason that controls everything in the universe. Virtue is therefore a will in conformity with the divine universal plan: 'a life according to nature.'

The emphasis upon virtue in Stoic literature reflects their view that ethics is the most important part of human knowledge. The Stoics saw politics as a subdivision of ethics, and even logic and physics were treated as subordinate studies to ethical doctrine.

Although, theoretically, all men possess reason and are capable of virtue, in practice only very few men—the Stoic Sages—are virtuous. Reason in most men is perverted; such perversions of reason are passions or emotions, and the ideal for the true Stoic is to rid himself of emotions in order to allow reason to show him the good. The ideal Stoic is therefore the passionless man whose every action is dictated by pure reason, and whose life is the epitome of virtue. Like Socrates, the Stoics contended that knowledge is a prerequisite of virtue, and, like Socrates, they contended that virtue is its own reward. Man ought to be good because that is the way of nature. To do one's duty may not bring pleasure—in fact very often duty is painful—but it must still be done. It is this more than anything which highlights the essential difference between Stoic and Epicurean and expresses the popular meaning of the term 'stoical'.

A further dissimilarity to Epicureanism lay in the Stoic view of man as naturally social; that is, able to develop naturally only in a community with other men. But unlike Plato and Aristotle, Zeno and his successors, particularly Chrysippus, saw little worth in the city state. The kind of community which the early Stoics saw as ideal for man's development was the City of the World: the *'cosmopolis'*. The whole universe is seen as a single community in which the gods and the wise men are the true citizens, ruled by natural law and free from the corrupt human laws and institutions based upon passion rather than reason. Although the mass of mankind cannot be regarded as true citizens, nevertheless they are inhabitants of the cosmopolis, and are entitled to be ruled according to the laws of nature.

It follows that each man is a citizen of two cities and subject to two sets of laws, human and natural (or divine). The former creates institutional differences between men; the latter treats all men as equals. Under natural law there can be no natural differences between Greeks and Barbarians or between free men and slaves. However, despite the egalitarianism of the Stoic creed, the emphasis of the founders upon the superiority of the wise man to the fool prevented it from becoming a revolutionary or even a popular creed. Its emphasis upon individual virtue and its contempt for externals led to the passive acceptance of unnatural institutions, such as slavery, since they were of no account. Stoicism always remained the doctrine of the educated upper classes of Greece and Rome.

Very little remains of the writings of the early Stoics, and therefore the extract concerned with Zeno is from the indispensable Diogenes Laertius whose *Lives and Opinions of the Philosophers*, written in the third century A.D., draws upon many sources and is relatively reliable (Ex. 12).

Zeno's successor, Cleanthes (an ex-boxer), who was head of the school for thirty years (263-232 B.C.), is represented by one of his few surviving poems, the moving 'Hymn to Zeus' (Ex. 13). A good deal of the voluminous writings of Chrysippus survive. He was the successor of Cleanthes as head of the Stoic School at the end of the third century B.C., but since he contributed little to the political or ethical aspects of Stoicism no extract from his works is given.

FURTHER READING

Texts

C. Bailey (ed.): *Epicurus. The Extant Remains* (Clarendon Press 1926)
Diogenes Laertius: *Lives and Opinions of the Philosophers* (G. Bell 1891)

Commentaries
E. Barker: *From Alexander to Constantine* (Clarendon Press 1956)
N. W. De Witt: *Epicurus and his Philosophy* (University of Minnesota Press 1954)
A. A. Long: *Hellenistic Philosophy* (Duckworth, London 1974)
J. M. Rist: *Stoic Philosophy* (Cambridge University Press 1969)
W. Tarn and G. T. Griffiths: *Hellenistic Civilization* (Methuen 1966)
E. Zeller: *Stoics, Epicureans and Sceptics* (Russell & Russell, N.Y. 1962)

10a EPICURUS: LETTER TO MENOECEUS

For the assertions of the many about the Gods are not anticipations, but false opinions. And in consequence of these, the greatest evils which befall wicked men, and the benefits which are conferred on the good, are all attributed to the Gods; for they connect all their ideas of them with a comparison of human virtues, and everything which is different from human qualities, they regard as incompatible with the divine nature.

Accustom yourself also to think death a matter with which we are not at all concerned, since all good and all evil is in sensation, and since death is only the privation of sensation. On which account, the correct knowledge of the fact that death is no concern of ours, makes the mortality of life pleasant to us, inasmuch as it sets forth no illimitable time, but relieves us for the longing for immortality. For there is nothing terrible in living to a man who rightly comprehends that there is nothing terrible in ceasing to live; so that he was a silly man who said that he feared death, not because it would grieve him when it was present, but because it did grieve him while it was future. For it is very absurd that that which does not distress a man when it is present, should afflict him when only expected. Therefore, the most formidable of all evils, death, is nothing to us, since, when we exist, death is not present to us; and when death is present, then we have no existence. It is no concern then either of the living or of the dead; since to the one it has no existence, and the other class has no existence itself. But people in general, at times flee from death as the greatest of evils, and at times wish for it as a rest from the evils in life. Nor is the not living a thing feared, since living is not connected with it: nor does the wise man think not living an evil; but, just as he chooses food, not preferring that which is most abundant, but that which is nicest; so too, he enjoys time, not measuring it as to whether it is of the greatest length, but as to whether it is most agreeable. . . . And we must consider that some of the passions are natural, and some empty; and of the natural ones some are necessary, and some merely natural. And of the necessary ones some are necessary to happiness, and others, with regard to the exemption of the body, from trouble; and others with respect to living itself; for a correct theory, with regard to these things, can refer all choice and avoidance to the health of the body and the freedom from disquietude of the soul. Since this is the end of living happily; for it is for the sake of this that we do everything, wishing to avoid grief and fear; and when once this is the case, with respect to us, then the storm of the soul is, as I may say, put an end to; since the animal is unable to go as if to something deficient, and to seek something different from that by which the good of the soul and body will be perfected.

For then we have need of pleasure when we grieve, because pleasure is not present; but when we do not grieve; then we have no need of pleasure; and on this account, we affirm, that pleasure is the beginning and end of living happily; for we have recognized this as the first good, being connate with us; and with reference to it, it is that we begin every choice and avoidance; and to this we come as if we judged of all good by passion as the standard; and, since this is the first good and connate with us, on this account we do not choose every pleasure, but at times we pass over many pleasures when any difficulty is likely to ensue from them; and we think many pains better than pleasures, when a greater pleasure follows them, if we endure the pain for a time.

Every pleasure is therefore a good on account of its own nature, but it does not follow that every pleasure is worthy of being chosen; just as every pain is an evil, and yet every pain must not be avoided. But it is right to estimate all these things by the measurement and view of what is suitable and unsuitable; for at times we may feel the good as an evil, and at times, on the contrary, we may feel the evil as good. And, we think, contentment a great good, not in order that we may never have but a little, but in order that, if we have not much, we may make use of a little, being genuinely persuaded that those men enjoy luxury most completely who are the best able to do without it; and that everything which is natural is easily provided, and what is useless is not easily procured. And simple flavours give as much pleasure as costly fare, when everything that can give pain, and every feeling of want, is removed; and corn and water give the most extreme pleasure when any one in need eats them. To accustom one's self, therefore, to simple and inexpensive habits is a great ingredient in the perfecting of health, and makes a man free from hesitation with respect to the necessary uses of life. And when we, on certain occasions, fall in with more sumptuous fare, it makes us in a better disposition towards it, and renders us fearless with respect to fortune. When, therefore, we say that pleasure is a chief good, we are not speaking of the pleasures of the debauched man, or those which lie in sensual enjoyment, as some think who are ignorant, and who do not entertain our opinions, or else interpret them perversely; but we mean the freedom of the body from pain, and of the soul from confusion. For it is not continued drinkings and revels, or the enjoyment of female society, or feasts of fish and other such things, as a costly table supplies, that make life pleasant, but sober contemplation, which examines into the reasons for all choice and avoidance, and which puts to flight the vain opinions from which the greater part of the confusion arises which troubles the soul.

(Diogenes Laertius, *Lives and Opinions of the Philosophers*, tr. C. D. Yonge, pp. 469-71, G. Bell and Sons, London 1891.)

10b   EPICURUS: PRINCIPAL DOCTRINES

It is not possible to live pleasantly without living prudently, and honourably, and justly; nor to live prudently, and honourably, and justly, without living pleasantly. But he to whom it does not happen to live prudently, honourably, and justly, cannot possibly live pleasantly.

For the sake of feeling confidence and security with regard to men, and not with reference to the nature of government and kingly power being a good, some men have wished to be eminent and powerful, in order that others might attain this feeling by their means; thinking that so they would secure safety as far as men are concerned. So that, if the life of such men is safe, they have attained to the nature of good; but if it is not safe, then they have failed in obtaining that for the sake of which they originally desired power according to the order of nature.

Irresistible power and great wealth may, up to a certain point, give us security as far as men are concerned; but the security of men in general depends upon the tranquillity of their souls, and their freedom from ambition.

Natural justice is a covenant of what is suitable, leading men to avoid injuring one another, and being injured.

Those animals which are unable to enter into an argument of this nature, or to guard against doing or sustaining mutual injury, have no such thing as justice or injustice. And the case is the same with those nations, the members of which are either unwilling or unable to enter into a covenant to respect their mutual interests.

Justice has no independent existence; it results from mutual contracts, and establishes itself wherever there is a mutual engagement to guard against doing or sustaining mutual injury.

Injustice is not intrinsically bad; it has this character only because there is joined with it a fear of not escaping those who are appointed to punish actions marked with that character.

It is not possible for a man who secretly does anything in contravention of the agreement which men have made with one another, to guard against doing, or sustaining mutual injury, to believe that he shall always escape notice, even if he have escaped notice already ten thousand times; for, till his death, it is uncertain whether he will not be detected.

In a general point of view, justice is the same thing to every one; for there is something advantageous in mutual society. Nevertheless, the difference of place, and divers other circumstances, make justice vary.

(Laertius, op. cit., pp. 474-5, 478.)

11 DIOGENES THE CYNIC (DIOGENES LAERTIUS: LIVES OF THE PHILOSOPHERS)

He used to say that there was nothing whatever in life which could be brought to perfection without practice, and that that alone was able to overcome every obstacle; that, therefore, as we ought to repudiate all useless toils, and to apply ourselves to useful labours, and to live happily, we are only unhappy in consequence of most exceeding folly. For the very contempt of pleasure, if we only inure ourselves to it, is very pleasant; and just as they who are accustomed to live luxuriously, are brought very unwillingly to adopt the contrary system; so they who have been originally inured to that opposite system, feel a sort of pleasure in the contempt of pleasure.

This used to be the language which he held, and he used to show in practice, really altering men's habits, and deferring in all things rather to the principles of nature than to those of law; saying that he was adopting the same fashion of life as Hercules had, preferring nothing in the world to liberty; and saying that everything belonged to the wise, and advancing arguments such as I mentioned just above. For instance: every thing belongs to the Gods; and the Gods are friends to the wise; and all the property of friends is held in common; therefore everything belongs to the wise. He also argued about the law, that without it there is no possibility of a constitution being maintained; for without a city there can be nothing orderly, but a city is an orderly thing; and without a city there can be no law; therefore law is order. And he played in the same manner with the topics of noble birth, and reputation, and all things of that kind, saying that they were all veils, as it were, for wickedness; and that that was the only proper constitution which consisted in order. Another of his doctrines was that all women ought to be possessed in common; and he said that marriage was a nullity, and that the proper way would be for every man to live with her whom he could persuade to agree with him. And on the same principle he said, that all people's sons ought to belong to every one in common; and there was nothing intolerable in the idea of taking anything out of a temple, or eating any animal whatever, and that there was no impiety in tasting even human flesh; as is plain from the habits of foreign nations; and he said that this principle might be correctly extended to every case and every people. For he said that in reality everything was a combination of all things. For that in bread there was meat, and in vegetables there was bread, and so there were some particles of all other bodies in everything, communicating by invisible passages and evaporating.

(Laertius, op. cit., pp. 244-5.)

12 ZENO (DIOGENES LAERTIUS: LIVES OF THE PHILOSOPHERS

They say that the first inclination which an animal has is to protect itself, as nature brings herself to take an interest in it from the beginning, as Chrysippus affirms in the first book of his treatise on Ends; where he says, that the first and dearest object to every animal is its own existence, and its consciousness of that existence. For that it is not natural for any animal to be alienated from itself, or even to be brought into such a state as to be indifferent to itself, being neither alienated from nor interested in itself. It remains, therefore, that we must assert that nature has bound the animal to itself by the greatest unanimity and affection; for by that means it repels all that is injurious, and attracts all that is akin to it and desirable. But as for what some people say, that the first inclination of animals is to pleasure, they say what is false. For they say that pleasure, if there be any such thing at all, is an accessory only, which nature, having sought it out by itself, as well as those things which are adapted to its constitution, receives incidentally in the same manner as animals are pleased, and plants made to flourish.

Moreover, say they, nature makes no difference between animals and plants, when she regulates them so as to leave them without voluntary motion or sense; and some things too take place in ourselves in the same manner as in plants. But, as inclination in animals tends chiefly to the point of making them pursue what is appropriate to them, we may say that their inclinations are regulated by nature. And as reason is given to rational animals according to a more perfect principle, it follows, that to live correctly according to reason, is properly predicated of those who live according to nature. For nature is as it were the artist who produces the inclination.

On which account Zeno was the first writer who, in his treatise on the Nature of Man, said, that the chief good was confessedly to live according to nature; which is to live according to virtue, for nature leads us to this point. And in like manner Cleanthes speaks in his treatise on Pleasure, and so do Posidonius and Hecaton in their essays on Ends as the Chief Good. And again, to live according to virtue is the same thing as living according to one's experience of those things which happen by nature; as Chrysippus explains it in the first book of his treatise on the Chief Good. For our individual natures are all parts of universal nature; on which account the chief good is to live in a manner corresponding to nature, and that means corresponding to one's own nature and to universal nature; doing none of those things which the common law of mankind is in the habit of forbidding, and that common law is identical with that right reason which pervades everything, being the same with Jupiter, who is the regulator and chief manager of all existing things.

Again, this very thing is the virtue of the happy man and the perfect happiness of life when everything is done according to a harmony with the genius of each individual with reference to the will of the universal governor and manager of all things. Diogenes, accordingly, says expressly that the chief good is to act according to sound reason in our selection of things according to our nature. And Archidemus defines it to be living in the discharge of all becoming duties. Chrysippus again understands that the nature, in a manner corresponding to which we ought to live, is both the common nature, and also human nature in particular; but Cleanthes will not admit of any other nature than the common one alone, as that to which people ought to live in a manner corresponding; and repudiates all mention of a particular nature. And he asserts that virtue is a disposition of the mind always consistent and always harmonious; that one ought to seek it out for its own sake, without being influenced by fear or hope by any external influence. Moreover, that it is in it that happiness consists, as producing in the soul the harmony of a life always consistent with itself; and that if a rational animal goes the wrong way, it is because it allows itself to be misled by the deceitful appearances of exterior things, or perhaps by the instigation of those who surround it; for nature herself never gives us any but good inclinations. . . .

Again, the Stoics, as for instance, Chrysippus, in the first book of his work on Lives, say, that the wise man will take a part in the affairs of the state, if nothing hinders him. For that he will restrain vice, and excite men to virtue. Also, they say that he will marry, as Zeno says, in his Republic, and beget children. Moreover, that the wise man will never form mere opinions, that is to say, he will never agree to anything that is false; and that he will become a Cynic; for that Cynicism is a short path to virtue, as Apollodorus calls it in his Ethics; that he will even eat human flesh, if there should be occasion; that he is the only free man, and that the bad are slaves; for that freedom is a power of independent action, but slavery a deprivation of the same. That there is besides, another slavery, which consists in subjection, and a third which consists in possession and subjection; the contrary of which is masterhood, which is likewise bad.

And they say, that not only are the wise free, but that they are also kings, since kingly power is an irresponsible dominion, which can only exist in the case of the wise man, as Chrysippus says in his treatise on the Proper Application of his Terms made by Zeno; for he says that a ruler ought to give decisions on good and evil, and that none of the wicked understand these things. In the same way, they assert that they are the only people who are fit to be magistrates or judges, or orators, and that none of the bad are qualified for these tasks. Moreover, that they are free from all error, in consequence of their not being prone to any wrong actions. Also, that they are unconnected with injury, for that they never injure any one else, nor themselves. Also, that they are not pitiful, and that they never make allowance for any one; for that they do not relax the punishments appointed by law, since yielding, and pity, and mercifulness itself, never exist in any of their souls, so as to induce an affectation of kindness in respect of punishment; nor do they ever think any punishment too severe. . . . However, Panaetius and Posidonius do not admit that virtue has sufficiency of itself, but say that there is also need of good health, and competency, and strength. And their opinion is that a man exercises virtue in everything, as Cleanthes asserts, for it cannot be lost; and the virtuous man on every occasion exercises his soul, which is in a state of perfection.

Again, they say that justice exists by nature, and not because of any definition or principle; just as law does, or right reason, as Chrysippus tells us in his treatise on the Beautiful. . . .

And as there are three kinds of lives; the theoretical, the practical, and the logical; they say that the last is the one which ought to be chosen. For that a logical, that is a rational, animal was made by nature on purpose for speculation and action. And they say that a wise man will very rationally take himself out of life, either for the sake of his country or of his friends, or if he be in bitter pain, or under the affliction of mutilation, or incurable disease. And they also teach that women ought to be in common among the wise, so that whoever meets with any one may enjoy her, and this doctrine is maintained by Zeno in his Republic, and by Chrysippus in his treatise on Polity, and by Diogenes the Cynic, and by Plato; and then, say they, we shall love all boys equally after the manner of fathers, and all suspicion on the ground of undue familiarity will be removed.

They affirm too, that the best of political constitutions is a mixed one, combined of democracy, and kingly power and aristocracy.

(Laertius, op. cit., pp. 290–2, 303–4, 306–7.)

13   CLEANTHES: HYMN TO ZEUS

O God most glorious, called by many a name,
Nature's great King, through endless years the same;
Omnipotence, who by thy just decree
Controllest all, hail, Zeus, for unto thee
Behooves they creatures in all lands to call.
We are thy children, we alone, of all
On earth's broad ways that wander to and fro,
Bearing thine image wheresoe'er we go.
Wherefore with songs of praise thy power I will forth show.
Lo! yonder heaven, that round the earth is wheeled,
Follows thy guidance, still to thee doth yield
Glad homage; thine unconquerable hand
Such flaming minister, the levin-brand,
Wieldeth, a sword two-edged, whose deathless might
Pulsates through all that Nature brings to light;
Vehicle of the universal Word, that flows
Through all, and in the light celestial glows
Of stars both great and small. O King of Kings
Through ceaseless ages, God, whose purpose brings
To birth, whate'er on land or in the sea
Is wrought, or in high heaven's immensity;
Save what the sinner works infatuate.
Nay, but thou knowest to make crooked straight:
Chaos to thee is order: in thine eyes
The unloved is lovely, who did'st harmonize
Things evil with things good, that there should be
One Word through all things everlastingly.
One Word—whose voice alas! the wicked spurn;
Insatiate for the good their spirits yearn:
Yet seeing see not, neither hearing hear
God's universal law, which those revere
By reason guided, happiness who win.
The rest, unreasoning, diverse shapes of sin
Self-prompted follow: for an idle name
Vainly they wrestle in the lists of fame:
Others inordinately Riches woo,
Or dissolute, the joys of flesh pursue.
Now here, now there they wander, fruitless still,
For ever seeking good and finding ill.
Zeus the all-bountiful, whom darkness shrouds,

Whose lightning lightens in the thunder clouds;
Thy children save from error's deadly sway:
Turn thou the darkness from their souls away:
Vouchsafe that unto knowledge they attain;
For thou by knowledge art made strong to reign
O'er all, and all things rulest righteously.
So by thee honoured, we will honour thee,
Praising thy works continually with songs,
As mortals should; nor higher meed belongs
E'en to the gods, than justly to adore
The universal law for evermore.

(tr. J. Adam)

CHAPTER 6

Roman Political Thought

There is little that is original in Roman philosophy. The Romans seem to have had scant liking for philosophical discourse for its own sake, as is emphasized by a senate decree of 161 B.C. banishing philosophers and teachers of rhetoric from the city. Their talents lay rather in administration and law; the philosophy they followed was drawn from Greek sources, and was studied not so much for its own sake as for its supposed benefits. The Romans needed an ethic which would provide the justification for their growing imperialism and their stern concept of duty. The necessary ethic could not be supplied by Plato and Aristotle, even though the writings of these philosophers were known and admired, because of their single-minded concern with the morality of the city state which was becoming more and more irrelevant to the Roman situation. The philosophy of Epicurus likewise had little to offer since it considered pleasure rather than duty to be the aim of human life, and emphasized the conventional nature of morality. It is not surprising, therefore, that Stoicism in a modified form became the political and moral philosophy of educated Romans.

The Middle Stoa

Panaetius

The founder of the Middle Stoa in which the philosophy of Stoicism was modified and made acceptable to Rome, was Panaetius of Rhodes who was head of the school towards the end of the second century B.C. He and his friend Polybius were closely associated with members of the group of Roman aristocrats known as the Scipionic Circle who were enthusiastically attempting to acquire Greek culture. The difficulty of accepting the Stoicism of Zeno and his immediate successors lay in the elements of Cynicism which it contained. What Panaetius did was to purge Stoicism of its elements of Cynicism and to introduce elements from the city-state philosophers.

The intellectual arrogance of the early Stoics, who stressed the superiority of the wise to the foolish, was abandoned and replaced by

the egalitarian view that all men may have sufficient reason to understand the law of nature (Ex. 14a). The content of 'nature' was
broadened to include, in addition to the former narrow conception of
individual virtue, other elements of the good life, such as physical
health and aesthetic appreciation.

In contrast to the early Stoics who had tended to regard human institutions with contempt, Panaetius saw an important place for them,
particularly for the state which answers the human needs for
gregariousness, security, and the protection of property rights. In place
of the Cynic and early Stoic emphasis upon individual self-sufficiency,
he allows for ambition and other natural feelings such as love and
loyalty. Duty might therefore include political services to the state, and
the desire for political leadership is acceptable provided that the as-
pirant has the true Stoic morality (Ex. 14b).

In common with so much Stoic literature, little remains of
Panaetius's writings. The extracts are taken from Cicero's *De Officiis*
(Moral Duties), of which the first two books are generally regarded as
being based upon the ideas of Panaetius.

Polybius

Polybius was a Greek who, as a consequence of his political activities, was forcibly taken to Rome in 167 B.C. As a result of his friendship
with Scipio Aemilianus he became a privileged resident of Rome and
developed a considerable admiration for the Roman political constitution. He was responsible for writing the first history of Rome and
the first study of Roman political institutions. He observed the military
success of Rome and its stability, and concluded that the reason lay in
its constitution.

In the sixth book of his *Universal History*, he discusses his cyclical
theory of constitutional change, which owes a good deal to Book VIII
of Plato's *Republic*. History tends to develop in an orderly way so that
if one knows what has happened in the past, it becomes possible to pre-
dict what will happen in the future. Everything is subject to a natural
law of growth and decay, so that unmixed constitutions degenerate in a
predictable manner. His classification of constitutions is reminiscent of
that in Aristotle's *Politics*. Monarchy decays into tyranny, aristocracy
becomes oligarchy, and democracy degenerates into ochlocracy (mob-
rule) (Ex. 15).

The first ruler was the physically strongest; such rule develops into
true kingship when the ruler discovers that social harmony is impossible without just laws based upon reason. In time, kings come to
inherit their thrones and begin to regard themselves as superior to their
subjects; reason gives way to unbridled appetite and tyranny is established. The people's leaders overthrow all forms of one-man rule and

set up an aristocracy. Eventually they too are corrupted by power, appetite again supplants reason, and the oligarchs are in turn deposed by the people who see their only hope in a democracy. Democracy degenerates into mob-rule where the masses are violent and corrupt, and where force, terror, and expropriation of property become commonplace. Finally, a strong man rises from the ruins and the whole cycle begins again.

Polybius bases his account of constitutional change mainly upon Greek experience. The reason for the impressive record of stability held by Rome is its adoption of a mixed form of constitution in which the various elements are in equilibrium. Polybius sees three such elements: the monarchic element in the consuls; the aristocratic element in the senate; the popular element in the assemblies. Each part, besides possessing an important constitutional function, checks or supports the others thereby preventing for a time the process of degeneration which would occur if any part grew too powerful. However, even the mixed constitution cannot for ever resist the dangers which come from prosperity and the possession of power. The people will become greedy for wealth and office, and ultimately even Rome will degenerate to mob-rule.

Cicero (106–43 B.C.)

In a selection of writings on political ideas it might seem strange to include extracts from a writer who added nothing original to the political thought of his time. Cicero, the Roman orator and statesman, was such a writer. He was a borrower rather than an originator; his extensive writings on political philosophy are simply transcriptions of the great Greek political works such as those of Plato, Aristotle, Polybius and Panaetius. But Cicero's political books have a twofold importance for us. First, he gives us in a stylish and concise form all the important Stoic doctrines of his period. Secondly, his influence in the transmission of these doctrines to the Roman world was pre-eminent. His books were widely read and the ideas therein absorbed by many who would otherwise have had little or no contact with Greek thought.

His intention in compiling his works: *De Re Publica* (*the Republic*), *De Legibus* (*The Laws*), and *De Officiis* (*Moral Duties*), was to show that Roman constitutional history and politics could be interpreted according to the political theory of the Greeks. For example, he follows Polybius very closely in his views on constitutional change and the excellence of the mixed constitution (Ex. 16a), and follows Plato and Panaetius in his theory that the best men should rule.

Perhaps the most significant of the ideas given expression by Cicero were the Stoic notions of justice and the law of nature. He sees the state as a natural association, as literally a 'commonwealth' united in its members' agreement about justice (Ex. 16b). The implication is that the people are the source of authority in the state, and this theory remained a maxim of Roman political and legal thought even during the period of empire. On the face of it, the theory seemed to be contradicted by the facts since the Roman empire was governed by a monarch. It was argued by the Roman lawyers, however, that the people had given their authority to the emperor for him to use it on their behalf. Whether the people had any right to demand the return of their gift was a problem that exercised the minds of constitutional lawyers as late as the twelfth century A.D. when the study of Roman law was revived.

An equally important implication of Cicero's statement, which is developed at length in *De Legibus*, is that the state must be governed in accordance with 'justice' which corresponds to the 'divine reason' or 'natural law' of the Stoics (Ex. 16c). The introduction of the concept of *Jus Naturale* (natural law) and its popularization among Romans of the educated classes was possibly Cicero's most significant contribution to political thought. His purpose in expounding this concept was to show that justice and law are not mere conventions to be determined by men according to whim, but, on the contrary, are absolute norms of conduct to be obeyed regardless of time and place. These norms or standards are the content of the natural law which, being the law of divine reason, is clearly unchangeable. Of all creatures man alone possesses the faculty of being able to choose between alternative courses of moral behaviour—between the absolutely 'right' and the absolutely 'wrong'. To choose the right course of action is in accordance with the natural law and it is the faculty of reason which enables a man to so choose. It follows that for the just man conformity to the natural law must always take precedence over the law of his state, so that if the two conflict, the former must be obeyed. Many eminent Stoics did, in fact, find themselves in this predicament and had to face the consequences of political disobedience or commit suicide.

The corollary of the theory of natural law as stated by Cicero was his statement of natural human equality. This, possibly more than any other single concept, illustrates the advance made in political theory since the time of Aristotle. For the philosophers of the city state, man is naturally a citizen, Greeks are superior to non-Greeks, free men are superior to slaves, the intellectual is superior to the manual worker. To the later Stoics as recorded by Cicero, nature has given all men reason; all men are therefore governed by the unchangeable world-wide law of nature, and are thus naturally equal.

The Later Stoa
This is the term normally used to denote the final phase in the

development of Stoic philosophy, of which the statesman, Seneca, the freed slave, Epictetus, and the philosopher-emperor, Marcus Aurelius, can be regarded as the most outstanding exponents. Most of the philosophic positions adopted by writers of this period (the first two centuries A.D.) had already been at least hinted at by Cicero and his predecessors, although there is a difference of emphasis possibly stemming from the changed social and political conditions of the Empire compared with the last years of the Republic.

Seneca (5 B.C.-65 A.D.)

Born in Spain, Seneca was educated in Rome and lived most of his life there where he became known as a literary stylist and philosopher. He had, besides, political ambitions, and held a number of offices including that of tutor and then minister to Nero. He was implicated in a plot against Nero's life and condemned to death, but was allowed to commit suicide, an act which conformed to the Stoic ethic. Not all of his activities so conformed—particularly to his own moral preaching on the virtues of honesty and spirituality.

Seneca's main significance in the development of later Stoicism derives from his treatment of the notion (which originated with Posidonius of the Middle Stoa) that, at some time in the distant past, men had lived happily and innocently in a society completely devoid of the institutions of civilization. In this 'golden age' all material things were held in common and neither slavery nor coercive government were present. Such an existence was orderly and just since the wisest members of the community guided the others according to the rules of nature. Their idyllic way of life was terminated by the introduction into the community of avarice. Avarice led to private property; the desire for wealth and power infected the rulers and the guidance of the wise was replaced by tyranny. To control the tyrants laws were made and order restored. The state and government and the institution of private property are therefore seen by Seneca as the result of man's corruption; as conventional institutions rather than natural ones (Ex. 17).

The development of institutions was not without important benefits. Although happy in his natural state, man had been ignorant. His virtue was therefore a consequence of his ignorance of vice. Moral perfection demands a positive abstention from evil so that, as Aristotle had formerly pointed out, evil must exist for good to be done. Hence the conventional institutions of man, although originating in evil, possess an ability to promote the good and to further man's moral stature.

Marcus Aurelius (122-180 A.D.)

The final extract taken from Stoic writings is from the *Meditations* of the emperor Marcus Aurelius. These notes represent a record of his thoughts on his inward spiritual life and were never intended for any-one other than the author to read. His Stoicism is eclectic, containing a good deal of Platonism, but drawing most from the thought of Epic-tetus. His writing like that of most of the later Stoics is in a pessimistic vein, preaching the futility of all earthly things such as political loyal-ties (Ex. 18). Unlike the Christians who took substantially the same view, Marcus had nothing positive with which to console himself. Belief in the immortality of the soul, so confidently expressed by the Christians, was regarded by the Stoics as highly doubtful.

Roman Law

The most important intellectual contribution of Rome was in the field of legal rather than political theory. The earliest Roman law was in the form of unwritten custom which in time became codified in the 'Twelve Tables.' This was the *jus civile*, the positive civil law binding on the citizens of the Roman state. In the fourth century B.C. the office of *praetor* was created to relieve the *consuls* of their judicial functions and, as Roman power and territory expanded and the administration of the law became more complex, so more *praetors* were created.

In 247 B.C. the office of *praetor peregrinus* was created. This was a special judge concerned with the law relating to transactions and dis-putes involving foreigners living in Roman territory. The *jus civile* could not be invoked in such cases since it was applicable only to Roman citizens and foreigners had no rights under it. Hence, in arriv-ing at decisions, the *praetor peregrinus* was forced to rely upon gener-ally held concepts of justice and fairness, which were drawn not only from Rome, but also from the ideas implicit in the legal systems of other races such as the Greeks and the Phoenicians. From the decisions published by the *praetor* there gradually developed a body of law which was assumed to represent principles of justice applicable to citizens of all states. This body of law became known as the *jus gentium*, the law of peoples. Because it was more equitable and more adaptable to the changing times than the *jus civile*, the *jus gentium* came to have an in-creasingly great influence on all legal decisions until eventually the two systems of law virtually merged.

The term *jus naturale*, of course, was a translation from the Greek of the Stoic term, natural law. It was a relatively common-place notion among lawyers after the time of Cicero and was generally thought of as a set of principles conforming to universal laws of reason. It was a philosophical concept rather than a strictly legal one, although its relationship to the other concepts of *jus* was a matter of dispute bet-ween the Roman jurists of the second and third centuries A.D. The Stoic originators of the notion of natural law had used it to show what the ideal pattern of virtuous behaviour should be. The jurists, on the other hand, tended to regard the *jus naturale* as a standard of rationality, in the light of which ambiguities in the positive law could be removed and gaps filled up. There was never the remotest possibility that the lawyers would use the *jus naturale* as an ideal against which the validity of the *jus civile* could be judged. Provided that the positive law was properly made, any discrepancy between it and the natural law might be regarded by the lawyers as regrettable but to have no legal significance in the sense of invalidating the positive law.

Even so, the existence of the concept of *jus naturale* was highly significant in that it led men to question the morality of laws that differed substantially from the law of nature. It became possible to envisage an 'unjust' law; a law which was purely conventional and did not conform to the ideal standard set by rational nature. The principle of human equality as a derivation from *jus naturale* was accepted by most of the Roman lawyers and one of the effects of this was a gradual amelioration in the treatment of subject peoples and slaves.

The Roman Lawyers

The great Roman jurists—the *juris consulti*—were the men responsible for the development and recording of Roman law. The most important jurists, such as Gaius, Ulpian, Paulus and Florentinus, lived in the latter part of the second century and the early part of the third century A.D. Apart from the writings of Gaius, whose legal textbook, the *Institutes*, still survives, knowledge of the work of the lawyers of this period comes from the *Corpus Juris Civilis* compiled by the lawyers of the emperor Justinian's court in the sixth century A.D. This legal compilation included the *Codex*, a condensation of the most important imperial legislation, the *Institutes*, a manual for law students, and the *Digest*, a textbook compiled from fragments of the most significant legal writings. These three books preserved in an easily accessible form the essence of Roman legal theory as it was in the second and third centuries.

Gaius

Gaius, a contemporary of Marcus Aurelius, who wrote in about 160 A.D., considers *jus* to be two-fold. He recognizes the *jus civile* as 'the special law of that state' and *jus gentium* as 'the law observed by all mankind' and established by 'natural reason'. It seems clear, therefore, that Gaius, who rarely uses the term *jus naturale,* has no conception of any important difference between it and the *jus gentium* (Ex. 19).

In a later passage in his *Institutes*, Gaius says that slavery exists under the *jus gentium*. This would seem to imply that he considers the institution of slavery to be rational and just, although he never positively states this, relying instead on the observation that slavery exists among all nations.

In the *Digest,* Gaius is quoted as stating that private property is warranted under the *jus gentium:* 'what belongs to no one is allowed by natural reason to the first taker'. Most of the lawyers take a similar position regarding the ownership of property; that it is rational, universal and primitive. Possibly the sole exception is Hermogenianus, who seems to imply that private property did not exist in man's primitive, natural state, but later became a universal institution sanctioned by the *jus gentium.*

Ulpian

Ulpian, who wrote in about 222 A.D., considers *jus* to be three-fold. He regards the *jus naturale* as something akin to animal instinct rather than to natural reason: 'that which (nature) . . . has taught all animals.' (Ex. 20.) Hence, natural biological activities such as procreating and bringing up children are derived from the natural law. *Jus gentium,* on the other hand, is peculiar to the human race and is presumably a law of reason. It follows that for Ulpian, under the law of nature all men were originally born free and equal. The institution of slavery, which is thus against nature, arose from wars between nations which led to the taking of prisoners and their enslavement. As a universal practice it is warranted under the *jus gentium.*

A further important statement made by Ulpian is that concerning the authority of the emperor: 'what the emperor determines has the force of a statute.' The justification for the exercise of his unlimited personal authority is that the people have conferred their power and authority upon him. Ulpian's statement of this democratic-authoritarian paradox represents the generally held jurisprudential theory of the source of political authority.

FURTHER READING

Texts
Polybius: *Histories*
Cicero: *Moral Duties*
Cicero: *The Republic*
Cicero: *The Laws*
Seneca: *Letters from a Stoic* (Penguin 1969)
Marcus Aurelius: *Meditations*
Gaius: *Institutes* tr. F. de Zulueta (Clarendon Press 1946)
Justinian: *Institutes,* tr. J. B. Moyle (Clarendon Press 1945)

Commentaries

E. Barker: *From Alexander to Constantine* (Clarendon Press 1956)
R. W. and A. J. Carlyle: *History of Mediaeval Political Theory in the West*, vol. 1 (Blackwood 1962)
C. H. McIlwain: *The Growth of Political Thought in the West* (Macmillan, N. Y., 1932)
C. Morris: *Western Political Thought*, vol. 1, (Longmans 1967)
J. M. Rist: *Stoic Philosophy* (Cambridge University Press 1969)

14a   PANAETIUS OF RHODES (CICERO: DE OFFICIIS)

First of all, Nature has endowed every species of living creature with the instinct of self-preservation, of avoiding what seems likely to cause injury to life or limb, and of procuring and providing everything needful for life—food, shelter, and the like. A common property of all creatures is also the reproductive instinct (the purpose of which is the propagation of the species) and also a certain amount of concern for their offspring. But the most marked difference between man and beast is this: the beast, just as far as it is moved by the senses and with very little perception of past or future, adapts itself to that alone which is present at the moment; while man—because he is endowed with reason, by which he comprehends the chain of consequences, perceives the causes of things, understands the relation of cause to effect and of effect to cause, draws analogies, and connects and associates the present and the future—easily surveys the course of his whole life and makes the necessary preparations for its conduct.

Nature likewise by the power of reason associates man with man in the common bonds of speech and life; she implants in him above all, I may say, a strangely tender love for his offspring. She also prompts men to meet in companies, to form public assemblies and to take part in them themselves; and she further dictates, as a consequence of this, the effort on man's part to provide a store of things that minister to his comforts and wants—and not for himself alone, but for his wife and children and the others whom he holds dear and for whom he ought to provide; and this responsibility also stimulates his courage and makes it stronger for the active duties of life.

Above all, the search after truth and its eager pursuit are peculiar to man. And so, when we have leisure from the demands of business cares, we are eager to see, to hear, to learn something new, and we esteem a desire to know the secrets or wonders of creation as indispensable to a happy life. Thus we come to understand that what is true, simple, and genuine appeals most strongly to a man's nature. To this passion for discovering truth there is added a hungering, as it were, for independence, so that a mind well-moulded by Nature is unwilling to be subject to anybody save one who gives rules of conduct or is a teacher of truth or who, for the general good, rules according to justice and law. From this attitude come greatness of soul and a sense of superiority to worldly conditions.

And it is no mean manifestation of Nature and Reason that man is the only animal that has a feeling for order, for propriety, for moderation in word and deed. And so no other animal has a sense of beauty, loveliness, harmony in the visible world; and Nature and Reason, extending the analogy of this from the world of sense to the world of spirit, find that beauty, consistency, order are far more to be maintained in thought and deed, and the same Nature and Reason are careful to do nothing in an improper or unmanly fashion, and in every thought and deed to do or think nothing capriciously.

(Cicero, De Officiis, tr. W. Miller, Bk 1, ch. 4, pp. 13-17, Loeb Classical Library, London 1913.)

14b PANAETIUS OF RHODES (CICERO: DE OFFICIIS)

Now it seems to me, at least, that not only among the Medes, as Herodotus tells us, but also among our own ancestors, men of high moral character were made kings in order that the people might enjoy justice. For, as the masses in their helplessness were oppressed by the strong, they appealed for protection to some one man who was conspicuous for his virtue; and, as he shielded the weaker classes from wrong, he managed by establishing equitable conditions to hold the higher and the lower classes in an equality of right. The reason for making constitutional laws was the same as that for making kings. For what people have always sought is equality of rights before the law. For rights that were not open to all alike would be no rights. If the people secured their end at the hands of one just and good man, they were satisfied with that; but when such was not their good fortune, laws were invented, to speak to all men at all times in one and the same voice.

This, then is obvious: nations used to select for their rulers those men whose reputation for justice was high in the eyes of the people. If in addition they were also thought wise, there was nothing that men did not think they could secure under such leadership. Justice is, therefore, in every way to be cultivated and maintained, both for its own sake (for otherwise it would not be justice) and for the enhancement of personal honour and glory.

The man in an administrative office, however, must make it his first care that everyone shall have what belongs to him and that private citizens suffer no invasion of their property rights by act of the state. It was a ruinous policy that Philippus proposed when in his tribuneship he introduced his agrarian bill. . . . But in his public speeches on the measure he often played the demagogue, and that time viciously, when he said that 'there were not in the state two thousand people who owned any property.' That speech deserves unqualified condemnation, for it favoured an equal distribution of property; and what more ruinous policy than that could be conceived? For the chief purpose in the establishment of constitutional state and municipal governments was that individual property rights might be secured. For, although it was by Nature's guidance that men were drawn together into communities, it was in the hope of safeguarding their possessions that they sought the protection of cities.

(Cicero, op. cit., Bk 2, chs 12, 21, pp. 209-11, 249.)

15 POLYBIUS

What is the origin then of a constitution, and whence is it produced? Suppose that from floods, pestilences, failure of crops, or some such causes the race of man is reduced almost to extinction. Such things we are told have happened, and it is reasonable to think will happen again. Suppose accordingly all knowledge of social habits and arts to have been lost. Suppose that from the survivors, as from seeds, the race of man to have again multiplied. In that case I presume they would, like the animals, herd together; for it is but reasonable to suppose that bodily weakness would induce them to seek those of their own kind to herd with. And in that case too, as with the animals, he who was superior to the rest in strength of body or courage of soul would lead and rule them. For what we see happen in the case of animals that are without the faculty of reason, such as bulls, goats, and cocks,—among whom there can be no dispute that the strongest take the lead,—that we must regard as in the truest sense the teaching of nature. Originally then it is probable that the condition of life among men was this,—herding together like animals and following the strongest and bravest as leaders. The limit of this authority would be physical strength, and the name we should give it would be despotism. But as soon as the idea of family ties and social relation has arisen amongst such agglomerations of men, then is born also the idea of kingship, and then for the first time mankind conceives the notion of goodness and justice and their reverse . . .

When any one man stands out as the champion of all in a time of danger, and braves with firm courage the onslaught of the most powerful wild beasts, it is probable that such a man would meet with marks of favour and pre-eminence from the common people; while he who acted in a contrary way would fall under their contempt and dislike. From this, once more, it is reasonable to suppose that there would arise in the minds of the multitude a theory of the disgraceful and the honourable, and of the difference between them; and that one should be sought and imitated for its advantages, the other shunned. When, therefore, the leading and most powerful man among his people ever encourages such persons in accordance with the popular sentiment, and thereby assumes in the eyes of his subject the appearance of being the distributor to each man according to his deserts, they no longer obey him and support his rule from fear of violence, but rather from conviction of its utility, however old he may be, rallying round him with one heart and soul, and fighting against all who form designs against his government. In this way he becomes a *king* instead of a *despot* by imperceptible degrees, reason having ousted brute courage and bodily strength from their supremacy . . .

In old times those who were once thus selected, and obtained this office, grew old in their royal functions, making magnificent strongholds and surrounding them with walls and extending their frontiers, partly for the security of their subjects, and partly to provide them with abundance of the necessaries of life; and while engaged in these works they were exempt from all vituperation or jealousy; because they did not make their distinctive dress, food, or drink, at all conspicuous, but lived very much like the rest, and joined in the everyday employments of the common people. But when their royal power became hereditary in their family, and they found every necessary for security ready to their hands, as well as more than was necessary for their personal support, then they gave the rein to their appetites; imagined that rulers must needs wear different clothes from those of subjects; have different and elaborate luxuries of the table; and must even seek sensual indulgence, however unlawful the source, without fear of denial. These things having given rise in the one case to jealousy and offence, in the other to outburst of hatred and passionate resentment, the kingship became a tyranny: the first step in disintegration was taken; and plots began to be formed against the government, which did not now proceed from the worst men but from the noblest, most high-minded, and most courageous, because these are the men who can least submit to the tyrannical acts of their rulers.

But as soon as the people got leaders, they co-operated with them against the dynasty for the reasons I have mentioned; and then *kingship* and *despotism* were alike entirely abolished, and *aristocracy* once more began to revive and start afresh. For in their immediate gratitude to those who had deposed the despots, the people employed them as leaders, and entrusted their interests to them; who, looking upon this charge at first as a great privilege, made the public advantage their chief concern, and conducted all kinds of business, public or private, with diligence and caution. But when the sons of these men received the same position of authority from their fathers,—having had no experience of misfortunes, and none at all of civil equality and freedom of speech, but having been bred up from the first under the shadow of their fathers' authority and lofty position,—some of them gave themselves up with passion to avarice and unscrupulous love of money, others to drinking and the boundless debaucheries which accompanies it, and others to the violation of women or the forcible appropriation of boys; and so they turned an *aristocracy* into an *oligarchy*. But it was not long before they roused in the minds of the people the same feelings as before; and their fall therefore was very like the disaster which befel the tyrants.

For no sooner had the knowledge of the jealousy and hatred existing in the citizens against them emboldened some one to oppose the government by word or deed, than he was sure to find the whole people ready and prepared to take his side. Having then got rid of these rulers by assassination or exile, they do not venture to set up a king again, being still in terror of the injustice to which this led before; nor dare they intrust the common interests again to more than one, considering the recent example of their misconduct: and therefore, as the only sound hope left them is that which depends upon themselves, they are driven to take refuge in that; and so changed the constitution from an oligarchy to a *democracy*, and took upon themselves the superintendence and charge of the state. And as long as any survive who have had experience of oligarchical supremacy and domination, they regard their present constitution as a blessing, and hold equality and freedom as of the utmost value. But as soon as a new generation has arisen, and the democracy has descended to their children's children, long association weakens their value for equality and freedom, and some seek to become more powerful than the ordinary citizens; and the most liable to this temptation are the rich. So when they begin to be fond of office, and find themselves unable to obtain it by their own unassisted efforts and their own merits, they ruin their estates, while enticing and corrupting the common people in every possible way. By which means when, in their senseless mania for reputation, they have made the populace ready and greedy to receive bribes, the virtue of democracy is destroyed, and it is transformed into a government of violence and the strong hand. For the mob, habituated to feed at the expense of others, and to have its hopes of a livelihood in the property of its neighbours, as soon as it has got a leader sufficiently ambitious and daring, being excluded by poverty from the sweets of civil honours, produces a reign of mere violence. Then come tumultuous assemblies, massacres, banishments, redivisions of land; until, after losing all trace of civilization, it has once more found a master and a despot.

This is the regular cycle of constitutional revolutions, and the natural order in which constitutions change, are transformed, and return again to their original stage. If a man have a clear grasp of these principles he may perhaps make a mistake as to the dates at which this or that will happen to a particular constitution; but he will rarely be entirely mistaken as to the stage of growth or decay at which it has arrived, or as to the point at which it will undergo some revolutionary change. However, it is in the case of the Roman constitution that this method of inquiry will most fully teach us its formation, its growth, and zenith, as well as the changes awaiting it in the future; for this, if any constitution ever did, owed, as I said just now, its original foundation and growth to natural causes, and to natural causes will owe its decay. My subsequent narrative will be the best illustration of what I say.

(Polybius, *Histories,* tr. E.S. Shuckburgh, Bk 6, pp. 461-6, Macmillan, London 1889.)

16a   CICERO: THE MIXED CONSTITUTION

Kingship, in my opinion, is by far the best of the three primary forms, but a moderate and balanced form of government which is a combination of the three good simple forms is preferable even to the kingship. For there should be a supreme and royal element in the State, some power also ought to be granted to the leading citizens, and certain matters should be left to the judgment and desires of the masses. Such a constitution, in the first place, offers in a high degree a sort of equality, which is a thing free men can hardly do without for any considerable length of time, and, secondly, it has stability. For the primary forms already mentioned degenerate easily into the corresponding perverted forms, the king being replaced by a despot, the aristocracy by an oligarchical faction, and the people by a mob and anarchy; but whereas these forms are frequently changed into new ones, this does not usually happen in the case of the mixed and evenly balanced constitution, except through great faults in the governing class. For there is no reason for a change when every citizen is firmly established in his own station, and there underlies it no perverted form into which it can plunge and sink.

(Cicero, *De Republica*, tr. C. W. Keyes, Bk 1, ch. 45, pp. 103-5, Loeb Classical Library, London 1928.)

16b CICERO: THE GOOD COMMONWEALTH

Scipio. Well, then, a commonwealth is the property of a people. But a people is not any collection of human beings brought together in any sort of way, but an assemblage of people in large numbers associated in an agreement with respect to justice and a partnership for the common good. The first cause of such an association is not so much the weakness of the individual as a certain social spirit which nature has implanted in man. For man is not a solitary or unsocial creature, but born with such a nature that not even under conditions of great prosperity of every sort [is he willing to be isolated from his fellow men.] . . .

About fifteen lines are lost. The following fragment may be part of the missing passage.

. . . In a short time a scattered and wandering multitude had become a body of citizens by mutual agreement. . . .

. . . certain seeds, as we may call them, for [otherwise] no source for the other virtues nor for the State itself could be discovered. Such an assemblage of men, therefore, originating for the reason I have mentioned, established itself in a definite place, at first in order to provide dwellings; and this place being fortified by its natural situation and by their labours, they called such a collection of dwellings a town or city, and provided it with shrines and gathering places which were common property. Therefore every people, which is such a gathering of large numbers as I have described, every city, which is an orderly settlement of a people, every commonwealth, which, as I said, is 'the property of a people,' must be governed by some deliberative body if it is to be permanent. And this deliberative body must, in the first place, always owe its beginning to the same cause as that which produced the State itself. In the second place, this function must either be granted to one man, or to certain selected citizens, or must be assumed by the whole body of citizens. And so when the supreme authority is in the hands of one man, we call him a king, and the form of this State a kingship. When selected citizens hold this power, we say that the State is ruled by an aristocracy. But a popular government (for so it is called) exists when all the power is in the hands of the people. And any one of these three forms of government (if only the bond which originally joined the citizens together in the partnership of the State holds fast), though not perfect or in my opinion the best, is tolerable, though one of them may be superior to another. For either a just and wise king, or a select number of leading citizens, or even the people itself, though this is the least commendable type, can nevertheless, as it seems, form a government that is not unstable, provided that no elements of injustice or greed are mingled with it.

(Cicero, *De Republica*, Bk 1, ch. 25, pp. 65-7.)

16c   CICERO: THE LAWS OF NATURE

XXII. . . . True law is right reason in agreement with nature; it is of universal application, unchanging and everlasting; it summons to duty by its commands, and averts from wrongdoing by its prohibitions. And it does not lay its commands or prohibitions upon good men in vain, though neither have any effect on the wicked. It is a sin to try to alter this law, nor is it allowable to attempt to repeal any part of it, and it is impossible to abolish it entirely. We cannot be freed from its obligations by senate or people, and we need not look outside ourselves for an expounder or interpreter of it. And there will not be different laws at Rome and at Athens, or different laws now and in the future, but one eternal and unchangeable law will be valid for all nations and all times, and there will be one master and ruler, that is, God, over us all, for he is the author of this law, its promulgator, and its enforcing judge. Whoever is disobedient is fleeing from himself and denying his human nature, and by reason of this very fact he will suffer the worst penalties, even if he escapes what is commonly considered punishment. . . .

XV. The most foolish notion of all is the belief that everything is just which is found in the customs or laws of nations. Would that be true, even if these laws had been enacted by tyrants? If the well-known Thirty had desired to enact a set of laws at Athens, or if the Athenians without exception were delighted by the tyrants' laws, that would not entitle such laws to be regarded as just, would it? No more, in my opinion, should that law be considered just which a Roman interrex proposed, to the effect that a dictator might put to death with impunity any citizen he wished, even without a trial. For Justice is one; it binds all human society, and is based on one Law, which is right reason applied to command and prohibition. Whoever knows not this Law, whether it has been recorded in writing anywhere or not, is without Justice.

But if Justice is conformity to written laws and national customs, and if, as the same persons claim, everything is to be tested by the standard of utility, then anyone who thinks it will be profitable to him will, if he is able, disregard and violate the laws. It follows that Justice does not exist at all, if it does not exist in Nature, and if that form of it which is based on utility can be overthrown by that very utility itself. And if Nature is not to be considered the foundation of Justice, that will mean the destruction [of the virtues on which human society depends]. For where then will there be a place for generosity, or love of country, or loyalty, or the inclination to be of service to others or to show gratitude for favours received? For these virtues originate in our natural inclination to love our fellow-men, and this is the foundation of Justice. Otherwise not merely consideration for men but also rites and pious observances in honour of the gods are done away with; for I think that these ought to be maintained, not through fear, but on account of the close relationship which exists between man and God. XVI. But if the principles of Justice were founded on the decrees of peoples, the edicts of princes, or the decisions of judges, then Justice would sanction robbery and adultery and forgery of wills, in case these acts were approved by the votes or decrees of the populace. But if so great a power belongs to the decisions and decrees of fools that the laws of Nature can be changed by their votes, then why do they not ordain that what is bad and baneful shall be considered good and salutary? Or, if a law can make Justice out of Injustice, can it not also make good out of bad? But in fact we can perceive the difference between good laws and bad by referring them to no other standard than Nature; indeed, it is not merely Justice and Injustice which are distinguished by Nature, but also and without exception things which are honourable and dishonourable. For since an intelligence common to us all makes things known to us and formulates them in our minds, honourable actions are ascribed by us to virtue, and dishonourable actions to vice; and only a madman would conclude that these judgments are matters of opinion, and not fixed by Nature.

(Cicero, *De Republica,* Bk 3, ch. 22, p. 211; Cicero, *De Legibus,* tr. C. W. Keyes, Bk 1, Chs 15, 16, pp. 343–7, Loeb Classical Library, London 1928.)

17   SENECA

The first men on this earth, however, and their immediate descendants, followed nature unspoiled; they took a single person as their leader and their law, freely submitting to the decisions of an individual of superior merit. . . .

In that age, then, which people commonly refer to as the Golden Age, government, so Posidonius maintains, was in the hands of the wise. They kept the peace, protected the weaker from the stronger, urged and dissuaded, pointed out what was advantageous and what was not. Their ability to look ahead ensured that their peoples never went short of anything, whilst their bravery averted dangers and their devotedness brought well-being and prosperity to their subjects. To govern was to serve, not to rule. No one used to try out the extent of his power over those to whom he owed that power in the first place. And no one had either reason or inclination to perpetrate injustice, since people governing well were equally well obeyed, and a king could issue no greater threat to disobedient subjects than that of his own abdication. . . .

What race of men could be luckier? Share and share alike they enjoyed nature. She saw to each and every man's requirements for survival like a parent. What it all amounted to was undisturbed possession of resources owned by the community. I can surely call that race of men one of unparalleled riches, it being impossible to find a single pauper in it.

Into this ideal state of things burst avarice, avarice which in seeking to put aside some article or other and appropriate it to its own use, only succeeded in making everything somebody else's property and reducing its possessions to a fraction of its previously unlimited wealth. Avarice brought in poverty, by coveting a lot of possessions losing all that it had. This is why although it may endeavour to make good its losses, may acquire estate after estate by buying out or forcing out its neighbours, enlarge country properties to the dimensions of whole provinces, speak of 'owning some property' when it can go on a long tour overseas without once stepping off its own land, there is no extension of our boundaries that can bring us back to our starting point. When we have done everything within our power, we shall possess a great deal: but we once possessed the world.

The earth herself, untilled, was more productive, her yields being more than ample for the needs of peoples who did not raid each other. With any of nature's products, men found as much pleasure in showing others what they had discovered as they did in discovering it. No one could outdo or be outdone by any other. All was equally divided among people living in complete harmony. The stronger had not yet started laying hands on the weaker; the avaricious person had not yet started hiding things away, to be hoarded for his own private use, so shutting the next man off from actual necessities of life; each cared as much about the other as about himself. Weapons were unused; hands still unstained with human blood had directed their hostility exclusively against wild beasts. . . .

This was a home in conformity with nature, a home in which one enjoyed living, and which occasioned neither fear of it nor fears for it, whereas nowadays our own homes count for a large part of our feeling of insecurity.

But however wonderful and guileless the life they led, they were not wise men; this is a title that has come to be reserved for the highest of all achievements. All the same, I should be the last to deny that they were men of exalted spirit, only one step removed, so to speak, from the gods. There can be no doubt that before this earth was worn out it produced a better type of offspring. But though they all possess a character more robust than that of today, and one with a greater aptitude for hard work, it is equally true that their personalities fell short of genuine perfection. For nature does not give a man virtue: the process of becoming a good man is an art. Certainly they did not go in search of gold or silver or the various crystalline stones to be found in the nethermost dregs of the earth. They were still merciful even to dumb animals. Man was far and away from killing man, not out of fear or provocation, but simply for entertainment. They had yet to wear embroidered clothing, and had yet to have gold woven into robes, or even mine it. But the fact remains that their innocence was due to ignorance and nothing else. And there is a world of difference between, on the one hand, choosing not to do what is wrong and, on the other, not knowing how to do it in the first place. They lacked the cardinal virtues of justice, moral insight, self-control and courage. There were corresponding qualities, in each case not unlike these, that had a place in their primitive lives; but virtue only comes to a character which has been thoroughly schooled and trained and brought to a pitch of perfection by unremitting practice. We are born for it, but not with it. And even in the best of people, until you cultivate it there is only the material for virtue, not virtue itself.

(Seneca, *Letters from a Stoic*, tr. R. Campbell, no. 90, pp. 162–3, 174–7, Penguin, Harmondsworth 1969.)

18   MARCUS AURELIUS

4. If our intellectual part is common, the reason also, in respect of which we

are rational beings, is common: if this is so, common also is the reason which commands us what to do, and what not to do; if this is so, there is a common law also; if this is so, we are fellow citizens; if this is so, we are members of some political community; if this is so, the world is in a manner a state. For of what other common political community will anyone say that the whole human race are members? And from this common political community comes also our very intellectual faculty and reasoning faculty and our capacity for law; or whence do they come? For as my earthly part is a portion given to me from certain earth, and that which is watery from another element, and that which is hot and fiery from some peculiar source (for nothing comes out of that which is nothing, as nothing also returns to non-existence), so also the intellectual part comes from some source. . . .

23. Everything harmonizes with me, which is harmonious to thee, O Universe. Nothing for me is too early nor too late, which is in due time for thee. Everything is fruit to me which thy seasons bring, O Nature: from thee are all things, in thee are all things, to thee all things return. The poet says, 'Dear city of Cecrops'; and wilt not thou say, 'Dear city of Zeus'? . . .

44. But if however the gods determine about none of the things which concern us, I am able to determine about myself, and I can inquire about that which is useful; and that is useful to every man which is conformable to his own constitution and nature. But my nature is rational and social; and my city and country, so far as I am Antoninus, is Rome, but so far as I am a man, it is the world. The things then which are useful to these cities are alone useful to me.

(Marcus Aurelius, *Meditations*, tr. G. Long, ch. 4, paras 4, 23, pp. 95, 98; ch. 6, para 44, pp. 127-8, G. Bell, London 1891.)

19 GAIUS

Every people that is governed by statutes and customs observes partly its own peculiar law and partly the common law of all mankind. That law which a people establishes for itself is peculiar to it, and is called *ius ciuile* (civil law) as being the special law of that *ciuitas* (State); while the law that natural reason establishes among all mankind is followed by all peoples alike, and is called *ius gentium* (law of nations, or law of the world) as being the law observed by all mankind. Thus the Roman people observes partly its own peculiar law and partly the common law of mankind. This distinction we shall apply in detail at the proper places. . . .

Slaves are in the *potestas* of their masters. This *potestas* is *iuris gentium*, for it is observable that among all nations alike masters have power of life and death over their slaves, and whatever is acquired through a slave is acquired for his master. But at the present day neither Roman citizens nor any other persons subject to the rule of the Roman people are allowed to treat their slaves with excessive and causeless harshness. For by a constitution of the late emperor Antoninus it is laid down that one who without cause kills his own slave is as much amenable to justice as one who kills another's. . . .

Ownership of some things is acquired under the law of nations, that law which owing to natural reason is observed amongst all men alike, of other things under the civil law, that is to say the proper law of each man's state. And since the law of nations is the older law, having been born along with the human race itself, it is necessary to treat of it first. Now all animals which are captured on land or sea or in the air, that is to say wild beasts, birds, and fish, become the property of their captors.

(*The Institutes of Gaius*, tr. F. de Zulueta, Bk 1, pp. 3, 17, Clarendon Press, Oxford 1946.)

20 ULPIAN (THE *INSTITUTES* OF JUSTINIAN)

The study of law consists of two branches, law public, and law private. The former relates to the welfare of the Roman State; the latter to the advantage of the individual citizen. Of private law then we may say that it is of threefold origin, being collected from the precepts of nature, from those of the law of nations, or from those of the civil law of Rome.

OF THE LAW OF NATURE: THE LAW OF NATIONS, AND THE CIVIL LAW

The law of nature is that which she has taught all animals; a law not peculiar to the human race, but shared by all living creatures, whether denizens of the air, the dry land, or the sea. Hence comes the union of male and female, which we call marriage; hence the procreation and rearing of children, for this is a law by the knowledge of which we see even the lower animals are distinguished. The civil law of Rome, and the law of all nations, differ from each other thus. The laws of every people governed by statutes and customs are partly peculiar to itself, partly common to all mankind. Those rules which a state enacts for its own members are peculiar to itself, and are called civil law: those rules prescribed by natural reason for all men are observed by all peoples alike, and are called the law of nations. Thus the laws of the Roman people are partly peculiar to itself, partly common to all nations; a distinction of which we shall take notice as occasion offers. . . . But the law of nations is common to the whole human race; for nations have settled certain things for themselves as occasion and the necessities of human life required. For instance, wars arose, and then followed captivity and slavery, which are contrary to the law of nature; for by the law of nature all men from the beginning were born free. The law of nations again is the source of almost all contracts; for instance, sale, hire, partnership, deposit, loan for consumption, and very many others.

Our law is partly written, partly unwritten, as among the Greeks. The written law consists of statutes, plebiscites, senatusconsults, enactments of the Emperors, edicts of the magistrates, and answers of those learned in the law. A statute is an enactment of the Roman people, which it used to make on the motion of a senatorial magistrate, as for instance a consul. A plebiscite is an enactment of the commonalty, such as was made on the motion of one of their own magistrates, as a tribune. . . . Again, what the Emperor determines has the force of a statute, the people having conferred on him all their authority and power by the *lex regia,* which was passed concerning his office and authority. Consequently, whatever the Emperor settles by rescript, or decides in his judicial capacity, or ordains by edicts, is clearly a statute: and these are what are called constitutions. . . . The unwritten law is that which usage has approved: for ancient customs, when approved by consent of those who follow them, are like statute. And this division of the civil law into two kinds seems not inappropriate, for it appears to have originated in the institutions of two states, namely Athens and Lacedaemon; it having been usual in the latter to commit to memory what was observed as law, while the Athenians observed only what they had made permanent in written statutes.

But the laws of nature, which are observed by all nations alike, are established, as it were, by divine providence, and remain ever fixed and immutable: but the municipal laws of each individual state are subject to frequent change, either by the tacit consent of the people, or by the subsequent enactment of another statute.

(*The Institutes of Justinian*, tr. J. B. Moyle, 5th edn, pp. 3-6, Clarendon Press, Oxford 1913.)

PART TWO

Christian Political Ideas

CHAPTER 7

The Political Theory of the New Testament

The Middle Ages produced a great deal of political literature. Some of it was a response to current political events, such as the literary activity stimulated by the investiture controversy of the eleventh century. Some developed from sources outside the main stream of Christian thought as in the case of the Aristotelian synthesis of the thirteenth century. Much of it, however, was a commentary on statements which had occurred in the gospels and the epistles of the New Testament.

Natural Law

Few of the political ideas of the New Testament were new. Most of them were the product of an acquaintance with Greek and Jewish philosophy which St Paul, in particular, possessed. The reference to natural law in Paul's Epistle to the Romans is an example (Ex. 21a). This appears to be the only distinct reference in the whole of the Bible, but it clearly refers to a law recognized by reason distinct from the positive law of any state. There seems to be little difference between the Pauline and Stoic concepts of natural law. Natural law remained an important element in philosophical discussion throughout the Middle Ages although there was a tendency, at least until the thirteenth century, to regard it as an ideal, unattainable except for those touched by God's grace.

Equality

The notion of human equality was never far from that of the law of nature in pagan philosophy. So, in the New Testament, we find the conception of a universal brotherhood of man in which differences of race and status are of merely superficial imporance. In language which recalls the first chapters of Aristotle's *Politics,* Paul uses an organic analogy to illustrate his conception of the universal community (Ex. 21b).

The Duty of Obedience

Jesus of Nazareth, who was executed as a political conspirator, had little to say of a political nature if the gospels are to be believed. His statement: 'My kingdom is not of this world', implied that his main purpose was to show men the individual road to the kingdom of heaven rather than to teach political attitudes. Possibly the most important political utterance attributed to Jesus was that made in answer to the Pharisees who had attempted to trick him into proclaiming his opposition to Roman authority, and the Herodians who wished him to declare his full collaboration (Ex. 21c). A less subtle answer would have associated him with one side or the other. His statement that a duty is owed to both God and Caesar can be regarded as the original statement of what in the Middle Ages was to be called the 'doctrine of the two swords' or 'two spheres' of rightful authority.

Jesus's view that it is right to pay tribute to the secular ruler is echoed in what is probably the most politically significant passage in the Bible: Paul's statement to the Romans that obedience to secular authority is commanded by God (Ex. 21d,i). This became the standard theory of political obligation held by political writers throughout the Middle Ages. There does not appear to be, in this Pauline passage or in a similar one in the first epistle of Peter (Ex. 21d,ii), any differentiation made between the just and the unjust ruler, although the implication is that rulers are likely to be on the side of righteousness. Paul says nothing about what the subject should do if he is commanded to sin or to act against his conscience. Later medieval writers invariably interpreted Paul to mean that in such cases disobedience would be a duty, but on no account would rebellion be justified.

Much speculation has taken place on why Paul (and the pseudonymous author of the Petrine epistle) emphasized so earnestly the divine nature of civil authority. There are at least two major reasons. The first is that Paul, an ex-Pharisee, would naturally be familiar with the Jewish teaching which accepted that kings were ordained of God. Scriptural evidence for this teaching was provided by the Old Testament Book of Samuel which relates how Saul was anointed king by Samuel with the blessing of Jahweh. The second reason is to do with political expediency. Many of the early Christian converts were prone to regard their new-found liberty from the restrictions of the Mosaic law as a first step towards an 'antinomian' attitude of complete freedom from the laws of the civil authorities. Their attitude was supported by the eschatological teaching of Jesus who seems to have predicted his second coming and the imminence of the end of the world. Clearly, such a belief in the transitory nature of things was unlikely to foster an acceptance of the existing order, particularly when the existing order was demonstrably less than perfect. The danger therefore was anarchy. Paul must have realized that the survival of the Christian Church, even in the short period prior to the second coming depended upon its members coming to terms with the secular authorities.

Slavery

Pauline statements concerning slavery show a similar respect for authority. Consistent with his views on human equality, he sees the distinction between the free man and the slave as of only superficial importance, although he nowhere suggests that the institution of slavery is in any sense unlawful. In fact, in the letter to Philemon (Ex. 21e,i), he explains that he is returning the runaway slave Onesimus to his master, although it is clear that he expects Philemon to behave towards his slave in the forgiving spirit of brotherly love. In Paul's letter to the Ephesians (Ex. 21e,ii), he writes that the slave has a religious duty to obey his master in a spirit of ungrudging service. Paul's attitude to slavery is thus one of acceptance of an institution which, while presumably burdonsome to the slave, was unimportant in the eyes of God. We find no implication that slaves should seek their freedom, but Paul clearly regards it as important that their treatment should be as fair as possible.

Private Property

References to property in the Pauline epistles are few and relatively trivial. However, in the Gospels there occurs a statement by Jesus on the subject of property which became an often quoted reference during the Middle Ages by those seeking to criticize the wealth of the Church (Ex. 21f,i). The interpretation of this passage has been much disputed, but normally it was taken to mean that the possession of wealth makes it more difficult to follow a righteous life. The words of the Magnificat in the Gospel of St Luke also stress the disadvantages of possessing wealth: 'He hath filled the hungry with good things; and the rich he hath sent empty away.'

The first chapters of the Acts of the Apostles describing the early church in Jerusalem indicate that its members were following the advice of Jesus to renounce private property. 'And all that believed were together, and had all things common; and sold their possessions and goods, and parted them to all men, as every man had need.' A later passage (Ex. 21f,ii), refers again to the communism practised by the early Christians and, in the story of Ananias, points to the penalty exacted by God for reverting to private ownership.

The most extreme statement of opposition to material wealth was made in the epistle of James, the leader of the Jerusalem Christians and traditionally the brother of Jesus (Ex. 21f,iii). The abandoning of private possessions had never been a condition of membership of the Christian Church and by the time that James wrote the early communism had apparently begun to break down. James denounces the rich and those who pay special attention to them, and seems to regard the rich as evil and the poor as good. Such radical class-consciousness is not typical of early Christian thought, and it has even been suggested that the epistle is the work of a non-Christian who ascribed its authorship to James in order to secure for it a spurious authenticity.

FURTHER READING

Text
The New Testament (authorized edition)

Commentaries
E. Barker: *From Alexander to Constantine* (Clarendon Press 1956)
R. W. and A. J. Carlyle: *History of Mediaeval Political Theory in the West*, vol. I (Blackwood 1962)

21a   ST PAUL: NATURAL LAW

11 For there is no respect of persons with God.
12 For as many as have sinned without law shall also perish without law: and as many as have sinned in the law shall be judged by the law;
13 (For not the hearers of the law are just before God, but the doers of the law shall be justified.
14 For when the Gentiles, which have not the law, do by nature the things contained in the law, these, having not the law, are a law unto themselves:
15 Which shew the work of the law written in their hearts, their conscience also bearing witness, and their thoughts the meanwhile accusing or else excusing one another;)
16 In the day when God shall judge the secrets of men by Jesus Christ according to my gospel.

(St Paul: Epistle to the Romans, ch. 2.)

21b   ST PAUL: THE ORGANIC COMMUNITY

12 For as the body is one, and hath many members, and all the members of that one body, being many, are one body: so also is Christ.
13 For by one Spirit are we all baptized into one body, whether we be Jews or Gentiles, whether we be bond or free; and have been all made to drink into one Spirit.
14 For the body is not one member, but many.
15 If the foot shall say, Because I am not the hand, I am not of the body; is it therefore not of the body?

16 And if the ear shall say, Because I am not the eye, I am not of the body; is it therefore not of the body?

17 If the whole body were an eye, where were the hearing? If the whole were hearing, where were the smelling?

18 But now hath God set the members every one of them in the body, as it hath pleased him.

19 And if they were all one member, where were the body?

20 But now are they many members, yet but one body.

(St Paul: Epistle to the Corinthians, ch. 12.)

21c JESUS OF NAZARETH: THE TWO POWERS

15 Then went the Pharisees, and took counsel how they might entangle him in his talk.

16 And they sent out unto him their disciples with the Herodians, saying, Master, we know that thou art true, and teachest the way of God in truth, neither carest thou for any man: for thou regardest not the person of men.

17 Tell us therefore, What thinkest thou? Is it lawful to give tribute unto Caesar, or not?

18 But Jesus perceived their wickedness, and said, Why tempt ye me, ye hypocrites?

18 Shew me the tribute money. And they brought unto him a penny.

20 And he saith unto them, Whose is this image and superscription?

21 They say unto him, Caesar's. Then saith he unto them, Render therefore unto Caesar the things which are Caesar's; and unto God the things that are God's.

22 When they had heard these words, they marvelled, and left him, and went their way.

(Gospel according to Matthew, ch. 22.)

21d ST PAUL and ST PETER: OBEDIENCE TO AUTHORITY

(i) Let every soul be subject unto the higher powers. For there is no power but of God: the powers that be are ordained of God.

2 Whosoever therefore resisteth the power, resisteth the ordinance of God: and they that resist shall receive to themselves damnation.

3 For rulers are not a terror to good works, but to the evil. Wilt thou then not be afraid of the power? do that which is good, and thou shalt have praise of the same:

4 For he is the minister of God to thee for good. But if thou do that which is evil, be afraid; for he beareth not the sword in vain: for he is the minister of God, a revenger to execute wrath upon him that doeth evil.

5 Wherefore ye must needs be subject, not only for wrath, but also for conscience sake.

6 For for this cause pay ye tribute also: for they are God's ministers, attending continually upon this very thing.
7 Render therefore to all their dues: tribute to whom tribute is due; custom to whom custom; fear to whom fear; honour to whom honour.

(ii) 13 Submit yourselves to every ordinance of man for the Lord's sake: whether it be to the king, as supreme;
14 Or unto governors, as unto them that are sent by him for the punishment of evildoers, and for the praise of them that do well.
15 For so is the will of God, that with well doing ye may put to silence the ignorance of foolish men:
16 As free, and not using your liberty for a cloke of maliciousness, but as the servants of God.
17 Honour all men. Love the brotherhood. Fear God. Honour the king.
18 Servants, be subject to your masters with all fear; not only to the good and gentle, but also to the froward.
19 For this is thankworthy, if a man for conscience toward God endure grief, suffering wrongfully.
20 For what glory is it, if, when ye be buffeted for your faults, ye shall take it patiently? but if, when ye do well, and suffer for it, ye take it patiently, this is acceptable with God.
21 For even hereunto were ye called: because Christ also suffered for us, leaving us an example, that ye should follow his steps.

((i) St Paul: Epistle to the Romans, ch. 13; (ii) St Peter: First Epistle, ch. 2.)

21e   ST PAUL: SLAVERY

(i) 10 I beseech for thee for my son Onesimus, whom I have begotten in my bonds:
11 Which in time past was to thee unprofitable, but now profitable to thee and to me:
12 Whom I have sent again: thou therefore receive him, that is, mine own bowels:
13 Whom I would have retained with me, that in thy stead he might have ministered unto me in the bonds of the gospel:
14 But without thy mind would I do nothing; that thy benefit should not be as it were of necessity, but willingly.
15 For perhaps he therefore departed for a season, that thou shouldest receive him for ever;
16 Not now as a servant, but above a servant, a brother beloved, specially to me, but how much more unto thee, both in the flesh, and in the Lord?
17 If thou count me therefore a partner, receive him as myself.
18 If he hath wronged thee, or oweth thee ought, put that on mine account.

(ii) 5 Servants, be obedient to them that are your masters according to the flesh, with fear and trembling, in singleness of your heart, as unto Christ;

6 Not with eyeservice, as menpleasers; but as the servants of Christ, doing the will of God from the heart;
7 With good will doing service, as to the Lord, and not to men:
8 Knowing that whatsoever good thing any man doeth, the same shall he receive of the Lord, whether he be bond or free.
9 And, ye masters, do the same things unto them, forbearing threatening: knowing that your Master also is in heaven; neither is there respect of persons with him.

((i) St Paul: Epistle to Philemon; (ii) Epistle to the Ephesians, ch. 6.)

21f JESUS, ACTS and ST JAMES: PROPERTY

(i) 18 And a certain ruler asked him, saying, Good Master, what shall I do to inherit eternal life?
19 And Jesus said unto him, Why callest thou me good? none is good, save one, that is, God.
20 Thou knowest the commandments, Do not commit adultery, Do not kill, Do not steal, Do not bear false witness, Honour thy father and thy mother.
21 And he said, All these have I kept from my youth up.
22 Now when Jesus heard these things, he said unto him, Yet lackest thou one thing: sell all that thou hast, and distribute unto the poor, and thou shalt have treasure in heaven: and come, follow me.
23 And when he heard this, he was very sorrowful: for he was very rich.
24 And when Jesus saw that he was very sorrowful, he said, How hardly shall they that have riches enter into the kingdom of God!
25 For it is easier for a camel to go through a needle's eye, than for a rich man to enter into the kingdom of God.
26 And they that heard it said, Who then can be saved?
27 And he said, The things which are impossible with men are possible with God.
28 Then Peter said, Lo, we have left all, and followed thee.
29 And he said unto them, Verily I say unto you, There is no man that hath left house, or parents, or brethren, or wife, or children, for the kingdom of God's sake,
30 Who shall not receive manifold more in this present time, and in the world to come life everlasting.

(ii) 32 And the multitude of them that believed were of one heart and of one soul: neither said any of them that ought of the things which he possessed was his own; but they had all things common.
33 And with great power gave the apostles witness of the resurrection of the Lord Jesus: and great grace was upon them all.
34 Neither was there any among them that lacked: for as many as were possessors of lands or houses sold them, and brought the prices of the things that were sold,
35 And laid them down at the apostles' feet: and distribution was made unto

every man according as he had need.
36 And Joses, who by the apostles was surnamed Barnabas, (which is, being interpreted, The son of consolation,) a Levite, and of the country of Cyprus.
37 Having land, sold it, and brought the money, and laid it at the apostles' feet.

Chapter 5

But a certain man named Ananias, with Sapphira his wife, sold a possession,
2 And kept back part of the price, his wife also being privy to it, and brought a certain part, and laid it at the apostles' feet.
3 But Peter said, Ananias, why hath Satan filled thine heart to lie to the Holy Ghost, and to keep back part of the price of the land?
4 Whiles it remained, was it not thine own? and after it was sold, was it not in thine own power? why hast thou conceived this thing in thine heart? thou has not lied unto men, but unto God.
5 And Ananias hearing these words fell down, and gave up the ghost: and great fear came on all them that heard these things.
6 And the young men arose, wound him up, and carried him out, and buried him.

(iii) My brethren, have not the faith of our Lord Jesus Christ, the Lord of glory, with respect of persons.
2 For if there come unto your assembly a man with a gold ring, in goodly apparel, and there come in also a poor man in vile raiment;
3 And ye have respect to him that weareth the gay clothing, and say unto him, Sit thou here in a good place; and say to the poor, Stand thou there, or sit here under my footstool:
4 Are ye not then partial in yourselves, and are become judges of evil thoughts?
5 Hearken, my beloved brethren, Hath not God chosen the poor of this world rich in faith, and heirs of the kingdom which he hath promised to them that love him?
6 But ye have despised the poor. Do not rich men oppress you, and draw you before the judgment seats?
7 Do not they blaspheme that worthy name by the which ye are called?
8 If ye fulfil the royal law according to the scripture, Thou shalt love thy neighbour as thyself, ye do well:
9 But if ye have respect to persons, ye commit sin, and are convinced of the law as transgressors.

((i) Gospel according to Luke, ch. 18; (ii) Acts of the Apostles, chs 4-5; (iii) Epistle of James, ch. 2.)

CHAPTER 8

St Augustine and the Growth of Christianity

In his monumental work, *The Decline and Fall of the Roman Empire*, the historian, Edward Gibbon, attributed the growth of the Christian Church before the time of Constantine to five main causes. First, 'the inflexible and . . . intolerant zeal of the Christians'. Secondly, 'the doctrine of a future life'. Thirdly, 'the miraculous powers ascribed to the primitive church'. Fourthly, 'the pure and austere morals of the Christians'. Fifthly, 'the union and discipline of the Christian republic which gradually formed an independent and increasing state in the heart of the Roman Empire'. It would probably be true to say that the fifth factor—the political one—was the most important, particularly in the conversion of Constantine.

The Christians in the Roman Empire had endured sporadic persecution since the time of Nero. Even during the reign of virtuous emperors such as Marcus Aurelius, the Christian community was seen as a threat to the civil order and persecution continued, as may be illustrated by the execution of the Christian apologist, Justin Martyr. In conformity with St Paul's teaching regarding obedience to the secular ruler, Christians acknowledged the authority of the emperor in political matters, but they could not accept the notion of a deified emperor as symbolizing the power of the state. Persecution reached its bloodiest climax in A.D. 303 when Diocletian attempted, unsuccessfully, to crush the Christian community once and for all.

Constantine

Although the first official decree granting toleration towards Christianity was made by Diocletian's son-in-law, Galerius, it was the latter's co-emperor, Constantine, who was responsible for the final triumph of Christianity in the Roman Empire. Constantine recognized that the highly organized, militant Christian sect was an important and effective source of political power. Competing religious sects, such as Mithraism, tended to be too tolerant to act as an important focus of opposition to the Christians and, furthermore, much of the army seems to have favoured Christianity. Constantine, therefore, had little to lose and a great deal to gain by attracting the goodwill of Christians, which he did by granting religious toleration in A.D. 313 in the Edict of Milan (Ex. 22). However one regards the story of Constantine's vision and his subsequent defeat of his rival, Maxentius, there is no reason to doubt his genuine religious conviction, which culminated in his baptism in the year of his death.

Schisms and heresies had been characteristic of the Christian sect since the Gnostic movement of the early second century, but with the cessation of external persecution even more energy was channelled into heretical struggles. The most important heresy in Constantine's reign was Arianism, the doctrine expounded by the Alexandrian priest, Arius, that God the father had created Christ the son, and therefore that the latter was inferior to the former. Constantine realized the potential political dangers of a division in the Church and offered himself as a mediator in the dispute. At the Council of Nicaea in 325, the assembled Christian bishops condemned the Arian heresy and supported the formula provided by Athanasius whose Nicene creed remains the cornerstone of orthodox Christian doctrine.

Theodosius

The alliance between Constantine and the orthodox Christian bishops was not continued by his successors, several of whom, including Constantine's son, Constantius II, favoured Arianism. Eventually, however, under the reign of Theodosius in 379, Catholic Christianity was established as the official religion of the Roman Empire, all other sects being prohibited. Once more the main reason was political. The empire was threatened within by disunity, and from without at the imperial frontiers by the barbarian tribesmen from the north. Theodosius saw the only possible answer to his problems in an alliance with the Church which, with its emphasis upon obedience to the secular government, he hoped would help to strengthen and unify the Roman state.

His expectations, at least in the Western Empire, were frustrated. Even during his reign the powerful Visigothic tribe constituted an ever-present danger to the Empire, and when he died in 395 the Goths under their newly elected king, Alaric the Bold, rose in revolt. Alaric's campaigns culminated in the sack of the city of Rome in 410.

Saint Augustine (354–430)

It is in the context of the sack of Rome and its aftermath that we must examine the political ideas of Augustine, the most outstanding figure in early Christian thought. The son of a pagan father and a Christian mother, Augustine was brought up as a pagan and became a Manichaean in about 374. The main feature of the Manichaean doctrine was a dualism which conceived of the universe as governed by the two opposing powers of good and evil, light and darkness. Unable for long to accept the independent reality of evil, Augustine embraced Neoplatonism which, in its identification of evil with the unreal material world and its exaltation of the real world of absolute spirit, fitted in well with his own metaphysical outlook. Despite this, Augustine was eventually repelled by the intellectual arrogance of the Neoplatonists and their dogmatic rationalism, and was led to an interest in Christianity. His conversion came about partly as a result of hearing St Ambrose preach in Milan, and partly from a study of the Pauline epistles. He was baptized in 387 and became Bishop of Hippo in north Africa in 396.

The fall of Rome in 410 came as a cataclysmic shock to the in habitants of the empire, pagans and Christians alike. For centurie Rome had been regarded as the centre of the civilized world; it had symbolized secular authority and was gradually also becoming the symbol for ecclesiastical authority. Many pagans attributed its fall to the abandonment of the old religion, and, furthermore, blamed the Christians for undermining the Roman martial spirit and even for sec retly working towards the realization of the end of the world. Augus tine took upon himself the task of answering these charges, and his book *De Civitate Dei* (*The City of God*) written in the years 413 to 426 is an attempt to refute the pagan accusations.

The work is divided into twenty-two books of which the first ten are concerned with rejecting the anti-Christian arguments. The last twelve books show Augustine's conception of society and attempt to en courage Christians by demonstrating that although earthly cities such as Rome may be destroyed, it is possible to conceive of a permanen and changeless city. This, of course, is the City of God to which the title of the book refers.

The Two Cities

The conception of the two cities, the heavenly and the earthly, was perhaps the most important political idea contributed by Augustine. I was not a completely original one, however. He drew upon a number of early, vaguely expressed notions in order to construct his theory The Stoic *cosmopolis* to which belonged all wise and virtuous men was clearly one element. Another was the early Christian conception of the community in Christ. St Paul speaks of 'the Lord's fellowship', and 'citizens of heaven'. A third element was the Neoplatonic division bet ween the higher 'real' world of form and spirit (the good), and th lower world of matter (the evil). Augustine was not even the firs thinker to synthesize these elements; Tychonius, a Donatist writer, had already produced a theory of two societies. What Augustine pre eminently did was to make the theory an integral part of orthodox Christian philosophy until it was displaced by the revived Aristotelianism of the thirteenth century.

The City of God (*Civitas Dei*) began when God created the angels who were its first inhabitants (Ex. 23a). It contains, in addition, the saints in heaven and those on earth who are predestined for salvation. It was founded on earth by Seth who was born after Cain killed Abel. The earthly city (*civitas terrena*) began with the fall of Satan and contains the souls in hell and those on earth who are predestined to damnation, the 'reprobate'. Its earthly foundation was by Cain. It is clear that Augustine sees the two cities as those of the good and the evil respectively, and the progress of history as the struggle between the two. Each exists on earth as well as in the supernatural world, although the members of each on earth mingle together and will only be separated at the Last Judgement which signifies the final victory of the City of God over its evil counterpart.

The theological conceptions of 'original sin' and 'predestination', are central to Augustine's system of philosophy. All men inherit the sin of Adam and are thus themselves depraved, deserving only eternal damnation. Most men are in fact damned; these are the 'reprobate' who, after death, suffer an eternity of torment in the fires of hell. But some are saved. They are the 'elect' who, through the gift of God's grace, are brought to the true faith in Christ and are hence able to follow a life of virtue. When they die, their souls ultimately enjoy an eternity of heavenly bliss. It is important to note that salvation for the few is not the result of their virtuous life. Because of original sin, no man can be good unless he is predestined by God to receive the free gift of faith. Why some men rather than others are chosen for election is a mystery that man cannot comprehend, although Augustine appears to think that the total number of those predestined for salvation is equivalent to the total number of empty places in heaven vacated by the fallen angels.

Secular Government

Augustine's preoccupation with the sinfulness of fallen man goes much of the way towards explaining his theory of government. We have already examined one important influence in this theory: Seneca's conception of government as a convention of man made necessary by the introduction into natural society of greed and private property. St Irenaeus, a second-century Christian writer, echoes Seneca's theory in his book *Against Heresies*, which contains a very similar statement about the origin of government (Ex. 24). According to Irenaeus, secular government was imposed by God upon sinful man in order that human wickedness should be minimized. Augustine's theory is cast in the same mould. Originally man was created to have authority over other life forms but not over men. The 'fall' led to the sins of ambition, greed, and lust for power. Greed led to the establishment of private property, and the lust for power led to the domination of man over man in the institutions of government and slavery (Ex. 23b). Paradoxically, these institutions established in sin are the means by which God both punishes and remedies the sin of man. Civil government and slavery by imposing servitude on man punish him for Adam's sin and yet at the same time, by imposing constraints on his actions, reduce his opportunities for sinning.

Augustine does not completely identify his earthly city with civil society. The *civitas terrena* includes only the reprobate, whereas civil society includes all men, elect as well as reprobate. It follows that if civil government is binding upon all men, no one may resist or even judge the actions of the ruler because his authority is from God. In this, Augustine closely follows St Paul. Even an evil ruler such as Nero may not be resisted, although passive disobedience would doubtless be called for in the event of a command to sin. Such a ruler must be accepted as a divine punishment for the people's sins.

Secular rule is therefore a conventional device imposed by man upon man with the approval of God, which has the effect of making man less sinful. It cannot make him good; goodness comes only from God's grace and is thus confined to the elect. It follows that Augustine's theory of the natural law must be substantially different from that of the Stoics. Whereas they had considered the law of nature to be a perfect standard of conduct attainable by all rational creatures, Augustine sees it as a norm of conduct unattainable since the Fall by any except the members of the City of God, the predestined elect. Sin has severed most men from their original natural state; only grace can restore them to it.

Augustine's treatment of the concept of 'peace' illustrates this point (Ex. 23c). All men and all societies require peace for a tolerable existence. But 'peace' is used by Augustine in two senses. On the one hand it means simply the absence of conflict: concord between men. It is the kind of peace that secular government exists to provide and is the only kind attainable by members of the *civitas terrena*. This type of peace is not undervalued by Augustine; it is a good but not the highest good. Law and order are essential for the inhabitants of both cities. The other kind of peace is more positive. It is almost equivalent to a Platonic 'form' in that it is perfect order and harmony, 'the perfectly ordered and harmonious enjoyment of God, and of one another in God.' Such a peace can be attained only by members of the *Civitas Dei* and hence, on earth, it is available only to the 'elect'.

As with peace, so with justice. Perfect justice (*vera justitia*) is a characteristic of the heavenly city alone (Ex. 23d). It must therefore be the case that Rome, as indeed any other civil society, was never a 'true commonwealth' since Cicero in *De Re Publica* (*The Republic*) had defined the commonwealth in terms of justice. Augustine sympathizes with Cicero's definition: 'without justice, what are kingdoms but great robberies?'

Nevertheless, Augustine cannot leave it at that. Such a conclusion would be inconsistent with his theory that the state is essential as a remedy for sin. Hence, just as earthly states aim at a second-rate peace, so they achieve a second-rate justice—an internal order based upon common agreement as to the things that the people respect. Using such a definition, Augustine concludes that it is possible to apply the term 'commonwealth' to existing civil societies even though they do not possess true justice.

Church and Civil Society

Neither of Augustine's two cities can be at all closely identified with actual institutions. We have seen that civil society includes pilgrim members of the heavenly city as well as the reprobate, and, by the same token, the Church includes members of the earthly city as well as the elect. It was on this latter point that Augustine quarrelled with the Donatists—a schismatic sect which argued that the visible Church should contain only the pure, and that the sacraments were valid only when administered by a priest who was himself morally pure. Rejecting this view, Augustine contended that a Church comprising only the elect implied that men could usurp God's function of discriminating between those with the gift of grace and those without. In addition, even if such discrimination were possible, such a Church would be unable to fulfil its function of providing spiritual direction for all men.

On the question of the relationship between Church and secular society, Augustine, unlike later writers, had no fully developed position. He realizes, however, the necessity for cooperation between the two, since the carrying out of the Church's sacramental and doctrinal functions depended upon a stable and peaceful political order. Furthermore, he regards the state as an important aid in promoting religious uniformity; he expresses quite forcibly his agreement with the anti-heresy laws which were aimed at the Donatists. It is possible to perceive here the seeds of the later Gelasian doctrine of the two swords.

The emphasis placed by Augustine upon the desirability of cooperation between the secular and the spiritual authorities contradicts once more any interpretation which seeks to identify these institutions with his two cities. History, for Augustine, is essentially the conflict, rather than the cooperation, between the heavenly and the earthly cities, beginning with the division among the angels and culminating in the final victory of the City of God at the end of the world. This optimistic vision of historical progress was the more remarkable coming at a time when it was evident that the collapse of Roman civilization was imminent. Augustine's *De Civitate Dei*, with its curious blend of despair for the mass of depraved mankind and optimism for the victory of good over evil, remained until the late Middle Ages a work of unparalleled influence.

FURTHER READING

Text
St Augustine: *De Civitate Dei*

Commentaries
E. Barker: *Essays on Government* (Clarendon Press 1951)
R. W. and A. J. Carlyle: *History of Mediaeval Political Theory in the West*, vol. 1 (Blackwood 1962)
H. A. Deane: *Political and Social Ideas of St Augustine* (Columbia University Press 1966)
J. N. Figgis: *The Political Aspects of St Augustine's 'City of God'* (Longmans 1921)

22   EDICT OF MILAN

2. When we, Constantine and Licinius, Emperors, met at Milan in conference concerning the welfare and security of the realm, we decided that of the things that are of profit to all mankind, the worship of God ought rightly to be our first and chiefest care, and that it was right that Christians and all others should have freedom to follow the kind of religion they favoured; so that the God who dwells in heaven might be propitious to us and to all under our rule. 4. We therefore announce that, notwithstanding any provisions concerning the Christians in our former instructions, all who choose that religion are to be permitted to continue therein, without any let or hindrance, and are not to be in any way troubled or molested. 6. Note that at the same time all others are to be allowed the free and unrestricted practice of their religions; for it accords with the good order of the realm and the peacefulness of our times that each should have freedom to worship God after his own choice; and we do not intend to detract from the honour due to any religion or its followers. 7. Moreover, concerning the Christians, we before gave orders with respect to the places set apart for their worship. It is now our pleasure that all who have bought such places should restore them to the Christians, without any demand for payment. . . .

[8.9. Churches received by gift and any other places formerly belonging to Christians to be restored. Owners may apply for compensation.]

10. You are to use your utmost diligence in carrying out these orders on behalf of the Christians, that our command may be promptly obeyed, for the fulfilment of our gracious purpose in establishing public tranquillity.
11. So shall that divine favour which we have already enjoyed, in affairs of the greatest moment, continue to grant us success, and thus secure the happiness of the realm.

(H. Bettenson, ed, *Documents of the Christian Church,* pp. 22–3, Oxford University Press, 1967.)

23a ST AUGUSTINE: THE TWO CITIES

I trust we have already done justice to these great and difficult questions regarding the beginning of the world, or of the soul, or of the human race itself. This race we have distributed into two parts, the one consisting of those who live according to man, the other of those who live according to God. And these we also mystically call the two cities, or the two communities of men, of which the one is predestined to reign eternally with God, and the other to suffer eternal punishment with the devil. This, however, is their end, and of it we are to speak afterwards. At present, as we have said enough about their origin, whether among the angels, whose numbers we know not, or in the two first human beings, it seems suitable to attempt an account of their career, from the time when our two first parents began to propagate the race until all human generation shall cease. For this whole time or world-age, in which the dying give place and those who are born succeed, is the career of these two cities concerning which we treat.

Of these two first parents of the human race, then, Cain was the first-born, and he belonged to the city of men; after him was born Abel, who belonged to the city of God. For as in the individual the truth of the apostle's statement is discerned, 'that is not first which is spiritual, but that which is natural, and afterward that which is spiritual,' whence it comes to pass that each man, being derived from a condemned stock, is first of all born of Adam evil and carnal, and becomes good and spiritual only afterwards, when he is graffed into Christ by regeneration: so was it in the human race as a whole. When these two cities began to run their course by a series of deaths and births, the citizen of this world was the first-born, and after him the stranger in this world, the citizen of the city of God, predestinated by grace, elected by grace, by grace a stranger below, and by grace a citizen above. By grace,—for so far as regards himself he is sprung from the same mass, all of which is condemned in its origin; but God, like a potter (for this comparison is introduced by the apostle judiciously, and not without thought), of the same lump made one vessel to honour, another to dishonour. But first the vessel to dishonour was made, and after it another to honour. For in each individual, as I have already said, there is first of all that which is reprobate, that from which we must begin, but in which we need not necessarily remain; afterwards is that which is well-approved, to which we may by advancing.attain, and in which, when we have reached it we may abide. Not, indeed, that every wicked man shall be good, but that no one will be good who was not first of all wicked; but the sooner any one becomes a good man, the more speedily does he receive this title, and abolish the old name in the new. Accordingly, it is recorded of Cain that he built a city, but Abel, being a sojourner, built none. For the city of the saints is above, although here below it begets citizens, in whom it sojourns till the time of its reign arrives, when it shall gather together all in the day of the resurrection; and then shall the promised kingdom be given to them, in which they shall reign with their Prince, the King of the ages, time without end.

(St Augustine, *The City of God*, tr. M. Dods, Bk 15, ch. 1, pp. 49-51, T. and T. Clark, Edinburgh 1872.)

23b   ST AUGUSTINE: THE ORIGIN OF SERVITUDE

This is prescribed by the order of nature: it is thus that God has created man. For 'let them,' He says, 'have dominion over the fish of the sea, and over the fowl of the air, and over every creeping thing which creepeth on the earth.' He did not intend that His rational creature, who was made in His image, should have dominion over anything but the irrational creation,—not man over man, but man over the beasts. And hence the righteous men in primitive times were made shepherds of cattle rather than kings of men, God intending thus to teach us what the relative position of the creatures is, and what the desert of sin; for it is with justice, we believe, that the condition of slavery is the result of sin. And this is why we do not find the word 'slave' in any part of Scripture until righteous Noah branded the sin of his son with this name. It is a name, therefore, introduced by sin and not by nature. The origin of the Latin word for slave is supposed to be found in the circumstance that those who by the law of war were liable to be killed were sometimes preserved by their victors, and were hence called servants. And these circumstances could never have arisen save through sin. For even when we wage a just war, our adversaries must be sinning; and every victory, even though gained by wicked men, is a result of the first judgment of God, who humbles the vanquished either for the sake of removing or of punishing their sins. Witness that man of God, Daniel, who, when he was in captivity, confessed to God his own sins and the sins of his people, and declares with pious grief that these were the cause of the captivity. The prime cause, then, of slavery is sin, which brings man under the dominion of his fellow,—that which does not happen save by the judgment of God, with whom is no unrighteousness, and who knows how to award fit punishments to every variety of offence. But our Master in heaven says, 'Every one who doeth sin is the servant of sin.' And thus there are many wicked masters who have religious men as their slaves, and who are yet themselves in bondage; 'for of whom a man is overcome, of the same is he brought in bondage'. And beyond question it is a happier thing to be a slave of a man than of a lust; for even this very lust of ruling, to mention no others, lays waste men's hearts with the most ruthless dominion. Moreover, when men are subjected to one another in a peaceful order, the lowly position does as much good to the servant as the proud position does harm to the master. But by nature, as God first created us, no one is the slave either of man or of sin. This servitude is, however, penal, and is appointed by that law which enjoins the preservation of the natural order and forbids its disturbance; for if nothing had been done in violation of that law, there would have been nothing to restrain by penal servitude. And therefore the apostle admonishes slaves to be subject to their masters, and to serve them heartily and with good-will, so that, if they cannot be freed by their masters, they may themselves make their slavery in some sort free, by serving not in crafty fear, but in faithful love, until all unrighteousness pass away, and all principality and every human power be brought to nothing, and God be all in all.

(St Augustine, op. cit., Bk 19, ch. 15, pp. 323-5.)

23c ST AUGUSTINE: THE TWO TYPES OF PEACE

The earthly city, which does not live by faith, seeks an earthly peace, and the end it proposes, in the well ordered concord of civic obedience and rule, is the combination of men's wills to attain the things which are helpful to this life. The heavenly city, or rather the part of it which sojourns on earth and lives by faith, makes use of this peace only because it must, until this mortal condition which necessitates it shall pass away. Consequently, so long as it lives like a captive and a stranger in the earthly city, though it has already received the promise of redemption, and the gift of the Spirit as the earnest of it, it makes no scruple to obey the laws of the earthly city, whereby the things necessary for the maintenance of this mortal life are administered; and thus, as this life is common to both cities so there is a harmony between them in regard to what belongs to it. But, as the earthly city has had some philosophers whose doctrine is condemned by the divine teaching, and who, being deceived either by their own conjectures or by demons, supposed that many gods must be invited to take an interest in human affairs, and assigned to each a separate function and a separate department,—to one the body, to another the soul; and in the body itself, to one the head, to another the neck, and each of the other members to one of the gods; and in like manner, in the soul, to one god the natural capacity was assigned, to another education, to another anger, to another lust; and so the various affairs of life were assigned,— cattle to one, corn to another, wine to another, oil to another, the woods to another, money to another, navigation to another, wars and victories to another, marriages to another, births and fecundity to another, and other things to other gods: and as the celestial city, on the other hand, knew that one God only was to be worshipped, and that to Him alone was due that service which the Greeks call λατρεία, and which can be given only to a god, it has come to pass that the two cities could not have common laws of religion, and that the heavenly city has been compelled in this matter to dissent, and to become obnoxious to those who think differently, and to stand the brunt of their anger and hatred and persecutions, except in so far as the minds of their enemies have been alarmed by the multitude of the Christians and quelled by the manifest protection of God accorded to them. This heavenly city, then, while it sojourns on earth, calls citizens out of all nations, and gathers together a society of pilgrims of all languages, not scrupling about diversities in the manners, laws, and institutions whereby earthly peace is secured and maintained, but recognising that, however various these are, they all tend to one and the same end of earthly peace. It therefore is so far from rescinding and abolishing these diversities, that it even preserves and adopts them, so long only as no hindrance to the worship of the one supreme and true God is thus introduced. Even the heavenly city, therefore, while in its state of pilgrimage, avails itself of the peace of earth, and, so far as it can without injuring faith and godliness, desires and maintains a common agreement among men regarding the acquisition of the necessaries of life, and makes this earthly peace bear upon the peace of heaven; for this alone can be truly called and esteemed the peace of the reasonable creatures, consisting as it does in the perfectly ordered and harmonious enjoyment of God and of one another in God. When we shall have reached that peace, this mortal life shall give place to one that is eternal, and our body shall be no more this animal body which by its corruption weighs down the soul, but a spiritual body feeling no want, and in all its members subjected to the will. In its pilgrim state the heavenly city possesses this peace by faith; and by this faith it lives righteously when it refers to the attainment of that peace every good action towards God and man; for the life of the city is a social life. . . .

The peace of the body then consists in the duly proportioned arrangement of its parts. The peace of the irrational soul is the harmonious repose of the appetites, and that of the rational soul the harmony of knowledge and action. The peace of body and soul is the well-ordered and harmonious life and health of the living creature. Peace between man and God is the well-ordered obedience of faith to eternal law. Peace between man and man is well-ordered concord. Domestic peace is the well-ordered concord between those of the family who rule and those who obey. Civil peace is a similar concord among the citizens. The peace of the celestial city is the perfectly ordered and harmonious enjoyment of God, and of one another in God. The peace of all things is the tranquillity of order.

(St Augustine, op. cit., Bk 19, ch. 17, pp. 326-8; ch. 13, p. 319.)

23d   ST AUGUSTINE: JUSTICE AND THE STATE

This, then, is the place where I should fulfil the promise I gave in the second book of this work, and explain, as briefly and clearly as possible, that if we are to accept the definitions laid down by Scipio in Cicero's *De Republica,* there never was a Roman republic; for he briefly defines a republic as the weal of the people. And if this definition be true, there never was a Roman republic, for the people's weal was never attained among the Romans. For the people, according to his definition, is an assemblage associated by a common acknowledgment of right and by a community of interests. And what he means by a common acknowledgment of right he explains at large, showing that a republic cannot be administered without justice. Where, therefore, there is no true justice there can be no right. For that which is done by right is justly done, and what is unjustly done cannot be done by right. For the unjust inventions of men are neither to be considered nor spoken of as rights; for even they themselves say that right is that which flows from the fountain of justice, and deny the definition which is commonly given by those who misconceive the matter, that right is that which is useful to the stronger party. Thus, where there is not true justice there can be no assemblage of men associated by a common acknowledgment of right, and therefore there can be no people, as defined by Scipio or Cicero; and if no people, then no weal of the people, but only of some promiscuous multitude unworthy of the name of people. Consequently, if the republic is the weal of the people, and there is no people if it be not associated by a common acknowledgment of right, and if there is no right where there is no justice, then most certainly it follows that there is no republic where there is no justice. Further, justice is that virtue which gives every one his due. Where, then, is the justice of man, when he deserts the true God and yields himself to impure demons? Is this to give every one his due? Or is he who keeps back a piece of ground from the purchaser, and gives it to a man who has no right to it, unjust, while he who keeps back himself from the God who made him, and serves wicked spirits, is just? . . .

To confirm this reasoning, there is added an eminent example drawn from nature: for 'why,' it is asked, 'does God rule man, the soul the body, the reason the passions and other vicious parts of the soul?' This example leaves no doubt that, to some, servitude is useful; and indeed, to serve God is useful to all. And it is when the soul serves God that it exercises a right control over the body; and in the soul itself the reason must be subject to God if it is to govern as it ought the passions and other vices. Hence, when a man does not serve God, what justice can we ascribe to him, since in this case his soul cannot exercise a just control over the body, nor his reason over his vices? And if there is no justice in such an individual, certainly there can be none in a community composed of such persons. Here, therefore, there is not that common acknowledgment of right which makes an assemblage of men a people whose affairs we call a republic. And why need I speak of the advantageousness, the common participation in which, according to the definition, makes a people? For although, if you choose to regard the matter attentively, you will see that there is nothing advantageous to those who live godlessly, as everyone lives who does not serve God but demons, whose wickedness you may measure by their desire to receive the worship of men though they are most impure spirits, yet what I have said of the common acknowledgment of right is enough to demonstrate that, according to the above definition, there can be no people, and therefore no republic, where there is no justice. . . .

But if we discard this definition of a people, and, assuming another, say that a people is an assemblage of reasonable beings bound together by a common agreement as to the objects of their love, then, in order to discover the character of any people, we have only to observe what they love. Yet whatever it loves, if only it is an assemblage of reasonable beings and not of beasts, and is bound together by an agreement as to the objects of love, it is reasonably called a people; and it will be a superior people in proportion as it is bound together by higher interests, inferior in proportion as it is bound together by lower. According to this definition of ours, the Roman people is a people, and its weal is without doubt a commonwealth or republic. But what its tastes were in its early and subsequent days, and how it declined into sanguinary seditions and then to social and civil wars, and so burst asunder or rotted off the bond of concord in which the health of a people consists, history shows, and in the preceding books I have related at large. And yet I would not on this account say either that it was not a people, or that its administration was not a republic, so long as there remains an assemblage of reasonable beings bound together by a common agreement as to the objects of love. But what I say of this people and of this republic I must be understood to think and say of the Athenians or any Greek state, of the Egyptians, of the early Assyrian Babylon, and of every other nation, great or small, which had a public government. For, in general, the city of the ungodly which did not obey the command of God that it should offer no sacrifice save to Him alone, and which, therefore, could not give to the soul its proper command over the body, nor to the reason its just authority over the vices, is void of true justice.

(St Augustine, op. cit., Bk 19, ch. 21, pp. 330-3; ch. 24, pp. 339-40.)

24   IRENAEUS

As therefore the devil lied at the beginning, so did he also in the end, when he said, 'All these are delivered unto me, and to whomsoever I will I give them.' For it is not he who has appointed the kingdoms of this world, but God; for 'the heart of the king is in the hand of God.' And the Word also says by Solomon, 'By me kings do reign, and princes administer justice. By me chiefs are raised up, and by me kings rule the earth.' Paul the apostle also says upon this same subject: 'Be ye subject to all the higher powers; for there is no power but of God: now those which are have been ordained of God.' And again, in reference to them he says, 'For he beareth not the sword in vain; for he is the minister of God, the avenger for wrath to him who does evil.' Now, that he spake these words, not in regard to angelical powers, nor of invisible rulers—as some venture to expound the passage—but of those of actual human authorities, [he shows when] he says, 'For this cause pay ye tribute also: for they are God's ministers, doing service for this very thing.' This also the Lord confirmed, when He did not do what He was tempted to by the devil; but He gave directions that tribute should be paid to the tax-gatherers for Himself and Peter; because 'they are the ministers of God, serving for this very thing.'

For since man, by departing from God, reached such a pitch of fury as even to look upon his brother as his enemy, and engaged without fear in every kind of restless conduct, and murder, and avarice; God imposed upon mankind the fear of man, as they did not acknowledge the fear of God, in order that, being subjected to the authority of men, and kept under restraint by their laws, they might attain to some degree of justice, and exercise mutual forbearance through dread of the sword suspended full in their view, as the apostle says: 'For he beareth not the sword in vain; for he is the minister of God, the avenger for wrath upon him who does evil.' And for this reason too, magistrates themselves, having laws as a clothing of righteousness whenever they act in a just and legitimate manner, shall not be called in question for their conduct, nor be liable to punishment. But whatsoever they do to the subversion of justice, iniquitously, and impiously, and illegally, and tyrannically, in these things shall they also perish; for the just judgment of God comes equally upon all, and in no case is defective. Earthly rule, therefore, has been appointed by God for the benefit of nations, and not by the devil, who is never at rest at all, nay, who does not love to see even nations conducting themselves after a quiet manner, so that under the fear of human rule, men may not eat each other up like fishes; but that, by means of the establishment of laws, they may keep down an excess of wickedness among the nations. And considered from this point of view, those who exact tribute from us are 'God's ministers, serving for this very purpose.'

As, then, 'the powers that be are ordained of God,' it is clear that the devil lied when he said, 'These are delivered unto me; and to whomsoever I will, I give them.' For by the law of the same Being as calls men into existence are kings also appointed, adapted for those men who are at the time placed under their government. Some of these [rulers] are given for the correction and the benefit of their subjects, and for the preservation of justice; but others, for the purposes of fear and punishment and rebuke: others, as [the subjects] deserve it, are for deception, disgrace, and pride; while the just judgment of God, as I have observed already, passes equally upon all.

(Irenaeus, *Against Heresies,* Bk 5, ch. 24 in *The Ante-Nicene Christian Library,* vol. IX, pp. 119-20, T. and T. Clark, Edinburgh 1869.)

CHAPTER 9

The Development of the Papacy

The political thought of a large part of the Middle Ages is dominated by speculations about the sources of political and ecclesiastical authority and the problem of the exact nature of the relationship between the two authorities. We shall defer until the next chapter an examination of the various views about the origin of secular authority, and consider here the development of the theory of papal supremacy.

The early Christian communities at Rome and elsewhere held authority in common, although within each congregation some individuals would be given titles such as 'bishop' or 'presbyter'. It was not until the early third century that the office of bishop developed into a position of institutional leadership, most probably because of the need for a more highly organized structure to protect the Church against schisms and heresies. The rise of the Roman Church to pre-eminence during the course of the third century was largely due to such Christian Fathers as Irenaeus and Tertullian, who pointed to the superiority of those churches which could trace their origins to one of the apostles. As the Roman Church could claim not one, but two apostles as its founders (Peter and Paul), there was a clear case for regarding it as specially favoured.

The special authority of the Roman Church was not a legal or constitutional one, but by the time of the Constantinean Settlement of 313 it had a well-established superior moral authority compared with the other Christian churches. The position of the bishop of Rome gradually assumed a parallel expansion in prestige. Damasus, a Pope of the late fourth century, consistently refers to the Roman Church as the 'apostolic see' and the 'see of St Peter'. The special position of Peter in bearing Christ's commission as head of the Roman Church was indicated by the passage in the Matthean gospel which was quoted continually in defence of the principle of papal monarchy (Ex. 25). Siricius, the successor of Damasus and the first Roman bishop to use the title of 'Pope', referred to himself as the heir of St Peter and as such claimed responsibility for all the Christian congregations. Siricius's statement was contained in the earliest known example of a papal decretal—a form of authoritative letter which tended to strengthen the papal claim to universal spiritual authority.

The Letter of 'Clement' to James

By the late fourth century the importance of St Peter compared with the other apostles was generally recognized and the story of his martyrdom in Rome was widely believed to be true. The link between Peter and the Roman Church was therefore established. But no scriptural writing existed which referred to any successor of St Peter. A document was forged in the late second century for the purpose of supplying the necessary reference. This was the famous *Epistola Clementis,* originally written in Greek and translated into Latin at the end of the fourth century. It purported to be a letter written by Clement, an early bishop of Rome, to James, the brother of Jesus, who was the bishop of the Christian congregation in Jerusalem. The writer claims that Peter, not long before his death, appointed him (Clement) to be his successor as head of the Christian Church and passed to Clement his 'binding and loosing powers', that, is, his authority to make decisions that would automatically be ratified in heaven (Ex. 26).

Walter Ullmann has said: 'Historically and doctrinally it would be difficult to find a parallel for a product that has exercised such enduring influence as the *Epistola Clementis.*' Throughout the Middle Ages this document was quoted as the vital piece of evidence which supported the principle of papal succession to the monarchy exercised by St Peter over the whole Christian Church.

Pope Leo I (440–461)

The pre-eminence of the Roman bishop over the whole Church was firmly asserted by Leo I. He was the first pope to assume the old pagan imperial title of *Pontifex Maximus* which had been discarded by Christian emperors. In his third sermon he refers to his position as the 'unworthy heir of St Peter' (Ex. 27). The importance of this formula for the development of the papal monarchy is difficult to over-estimate. Leo used his knowledge of Roman law to provide papalists with a durable theory of Church government. Peter's binding and loosing powers (as opposed to his personal merits) were seen by Leo as independent of the man himself, and hence could be transmitted and inherited. It followed therefore that the personal qualities of a pope were unimportant; although 'unworthy' he had precisely the same powers as St Peter and his orders and decrees had precisely the same validity. It was this demarcation between the office and the character of the person exercising it that later allowed the Church to regard as legitimate the decrees of even the most morally debased popes.

The notion of inheritance of the Petrine powers had another

important theoretical consequence. It meant that each pope inherited his powers directly from Peter and hence succeeded Peter directly. Leo was the first pope to claim the 'plenitude of power' (*plenitudo potestatis*), a phrase which was to undergo an expansion of meaning in the later Middle Ages. In this period, however, it referred to the government of the Church and had nothing to do with the sacramental functions of the bishop of Rome, let alone any claim to secular authority. The consequence of Leo's claim was to allow a lay person to inherit the Petrine powers, provided he was validly elected as pope and had been baptized as a Christian. A further consequence of the Leonine thesis was the legal impossibility of depriving a pope of his administrative powers.

Pseudo-Denys (c. 480)

An interesting and influential writer of the late fifth century was the pseudonymous author of a number of mystical works, who referred to himself as Dionysius or Denys the Areopagite, the follower of St Paul mentioned in the Acts of the Apostles (ch. 17, v.33-4). Denys was responsible for introducing the idea of *hierarchy*: the Neoplatonic concept of an order based upon an interrelationship of grades and ranks, each with its own special function (Ex. 28). Such a hierarchical order exists throughout the universe, in heaven as well as upon earth. God, the perfect unity, is the source of all power and the author of hierarchical order. All power therefore flows from God and is distributed according to the ranks of the celestial hierarchy, the various categories of angels. From the lower angels power is transmitted to the ecclesiastical hierarchy which, being a copy of the hierarchy of heaven, must be organized according to the monarchic principle.

The hierarchical theory of pseudo-Denys therefore fitted very neatly into the papal system whereby the monarchic ruler delegated limited authority to subordinates. It emphasized that the Church possessed no autonomous powers; what powers it had came from the pope who had received them ultimately from God.

Pope Gelasius I (492-496)

With the various theoretical formulations of his position, the pope's supremacy in the Church had been established, at least to the satisfaction of clerics. But since the time of Constantine, the emperors also had claimed the right to rule the Church. This may be illustrated by two episodes. The first was concerned with the excommunication of the Emperor Theodosius by St Ambrose in 390. The response of Theodosius was to deny the right of any bishop to criticize his actions and to assert his right as emperor to rule the Church. The second case concerned the Emperor Zeno who, in the *Henoticon* issued in 482, sought to reconcile two opposing views about the nature of Christ; the orthodox view which had been defined at the Council of Chalcedon in 451, and the Monophysite view which had been condemned at that council. By this attempted reconciliation the emperor implied that he possessed the right to define theological doctrine, and challenged those clerics who considered that the Church should manage its own doctrinal affairs without help or hindrance from the secular authorities.

The challenge was vigorously met by the popes; first by Felix II and then most importantly by Gelasius I, whose firm line with the emperor was partly the result of the political circumstances of the time. This was the period during which the Gothic invasions had destroyed the power of the Byzantine emperor in Italy, and Gelasius considered that he could rely on the protection of the Gothic king, Theodoric. In a series of letters and tracts, Gelasius attempted to set out the principles which should govern the relationship between 'the secular and the spiritual authorities. His famous theory of the 'two swords' was to be accepted and constantly referred to for the whole period of the Middle Ages.

In his fourth *tractate* (Ex. 29a), Gelasius states that before the coming of Christ some men, such as Melchisedech, were legitimately both kings and priests. Christ, the true king and priest, being aware of human weakness, distinguished between the two offices, giving to each its own functional sphere. He ordained that until his return to earth the two offices should never again be held by a single individual.

The relationship between the two areas of authority is developed by Gelasius in a letter written to the Emperor in 494 (Ex. 29b). The world is ruled by two authorities, the sacerdotal (priestly) power and the regal power. Each has a sphere in which his authority is exercised, the spiritual and the temporal. Gelasius implied that the priestly power is superior to the royal, since the priests 'render account even for rulers of men at the divine judgement'. The emperor must submit to the judgement of the priests in matters pertaining to the sacraments and salvation, and likewise the priests must obey the laws made by the emperor in the temporal sphere. The authority in each sphere comes from God, and in the spiritual sphere God has given the supreme authority to the bishop of Rome.

The importance of the theory of Gelasius for later centuries can hardly be exaggerated. His conception of two authorities, each supreme in his own sphere but each subordinate in the other, established the theoretical position of royal and papal authority for the whole medieval period. There were two particularly important consequences for political thought. The first was the difficulty of deciding what actions were spiritual and what secular. The second was the implied superiority of the spiritual over the temporal authority. The first consequence led to the great disputes between emperors and popes, notably the investiture conflict of the eleventh century (see Ch. 10). The second was indirectly responsible for the growth of the papal claims to supreme power in both spheres which came to a climax in the thirteenth century.

Pope Gregory I (590-604)

By the late sixth century the old imperial order in the west had completely broken down. The Western Empire had disappeared and had been replaced by Germanic monarchies. The attempt by Justinian to recover Italy for the Eastern Empire had failed in the face of the Lombard invaders, and even the Roman Church was fighting for survival. It was at this time that Gregory was elected pope. During his pontificate he was largely responsible for saving Rome from the Lombards, in the course of which operation he took into his own hands the administration of Roman public and social affairs and even, for a time, the function of provisioning the imperial garrison. Such activities won an increased prestige for the papacy and laid the foundations of the pope's secular power over the city of Rome and its environs.

Although the Western Empire had fallen to the barbarians, the Eastern Empire remained and the emperor in Constantinople (Byzantium) was the heir to the unbroken imperial tradition. As such he retained in his single person the authority of both state and Church. He was at the same time both emperor and pope and could not therefore accept the claim of the bishop of Rome to govern the whole Church. Realistically, Gregory did not attempt to press the papal claim to jurisdictional primacy in the east; instead he turned to the west and sent missionaries to Gaul and Britain. In this way the most remote areas of western Europe were led to accept papal supremacy and it was largely through British missionaries that eventually the rest of western Europe was converted to Roman Christianity.

Gregory's political ideas were concerned with his theory of the origin of government and with the concept of obedience to secular rulers. His theory of government, as we might expect, is very similar to that of St Augustine and the other patristic writers. In man's primitive, natural society there was no coercive government as man was not created to lord it over his fellow men. Such government was introduced through man's sin and although against nature, is perfectly legitimate in man's corrupted state, being the divinely sanctioned remedy and punishment for sin. Only in one detail does Gregory differ from the patristic tradition and that is his suggestion that even in man's natural state there were differences of rank and degree (Ex. 30a). This is proved by the example of the angelic hierarchy; a clear reference to pseudo-Denys.

All rulers derive their authority from God. Even the most evil tyrant, whom Gregory sees as a divine punishment for the sins of the people, receives the divine authority and must be reverenced and obeyed. Not only must subjects submit to evil rulers, but they must not even criticize their evil conduct (Ex. 30b). There is little doubt that Gregory goes much further than any of his predecessors in exalting the divine authority of the ruler: his sentiments are similar to those uttered by the exponents of the theory of Divine Right of Kings in the sixteenth and seventeenth centuries. The deferential character of Gregory's own relationships with secular monarchs is nowhere better illustrated than in his letter to the Emperor Maurice (Ex. 30c). Here he points out that a law made by Maurice which prevents a public servant from becoming a monk is unjust and impious. Nevertheless, he ends the letter by agreeing to act as an agent for the promulgation of the law.

The Donation of Constantine

Until the eighth century, papal literature had confined itself to propagating the theory of the primacy of the pope over the Church alone. It had faithfully conformed to the Gelasian principle of the separation of the two authorities, spiritual and temporal. However, in the document known as the *Donation of Constantine*, forged probably about the year 750, a basis was laid for the future papal claims to secular as well as to spiritual authority. The forgery was produced in order to provide a legalistic argument for Pope Stephen II in his attempt to secure the help of the Franks against the Lombards who were once more threatening the city of Rome. As a result of Stephen's negotiations with Pippin, the Frankish king, the Lombards were defeated in battle and the territory that they had taken was handed over to the pope. The Byzantine emperor naturally objected to Pippin's action but the latter refused to restore the lands to the emperor on the grounds that they belonged to St Peter and his papal successors.

The grounds for this curious action were contained in the *Donation of Constantine*. According to the writer of the document, Constantine, on the eve of his departure for Byzantium, handed to the pope (Silvester) all the insignia of imperial authority together with his 'provinces, palaces and districts of the city of Rome and Italy and the regions of the west' (Ex. 31). The consequences of this supposed gift were two-fold. First, it provided the popes with a legal claim to temporal sovereignty over Rome and its surrounding districts such as the Exarchate of Ravenna. This claim was duly accepted by Pippin and these territories became the Papal States (or Patrimony of St Peter) which lasted until 1870. The second consequence was that Constantine and his successors in Byzantium wore the imperial crown only because they were suffered to by the pope. If he wished, the pope could withdraw the emperor's authority and assume it himself. This latter interpretation was of little importance at the time. It became significant in the twelfth century when the papal claims to complete authority in both spheres were being developed.

Tentative claims to papal secular authority were made in the ninth century. *The Pseudo-Isidorean Decretals*, forged in about the year 850 by the Frankish clergy, purported to be a collection of papal decretals from the time of the apostles down to the time of the genuine Isidore of Seville. They contained statements about the superiority of the spiritual to the secular authority which were eagerly seized upon by papal writers in the succeeding centuries. Two important popes of the ninth century, Nicholas I and Adrian II, made use of *Pseudo-Isidore* in their attempts to exert their authority over secular rulers. In the letters of these two popes can be seen similar sentiments to those which in later centuries were used by Gregory VII and Innocent III to justify the superiority of the *sacerdotium* over the *regnum*.

FURTHER READING

Texts

Pseudo-Clement: *Epistle to St James* in *The Ante-Nicene Fathers*, vol. 8 (Buffalo 1886)

Leo I: *Letters and Sermons* in *A Select Library of Nicene and Post-Nicene Fathers*, 2nd series, vol. 12 (Michigan 1956)

Dionysius the Areopagite: *Celestial Hierarchies* (Shrine of Wisdom 1965)

Gregory I: *Book of Pastoral Rule and Selected Epistles* in *A Select Library of Nicene and Post-Nicene Fathers*, 2nd series, vol. 12 (Michigan 1956)

Commentaries

G. Barraclough: *The Medieval Papacy* (Thames & Hudson 1968)

R. W. and A. J. Carlyle: *History of Mediaeval Political Theory in the West* (Blackwood 1962)

W. Ullmann: *A Short History of the Papacy in the Middle Ages* (Methuen 1972)

W. Ullmann: *History of Political Thought: The Middle Ages* (Penguin 1970)

25 JESUS OF NAZARETH

13 When Jesus came into the coasts of Caesarea Philippi, he asked his disciples, saying, Whom do men say that I the Son of man am?
14 And they said, Some say that thou art John the Baptist: some, Elias; and others, Jeremias, or one of the prophets.
15 He saith unto them, But whom say ye that I am?

16 And Simon Peter answered and said, Thou art the Christ, the Son of the living God.

17 And Jesus answered and said unto him, Blessed art thou, Simon Bar-jona: for flesh and blood hath not revealed it unto thee, but my Father which is in heaven.

18 And I say also unto thee, That thou art Peter, and upon this rock I will build my church; and the gates of hell shall not prevail against it.

19 And I will give unto thee the keys of the kingdom of heaven: and whatsoever thou shalt bind on earth shall be bound in heaven: and whatsoever thou shalt loose on earth shall be loosed in heaven.

20 Then charged he his disciples that they should tell no man that he was Jesus the Christ.

(Gospel according to Matthew, ch. 16.)

26 PSEUDO-CLEMENT

Clement to James, the lord, and the bishop of bishops, who rules Jerusalem, the holy church of the Hebrews, and the churches everywhere excellently founded by the providence of God, with the elders and deacons, and the rest of the brethren, peace be always.

Chap. I—Peter's Martyrdom

Be it known to you, my lord, that Simon, who, for the sake of the true faith, and the most sure foundation of his doctrine, was set apart to be the foundation of the Church, and for this end was by Jesus Himself, with His truthful mouth, named Peter, the first-fruits of our Lord, the first of the apostles; . . . he himself, by reason of his immense love towards men, having come as far as Rome, clearly and publicly testifying, in opposition to the wicked one who withstood him, that there is to be a good King over all the world, while saving men by his God-inspired doctrine, himself, by violence, exchanged this present existence for life.

Chap. II—Ordination of Clement

But about that time, when he was about to die, the brethren being assembled together, he suddenly seized my hand, and rose up, and said in presence of the church: 'Hear me, brethren and fellow-servants. Since, as I have been taught by the Lord and Teacher Jesus Christ, whose apostle I am, the day of my death is approaching, I lay hands upon this Clement as your bishop; and to him I entrust my chair of discourse, even to him who has journeyed with me from the beginning to the end, and thus has heard all my homilies—who, in a word, having had a share in all my trials, has been found stedfast in the faith; whom I have found, above all others, pious, philanthropic, pure, learned, chaste, good, upright, large-hearted, and striving generously to bear the ingratitude of some of the catechumens. Wherefore I communicate to him the power of binding and loosing, so that with respect to everything which he shall ordain in the earth, it shall be decreed in the heavens. For he shall bind what ought to be bound, and loose what ought to be loosed, as knowing the rule of the Church. Therefore hear him, as knowing that he who grieves the president of the truth, sins against Christ, and offends the Father of all. Wherefore he shall not live; and therefore it becomes him who presides to hold the place of a physician, and not to cherish the rage of an irrational beast.'

Chap. III—Nolo Episcopari

While he thus spoke, I knelt to him, and entreated him, declining the honour and the authority of the chair. But he answered: 'Concerning this matter do not ask me; for it has seemed to me to be good that thus it be, and all the more if you decline it. For this chair has not need of a presumptuous man, ambitious of occupying it, but of one pious in conduct and deeply skilled in the word *of God*. But show me a better *than yourself*, who has travelled more with me, and has heard more of my discourses, and has learned better the regulations of the Church, and I shall not force you to do well against your will. But it will not be in your power to show me your superior; for you are the choice first-fruits of the multitudes saved through me. . . .'

Chap. XIX—Installation of Clement

Having thus spoken, he laid his hands upon me in the presence of all, and compelled me to sit in his own chair. And when I was seated, he immediately said to me: 'I entreat you, in the presence of all the brethren here, that whensoever I depart from this life, as depart I must, you send to James the brother of the Lord a brief account of your reasonings from your boyhood, and how from the beginning until now you have journeyed with me, hearing the discourses preached by me in every city and *seeing* my deeds. And then at the end you will not fail to inform him of the manner of my death, as I said before. For that event will not grieve him very much, when he knows that I piously went through what it behoved me to suffer. And he will get the greatest comfort when he learns, that not an unlearned man, or one ignorant of life-giving words, or not knowing the rule of the Church, shall be entrusted with the chair of the teacher after me.

(*Epistle of Clement to James*, in *The Ante-Nicene Fathers*, Christian Literature Co, Buffalo 1886.)

27 POPE LEO THE GREAT

I. As often as God's mercy deigns to bring round the day of His gifts to us, there is, dearly-beloved, just and reasonable cause for rejoicing, if only our appointment to the office be referred to the praise of Him who gave it. For though this recognition of God may well be found in all His priests, yet I take it to be peculiarly binding on me, who, regarding my own utter insignificance and the greatness of the office undertaken, ought myself also to utter that exclamation of the Prophet, 'Lord, I heard Thy speech and was afraid: I considered Thy works and was dismayed.' For what is so unwonted and so dismaying as labour to the frail, exaltation to the humble, dignity to the undeserving? And yet we do not despair nor lose heart, because we put our trust not in ourselves but in Him who works in us. And hence also we have sung with harmonious voice the psalm of David, dearly beloved, not in our own praise, but to the glory of Christ the Lord. For it is He of whom it is prophetically written, 'Thou art a priest for ever after the order of Melchizedeck,' that is, not after the order of Aaron, whose priesthood descending along his own line of offspring was a temporal ministry, and ceased with the law of the Old Testament, but after the order of Melchizedeck, in whom was prefigured the eternal High Priest. And no reference is made to his parentage because in him it is understood that He was portrayed, whose generation cannot be declared. And finally, now that the mystery of this Divine priesthood has descended to human agency, it runs not by the line of birth, nor is that which flesh and blood created, chosen, but without regard to the privilege of paternity and succession by inheritance, those men are received by the Church as its rulers whom the Holy Ghost prepares: so that in the people of God's adoption, the whole body of which is priestly and royal, it is not the prerogative of earthly origin which obtains the unction, but the condescension of Divine grace which creates the bishop.

II. Although, therefore, dearly beloved, we be found both weak and slothful in fulfilling the duties of our office, because, whatever devoted and vigorous action we desire to do, we are hindered by the frailty of our very condition; yet having the unceasing propitiation of the Almighty and perpetual Priest, who being like us and yet equal with the Father, brought down His Godhead even to things human, and raised His Manhood even to things Divine, we worthily and piously rejoice over His dispensation, whereby, though He has delegated the care of His sheep to many shepherds, yet He has not Himself abandoned the guardianship of His beloved flock. And from His overruling and eternal protection we have received the support of the Apostles' aid also, which assuredly does not cease from its operation: and the strength of the foundation, on which the whole superstructure of the Church is reared, is not weakened by the weight of the temple that rests upon it. For the solidity of that faith which was praised in the chief of the Apostles is perpetual: and as that remains which Peter believed in Christ, so that remains which Christ instituted in Peter. For when, as has been read in the Gospel lesson, the Lord had asked the disciples whom they believed Him to be amid the various opinions that were held, and the blessed Peter had replied, saying, 'Thou art the Christ, the Son of the living God,' the Lord says, 'Blessed art thou, Simon Bar-Jona, because flesh and flood hath not revealed it to thee, but My Father, which is in heaven. And I say to thee, that thou art Peter, and upon this rock will I build My church, and the gates of Hades shall not prevail against it. And I will give unto thee the keys of the kingdom of heaven. And whatsoever thou shalt bind on earth, shall be bound in heaven; and whatsoever thou shalt loose on earth, shall be loosed also in heaven.'

III. The dispensation of Truth therefore abides, and the blessed Peter perservering in the strength of the Rock, which he has received has not abandoned the helm of the Church, which he undertook. For he was ordained before the rest in such a way that from his being called the Rock, from his being pronounced the Foundation, from his being constituted the Doorkeeper of the kingdom of heaven, from his being set as the Umpire to bind and to loose, whose judgments shall retain their validity in heaven, from all these mystical titles we might know the nature of his association with Christ. And still to-day he more fully and effectually performs what is entrusted to him, and carries out every part of his duty and charge in Him and with Him, through Whom he has been glorified. And so if anything is rightly done and rightly decreed by us, if anything is won from the mercy of God by our daily supplications, it is of his work and merits whose power lives and whose authority prevails in his See. For this, dearly-beloved, was gained by that confession, which, inspired in the Apostle's heart by God the Father, transcended all the uncertainty of human opinions, and was endued with the firmness of a rock, which no assaults could shake. For throughout the Church Peter daily says, 'Thou art the Christ, the Son of the living God,' and every tongue which confesses the Lord, accepts the instruction his voice conveys. . . .

IV. And so, dearly beloved, with reasonable obedience we celebrate to-day's festival by such methods, that in my humble person he may be recognized and honoured, in whom abides the care of all the shepherds, together with the charge of the sheep commended to him, and whose dignity is not abated even in so unworthy an heir. And hence the presence of my venerable brothers and fellow-priests, so much desired and valued by me, will be the more sacred and precious, if they will transfer the chief honour of this service in which they have deigned to take part to him whom they know to be not only the patron of this see, but also the primate of all bishops.

(Leo I, *Sermon 3*, in *A Select Library of Nicene and Post-Nicene Fathers*, 2nd series, vol. XII, Wm. B. Eerdmans Publishing Co, Grand Rapids, Michigan 1956.)

28   PSEUDO-DIONYSIUS

Hierarchy is, in my opinion, a holy order and knowledge and activity which, so far as is attainable, participates in the Divine Likeness, and is lifted up to the illuminations given it from God, and correspondingly towards the imitation of God.

Now the Beauty of God, being unific, good, and the Source of all perfection, is wholly free from dissimilarity, and bestows Its own Light upon each according to his merit; and in the most divine Mysteries perfects them in accordance with the unchangeable fashioning of those who are being perfected harmoniously to Itself.

The aim of Hierarchy is the greatest possible assimilation to and union with God, and by taking Him as leader in all holy wisdom, to become like Him, so far as is permitted, by contemplating intently His most Divine Beauty. Also it moulds and perfects its participants in the holy image of God like bright and spotless mirrors which receive the Ray of the Supreme Deity Which is the Source of Light; and being mystically filled with the Gift of Light, it pours it forth again abundantly, according to the Divine Law, upon those below itself.

For it is not lawful for those who impart or participate in the holy Mysteries to over-pass the bounds of its sacred laws; nor must they deviate from them if they seek to behold, as far as is allowed, that Deific Splendour, and to be transformed into the likeness of those Divine Intelligences.

Therefore he who speaks of Hierarchy implies a certain perfectly holy Order in the likeness of the First Divine Beauty, ministering the sacred mystery of its own illuminations in hierarchical order and wisdom, being in due measure conformed to its own Principle.

For each of those who is allotted a place in the Divine Order finds his perfection in being uplifted, according to his capacity, towards the Divine Likeness; and what is still more divine, he becomes, as the Scriptures say, a fellow-worker with God, and shows forth the Divine Activity revealed as far as possible in himself. For the holy constitution of the Hierarchy ordains that some are purified, others purify; some are enlightened, others enlighten; some are perfected, others make perfect; for in this way the divine imitation will fit each one.

Inasmuch as the Divine Bliss (to speak in human terms) is exempt from all dissimilarity, and is full of Eternal Light, perfect, in need of no perfection, purifying, illuminating, perfecting, being rather Himself the holy Purification, Illumination, and Perfection, above purification, above light, supremely perfect, Himself the Origin of perfection and the Cause of every Hierarchy, He transcends in excellence all holiness.

I hold, therefore, that those who are being purified ought to be wholly perfected and free from all taint of unlikeness; those who are illuminated should be filled full with Divine Light, ascending to the contemplative state and power with the most pure eyes of the mind; those who are being initiated, holding themselves apart from all imperfection, should become participators in the Divine Wisdom which they have contemplated.

Further it is meet that those who purify should bestow upon others from their abundance of purity their own holiness; those who illuminate, as possessing more luminous intelligence, duly receiving and again shedding forth the light, and joyously filled with holy brightness, should impart their own overflowing light to those worthy of it; finally, those who make perfect, being skilled in the mystical participations, should lead to that consummation those who are perfected by the most holy initiation of the knowledge of holy things which they have contemplated.

Thus each order in the hierarchical succession is guided to the Divine co-operation, and brings into manifestation, through the Grace and Power of God, that which is naturally and supernaturally in the Godhead, and which is consummated by Him superessentially, but is hierarchically manifested for man's imitation, as far as is attainable, of the God-loving Celestial Intelligences.

(Dionysius the Areopagite, *Celestial Hierarchies*, ch. 3, pp. 37-9, Shrine of Wisdom, Brook, Surrey 1965.)

29a POPE GELASIUS I: SEPARATION OF PRIESTHOOD AND KINGSHIP

But if Emperors are afraid to attempt these things, and know that they do not fall within their own scant measure of power, which is permitted to judge only human affairs and not to take the lead in things divine: how then can they presume to judge those through whom things divine are administered? Before the coming of Christ it happened that certain men, although at that time they were only appointed to carry out worldly functions, were in a sense both kings and priests, because Scripture tells us that the Holy Melchisedech was such a person. And the devil imitated this among his own people, since he always strives to claim for himself, like a usurper, things pertaining to the worship of God, with the result that heathen Emperors were also called Supreme Pontiffs [*maximi pontifices*]. But after the coming of the true King and Pontiff, the Emperor no longer assumed the title of Pontiff, nor did the Pontiff lay claim to the royal supremacy. For even though the body of the true King and Pontiff is said to have embraced both these attributes in holy nobility, according to their participation in his majestic nature, so that a nation may be at once royal and priestly, yet Christ, thinking of human frailty, by a majestic disposition took the appropriate measure for the salvation of his people, and distinguished the sphere of each power by appropriate functions and distinct titles, wishing his people to be saved by the physic of humility and not be struck down again by human arrogance. Hence at the same time Christian Emperors needed bishops for the sake of eternal life, and bishops availed themselves of imperial decrees for the good order of temporal affairs. Hence the spiritual function might be immune from worldly interference, and 'No soldier of God might involve himself in the affairs of this life', and conversely no man who was involved in the affairs of this life might take charge of things divine. Hence both orders might be restrained and neither be boosted and exalted above the other, and each calling might become specially competent in certain kinds of function.

(Gelasius I, *Tractatus IV*, in B. Pullan, *Sources for the History of Medieval Europe*, pp. 46-7, Blackwell, Oxford 1966.)

29b POPE GELASIUS I: THEORY OF THE TWO SWORDS

There are two powers, august Emperor, by which this world is ruled from the beginning: the consecrated authority of the bishops, and the royal power [*auctoritas sacrata pontificum et regalis potestas*]. In these matters the priests bear the heavier burden because they will render account, even for rulers of men, at the divine judgment. Besides, most gracious son, you are aware that, although you in your office are the ruler of the human race, nevertheless you devoutly bow your head before those who are leaders in things divine and look to them for the means of your salvation; and in the reception and proper administration of the heavenly sacraments you know that you ought to submit to Christian order rather than take the lead, and in those matters follow their judgment without wanting to subject them to your will. For if, in matters relating to public law and order, Christian priests themselves obey your laws in the knowledge that your Empire is conferred upon you by heavenly disposition, and lest they appear to be resisting your judgment, which is unchallengeable in worldly affairs, then how eagerly one ought to obey those who are assigned to the administration of the hallowed mysteries! There is no slight danger to the bishops in not having spoken up for the worship of God as they should; and, which God forbid, there is no inconsiderable peril in store for those who behave contemptuously when they ought to be obedient. And if it be right that the hearts of the faithful should submit to all bishops everywhere who rightly administer the things that are divine, how much more then must they give their support to the bishop of this see, who, even by the supreme divine will, was to be superior to all other priests, and whom the Church has obediently honoured with universal loyalty!

(Gelasius I, 'Letter to Emperor Anastasius I', in B. Pullan, op. cit., p. 46.)

30a   GREGORY THE GREAT: THE PRINCIPLE OF HIERARCHY

Gregory to all the Bishops of Gaul who are under the kingdom of Childebert.

To this end has the provision of the divine dispensation appointed that there should be diverse degrees and distinct orders, that, while the inferiors show reverence to the more powerful and the more powerful bestow love on the inferiors, one contexture of concord may ensue of diversity, and the administration of all several offices may be properly borne. Nor indeed could the whole otherwise subsist; unless, that is, a great order of differences of this kind kept it together. Further, that creation cannot be governed, or live, in a state of absolute equality we are taught by the example of the heavenly hosts, since, there being angels and also archangels, it is manifest that they are not equal; but in power and rank, as you know, one differs from another. If then among these who are without sin there is evidently this distinction, who of men can refuse to submit himself willingly to this order of things which he knows that even angels obey? For hence peace and charity embrace each other mutually, and the sincerity of concord remains firm in the reciprocal love which is well pleasing to God.

(Gregory the Great, *Epistle 54* in *A Select Library of Nicene and Post-Nicene Fathers*, 2nd series, vol. XII, p. 183, Wm. B. Eerdmans Publishing Co, Grand Rapids, Michigan 1956.)

30b   GREGORY THE GREAT: OBEDIENCE TO RULERS (i)

Subjects are to be admonished that they judge not rashly the lives of their superiors, if perchance they see them act blamably in anything, lest whence they rightly find fault with evil they thence be sunk by the impulse of elation to

lower depths. They are to be admonished that, when they consider the faults of
their superiors, they grow not too bold against them, but, if any of their deeds
are exceedingly bad, so judge of them within themselves that, constrained by
the fear of God, they still refuse not to bear the yoke of reverence under them.
Which thing we shall show the better if we bring forward what David did (1
Sam xxiv. 4 *seq.*). For when Saul the persecutor had entered into a cave to ease
himself, David, who had so long suffered under his persecution, was within it
with his men. And, when his men incited him to smite Saul, he cut them short
with the reply, that he ought not to put forth his hand against the Lord's
anointed. And yet he rose unperceived, and cut off the border of his robe. For
what is signified by Saul but bad rulers, and what by David but good subjects?
Saul's easing himself, then, means rulers extending the wickedness conceived
in their hearts to works of woful stench, and their shewing the noisome
thoughts within them by carrying them out into deeds. Yet him David was
afraid to strike, because the pious minds of subjects, witholding themselves
from the whole plague of backbiting, smite the life of their superiors with no
sword of the tongue, even when they blame them for imperfection. And when
through infirmity they can scarce refrain from speaking, however humbly, of
some extreme and obvious evils in their superiors, they cut as it were silently
the border of their robe; because, to wit, when, even though harmlessly and
secretly, they derogate from the dignity of superiors, they disfigure as it were
the garment of the king who is set over them; yet still they return to
themselves, and blame themselves most vehemently for even the slightest
defamation in speech.

(Gregory the Great, *Book of Pastoral Rule,* ch. 4, p. 27, op. cit. Vol XII.)

30c   GREGORY THE GREAT: OBEDIENCE TO RULERS (ii)

On the arrival here of the most illustrious Longinus, I received the law of my
lords, to which, being at the time worn out by bodily sickness, I was unable to
make any reply. In it the piety of my lords has ordained that it shall not be
lawful for any one who is engaged in any public administration to enter on an
ecclesiastical office. And this I greatly commended, knowing by most evident
proof that one who is in haste to desert a secular condition and enter on an
ecclesiastical office is not wishing to relinquish secular affairs, but to change
them. But, at its being said in the same law that it should not be lawful for him
to become a monk, I was altogether surprised, seeing that his accounts can be
rendered through a monastery, and it can be arranged for his debts also to be
recovered from the place into which he is received. . . .

Let my lord enquire, I beg, what former emperor ever enacted such a law,
and consider more thoroughly whether it ought to have been enacted. . . .
Let your Piety, either by interpretation or alteration, modify the force of this
law, since the army of my lords against their enemies increases the more when
the army of God has been increased for prayer.

I indeed, being subject to your command, have caused this law to be
transmitted through various parts of the world; and, inasmuch as the law itself

s by no means agreeable to Almighty God, lo, I have by this my representation declared this to my most serene lords. On both sides, then, I have discharged my duty, having both yielded obedience to the Emperor, and not kept silence as to what I feel in behalf of God.

Gregory the Great, *Epistle 65*, p. 140, op. cit., Vol. XII.)

31   THE DONATION OF CONSTANTINE

In the name of the holy and undivided Trinity, the Father, the Son and the Holy Spirit. The Emperor Caesar Flavius Constantinus . . . to the most holy and blessed father of fathers, Silvester, Bishop of the Roman city and Pope; and to all his successors, the pontiffs, who shall sit in the chair of blessed Peter to the end of time; . . . For we wish you to know . . . that we have forsaken the worship of idols . . . and have come to the pure Christian faith, the true light and everlasting life. . . .

For when a horrible and filthy leprosy invaded all the flesh of my body and I was treated by many assembled doctors but could not thereby attain to health, there came to me the priests of the Capitol, who said I ought to erect a font on the Capitol and fill it with the blood of innocent children and that by bathing in it while it was warm I could be healed. According to their advice many innocent children were assembled; but, when the sacrilegious priests of the pagans wished them to be slaughtered and the font filled with their blood, our serenity perceived the tears of their mothers and I thereupon abhorred the project; and, pitying them, we ordered their sons to be restored to them, gave them vehicles and gifts and sent them back rejoicing to their homes. And when the day had passed, and the silence of night had descended upon us and the time of sleep had come, the apostles SS. Peter and Paul appeared to me saying, 'Since thou hast put an end to thy sins and hast shrunk from shedding the blood of the innocent, we are sent by Christ, our Lord God, to impart to thee a plan for the recovery of thy health. Hear therefore our advice and do whatever we bid thee. Silvester, bishop of the city of Rome, flying from thy persecutions, is in hiding with his clergy in the caverns of the rocks on Mount Serapte. When thou hast called him to thee, he will show thee the pool of piety; and, when he has thrice immersed thee therein, all the strength of this leprosy will leave thee. When that is done, make this return to thy Saviour, that by thy command all the churches throughout the world be restored; and purify thyself in this way, by abandoning all the superstition of idols and adoring and worshipping the living and true God, who alone is true, and devote thyself to His will. . . .'

Therefore I rose from sleep and followed the advice of the holy apostle. . . . The Blessed Silvester . . . imposed on me a period of penance . . . then the font was blessed and I was purified by a triple immersion. And when I was at the bottom of the font I saw a hand from heaven touching me. And I rose from the water cleansed . . . from the filthiness of leprosy. . . .

And so the first day after my reception of the mystery of Holy Baptism and the cure of my body from the filthiness of leprosy I understood that there is no other God than the Father, the Son and the Holy Spirit, whom most blessed Silvester, the Pope, preaches, a Trinity in unity and Unity in trinity. For all the gods of the nations, whom I have hitherto worshipped, are shown to be demons, the works of men's hands. And the same venerable father told us clearly how great power in heaven and earth our Saviour gave to His Apostle, blessed Peter. . . .' And when I learned these things at the mouth of the blessed Silvester, and found that I was wholly restored to health by the beneficence of blessed Peter himself, we—together with all our satraps and the whole senate, and the magnates and all the Roman people which is subject to the glory of our rule—considered that, since he is seen to have been set up as the vicar of God's Son on earth, the pontiffs who act on behalf of that prince of the apostles should receive from us and our empire a greater power of government than the earthly clemency of our imperial serenity is seen to have conceded to them; for we choose the same prince of the apostles and his vicars to be our constant witnesses before God. And inasmuch as our imperial power is earthly, we have decreed that it shall venerate and honour his most holy Roman Church and that the sacred see of blessed Peter shall be gloriously exalted above our empire and earthly throne. We attribute to him the power and glorious dignity and strength and honour of the Empire, and we ordain and decree that he shall have rule as well over the four principal sees, Antioch, Alexandria, Constantinople, and Jerusalem, as also over all the churches of God in all the world. And the pontiff who for the time being presides over that most holy Roman Church shall be the highest and chief of all priests in the whole world, and according to his decision shall all matters be settled which shall be taken in hand for the service of God or the confirmation of the faith of Christians. For it is right that the sacred law should have the centre of its power there where the Founder of the sacred laws, our Saviour, commanded blessed Peter to have the chair of his apostolate, and where, bearing the suffering of the cross, he accepted the cup of a blessed death and showed himself an imitator of his Lord and Master; and that there the nations should bow their necks in confession of Christ's name, where their teacher, blessed Paul, the apostle, offered his neck for Christ and was crowned with martyrdom . . .

To the holy apostles, my lords the most blessed Peter and Paul, and through them also the blessed Silvester, our father, supreme pontiff and universal pope of the city of Rome, and to the pontiffs, his successors, who to the end of the world shall sit in the seat of blessed Peter, we grant and by this present we convey our imperial Lateran palace, which is superior to and excels all palaces in the whole world; and further the diadem, which is the crown of our head; and the mitre; as also the super-humeral, that is, the stole which usually surrounds our imperial neck; and the purple cloak and the scarlet tunic and all the imperial robes; also the rank of commanders of the imperial cavalry. . . .

And we decree that those most reverend men, the clergy of various orders serving the same most holy Roman Church, shall have that eminence, distinction, power and precedence, with which our illustrious senate is gloriously adorned; that is, they shall be made patricians and consuls. And we ordain that they shall also be adorned with other imperial dignities. Also we decree that the clergy of the sacred Roman Church shall be adorned as are the imperial officers. . . .

Wherefore that the pontifical crown should not be made of less repute, but rather that the dignity of a more than earthly office and the might of its glory should be yet further adorned—lo, we convey to the oft-mentioned and most blessed Silvester, universal pope, both our palace, as preferment, and likewise all provinces, palaces and districts of the city of Rome and Italy and of the regions of the West; and, bequeathing them to the power and sway of him and the pontiffs, his successors, we do (by means of fixed imperial decision through this our divine, sacred and authoritative sanction) determine and decree that the same be placed at his disposal, and do lawfully grant it as a permanent possession to the holy Roman Church.

Wherefore we have perceived that our empire and the power of our government should be transferred and removed to the regions of the East and that a city should be built in our name in the best place in the province of Byzantium and our empire there established; for it is not right that an earthly emperor should have authority there, where the rule of priests and the head of the Christian religion have been established by the Emperor of heaven. . . .

(H. Bettenson, ed, *Documents of the Christian Church,* pp. 136-40, Oxford University Press, 1967.)

CHAPTER 10

The Clash between Regnum and Sacerdotium

The Condition of the Church in the Tenth and Eleventh Centuries

During the pontificate of Nicholas I in the mid-ninth century, the papacy appeared to have become a well established independent institution with claims to be able to dictate the morality of kings and emperors. Following Nicholas, however, the papacy suffered a catastrophic decline in prestige. Popes became the creations and puppets of Roman aristocratic political factions. Many were imprisoned and murdered, in some cases on the orders of their papal successors.

The moral degradation of the papacy was paralleled by the condition of the clergy. Many priests had violated their vows of celibacy and were living openly with wives and children. The practice of 'simony' was also rife. Simony was the purchase and sale of ecclesiastical benefices without regard to the merit or spiritual inclinations of the clerical purchaser. Livings went to those wealthy enough to purchase them, and it is easy to understand, therefore, how worldly rather than spiritual interests became uppermost in the minds of many priests.

The feudal structure of western Europe also tended towards the secularization of the clergy under the system of right by land ownership. German kings (including the Holy Roman Emperor) were inclined to regard all churches within their territories as part of their estates and hence under their jurisdiction. From this feudal conception and from the need to rely for administrative assistance upon the only literate group in a predominantly illiterate society, came the practice of 'lay investiture' whereby secular lords and rulers claimed the right to 'invest' suitable persons with high clerical status. It inevitably happened with increasing frequency that the criterion for 'suitability' was not spiritual integrity or theological learning, but a concern for worldly things and a desire to co-operate with one's feudal superiors.

The Cluniac Reforms

The tenth century, which saw the decline of the western Church, also witnessed the first significant movement for clerical reform. The movement, which was a response to the appalling conditions of the Church, had its most important source in the Burgundian monastery of Cluny. From here and from other new and reformed monastic institutions the influence of the reformers spread throughout the tenth and eleventh centuries. The reign of the Holy Roman Emperor, Henry III (1039–56), was instrumental in destroying the political influence of the Roman aristocracy over the papacy. Having deposed Gregory VI for simony in 1046, Henry was directly responsible for raising four reforming bishops to the papacy in succession. Of the four 'Cluniac' popes, only Leo IX lived long enough to make a decisive mark on the papal institution. It is an interesting paradox that the emperor, by his investiture of the reforming popes, prepared the way for the election of Gregory VII, the greatest reformer of all, who effectively abolished the practice of lay investiture.

The Investiture Contest (1075–1122)

Down to the death of Henry III in 1056, there appears to have been little opposition, in the ranks of the reformers, to the intervention of the emperor in the matter of papal elections. After his death, however, the reformers allied themselves, during the pontificate of Nicholas II, with the Normans who were enemies of the imperial government. The most significant measure introduced by Nicholas was the electoral decree of 1059 which, by giving the right of papal election to the cardinal bishops, effectively deprived both the Roman aristocracy and the emperor of any substantial influence (Ex. 32). The emperor retained the right of veto but he could no longer exercise any choice in the nomination.

The most outstanding of the reforming popes was Hildebrand, elected as Pope Gregory VII in 1073, without the assent of the emperor. His inflexible will to reform the worst abuses of the Church even against opposition was apparent from the beginning of his pontificate. In 1074 all priests who had acquired their offices through simony were ordered to be deposed, and in the same year the celebrations of Mass by married priests was prohibited. Much opposition to these measures was generated, particularly among the German clergy. In the following year (1075) Gregory was responsible for a decree which forbade lay investiture under pain of excommunication.

The stage was thus set for the confrontation between Gregory VII and the German king, Henry IV. Henry was one of the worst offenders in the practice of investing clerics, and as emperor he considered that he had the right to make clerical appointments in Italy. Although ostensibly the struggle was over the right to make such appointments, in reality the two forces were contesting each other's implicit claim to supremacy in both spheres.

The act which sparked off the conflict was the investiture of the Archbishop of Milan by Henry. The decree prohibiting lay investiture being too recent for this action to be overlooked, Gregory promptly warned Henry that failure to revoke the appointment would lead to his excommunication and deposition. Henry's response was to convene a council of German bishops at Worms in January 1076 which deposed the Pope. In a letter to Gregory communicating their decision, the bishops charged him with a large number of offences, including causing strife within the Church, irregular election, and fornication (Ex. 33).

The papal counter-attack was, predictably, the excommunication and deposition of the emperor and the releasing of subjects from their allegiance to him (Ex. 34a). Excommunication was, in Gregory's view, the only appropriate penalty for Henry's actions in disobeying God, maintaining contact with excommunicated persons and attempting to divide the Church. Excommunication in a Christian society meant virtual isolation from other men and, for a king, it meant that he was deprived of the ability to communicate and hence could not govern. Deposition went rather further. It implied that the ruler was no longer a fit person to govern a Christian community since he could not carry out the moral teaching of the Church. In short, excommunication rendered a ruler incapable of governing; deposition took away his right to govern.

Henry's reply to the papal action was contained in a letter written to Gregory in March 1076 in which he attempted to justify the royal position. Kings were responsible only to God and could be deposed only for heresy. Popes, on the other hand, could be judged and deposed by the king and the bishops. This rather crude statement was amplified in a summons addressed to the bishops to attend a council at Worms. In this document Henry refers to the doctrine of the two spheres of authority—the 'sacerdotium' and the 'regnum' (the priestly and the royal spheres). He accuses Hildebrand, the 'false monk', of attempting to destroy this two-fold order by usurping authority in both spheres.

The papal argument was set out in a letter sent by Gregory to Bishop Hermann of Metz in August 1076 (Ex. 34b). He cites a number of precedents for excommunicating a king and refers to the action of Pope Zachary in allegedly deposing the last of the Merovingian kings of France. He emphasizes that the Church has authority over all men, including kings, and rhetorically asks why the papacy should not have jurisdiction over temporal as well as over spiritual matters. In explaining why the priestly power is superior to the royal, he states that whereas the origin of the papacy was in divine grace, kingship had its origin in human sin.

In the following year political expediency compelled Henry to submit to the pope and to seek absolution. Soon after the humiliating episode at Canossa where Henry was eventually absolved by Gregory, the German princes elected an 'anti-king', Rudolph. The pope, claiming the authority to decide between the rival kings, summoned a meeting for that purpose to be held in Germany. The meeting was prevented from taking place by Henry. The pope once more excommunicated the emperor and declared his allegiance to Rudolph pointing out that Henry had not been restored to the imperial throne by his absolution at Canossa. This second excommunication, it must be noted, was on the ground that Henry had not accepted the papal authority to decide who should be the secular ruler of Germany. It certainly seemed as if Gregory was attempting to put into practice what he had earlier hinted at in his reference to papal jurisdiction over temporal matters.

The struggle over lay investiture stimulated a great amount of political controversy which found its written expression in the so-called 'publicistic tracts'. These tracts were concerned with the fundamental issues underlying the superficial quarrel over the right to create bishops. Two examples of such tracts were *Ad Gebehardum* by Manegold of Lautenbach on the papal side, and the *York Tracts* by an anonymous supporter of the royal authority.

Manegold of Lautenbach

In *Ad Gebehardum* written in about 1085, the author is concerned to reply to the imperialist arguments of Wenrich of Trier, a writer of little interest or originality. Manegold's arguments are, however, highly original for their time and of great interest in the history of political thought since they represent the first expression of what later was to be called the contract theory of government (Ex. 35). Manegold accepts the royal contention that the secular ruler possesses divine authority and therefore is above all other earthly authorities. But because the office is so great, the holder of the office should be a man of superior virtue so that he may justly exercise his power. A ruler is chosen by the people in order to defend them against injustice. If the ruler acts tyrannically then he has broken the compact or agreement under which he was elected. The people are no longer his subjects and presumably may rebel against him and elect another king. In terms of the current controversy, Manegold's theory implied approval of Gregory's action in deposing Henry in the sense that Gregory had publicly stated what already existed in fact, namely Henry's invalid title to rule.

Although Manegold's argument is original in political literature, he was only expressing a basic principle of medieval society. The

Coronation ceremonies of medieval kings involved the taking of reciprocal oaths by king and people. The king swore to rule justly and the people (through their representatives) swore obedience. Hence the theory of contract, which was to be so important in the sixteenth century, was a direct descendant of the feudal compact between king and people which underlay the constitution of the medieval state.

Anonymous of York

The *York Tracts (Tractatus Eboracenses)* were written in 1100 or 1101 by an anonymous theologian in order to defend the position of Henry I of England in his dispute with the Church over yet another instance of lay investiture. His support of the royal authority led the writer to attack the primatial claims of the papacy (Ex. 36).

The argument of the tracts is that the popes had misinterpreted Christ's words to Peter in the Matthean passage. Christ's statement did not specifically apply to Peter but to all the apostles equally. Hence all the apostles were equal, and there is therefore no biblical evidence for the papal claim to exercise monarchy in the Church.

In the fourth tract the author asserts the superiority of the *regnum* over the *sacerdotium*. Having demonstrated the absence of any link between Christ and the pope, he now attempts to show a close relationship between Christ and the king. Both kings and priests are anointed by God to rule over Christians in accordance with the principle expressed by Pope Gelasius. Kings by their actions have shown how necessary secular authority is for the defence of the Church. Priest and king represent the two natures of Christ. His human nature is represented by the *sacerdotium;* his divine nature by the *regnum.* Christ was King from eternity and, in that status, equal to the Father. His priesthood represented the assumption of human nature and is thus in status inferior to the Father. Therefore the kingly power exercised by Christ was superior to the priestly power that he exercised, in the same way that his divine status was clearly superior to his human status.

A Christian king is the earthly counterpart of Christ in that he possesses both regal and sacerdotal powers. Just as Christ invoked his kingly power to make himself a priest, so a king by his royal power institutes the priesthood. The priest therefore is the inferior of the king who appoints him, although such appointment is by virtue of the king's divine authority.

The Concordat of Worms

The struggle over investiture continued for many years after the deaths of the original protagonists. In 1122 Henry V and Pope Calixtus II agreed to a compromise over the investiture in the Concordat of

Worms. Under the terms of this settlement, the election of bishops and abbots was to follow the correct ecclesiastical procedure although it was agreed that the king should have the right to decide in the case of any dispute between the parties (Ex. 37). The result of the conflict was therefore a face-saving formula which, by limiting secular interference, did have the beneficial effect of improving the calibre of the higher priesthood.

Honorius of Augsburg

The twelfth century witnessed the papacy develop its claims to the 'plenitude of power' in both spheres to the point when, in the pontificate of Innocent III at the end of the century, its primacy was well-nigh established. The two most influential writers who supported the papal hierocratic position were Honorius of Augsburg and John of Salisbury.

Summa Gloria by Honorius of Augsburg was probably written soon after the Concordat of Worms and was an attempt to show the superiority of the *sacerdotium* to the *regnum* (Ex. 38). The two sons of Adam, Abel and Cain, represent the priesthood and the kingship respectively. The superiority of Abel to Cain parallels the superiority of the priestly to the royal authority. When Moses led his people out of Egypt he appointed priests, not kings, to govern them until the time when God through Samuel anointed Saul as king. After the Babylonian exile priests once more ruled the Jews until the arrival of Christ who was both king and priest. Christ established laws for the Church and instituted the *sacerdotium* to exercise authority over the Church. He made Peter the recipient of sacerdotal authority which was inherited from him by his papal successors. Thus, from the time of Christ to the time of Pope Silvester, the Church was again ruled solely by priests.

Honorius follows this original account of Judeo-Christian history by an even more individual and extreme interpretation of the eighth-century *Donation of Constantine*. As a result of his conversion the Emperor Constantine had placed his crown upon the head of Pope Silvester decreeing that in future no person could become emperor without papal consent. By this grant, Silvester and his successors were given the sole right of disposing of the Empire.

However, realizing that priests were not appropriate persons to rule in the secular sphere, Silvester had handed back to Constantine his sword and his crown so that Constantine and his kingly successors should be responsible for the physical suppression of evil. From that time, it was the custom for the Church to have kings for secular judgements and for secular judgements only. The priesthood which is responsible for establishing the kingship is therefore superior to it.

The doctrine of Honorius is novel for its time and seems to go much further than any previous theory towards the view that all authority, both spiritual and temporal, is vested in the pope. This notion is hinted at by Gregory VII in his letter to Hermann (see above, Ex. 34b), but is made explicit by Honorius. This being so, it is curious that he does not use his theory of the source of authority to show that unjust kings should be resisted. In fact, his position on obedience to secular authority seems to be little different to that of the Christian fathers.

John of Salisbury (1115-1180)

As well as being an important member of the ecclesiastical hierarchy, John of Salisbury was one of the outstanding writers of the twelfth-century renaissance. His book, *Policraticus (The Statesman's Book)*, written between 1155 and 1159 was, without doubt, the most influential systematic work of political philosophy since the time of St Augustine. It is especially interesting and important in that it represents the final development of medieval political speculation before the revival of Aristotle in the thirteenth century.

The Organic Commonwealth

John uses the term 'commonwealth' *(res publica)* to describe civil society, although the term is hardly appropriate to the feudal structure. He defines it in organic terms, comparing it to a living body ruled by reason (Ex. 39a). The organic analogy, while not rare in medieval writings , had never been made the basis of such a detailed comparison. John compares the priesthood to the soul of the living person, and, as the soul rules the body, so therefore should the *sacerdotium* rule over the body politic. The secular ruler is seen as the head of the body and is subject only to God and his priestly agents on earth. Other parts of the body are in turn compared to the senate, judges, provincial governors, officials, etc. All have their particular functions which must be performed interdependently if the good of the commonwealth is to be achieved.

The Church and the Law

John's view of the relationship between spiritual and secular authority was similar in some respects to that of his predecessor, Honorius of Augsburg. The prince receives the secular sword from the Church which considers only the spiritual sword to be appropriate for the use of priests (Ex. 39b). The superiority of the *sacerdotium* is such that even Constantine reverenced its decrees as if they had come from God. In referring to the Emperor Theodosius, John states that Ambrose had not only excommunicated him but also suspended him from his office. He reinforces his argument that both swords are in the control of the sacerdotal power by instancing the deposition of Saul by

Samuel. The superiority of the religious sphere is nowhere better illustrated than in the passage where John considers the priesthood to be the agency by which divine law is transmitted. As such, priests must be immune from all secular interference including the courts. Clergy and the holy places are to be protected against injury by the enforcement of the death penalty for such sacrilegious acts (Ex. 39c).

The legitimate ruler is distinguished from the tyrant by the fact that he governs according to law (Ex. 39d). A true prince possesses a share of divine authority and uses it to punish evil-doers and reward the good. John has no sympathy with the view that the prince may be above the law or that he might override it. The prince must govern according to the law of God; human laws therefore must conform to the teaching of the Church which is the authoritative interpreter of the divine law (Ex 39e). Thus the ruler, when legislating, must seek the advice of priests who alone are qualified to pronounce upon justice.

Tyranny

Unlike the true prince who rules according to the divine law of God, the tyrant rules by force. The law means nothing to him and he will inevitably reduce the people to slavery. The origin of tyranny is iniquity and injustice; the tyrant resembles the Devil himself. It is therefore fitting that the tyrant should be killed (Ex. 39f). In another passage (not quoted) the slaying of a tyrant is justified in the phrase: 'He who takes the sword shall perish by the sword.'

John's advocacy of tyrannicide is the first theory of its kind to be encountered in the Middle Ages, although it is only a comparatively small step from the various theories justifying deposition which we have examined earlier. One feels, however, that the author of *Policraticus* is not entirely happy with his conclusion. He regards it as unlawful for a tyrant to be killed by one who is bound to him by an oath of fealty, or to be done to death by the administration of poison. Moreover, he seems to refer to the early Christian doctrine that an evil prince is part of God's punishment for sinful man. There is here an obvious inconsistency with the doctrine of tyrannicide of which John is perhaps uneasily aware.

Innocent III (1198-1216)

The pontificate of Innocent III is often regarded as marking the zenith of the medieval papacy. There is some doubt as to whether Innocent claimed the right to exercise power in both spheres, but no doubt whatsoever of his claim to exalted status. In an early sermon he refers to himself as above all peoples, endowed with unlimited power (*in plenitudinem potestatis*), less than God but more than man, judging all but judged only by God. As the 'vicar of Christ' the pope, in Innocent's view, is the true monarch over all Christians in exactly the same way that Christ was.

Although he may not have claimed direct secular authority, except over the Papal States, Innocent did claim a special authority in the case of the Empire. In the decretal *Venerabilem* of 1202 he asserts the right of the pope to approve the candidate for the imperial throne (Ex. 40a). Throughout his pontificate he continually claimed the right to intervene in disputes between secular rulers, such as the one between Philip of France and John of England. A further example of Innocent's claim to exercise special secular authority was the case of his quarrel with King John which led to England being taken under the special protection of the papacy. In a letter to John, he restates his position as vicar of Christ and points to John's temporal submission of the kingdom to the Pope (Ex. 40b).

Innocent IV (1243–1254)

As we have seen above, Innocent III held generally to the doctrine of the two swords, although believing in the superiority of the spiritual to the temporal sword and enlarging the area in which the papacy could exercise its authority. A later pope, Gregory IX, went rather further in claiming that Constantine had transferred the Empire to the papacy, and that the Church had then delegated the temporal sword to secular rulers to be used under its control. There is an obvious similarity here to the theory of Honorius of Augsburg.

Innocent IV went even further. He considered that even before Constantine all temporal authority belonged to the Church and that the so-called 'Donation' was simply a belated recognition of this fact. Constantine was therefore renouncing his illegitimate authority and returning it to its proper place (Ex. 41). Elsewhere Innocent claims the right of the pope to intervene in the secular courts in cases of injustice and even asserts that the pope should take the throne during an imperial vacancy. It would be true to conclude that Innocent IV considered that he possessed all temporal as well as all spiritual authority.

FURTHER READING

Texts

H. Bettenson: *Documents of the Christian Church* (Oxford University Press 1967)

E. Lewis: *Medieval Political Ideas* (Routledge & Kegan Paul 1954)

John of Salisbury: *Policraticus,* tr. J. Dickinson (Russell & Russell, NY, 1963)

Commentaries

R. W. and A. J. Carlyle: *History of Mediaeval Political Theory in the West*, vol. 4 (Blackwood 1962)

C. H. McIlwain: *The Growth of Political Thought in the West* (Macmillan, N.Y., 1932)

J. B. Morrall: *Political Thought in Medieval Times* (Hutchinson 1960)

J. M. Powell (ed): *Innocent III* (D. C. Heath & Co., Boston, 1963)

W. Ullmann: *History of Political Thought: The Middle Ages* (Penguin 1970)

W. Ullmann: *Principles of Government and Politics in the Middle Ages* (Methuen 1966)

32   POPE NICHOLAS II: DECREE ON PAPAL ELECTIONS

. . . We [Pope Nicholas II] decree and establish (3) that, on the death of the pontiff of this Roman universal church, the cardinal bishops shall first confer with most diligent consideration and then shall summon the cardinal clergy to join them; and afterwards the rest of the clergy and people shall give their assent to the new election. (4) That, lest the disease of venality creep in by any means, godly men shall take the chief part in the election of the pontiff, and the others shall follow their lead. This method of election is regular and in accordance with the rules and decrees of the Fathers . . . especially with the words of St Leo; 'No argument,' he says, 'will permit them to be considered bishops who have not been elected by the clergy, nor demanded by the people, nor consecrated by the bishops of the province with the approval of the metropolitan.' But since the Apostolic See is raised above all churches in the world and therefore can have no metropolitan over it, the cardinal bishops without doubt perform the function of a metropolitan, when they raise the elected pontiff to the apostolic eminence. (5) They shall elect someone from out of this [Roman] church, if a suitable candidate be found; if not, he shall be chosen from another church. (6) Saving the honour and reverence due to our beloved son Henry, who at present is acknowledged King and, it is hoped, will be Emperor, by God's grace; as we have granted to him and to such of his successors as obtain this right in person from the apostolic see. (7) But, if the perversity of evil and wicked men shall make it impossible to hold a pure, fair and free election in the city, the cardinal bishops with the godly clergy and catholic laymen, even though they be few, shall have the right and power to elect the pontiff of the Apostolic See in any place which they shall consider most convenient. (8) After an election has been clearly made, if the fierceness of war or the malignant endeavours of any man shall prevent him who is elected from being enthroned on the apostolic chair according to custom, the elected shall nevertheless have authority as Pope to rule the holy Roman church and to dispose of its resources, as we know that blessed Gregory did before his consecration. . . .

(H. Bettenson, ed., *Documents of the Christian Church*, pp. 140-1, Oxford University Press 1967.)

33 SYNOD OF WORMS: LETTER TO GREGORY VII

Although, when thou didst first seize the control of the church, it was clear to us how unlawful and wicked a thing thou hadst presumed to do contrary to right and justice with thy well-known arrogance; nevertheless we thought fit to draw a veil of indulgent silence over the evil beginnings of thine inauguration, hoping that these iniquitous preliminaries would be emended and cancelled by the integrity and diligence of the rest of thy reign. But now, as the lamentable condition of the whole church sadly proclaims, thou art consistently and pertinaciously faithful to thine evil beginnings, in the increasing iniquity of thine actions and decrees. . . . The flame of discord, which thou didst arouse with baneful factions in the Roman church, thou hast spread with senseless fury throughout all the churches of Italy, Germany, Gaul and Spain. For to the utmost of thy power thou hast deprived the bishops of all the power, known to have been divinely given to them by the grace of the Holy Spirit, Who operates above all in ordinations. Thou hast given all oversight over ecclesiastical matters to the passions of the mob. None is now acknowledged a bishop or a priest, unless by unworthy subservience he has obtained his office from thy magnificence. Thou hast thrown into wretched confusion all the vigour of the apostolic institution and that perfect mutuality of the members of Christ, which the teacher of the gentiles so often commends and inculcates. Thus, because of thine ambitious decrees—with tears it must be said—the name of Christ has all but perished. Who is not astounded by thine unworthy conduct in arrogating to thyself a new and unlawful power in order to destroy the due rights of the whole brotherhood? For thou dost assert that, if the mere rumour of a sin committed by a member of our flocks reaches thee, none of us has henceforth any power to bind or loose him, but thou only or he whom thou shalt specially delegate for the purpose. Who, that is learned in the sacred scriptures, does not see that this decree exceeds all madness? Wherefore . . . we have decided, by common consent, to make known to thee that on which we have hitherto kept silence, namely why thou canst not now, nor ever couldst preside over the apostolic see. Thou didst bind thyself with a corporal oath in the time of Emperor Henry of blessed memory that never in the Emperor's lifetime, nor in that of his son, our present reigning and glorious King, wouldst thou thyself accept the papacy, or, as far as in thee lay, wouldst thou suffer another to accept it, without the consent and approval of the father, while he was alive, or of the son while he lived. And there are today many bishops who witnessed that oath; who saw it with their eyes and heard it with their ears. Remember too how, when ambition to be pope moved several of the cardinals, to remove all rivalry on that occasion, thou didst bind thyself with an oath, on condition that they did the same, never to hold the papacy. See how faithfully thou hast kept these oaths!

Further, when a synod was held in the time of Pope Nicholas, whereat 125 bishops assisted, it was established and decreed under pain of anathema that none should ever be made Pope except by the election of the cardinals, the approbation of the people and the consent and authorization of the king. And of that decision and decree thou thyself wast the author, sponsor and signatory.

Also thou hast, as it were, filled the whole church with the stench of a grave scandal by living more intimately than is necessary with a woman not of thy kin. This is a matter of propriety rather than of morality; and yet this general complaint is everywhere made, that at the apostolic see all judgements and all decrees are the work of a woman, and that the whole church is governed by this new senate of a woman. . . .

Wherefore henceforth we renounce, now and for the future, all obedience unto thee—which indeed we never promised to thee. And since, as thou didst publicly proclaim, none of us has been to thee a bishop, so thou henceforth wilt be Pope to none of us.

(H. Bettenson, ed., op. cit., pp. 142-4.)

34a   POPE GREGORY VII: DEPOSITION OF HENRY IV

Especially to me, as thy representative, has been committed, and to me by thy grace has been given by God the power of binding and loosing in heaven and on earth. Relying, then, on this belief, for the honour and defence of thy church and in the name of God Almighty, the Father, the Son and the Holy Ghost, through thy power and authority, I withdraw the government of the whole kingdom of the Germans and of Italy from Henry the King, son of Henry the Emperor. For he has risen up against thy Church with unheard of arrogance. And I absolve all Christians from the bond of the oath which they have made to him or shall make. And I forbid anyone to serve him as king. For it is right that he who attempts to diminish the honour of thy church, shall himself lose the honour which he seems to have. And since he has scorned to show Christian obedience, and has not returned to the Lord whom he has deserted—holding intercourse with the excommunicate; committing many iniquities; despising my warnings, which, as thou art my witness, I have sent to him for his salvation, separating himself from thy church and trying to divide it—on thy behalf I bind him with the bond of anathema. Trusting in thee I thus bind him that the peoples may know and acknowledge that thou art Peter and that on thy rock the Son of the living God has built his church and that the gates of hell shall not prevail against it.

(H. Bettenson, ed., op. cit., pp. 144-5.)

34b   POPE GREGORY VII: LETTER TO THE BISHOP OF METZ

Now to those who say: 'A king may not be excommunicated,' although we are not bound to reply to such a fatuous notion, yet, lest we seem to pass over their foolishness impatiently we will recall them to sound doctrine by directing their attention to the words and acts of the holy fathers. Let them read what instructions St Peter gave to the Christian community in his ordination of St. Clement in regard to one who had not the approval of the pontiff. Let them learn why the Apostle said, 'Being prompt to punish every disobedience'; and of whom he said, 'Do not even take food with such people.' Let them consider why Pope Zachary deposed a king of the Franks and released all his subjects from their oaths of allegiance. Let them read in the records of St. Gregory how in his grants to certain churches he not merely excommunicated kings and dukes who opposed him but declared them deprived of their royal dignity. And let them not forget that St. Ambrose not only excommunicated the emperor Theodosius but forbade him to stand in the room of the priests within the church.

But perhaps those people would imagine that when God commended his Church to Peter three times saying, 'Feed my sheep,' he made an exception of kings! Why do they not see, or rather confess with shame that, when God gave to Peter as leader the power of binding and loosing in heaven and on earth he excepted no one, withheld no one from his power? For if a man says that he cannot be bound by the ban of the Church, it is evident that he could not be loosed by its authority, and he who shamelessly denies this cuts himself off absolutely from Christ. If the Holy Apostolic See, through the princely power divinely bestowed upon it, has jurisdiction over spiritual things, why not also over temporal things? When kings and princes of this world set their own dignity and profit higher than God's righteousness and seek their own honor, neglecting the glory of God, you know whose members they are, to whom they give their allegiance. Just as those who place God above their own wills and obey his commands rather than those of men are members of Christ, so those of whom we spoke are members of Antichrist. If then spiritual men are to be judged, as is fitting, why should not men of the world be held to account still more strictly for their evil deeds?

Perchance they imagine that royal dignity is higher than that of bishops; but how great the difference between them is, they may learn from the difference in their origins. The former came from human lust of power; the latter was instituted by divine grace. The former constantly strives after empty glory; the latter aspires ever toward the heavenly life. Let them learn what Anastasius the pope said to Anastasius the emperor regarding these two dignities, and how St. Ambrose in his pastoral letter distinguished between them. He said: 'If you compare the episcopal dignity with the splendor of kings and the crowns of princes, these are far more inferior to it than lead is to glistening gold.' And, knowing this, the emperor Constantine chose, not the highest, but the lowest seat among the bishops; for he knew that God resists the haughty, but confers his grace upon the humble.

Meantime, be it known to you, my brother, that, upon receipt of letters from certain of our clerical brethren and political leaders we have given apostolic authority to those bishops to absolve such persons excommunicated by us as have dared to cut themselves loose from the king. But as to the king himself, we have absolutely forbidden anyone to dare to absolve him until we shall have been made certain by competent witnesses of his sincere repentance and reparation; so that at the same time we may determine, if divine grace shall have visited him, in what form we may grant him absolution, to God's glory and his own salvation. For it has not escaped our knowledge that there are some of you who, pretending to be authorized by us, but really led astray by fear or the favor of men, would presume to absolve him if I [sic] did not forbid them, thus widening the wound instead of healing it. And if others, bishops in very truth, should oppose them, they would say that these were actuated, not by a sense of justice, but by personal hostility.

Moreover ordination and consecration by those bishops who dare to communicate with an excommunicated king become in the sight of God an execration, according to St. Gregory. For since they in their pride refuse to obey the Apostolic See, they incur the charge of idolatry, according to Samuel. If he is said to be of God who is stirred by divine love to punish crime, certainly he is not of God who refuses to rebuke the lives of carnal men so far as in him lies. And if he is accursed who withholds his sword from blood—that is to say, the world of preaching from destroying the life of the flesh—how much more is he accursed who through fear or favor drives his brother's soul into everlasting perdition! Furthermore you cannot find in the teaching of any of the holy fathers that men accursed and excommunicated can convey to others that blessing and that divine grace which they do not fear to deny by their actions.

(*The Correspondence of Pope Gregory VII*, tr. E. Emerton, Bk 4, pp. 103-5, Columbia University Press 1932.)

35 MANEGOLD OF LAUTENBACH

Therefore even as the royal dignity and authority excels all earthly authorities, so no infamous or shameful man is appointed to administer it, but he who no less in wisdom, justice, and piety than in place and dignity is superior to others. Therefore it is necessary that he who is to bear the charge of all and govern all should shine above others in greater grace of the virtues and should strive to administer with the utmost balance of equity the authority allotted to him. For the people do not exalt him above themselves in order to grant him a free opportunity to exercise tyranny against them, but that he may defend them from the tyranny and unrighteousness of others. Yet when he who has been chosen for the coercion of the wicked and the defence of the upright has begun to foster evil against them, to destroy the good, and himself to exercise most cruelly against his subjects the tyranny which he ought to repel, is it not clear that he deservedly falls from the dignity entrusted to him and that the people stand free of his lordship and subjection, when he has been evidently the first to break the compact for whose sake he was appointed? Nor can anyone justly and rationally accuse them of faithlessness, since it is quite evident that he first broke faith. For, to draw an example from baser things, if someone should entrust his pigs to be pastured to someone for a fitting wage, and afterwards learned that the latter was not pasturing them, but was stealing, slaughtering, and losing them, would he not remove him with reproaches from the care of the pigs, retaining also the promised wage? If, I say, this principle is maintained in regard to base things, that he is not considered indeed a swineherd who seeks not to pasture the pigs, but to scatter them, so much the more fittingly, by just and probable reason, in proportion as the condition of men is distinct from the nature of pigs, is he who attempts not to rule men, but to drive them into confusion, deprived of all the authority and dignity which he has received over men. . . . It is one thing to reign, another to exercise tyranny in the kingdom. For as faith and reverence ought to be given to emperors and kings for safeguarding the administration of a kingdom, so certainly, for good reason, if they break into the exercise of tyranny, without any breach of faith or loss of piety no fidelity or reverence ought to be paid them.

(Manegold of Lautenbach, *Ad Gebehardum*, in E. Lewis, *Medieval Political Ideas*, p. 165, Routledge and Kegan Paul, London 1954.)

36 YORK TRACTATES

Now some men divide this principate in the following way, saying that the priest has the principate of ruling souls, but the king that of ruling bodies, as if souls could be ruled without bodies and bodies without souls, which can by no means be done. For if bodies are well ruled it is necessary that souls also be well ruled, and *vice versa*, because both are ruled for the same purpose: that in the resurrection both may be saved together. However, if the king had only the principate of ruling the bodies of Christians, would he not have the principate of ruling the temple of God, which is holy? For the apostle says, 'Do you not know that your bodies are temples of the Holy Spirit?' [I Corinthians 6:19]. . . . Since these things are so, it is evident that the king has the principate of ruling those who have the sacerdotal dignity. Therefore, the king ought not to be excluded from the government of the holy church: that is, of the Christian people; because thus the kingdom of the church would be divided and made desolate. . . . And the bodies of Christians also would be badly ruled, if the regal power were separated from the church. Thus the holy fathers and the apostolic pontiffs, understanding this through divine providence, consecrated kings for the protection of the holy church and the defence of the catholic faith, because if gentiles and heretics had not been coerced by regal power, they would have brought the church and the catholic faith to confusion and nothingness. But Christian kings have repelled the gentiles from the church and have condemned heretics and eradicated their perverted doctrines deep within the bosom of the church; for they reigned together with Christ—or rather, in the kingdom of Christ they administered the Christian laws. For these things could not be done by sacerdotal power alone, and therefore the kingly power was necessary to the sacerdotal, that it might protect and defend it, and that the peace and security of the church might remain inviolate. In this, therefore, these two persons, namely the priest and the king, seem to represent Christ and bear his image.

For, as the blessed Augustine asserts in the first book of his *De Consensu Evangelistarum*, [ch. 3, sec. 5]: 'Our Lord Jesus Christ, the one true King and true Priest, has shown among our forefathers these two persons, each commended as having borne His likeness: the one for our rule, the other for our expiation.' And also we read in the Old Testament that these two persons were consecrated with the unction of holy oil and sanctified by divine blessing to this end: that they should bear the likeness and office of Christ in ruling His people and should present His image in the sacrament. Therefore, king and priest have a common unction of holy oil and spirit of sanctification and virtue of benediction, and the common name of God and Christ, and something in common to which that name deservedly applies. . . . The priest prefigured one nature of Christ: that is, Christ as Man; the king prefigured the other: that is, Christ as God. The latter, the higher nature by which He is equal to God the Father; the former, the lower nature by which He is less than the Father. . . .

Now we come to the New Testament, because in it also priests and kings are sanctified with the holy oil and consecrated with the chrism and the divine blessing. I think that what was said above of the Old Testament can be said also of the New, since they have more certainly and more truly been made sharers of the divine grace and the divine nature. For both priests and kings are one with God and His Christ; they are very Gods and Christs by the adoption of the Spirit, and in them also speaks Christ and the Holy Spirit; and in them He fulfills and performs His office; in them He hallows and reigns over and rules His people. Whence each is in the Spirit both Christ and God, and each in his office is the figure and image of Christ and God. The priest, of the Priest; the king, of the King. The priest, of His lower office and nature: that is, of His humanity; the king of the higher: that is, of His divinity. For Christ, God and Man, is the true and highest King and Priest. He is King, but from the eternity of His divinity, not made, not created, not below or diverse from the Father, but equal and one with the Father. But He is Priest from His assumption of humanity, made according to the order of Melchisedech and created, therefore, lower than the Father. . . . Hence, therefore, it appears that the royal power in Christ is greater than the sacerdotal power, and higher, in proportion as His divinity is greater and higher than His humanity. Wherefore, also, some think that likewise among men the royal power is greater and higher than the priestly, and the king greater and higher than the priest, as an imitation and emulation of the better and higher nature or power of Christ. Wherefore, they say, it is not contrary to the justice of God if the sacerdotal dignity is instituted through the regal and subjected to it, because even so it was done in Christ: He was made Priest through His own royal power and through His priesthood was subjected to the Father, to Whom through His kingship He was equal. But if anyone says that a priest is also a king—for everyone who rules can rightly be called a king—it would still seem better that the lesser king be instituted through the higher king. And those who hold this opinion can say that in the language of the holy benediction the king is called 'prince above all.'

Yet, although king and priest have certain common charismata of privileges and the same grace, they also have their own diverse offices. For though in ruling they seem to have a common grace, yet in certain respects it is applied differently to priests and kings, and each has a different grace in carrying out his ministry.

But if the priest is instituted through the king, he is not instituted through the power of man but through the power of God. Whence also the king is God and Christ, but through grace, so that, whatever he does, he does it not simply as man, but as made God and through grace. Or rather, He Who by His nature is God and Christ does this through His vicar, through whom He fulfills His office.

But now let us see what the king confers on the man who is to be created bishop by the prerogative of the pastoral staff. I think that he does not confer on him the order or right of priesthood, but what pertains to his right and reign: namely, the control of earthly things, and the guardianship of the church, and the power of ruling the people of God, which is the temple of the living God and the holy church, bride of our Lord Christ. . . .

(*York Tractates*, in E. Lewis, op. cit., pp. 563-6.)

37   THE CONCORDAT OF WORMS

1. *Agreement of Pope Calixtus II*

I, Calixtus, Bishop, servant of the servants of God, do grant to thee, beloved son, Henry—by the grace of God Emperor of the Romans, Augustus—that the elections of bishops and abbots of the German kingdom, who belong to that kingdom, shall take place in thy presence, without simony or any violence; so that if any dispute shall arise between the parties concerned, thou, with the counsel or judgement of the metropolitan and the co-provincial bishops, shalt give consent and aid to the party which has the more right. The one elected shall receive the regalia from thee by the sceptre and shall perform his lawful duties to thee on that account. . . . Concerning matters in which thou shalt make complaint to me, and ask aid—I, according to the duty of my office, will furnish aid to thee. I give unto thee true peace, and to all who are or have been of thy party in this conflict.

2. *Edict of the Emperor Henry V*

In the name of the holy and indivisible Trinity I, Henry . . . do surrender to God, and to the holy apostles of God, Peter and Paul, and to the Holy Catholic Church, all investiture through ring and staff; and do grant that in all the churches that are in my kingdom or empire there may be canonical election and free consecration. All the possessions and regalia of St Peter which, from the beginning of this discord unto this day, whether in the time of my father or in mine have been seized, and which I hold, I restore to that same Holy Roman Church. And I will faithfully aid in the restoration of those things which I do not hold. . . . And in matters where the Holy Roman Church shall ask aid I will grant it; and in matters concerning which it shall make complaint to me I will duly grant to it justice. . . .

(H. Bettenson, ed., op. cit., pp. 154-5.)

38 HONORIUS OF AUGSBURG

I. *That even as the spiritual excels the secular, so the priesthood excels the kingship*

Since the body of the faithful is divided into clergy and people, and since the clergy are assigned to the speculative life, but the people to the practical life, and since the one part is often called spiritual while the other is called secular, and since the one is governed by the sacerdotal rod, the other by the regal, many persons often inquire whether the priesthood ought rightly to be preferred in dignity to the kingship, or the kingship to the priesthood. To this question I might indeed be able to answer briefly that as the spiritual is preferred to the secular, or as the clergy excels the people in rank, so the priesthood transcends the kingship in dignity. But to the inexpert and those who are blinded by mere secular knowledge nothing seems certain unless it is confirmed by many Scriptural testimonies. Whence, that this question may be discussed more plainly, the root of the problem to be solved may be carefully examined from the beginning of the world.

II. *Adam prefigures Christ*

The first earthly Adam, created from clean earth, bore the image of the second celestial Adam, Who took flesh from a clean virgin. Adam begot two sons by his wife, because Christ was to beget clergy and people by His bride the church. For each son prefigures one order in his office.

Abel represents the priesthood. For Abel, who was a shepherd of sheep, typified the priesthood. . . . He was killed by his brother, because the priesthood is often oppressed by the kingship.

Cain represents the kingship. Moreover Cain, who cultivated the countryside and built a city in which he ruled, typified the kingship. We read that the Lord had no respect for his offerings because, as it is said, he had improperly usurped for himself the office of his brother. How much, therefore, the priesthood excels the kingship in excellence the Lord most evidently declares when He praises Abel the priest and approves his sacrifice but denounces Cain the king and rejects his offerings. . . .

VI. *Noah prefigures Christ*

Noah also, who ruled an ark full of diverse animals among the waves, typified Christ, Who rules His church crammed full of diverse kinds of people among the waves of time.

Shem represents the priesthood. His two sons, Shem and Japheth, most evidently bear the image of the priesthood and the kingship, and typify clergy and people. For Shem is said by the learned to have been Melchisedech, who is described as priest of the Most High; who also, as we read, was king of Salem, since at that time the ruler of any city was called king; who also is described as the firstborn, because in him true priesthood began.

Japheth represents the kingship. Moreover the Roman empire has been found to have proceeded from Japheth. . . .

X. *That Moses did not appoint a king, but a priest*

But now Moses, with the light of law, came to the forefront and cast out the darkness from within our minds. Leading the people of God out of Egypt, he established the Law and rights for them and appointed to govern them not a king but a priest; and the priesthood of the Law originated with his brother Aaron. Therefore, from the time of Moses to the time of Samuel, the people of God were ruled not by kings but by priests; and the judges, who seem to have been over the people in secular affairs, were controlled in all things by the decrees of the priests.

XI. *That Saul was subject to Samuel*

Moreover, when the people had refused to bear the mildness of priests and had decided to experience the greatness of kings, Samuel, prophet and priest, by divine command anointed a king for them and at the same time wrote the law of kingship. And the king obeyed Samuel in all things which befitted divine law. Likewise Samuel also obeyed the king in all things which belonged to the right of the kingship. . . .

XIV. *That priests once ruled the people alone*

Moreover, from the time of the Babylonian exile only priests ruled the people of God, because the kingship had totally ceased, until He came in the flesh . . . to Whom the sceptre of both kingship and priesthood was restored. Thus the kingship was frequently altered, but the priesthood remained always unimpaired, though sometimes disturbed. . . .

XV. *That Christ did not appoint a king but a priest*

The Lord Jesus Christ, true king and priest according to the order of Melchisedech, established laws and rights for His bride the church, and for her governance instituted not a kingship but a priesthood. And He set the Apostle Peter at the head of the priesthood. . . . This power of the priesthood Peter received from the Lord; this same power he left to his successors. Therefore, as from the time of Moses to that of Samuel only priests were over the people of God, so from the time of Christ to that of Silvester only priests ruled the church of God, and they established it with the best laws and customs and excellently taught it the way to the eternal fatherland. But kings everywhere attacked it and attempted in every way to turn it from the worship of the true God. . . .

XVI. *Whence the Christian empire*

. . . For the God of peace, the High Priest, changed the time of persecution to a time of peace, and the great King over all gods transformed the rebel empire of the pagans into a Christian kingdom.

XVII. *That Silvester crowned Constantine king*

Therefore Constantine, prince of the princes of the kingdom, was converted by Silvester, prince of the priests of the church, to the faith of Christ, and the whole world was clothed with the new rites of the Christian religion. And Constantine set the crown of the kingdom on the head of the Roman pontiff, and decreed by imperial authority that in the future no one should become

Roman emperor without apostolic consent. This privilege Silvester received from Constantine, this same privilege he left to his successors. And since the supreme charge of the priesthood and the kingship rested on Silvester's decision, this man, full of God, understanding that rebels cannot be subdued to priests by the sword of the word of God, but by the sword of the spirit, associated this same Constantine with himself as his fellow-worker in the fields of God and as defender of the church against pagans, Jews, and heretics. And he also entrusted to him the sword, that he might punish evildoers, and set on his head the crown of the kingdom, that he might reward the good.

XVIII. *That the church has constituted kings for herself*

Thus began the church's custom of having kings or judges for secular judgments, to repel with armed force pagans who infest the church or other enemies who attack it, and to subdue to the church by fear of punishment those within the church who rebel against divine laws. To kings, however, only secular judgments belong. . . . Therefore, inasmuch as the soul, which gives life to the body, is nobler than the body, and as spiritual things, which justify secular things, are of greater dignity than secular things, so the priesthood is of greater dignity than the kingship, which it establishes and ordains. . . .

XXVI. *That man is preferred not to man but to beasts*

For God did not set the first man over men but over beasts and brute animals, because judges are established over those who live irrationally and bestially only in so far as by fear they may recall them to the ways of mildness innate in human beings. Wherefore also God through Noah set Shem and Japheth over the posterity of the sinning son, because He subjected sinners to the priesthood and the kingship. Wherefore in the Gospel also, when the disciples said, 'Lord behold, here are two swords' [Luke 22:38], He confirmed these words by His authority, showing that two swords are necessary for the government of the church in the present life: the one spiritual, namely, the word of God, which the priesthood uses for the wounding of sinners; the other material, which the kingship uses for the punishment of those who are hardened in evil deeds. For it is necessary that the royal power subjugate with the material sword those rebels against the law of God who cannot be corrected by the sacerdotal stole.

(Honorius of Augsburg, *Summa Gloria*, in E. Lewis, op. cit., pp. 558–62.)

39a JOHN OF SALISBURY: THE ORGANIC COMMONWEALTH

A commonwealth, according to Plutarch, is a certain body which is endowed with life by the benefit of divine favor, which acts at the prompting of the highest equity, and is ruled by what may be called the moderating power of reason. Those things which establish and implant in us the practice of religion, and transmit to us the worship of God (here I do not follow Plutarch, who says 'of the Gods') fill the place of the soul in the body of the commonwealth. And therefore those who preside over the practice of religion should be looked up to and venerated as the soul of the body. For who doubts that the ministers of God's holiness are His representatives? Furthermore, since the soul is, as it were, the prince of the body, and has rulership over the whole thereof, so those whom our author calls the prefects of religion preside over the entire body. Augustus Caesar was to such a degree subject to the priestly power of the pontiffs that in order to set himself free from this subjection and have no one at all over him, he caused himself to be created a pontiff of Vesta, and thereafter had himself promoted to be one of the gods during his own life-time. The place of the head in the body of the commonwealth is filled by the prince, who is subject only to God and to those who exercise His office and represent Him on earth, even as in the human body the head is quickened and governed by the soul. The place of the heart is filled by the Senate, from which proceeds the initiation of good works and ill. The duties of eyes, ears, and tongue are claimed by the judges and the governors of provinces. Officials and soldiers correspond to the hands. Those who always attend upon the prince are likened to the sides. Financial officers and keepers (I speak now not of those who are in charge of the prisons, but of those who are keepers of the privy chest) may be compared with the stomach and intestines, which, if they become congested through excessive avidity, and retain too tenaciously their accumulations, generate innumerable and incurable diseases, so that through their ailment the whole body is threatened with destruction. The husbandmen correspond to the feet, which always cleave to the soil, and need the more especially the care and foresight of the head, since while they walk upon the earth doing service with their bodies, they meet the more often with stones of stumbling, and therefore deserve aid and protection all the more justly since it is they who raise, sustain, and move forward the weight of the entire body. Take away the support of the feet from the strongest body, and it cannot move forward by its own power, but must creep painfully and shamefully on its hands, or else be moved by means of brute animals.

(John of Salisbury, *Policraticus*, tr. J. Dickinson, Bk 5, ch. 2, pp. 64-5, Russell and Russell, New York 1963.)

39b   JOHN OF SALISBURY: RELATIONSHIP OF PRINCE TO THE CHURCH

This sword, then, the prince receives from the hand of the Church, although she herself has no sword of blood at all. Nevertheless she has this sword, but she uses it by the hand of the prince, upon whom she confers the power of bodily coercion, retaining to herself authority over spiritual things in the person of the pontiffs. The prince is, then, as it were, a minister of the priestly power, and one who exercises that side of the sacred offices which seems unworthy of the hands of the priesthood. For every office existing under, and concerned with the execution of, the sacred laws is really a religious office, but that is inferior which consists in punishing crimes, and which therefore seems to be typified in the person of the hangman. Wherefore Constantine, most faithful emperor of the Romans, when he had convoked the council of priests at Nicaea, neither dared to take the chief place for himself nor even to sit among the presbyters, but chose the hindmost seat. Moreover, the decrees which he heard approved by them he reverenced as if he had seen them emanate from the judgment-seat of the divine majesty. Even the rolls of petitions containing accusations against priests which they brought to him in a steady stream he took and placed in his bosom without opening them. And after recalling them to charity and harmony, he said that it was not permissible for him, as a man, and one who was subject to the judgment of priests, to examine cases touching gods, who cannot be judged save by God alone. And the petitions which he had received he put into the fire without even looking at them, fearing to give publicity to accusations and censures against the fathers, and thereby incur the curse of Cham, the undutiful son, who did not hide his father's shame. Wherefore he said, as is narrated in the writings of Nicholas the Roman pontiff, 'Verily if with mine own eyes I had seen a priest of God, or any of those who wear the monastic garb, sinning, I would spread my cloak and hide him, that he might not be seen of any.' Also Theodosius, the great emperor, for a merited fault, though not so grave a one, was suspended by the priest of Milan from the exercise of his regal powers and from the insignia of his imperial office, and patiently and solemnly he performed the penance for homicide which was laid upon him. Again, according to the testimony of the teacher of the gentiles, greater is he who blesses man than he who is blessed; and so he in whose hands is the authority to confer a dignity excels in honor and the privileges of honor him upon whom the dignity itself is conferred. Further, by the reasoning of the law it is his right to refuse who has the power to grant, and he who can lawfully bestow can lawfully take away. Did not Samuel pass sentence of deposition against Saul by reason of his disobedience, and supersede him on the pinnacle of kingly rule with the lowly son of Ysai? But if one who has been appointed prince has performed duly and faithfully the ministry which he has undertaken, as great honor and reverence are to be shown to him as the head excels in honor all the members of the body. Now he performs his ministry faithfully when he is mindful of his true status, and remembers that he bears the person of the *universitas* of those subject to him; and when he is fully conscious that he owes his life not to himself and his own private ends, but to others, and allots it to them accordingly, with duly ordered charity and affection.

(John of Salisbury, op. cit., Bk 4, ch. 3, pp. 9-11.)

39c JOHN OF SALISBURY: REVERENCE FOR THE CHURCH

In the persons of those who administer the divine laws, God is honoured or brought into contempt more than in the case of others because He regards their honour or dishonour as His own. Hence the scripture, 'I said, Ye are Gods'; and again 'The lips of the priest keep knowledge, and from his mouth they seek the law because he is the messenger of the Lord of Hosts.' Also the Gospel says, 'Who hears you, hears me; who receives you, receives me; and who rejects you, rejects Him that sent me'; and again, 'Who touches you, touches the pupil of my eye.'

The reverence which is to be shown to things is of many different kinds. For things are either corporeal, as shrines, and sacred places, and things dedicated to pious uses, and sacrifices performed visibly; or else incorporeal, as the laws which apply to sacred things, and disregard whereof is a sacrilege to be expiated by death or some other punishment of the severest kind, proportioned to the gravity of the offence. Therefore, to outrage the immunities of sacred things is to rebel against God Himself, and as it were condemn Him to slavery. And surely many arguments founded on the divine law could be brought forward in support of its provisions, but to prevent the audacity of a rival power from gainsaying it, the statutes of princes on this point are of broad and generous application, embodying reverence and approval of the Christian faith, and confirming in their entirety the privileges of churches, priests and all sacred places. For who has not heard of the ordinance of the prince whose memory is forever blessed—I speak of Archadius? 'If anyone has broken out into this species of sacrilege, namely of entering Catholic churches by force, and committing outrage against the ministers and priests, or in the sacred place itself, let notice be taken of the act by the rulers of the province, and let the governor of the province know that such injury to priests and ministers of the Catholic Church, and to the place which is theirs, and to the worship of God, must be punished by sentence of death upon those who are convicted thereof or who confess the crime. Nor let him wait until the punishment of the injury is demanded by the bishop, to whom is rather left the holy glory of pardon and forgiveness, but let it be a praiseworthy act for all or any to track down atrocities against priests or ministers as a public crime and acquire merit by taking vengeance therefor.' And likewise, 'It pleases our mercy that the clergy shall have nought to do with proceedings at law or those which pertain to our court, to the body whereof they are not attached.' And elsewhere, 'If the privileges of any holy church shall have been violated by audacity or neglected by dissimulation, let the offence be punished by a fine of five pounds of gold.' The nature of these privileges of churches and holy places and ministers is made clearly known by the law both divine and human, although it is now obvious from usage that they can only be determined before ecclesiastical judges; and if anyone lays violent hands on one of the clergy, he is to be punished by anathema . . .

(John of Salisbury, op. cit., Bk 5, ch. 5, pp. 80-1.)

39d JOHN OF SALISBURY: THE GOOD RULER

Between a tyrant and a prince there is this single or chief difference, that the latter obeys the law and rules the people by its dictates, accounting himself as but their servant. It is by virtue of the law that he makes good his claim to the foremost and chief place in the management of the affairs of the commonwealth and in the bearing of its burdens; and his elevation over others consists in this, that whereas private men are held responsible only for their private affairs, on the prince fall the burdens of the whole community. Wherefore deservedly there is conferred on him, and gathered together in his hands, the power of all his subjects, to the end that he may be sufficient unto himself in seeking and bringing about the advantage of each individually, and of all; and to the end that the state of the human commonwealth may be ordered in the best possible manner, seeing that each and all are members one of another. Wherein we indeed but follow nature, the best guide of life; for nature has gathered together all the senses of her microcosm or little world, which is man, into the head, and has subjected all the members in obedience to it in such wise that they will all function properly so long as they follow the guidance of the head, and the head remains sane. Therefore the prince stands on a pinnacle which is exalted and made splendid with all the great and high privileges which he deems necessary for himself. And rightly so, because nothing is more advantageous to the people than that the needs of the prince should be fully satisfied; since it is impossible that his will should be found opposed to justice. Therefore, according to the usual definition, the prince is the public power, and a kind of likeness on earth of the divine majesty. Beyond doubt a large share of the divine power is shown to be in princes by the fact that at their nod men bow their necks and for the most part offer up their heads to the axe to be struck off, and, as by a divine impulse, the prince is feared by each of those over whom he is set as an object of fear. And this I do not think could be, except as a result of the will of God. For all power is from the Lord God, and has been with Him always, and is from everlasting. The power which the prince has is therefore from God, for the power of God is never lost, nor severed from Him, but He merely exercises it through a subordinate hand, making all things teach His mercy or justice. 'Who, therefore, resists the ruling power, resists the ordinance of God,' in whose hand is the authority of conferring that power, and when He so desires, of withdrawing it again, or diminishing it. For it is not the ruler's own act when his will is turned to cruelty against his subjects, but it is rather the dispensation of God for His good pleasure to punish or chasten them. Thus during the Hunnish persecution, Attila, on being asked by the reverend bishop of a certain city who he was, replied, 'I am Attila, the scourge of God.' Whereupon it is written that the bishop adored him as representing the divine majesty. 'Welcome,' he said, 'is the minister of God,' and 'Blessed is he that cometh in the name of the Lord,' and with sighs and groans he unfastened the barred doors of the church, and admitted the persecutor through whom he attained straightway to the palm of martyrdom. For he dared not shut out the scourge of God, knowing that His beloved Son was scourged, and that the power of this scourge which had come upon himself was as nought except it came from God. If good men thus regard power as worthy of veneration even when it comes as a plague upon the elect, who should not venerate that power which is instituted by God for the punishment of evil-doers and for the reward of good men, and which is promptest in devotion and obedience to the laws? To quote the words of the Emperor, 'it is indeed a saying worthy of the majesty of royalty that the prince acknowledges himself bound by the Laws.' For the authority of the prince depends upon the authority of justice and law; and truly it is a greater thing than imperial power for the prince to place his government under the laws, so as to deem himself entitled to do nought which is at variance with the equity of justice.

(John of Salisbury, op. cit., Bk 4, ch. 1, pp. 3–5.)

39e JOHN OF SALISBURY: THE PROCESS OF LAW-MAKING

'And it shall be when he sitteth upon the throne of his kingdom that he shall write him a copy of this law of the Deuteronomy in a book.' Observe that the prince must not be ignorant of the law, and, though he enjoys many privileges, he is not permitted, on the pretext that his duties are military, to be ignorant of the law of God. He shall therefore write the law of the Deuteronomy, that is to say the second law, in the book of his heart; it being understood that the first law is that which is embodied in the letter; the second, that which the mystical insight learns from the first. For the first could be inscribed on tablets of stone; but the second is imprinted only on the purer intelligence of the mind. And rightly is the Deuteronomy inscribed in a book in the sense that the prince turns over in his mind the meaning of this law so that its letter never recedes from before his eyes. And thus he holds the letter firm, without permitting it in any wise to vary from the purity of the inner meaning. For the letter killeth, but the spirit giveth life, and it rests in his hands to give a mediating inter-pretation of human law and equity which must be at once necessary and general.

'Taken from the copy,' says the scripture, 'which is in the hands of the priests of the tribe of Levi.' And rightly so. Every censure imposed by law is vain if it does not bear the stamp of the divine law; and a statute or ordinance of the prince is a thing of nought if not in conformity with the teaching of the Church. This did not escape the notice of that most Christian prince, who required of his laws that they should not disdain to imitate the sacred canons. And not only are men enjoined to take priests as models for imitation, but the prince is expressly sent to the tribe of Levi to borrow of them. For lawful priests are to be hearkened to in such fashion that the just man shall close his ear utterly to reprobates and all who speak evil against them. But who are priests of the tribe of Levi? Those, namely, who without the incentive of avarice, without the motive of ambition, without affection of flesh and blood, have been introduced into the Church by the law. And not the law of the letter, which mortifieth, but the law of the spirit, which in holiness of mind. clean-ness of body, purity of faith and works of charity, giveth life. . . .

(John of Salisbury, op. cit., Bk 4, ch. 6, pp. 24-5.)

39f JOHN OF SALISBURY: THE TYRANT AND TYRANNY

Wherein the prince differs from the tyrant has already been set forth above when we were reviewing Plutarch's 'Instruction of Trajan'; and the duties of the prince and of the different members of the commonwealth were also care-fully explained at that point. Wherefore it will be easier to make known here, and in fewer words, the opposite characteristics of the tyrant. A tyrant, then, as the philosophers have described him, is one who oppresses the people by rulership based upon force, while he who rules in accordance with the laws is a prince. Law is the gift of god, the model of equity, a standard of justice, a like-ness of the divine will, the guardian of well-being, a bond of union and solidarity between peoples, a rule defining duties, a barrier against the vices and the destroyer thereof, a punishment of violence and all wrong-doing. The law is assailed by force or by fraud, and, as it were, either wrecked by the fury of the lion or undermined by the wiles of the serpent. In whatever way this comes to pass, it is plain that it is the grace of God which is being assailed, and that it is God himself who in a sense is challenged to battle. The prince fights for the laws and the liberty of the people; the tyrant thinks nothing done unless he brings the laws to nought and reduces the people to slavery. Hence the prince is a kind of likeness of divinity; and the tyrant, on the contrary, a likeness of the boldness of the Adversary, even of the wickedness of Lucifer, imitating him that sought to build his throne to the north and make himself like unto the Most High, with the exception of His goodness. For had he desired to be like unto Him in goodness, he would never have striven to tear from Him the glory of His power and wisdom. What he more likely did aspire to was to be equal with him in authority to dispense rewards. The prince, as the likeness of the Deity, is to be loved, worshipped and cherished; the tyrant, the likeness of wickedness, is generally to be even killed. The origin of tyranny is iniquity, and springing from a poisonous root, it is a tree which grows and sprouts into a baleful pestilent growth, and to which the axe must by all means be laid. For if iniquity and injustice, banishing charity, had not brought about tyranny, firm concord and perpetual peace would have possessed the peoples of the earth forever, and no one would think of enlarging his boundaries. Then kingdoms would be as friendly and peaceful, according to the authority of the great father Augustine, and would enjoy as undisturbed repose, as the separate families in a well-ordered state, or as different persons in the same family; or perhaps, which is even more credible, there would be no kingdoms at all, since it is clear from the ancient historians that in the beginning these were founded by iniquity as presumptuous encroachments against the Lord, or else were extorted from Him.

(John of Salisbury, op. cit., Bk 8, ch. 17, pp. 335-6.)

40a POPE INNOCENT III: DECRETAL: VENERABILEM

. . . We acknowledge, as we are bound, that the right and authority to elect a king (later to be elevated to the Imperial throne) belongs to those princes to whom it is known to belong by right and ancient custom; especially as this right and authority came to them from the Apostolic See, which transferred the Empire from the Greeks to the Germans in the person of Charles the Great. But the princes should recognize, and assuredly do recognize, that the right and authority to examine the person so elected king (to be elevated to the Empire) belongs to us who anoint, consecrate and crown him. For it is a generally observed rule that the examination of a person belongs to him who has the duty of the laying-on of hands. For suppose that the princes elected a sacrilegious man or an excommunicate, a tyrant or an imbecile, a heretic or a pagan; and that not just by a majority but unanimously, are we bound to anoint, consecrate and crown such a person? Of course not. . . .

And it is evident from law and custom that when in an election the votes of the princes are divided we may, after due warning and a fitting interval, favour one of the parties. . . . For if after such due notice the princes cannot or will not agree, will not the Apostolic See be without an advocate and defender, and thus be punished for their fault?

(H. Bettenson, ed., op. cit., pp. 156-7.)

40b POPE INNOCENT III: LETTER TO KING JOHN OF ENGLAND

The King of Kings and Lord of lords, Jesus Christ, a priest for ever after the order of Melchisedech, has so established in the Church His kingdom and His priesthood that the one is a kingdom of priests and the other a royal priesthood, as is testified by Moses in the Law and by Peter in his Epistle; and over all He has set one whom He has appointed as His Vicar on earth, so that, as every knee is bowed to Jesus, of things in heaven, and things in earth, and things under the earth, so all men should obey His Vicar and strive that there may be one fold and one shepherd. All secular kings for the sake of God so venerate this Vicar, that unless they seek to serve him devotedly they doubt if they are reigning properly. To this, dearly beloved son, you have paid wise attention; and by the merciful inspiration of Him in whose hand are the hearts of kings which He turns whithersoever He wills, you have decided to submit in a temporal sense yourself and your kingdom to him to whom you knew them to be spiritually subject, so that kingdom and priesthood, like body and soul, for the great good and profit of each, might be united in the single person of Christ's Vicar. He has deigned to work this wonder, who being alpha and omega has caused the end to fulfil the beginning and the beginning to anticipate the end, so that those provinces which from of old have had the Holy Roman Church as their proper teacher in spiritual matters should now in temporal things also have her as their peculiar sovereign. You, whom God has chosen as a suitable minister to effect this, by a devout and spontaneous act of will and on the general advice of your barons have offered and yielded, in the form of an annual payment of a thousand marks, yourself and your kingdoms of England and Ireland, with all their rights and appurtenances, to God and to SS Peter and Paul His apostles and to the Holy Roman Church and to us and our successors, to be our right and our property. . . .

(Innocent III, *Selected Letters*, ed. Cheney and Semple, no. 67, pp. 177-8, Nelson, London 1953.)

41 POPE INNOCENT IV

. . . It is imperceptive to suppose, not knowing how to seek out the origins of things, that the Apostolic See first obtained its rulership of the Empire from Prince Constantine, for this rulership is known to have lain with it both naturally and potentially at an earlier time. For the Lord Jesus Christ, the Son of God, as true man and true God, was true king and true priest after the order of Melchisedech, as he plainly showed by sometimes using for men's sake the honourable title of Royal Majesty and sometimes on their behalf performing the office of priest with his father. He therefore established not only a pontifical but also a royal monarchy in the Apostolic See, handing the reins at once of heavenly and of earthly Empire to St. Peter and his successors. This is sufficiently symbolized by there being more than one key, that it may be understood that the Vicar of Christ has received the power of judgment through the first key which we have received in temporal matters upon earth and through the other in spiritual matters in heaven. The same Constantine, being joined to the Catholic Church by the Christian faith, humbly resigned to the Church the unbounded despotism which he had unlawfully exercised abroad. As a monument to his resignation, a token and a sign full of mystical meaning, we, in reverend imitation of earlier fathers, retain the emblems of the princely status which he left. And Constantine received from the Vicar of Christ, the successor of Peter, the divinely regulated power of the Empire, that he might henceforth use it legitimately to punish the wicked and praise the good, and that, though he had previously abused the power allowed him, he might now be satisfied with the authority he was granted.

For the two swords of the two governments are contained within the bosom of the faithful Church, as the declaration of the apostle shows, in accordance with the authority of God; and hence no one who is not in the Church can have either sword. Peter is believed to have a right to both, since of the material sword the Lord did not say to him 'throw away your sword', but 'put it away in the sheath'—meaning, 'you are no longer to wield it personally'. He distinctly said '*your* sword' and '*your* sheath', so as to give a sign that his vicar, the head of the Church militant, although the actual use of this sword was forbidden him by divine prohibition, should have the authority by which the sword is used for the service of law, the punishment of evil and the protection of good. The power of this material sword is enfolded within the Church, but is unfolded through the Emperor, who receives it from the Church; and, being only latent and confined whilst in the bosom of the Church, it becomes real when it is transferred to the Prince. . . .

(Innocent IV, Bull, *Aeger, cui levia,* in B. Pullan, *Sources for the History of Medieval Europe,* pp. 218-19, Blackwell, Oxford 1966.)

CHAPTER 11

St Thomas Aquinas and Scholasticism

Scholasticism

The eleventh century witnessed a revival of learning in western Europe. Whereas in earlier centuries men had been content simply to transmit the culture of the pagans, they now began to examine it for its relevance to Christian theology. Logic was regarded as a particularly important study and was largely based upon those works of Aristotle translated as early as the sixth century. The new logical emphasis in learning was associated with the concurrent rise in importance of the cathedral schools such as Paris, Chartres, York and Lincoln, and the term 'scholastic' became applied to the scholar who studied philosophy in the belief that such knowledge would help him in his theological studies. Scholasticism, therefore, was that system of thought which aimed at the clarification of Christian faith with the help of reason. It dominated European culture until the end of the Middle Ages.

The era of scholasticism can be said to have begun with Gerbert of Aurillac (d. 1003), although St Anselm of Bec, 'the father of scholasticism', is certainly the most well known of the early scholastic philosophers. Anselm was an exponent of the doctrine of 'realism' in the current controversy over metaphysics. 'Realists' considered that universal qualities such as justice or whiteness were real entities. Their opponents, the 'nominalists', considered that such universals were merely names of properties which were useful in so far as they allowed discussion of concepts, but did not possess any independent reality. Roscelin of Compiègne was a prominent nominalist whose stance led him to attack the reality of the Trinity. Peter Abelard, perhaps the most notable of twelfth-century scholastics, proposed a compromise which, to some extent, reduced the acrimony of the controversy.

The Revival of Aristotle

The most important factor in the development of scholasticism in the twelfth and thirteenth centuries was the reintroduction of Aristotle's writings into western Europe. Although one or two of them existed in Latin translations in earlier centuries, it was not until the beginning of the twelfth century that the remainder began to filter into the west. They were mainly in Arabic translations from the Greek and came with the interpolated notes of Arab commentators such as Avicenna (d. 1031) and Averroes (d. 1198). By the middle of the thirteenth century, the *Nicomachean Ethics* and the *Politics* completed the number of Aristotle's works available to the Latin world.

The impact of these books on western scholarship was staggering. At first most Christian opinion was critical. Aristotle was regarded not only as pre-Christian, but also as anti-Christian. His views on 'nature' were seen as inconsistent with the orthodox Augustinian conception. His account of the immortality of the soul again could hardly be fitted into orthodox doctrine. A number of schoolmen, who became known as the Latin Averroists, managed to evade these obvious difficulties by their theory of 'double truth'; that is, that what might be true for philosophy could be untrue for theology because God had so willed it against reason. However, most orthodox theologians and philosophers remained suspicious of the newly introduced pagan learning and, during the pontificate of Gregory IX, the study of Aristotle was prohibited until his works had been properly 'examined and purified'.

Thomas Aquinas (1225-1274)

The necessary examination of Aristotle was done in the main by three Dominican friars: William of Moerbeke, Albertus Magnus and Thomas Aquinas. William of Moerbeke was responsible for the Latin translation, Albert for the work of bringing the understanding of Aristotle's philosophy to his contemporaries, and Thomas Aquinas for the supreme task of converting Aristotle into a pillar of Christian orthodoxy. Thomas's great work of reconciling the two realms of reason and faith, Aristotle and Augustine, took him the rest of his life, and his 'great synthesis' remains to this day the basis of Catholic philosophy.

Thomas's aim was the construction of a philosophical system which would embrace metaphysics, ethics and politics, and which could be integrated into orthodox Christian theology, largely based upon the teachings of Augustine and the Fathers. To do this he had to demonstrate that Aristotelean reason did not contradict faith but supported it. There were, however, great difficulties in the reconciliation of the two systems of thought. For instance, the Fathers had taught that the institutions of private property, slavery and government were not natural and originated in human sin which they were designed to punish and to correct. But Aristotle's *Politics* dogmatically asserted that all these institutions were natural.

Property and Slavery

In the matter of private property, Thomas manages to agree with both authorities (Ex. 42a). He agrees with Augustine that common ownership of goods exists naturally, but argues that it does not follow that natural law prohibits private ownership. Private ownership occurs because of agreement between men and hence is an addition to natural law, stemming from human reason. Thomas is, however, careful to point out that in cases of necessity, as where a man is starving, it is no sin to take the goods of another. Although a number of his statements on the matter seem to be contradictory, Aquinas arrives at a similar conclusion regarding the institution of slavery. Slavery did not exist in man's natural condition but arose through human reason as a result of sin.

The State and Government

Nowhere is Thomas closer to Aristotle's *Politics* than at the beginning of *De Regimine Principum* (*On Princely Rule*), where he adopts Aristotle's view that the state is a product of nature (Ex. 42b). He terms man 'naturally a social and political animal' destined by virtue of his natural gifts of reason and speech to live in society. If the state is natural to man then the Augustinian view that government was made necessary by the sin of Adam must obviously be incorrect. According to Thomas in the *Summa Theologica*, even before the fall there were natural inequalities between men which meant that some were better qualified than others to lead the community towards justice (Ex. 42c).

Augustine had argued that Adam's sin had doomed the human race to misery and depravity. The role of government was to act in a repressive manner so that the opportunities for sin would be lessened. It would not make men good—only God could do that through the gift of Grace—but it could make them less evil. Against this view, Aquinas held that man was a member of two orders: the natural and the supernatural. As part of the natural order man has a natural end in the good life. And as Aristotle had stated, the good life was achievable only in the state. Hence, in contradiction of the patristic conception, Thomas held that the state could make men good. But whereas Aristotle had seen man's natural end as his only one, Thomas was obliged to emphasize that man's supernatural end, the salvation of his soul, was of greater value.

The ruler of the community has therefore a duty to promote the common good by providing what is necessary for its welfare. He must provide peace and unity, moral direction and material well-being (Ex. 42d). For man to be truly good he must be spiritually directed by the priesthood, for the protection of which the state is also responsible. Both Church and civil society are therefore necessary in a Christian community, the former to cater for the welfare of the soul and the latter for the body. As the supernatural end of man is more important than his natural end, so the state must accept a place of subordination to the Church.

Law

The notion that the state is necessary for the good life led Aquinas to his theory of law, especially to his view that human laws must conform to the laws of nature and of God. He defines law as 'a rational ordering of things which concern the common good; promulgated by him who has charge of the community.' He distinguishes between four categories of Law:

1 *The Eternal Law*

This is the law which pervades the whole universe and is equated with the mind of God himself. All types of law are ultimately derived from God's eternal law, 'the ideal of divine wisdom considered as directing all actions and movements'. It bears a strong resemblance to the Stoic conception of the 'natural law'

2 *The Natural Law*

All creatures below man in the natural hierarchy participate in God's eternal law since they do not possess free will. All their actions are irrational impulses. Man, however, possessing rationality and free will, has the ability to choose between actions and may act in a way which is incompatible with the eternal law. He must therefore have a means of knowing what the eternal law requires of him. Such knowledge comes to him, as a result of rational reflection, in the form of guides to conduct based upon the needs of his nature. 'This participation in the eternal law by rational creatures is called the natural law' (Ex. 42e).

The precepts of the natural law can be derived from the natural inclinations of man. All creatures have a natural inclination to good, and in conformity with this fundamental principle, the major precepts of the natural law include the preservation of human life, the propagation of the species, and the inclinations to know the truth about God and to live in society. From these primary precepts reason may deduce secondary precepts concerned with more detailed matters. Unlike the major precepts which are always true and universally known, and the particular conclusions of speculative reason, such as geometrical truths, which are always true but not universally known, the conclusions of practical reason can be regarded as norms applicable only in the majority of cases.

3 *The Divine Law*

Throughout the Middle Ages there had been a tendency to confuse the concepts of natural law and divine law, or to identify one with the other. Thomas clearly differentiates the two, putting the law of nature into the category of human reason, and divine law into the category of revelation. Divine revelation, whether in the form of biblical writings or any other form, is a necessary supplement to natural law, pertaining to the supernatural, rather than to the natural, end of man. In the passage quoted (Ex. 42f), Aquinas provides four reasons why divine law is a necessity for man.

4 The Human Law
It is axiomatic for Thomas that human laws must be derived from natural law. If they do not conform to the common good as expressed by the law of nature, then the laws of the state are not true laws but mere unjust commands (Ex. 42g). The idea that men could and should be ruled by the law of nature was, of course, in conformity with Thomas's view of man as part of the natural order, and contradicted the patristic assumption that human laws originated in sin, and could not be the expression of man's original nature.

Aquinas shows in some detail the relationship of the human to the natural law. Some enacted laws are clearly rational deductions from general precepts of the law of nature, such as the law prohibiting murder. Others, which are concerned with particular applications of general principles, may differ from place to place, such as the sentence to be given for the crime of murder. In the latter case natural law does not prescribe a penalty and therefore the human law, while still conforming to natural law, is not a necessary conclusion from it.

Resistance to the Ruler
In an early work, the *Commentary on the Sentences of Peter Lombard*, Aquinas sets out with great clarity his views on the nature of the ruler's authority and on the obligation of the subject to obey the ruler (Ex. 42h). Obedience to authority is commanded in the scriptures (Romans XIII) because rightful authority is ordained by God. But there are a number of ways in which the authority of the ruler may fail to derive from God. In such cases, the prince becomes a tyrant and the subject need not (or, in some cases, must not) obey him.

Nothing is said in this passage about the right of rebellion against an unjust ruler, although there is a reference to Cicero's justification of the killing of Julius Caesar. In a later work, *De Regimine Principum (On Princely Government)*, Thomas, in discussing the relationship of the community to the ruler, considers that the best type of government is one where the monarch is chosen and restrained by the community. Such a monarchy would be the least likely to become tyrannical. If, however, a tyranny were to emerge, it would be better for the people to endure it for a time because even tyranny is preferable to anarchy. But if the tyranny becomes insupportable, then the tyrant may be legitimately removed by the agency of those who appointed him. In the last resort, God may be appealed to for aid (Ex. 42i).

Finally, in a passage in the *Summa Theologica*, Thomas seems to express his approval of rebellion against tyranny (Ex. 42j). A tyrant is one who rules for his own good rather than for the common good. Resistance to him is therefore not sedition provided that the harm caused by the rebellion is less than the harm resulting from a continuance of the tyrant's rule.

FURTHER READING

Text

St Thomas Aquinas: *Selected Political Writings*, ed. A. P. d'Entreves, tr. J. G. Dawson (Blackwell 1959)

Commentaries

A. P. d'Entreves: *Medieval Contributions to Political Thought* (Oxford University Press 1939)

T. Gilby: *Principality and Polity* (Longmans 1958)

E. Gilson: *The Philosophy of St Thomas Aquinas* (W. Heffer, Cambridge 1929)

W. Ullmann: *Principles of Government and Politics in the Middle Ages* (Methuen 1966)

42a ST THOMAS AQUINAS: PRIVATE PROPERTY

The common possession of things is to be attributed to natural law, not in the sense that natural law decrees that all things are to be held in common and that there is to be no private possession: but in the sense that there is no distinction of property on grounds of natural law, but only by human agreement; and this pertains to positive law, as we have already shown. Thus private property is not opposed to natural law, but is an addition to it, devised by the human reason.

What pertains to human law can in no way detract from what pertains to natural law or to divine law. Now according to the natural order, instituted by divine providence, material goods are provided for the satisfaction of human needs. Therefore the division and appropriation of property, which proceeds from human law, must not hinder the satisfaction of man's necessity from such goods. Equally, whatever a man has in superabundance is owed, of natural right, to the poor for their sustenance. So Ambrosius says, and it is also to be found in the *Decretum Gratiani* (Dist. XLVII): 'The bread which you withhold belongs to the hungry; the clothing you shut away, to the naked; and the money you bury in the earth is the redemption and freedom of the penniless.' But because there are many in necessity, and they cannot all be helped from the same source, it is left to the initiative of individuals to make provision from their own wealth, for the assistance of those who are in need. If, however, there is such urgent and evident necessity that there is clearly an immediate need of necessary sustenance,—if, for example, a person is in immediate danger of physical privation, and there is no other way of satisfying his need,—then he may take what is necessary from another person's goods, either openly or by stealth. Nor is this, strictly speaking, fraud or robbery.

(St Thomas Aquinas, *Selected Political Writings*, ed. A. P. d'Entreves, tr. J. G. Dawson, pp. 169-71, Blackwell, Oxford 1959.)

42b   ST THOMAS AQUINAS: MAN NATURALLY SOCIAL AND POLITICAL

When we consider all that is necessary to human life, however, it becomes clear that man is naturally a social and political animal, destined more than all other animals to live in community. Other animals have their food provided for them by nature, and a natural coat of hair. They are also given the means of defence, be it teeth, horns, claws, or at least speed in flight. Man, on the other hand, is not so provided, but having instead the power to reason must fashion such things for himself. Even so, one man alone would not be able to furnish himself with all that is necessary, for no one man's resources are adequate to the fullness of human life. For this reason the companionship of his fellows is naturally necessary to man.

Furthermore: other animals have a natural instinct for what is useful or hurtful to them; the sheep, for instance, instinctively senses an enemy in the wolf. . . . Man, on the other hand has a natural knowledge of life's necessities only in a general way. Being gifted with reason, he must use it to pass from such universal principles to the knowledge of what in particular concerns his well-being. Reasoning thus, however, no one man could attain all necessary knowledge. Instead, nature has destined him to live in society, so that dividing the labour with his fellows each may devote himself to some branch of the sciences, one following medicine, another some other science, and so forth. This is further evident from the fact that men alone have the power of speech which enables them to convey the full content of their thoughts to one another. Other animals show their feelings it is true, but only in a general way, as when a dog betrays its anger by barking and other animals in different ways. Man, then, is more able to communicate with his kind than any other animal, even those which appear to be the most gregarious, such as cranes, ants or bees. Solomon had this in mind when he said (*Ecclesiastes*, IV, 9): 'It is better for two to live together than solitary, for they gain by mutual companionship.' The fellowship of society being thus natural and necessary to man, it follows with equal necessity that there must be some principle of government within the society. For if a great number of people were to live, each intent only upon his own interests, such a community would surely disintegrate unless there were one of its number to have a care for the common good: just as the body of a man or of any other animal would disintegrate were there not in the body itself a single controlling force, sustaining the general vitality in all the members. As Solomon tells us (*Prov.* XI, 14): 'Where there is no ruler the people shall be scattered.' This conclusion is quite reasonable; for the particular interest and the common good are not identical.

(St Thomas Aquinas, op. cit., pp. 3-5.)

42c ST THOMAS AQUINAS: DOMINION AND SERVITUDE

Dominion is to be understood in two senses. In the first it is contrasted with servitude. So a master is one to whom another is subject as a slave. In the second sense it is to be understood in opposition to any form of subjection. In this sense one whose office it is to govern and control free men may also be called a lord. The first sort of dominion which is servitude did not exist between man and man in the state of innocence. Understood in the second way, however, even in the state of innocence, some men would have exercised control over others. The reason for this is that a slave differs from a free man in that the latter is 'a free agent of his own actions' as is said in the *Metaphysics*. A slave, however, is completely under the control of another. Thus a person rules another as a slave when the latter is ordered about solely for the benefit of the ruler. But since it is natural for every one to find pleasure in their own satisfaction, such satisfaction cannot be surrendered to another without suffering loss. Such dominion, then, cannot occur without the accompanying penalties of subjection; and for this reason could not have existed between man and man in the state of innocence.

The control of one over another who remains free, can take place when the former directs the latter to his own good or to the common good. And such dominion would have been found between man and man in the state of innocence for two reasons. First, because man is naturally a social animal; and in consequence men would have lived in society, even in the state of innocence. Now there could be no social life for many persons living together unless one of their number were set in authority to care for the common good. Many individuals are, as individuals, interested in a variety of ends. One person is interested in one end. So the Philosopher says (in the beginning of the *Politics*): 'Whenever a plurality is directed to one object there is always to be found one in authority, giving direction.' Secondly, if there were one man more wise and righteous than the rest, it would have been wrong if such gifts were not exercised on behalf of the rest; as is said in I *Peter*, 4: 'Every one using the grace he has received for the benefit of his fellows.'

(St Thomas Aquinas, op. cit., p. 105.)

42d ST THOMAS AQUINAS: THE COMMON GOOD

Because the aim of a good life on this earth is blessedness in heaven, it is the king's duty to promote the welfare of the community in such a way that it leads fittingly to the happiness of heaven; insisting upon the performance of all that leads thereto, and forbidding, as far as is possible, whatever is inconsistent with this end. . . . A king then, being instructed in the divine law, must occupy himself particularly with directing the community subject to him to the good life. In this connection he has three tasks. He must first establish the welfare of the community he rules; secondly, he must ensure that nothing undermines the well-being thus established; and thirdly he must be at pains continually to extend this welfare.

For the well-being of the individual two things are necessary: the first and most essential is to act virtuously (it is through virtue, in fact, that we live a good life); the other, and secondary requirement, is rather a means, and lies in a sufficiency of material goods, such as are necessary to virtuous action. Now man is a natural unit, but the unity of a community, which is peace, must be brought into being by the skill of the ruler. To ensure the well-being of a community, therefore, three things are necessary. In the first place the community must be united in peaceful unity. In the second place the community, thus united, must be directed towards well-doing. For just as a man could do no good if he were not an integral whole, so also a community of men which is disunited and at strife within itself, is hampered in well-doing. Thirdly and finally, it is necessary that there be, through the ruler's sagacity, a sufficiency of those material goods which are indispensable to well-being. Once the welfare of the community is thus ensured, it remains for the king to consider its preservation.

(St Thomas Aquinas, op. cit., pp. 79–81.)

42e ST THOMAS AQUINAS: THE NATURAL LAW

Since all things which are subject to divine providence are measured and regulated by the eternal law—as we have already shown—it is clear that all things participate to some degree in the eternal law; in so far as they derive from it certain inclinations to those actions and aims which are proper to them. But, of all others, rational creatures are subject to divine providence in a very special way; being themselves made participators in providence itself, in that they control their own actions and the actions of others. So they have a certain share in the divine reason itself, deriving therefrom a natural inclination to such actions and ends as are fitting. This participation in the eternal law by rational creatures is called the natural law. . . .

The order of the precepts of the natural law corresponds to the order of our natural inclinations. For there is in man a natural and initial inclination to good which he has in common with all substances; in so far as every substance seeks its own preservation according to its own nature. Corresponding to this inclination, the natural law contains all that makes for the preservation of human life, and all that is opposed to its dissolution. Secondly, there is to be found in man a further inclination to certain more specific ends, according to the nature which man shares with other animals. In virtue of this inclination there pertains to the natural law all those instincts 'which nature has taught all animals,' such as sexual relationship, the rearing of offspring, and the like. Thirdly, there is in man a certain inclination to good, corresponding to his rational nature: and this inclination is proper to man alone. So man has a natural inclination to know the truth about God and to live in society. In this respect there come under the natural law, all actions connected with such inclinations: namely, that a man should avoid ignorance, that he must not give offence to others with whom he must associate and all actions of like nature.

As we have just said, all those actions pertain to the natural law to which man has a natural inclination: and among such it is proper to man to seek to act according to reason. Reason, however, proceeds from general principles to matters of detail, as is proved in the *Physics* (Book I, 1). The practical and the speculative reason, however, go about this process in different ways. For the speculative reason is principally employed about necessary truths, which cannot be otherwise than they are; so that truth is to be found as surely in its particular conclusions as in general principles themselves. But practical reason is employed about contingent matters, into which human actions enter: thus, though there is a certain necessity in its general principles, the further one departs from generality the more is the conclusion open to exception.

So it is clear that as far as the general principles of reason are concerned, whether speculative or practical, there is one standard of truth or rightness for everybody, and that this is equally known by every one. With regard to the particular conclusions of speculative reason, again there is one standard of truth for all; but in this case it is not equally known to all: it is universally true, for instance, that the three interior angles of a triangle equal two right angles; but this conclusion is not known by everybody. When we come to the particular conclusions of the practical reason, however, there is neither the same standard of truth or rightness for every one, nor are these conclusions equally known to all. All people, indeed, realize that it is right and true to act according to reason. And from this principle we may deduce as an immediate conclusion that debts must be repaid. This conclusion holds in the majority of cases. But it could happen in some particular case that it would be injurious, and therefore irrational, to repay a debt; if for instance, the money repaid were used to make war against one's own country. Such exceptions are all the more likely to occur the more we get down to particular cases: take, for instance, the question of repaying a debt together with a certain security, or in some specific way. The more specialized the conditions applied, the greater is the possibility of an exception arising which will make it right to make restitution or not.

(St Thomas Aquinas, op. cit., pp. 113–15, 123–5.)

42f   ST THOMAS AQUINAS: THE DIVINE LAW

In addition to natural law and to human law there had of necessity to be also a divine law to direct human life: and this for four reasons. In the first place because it is by law that man is directed in his actions with respect to his final end. If, therefore, man were destined to an end which was no more than proportionate to his natural faculties, there would be no need for him to have any directive on the side of reason above the natural law and humanly enacted law which is derived from it. But because man is destined to an end of eternal blessedness, and this exceeds what is proportionate to natural human faculties as we have already shown, it was necessary that he should be directed to this end not merely by natural and human law, but also by a divinely given law.—Secondly: because of the uncertainty of human judgement, particularly in matters that are contingent and specific, it is often the case that very differing judgements are passed by various people on human activities; and from these there proceed different, and even contrary, laws. In order, therefore, that man should know without any doubt what he is to do and what to avoid, it was necessary that his actions should be directed by a divinely given law, which is known to be incapable of error.—Thirdly: because laws are enacted in respect of what is capable of being judged. But the judgement of man cannot reach to the hidden interior actions of the soul, it can only be about external activities which are apparent. Nevertheless, the perfection of virtue requires that a man should be upright in both classes of actions. Human law being thus insufficient to order and regulate interior actions, it was necessary that for this purpose there should also be a divine law.—Fourthly: because, as Augustine says (I *De Lib. Arb.*), human law can neither punish nor even prohibit all that is evilly done. For in trying to prevent all that is evil it would render impossible also much that is good; and thus would impede much that is useful to the common welfare and therefore necessary to human intercourse. In order, therefore, that no evil should go unforbidden and unpunished it was necessary that there should be a divine law which would prohibit all manner of sin.

(St Thomas Aquinas, op. cit., pp. 115-17.)

42g   ST THOMAS AQUINAS: THE HUMAN LAW

Just as in speculative reason we proceed from indemonstrable principles, naturally known, to the conclusions of the various sciences, such conclusions not being innate but arrived at by the use of reason; so also the human reason has to proceed from the precepts of the natural law, as though from certain common and indemonstrable principles, to other more particular dispositions. And such particular dispositions, arrived at by an effort of reason, are called human laws: provided that the other conditions necessary to all law, which we have already noted, are observed. So Cicero says (*De Invent. Rhetor.* II, 53): 'Law springs in its first beginnings from nature: then such standards as are judged to be useful become established by custom: finally reverence and holiness add their sanction to what springs from nature and is established by custom.' . . .

Saint Augustine says: 'There is no law unless it be just.' So the validity of law depends upon its justice. But in human affairs a thing is said to be just when it accords aright with the rule of reason: and, as we have already seen, the first rule of reason is the natural law. Thus all humanly enacted laws are in accord with reason to the extent that they derive from the natural law. And if a human law is at variance in any particular with the natural law, it is no longer legal, but rather a corruption of law.

But it should be noted that there are two ways in which anything may derive from natural law. First, as a conclusion from more general principles. Secondly, as a determination of certain general features. The former is similar to the method of the sciences in which demonstrative conclusions are drawn from first principles. The second way is like to that of the arts in which some common form is determined to a particular instance: as, for example, when an architect, starting from the general idea of a house, then goes on to design the particular plan of this or that house. So, therefore, some derivations are made from the natural law by way of formal conclusion: as the conclusion, 'Do no murder,' derives from the precept, 'Do harm to no man.' Other conclusions are arrived at as determinations of particular cases. So the natural law establishes that whoever transgresses shall be punished. But that a man should be punished by a specific penalty is a particular determination of the natural law.

Both types of derivation are to be found in human law. But those which are arrived at in the first way are sanctioned not only by human law, but by the natural law also; while those arrived at by the second method have the validity of human law alone.

(St Thomas Aquinas, op. cit., pp. 115, 129.)

42h ST THOMAS AQUINAS: DEFECTS IN AUTHORITY

We must observe that, as has been stated already, in the observance of a certain precept, obedience is connected with the obligation to such observance. But such obligation derives from the order of authority which carries with it the power to constrain, not only from the temporal, but also from the spiritual point of view, and in conscience; as the Apostle says (*Romans* XIII): and this because the order of authority derives from God, as the Apostle says in the same passage. For this reason the duty of obedience is, for the Christian, a consequence of this derivation of authority from God, and ceases when that ceases. But, as we have already said, authority may fail to derive from God for two reasons: either because of the way in which authority has been obtained, or in consequence of the use which is made of it. There are two ways in which the first case may occur. Either because of a defect in the person, if he is unworthy; or because of some defect in the way itself by which power was acquired, if, for example, through violence, or simony or some other illegal method. The first defect is not such as to impede the acquisition of legitimate authority; and since authority derives always, from a formal point of view, from God (and it is this which produces the duty of obedience), their subjects are always obliged to obey such superiors, however unworthy they may be. But the second defect prevents the establishment of any just authority: for whoever possesses himself of power by violence does not truly become lord or master. Therefore it is permissible, when occasion offers, for a person to reject such authority; except in the case that it subsequently became legitimate, either through public consent or through the intervention of higher authority. With regard to abuse of authority, this also may come about in two ways. First, when what is ordered by an authority is opposed to the object for which that authority was constituted (if, for example, some sinful action is commanded or one which is contrary to virtue, when it is precisely for the protection and fostering of virtue that authority is instituted). In such a case, not only is there no obligation to obey the authority, but one is obliged to disobey it, as did the holy martyrs who suffered death rather than obey the impious commands of tyrants. Secondly, when those who bear authority command things which exceed the competence of such authority; as, for example, when a master demands payment from a servant which the latter is not bound to make, and other similar cases. In this instance the subject is free to obey or to disobey.

(St Thomas Aquinas, op. cit., pp. 183–5.)

42i   ST THOMAS AQUINAS: REMEDIES AGAINST TYRANNY

Since government by one person, being the best, is to be preferred; and since, as we have shown, there is always a danger that it will develop into tyranny, which is the worst government, every precaution must be taken to provide the community with a ruler who will not become a tyrant. In the first place it is necessary that whoever of the possible candidates is proclaimed king shall be of such character that it is unlikely that he will become a tyrant. . . . Next, a monarchy should be so constituted that there is no opportunity for the king, once he is reigning, to become a tyrant. And, at the same time the kingly power should be so restricted that he could not easily turn to tyranny. The steps to be taken to this end will be considered later. Finally, we must consider the action to be taken should a king become tyrannical.

If the tyranny be not excessive it is certainly wiser to tolerate it in limited measure, at least for a time, rather than to run the risk of even greater perils by opposing it. For those who take action against a tyrant may fail in their object, and only succeed in rousing the tyrant to greater savagery. Even when action against a tyrant meets with success, this very fact breeds strife and grave discord among the populace, either in the moment of rebellion or after his overthrow when opinion in the community is factiously divided as to the new form of government. . . .

It seems then, that the remedy against the evils of tyranny lies rather in the hands of public authority than in the private judgement of individuals. In particular, where a community has the right to elect a ruler for itself, it would not be contrary to justice for that community to depose the king whom it has elected, nor to curb his power should he abuse it to play the tyrant. Nor should the community be accused of disloyalty for thus deposing a tyrant, even after a previous promise of constant fealty; for the tyrant lays himself open to such treatment by his failure to discharge the duties of his office as governor of the community, and in consequence his subjects are no longer bound by their oath to him. . . .

If on the other hand the right to appoint a king over a certain community belongs to some superior, then the remedy against tyrannical excess must be sought from him. Thus the Jews made complaint to Caesar Augustus against Archelaus, when the latter began to rule in the place of his father, Herod, in Judea and had begun to imitate his father's evil ways. . . .

Finally, when there is no hope of human aid against tyranny, recourse must be made to God the King of all, and the helper of all who call upon Him in the time of tribulation.

(St Thomas Aquinas, op. cit., pp. 29–33.)

42j ST THOMAS AQUINAS: REBELLION

Tyrannical government is unjust government because it is directed not to the common welfare but to the private benefit of the ruler. This is clear from what the Philosopher says in the *Politics*, Book III, and in the *Ethics*, Book VIII. Consequently the overthrowing of such government is not strictly sedition; except perhaps in the case that it is accompanied by such disorder that the community suffers greater harm from the consequent disturbances than it would from a continuance of the former rule. A tyrant himself is, in fact, far more guilty of sedition when he spreads discord and strife among the people subject to him, so hoping to control them more easily. For it is a characteristic of tyranny to order everything to the personal satisfaction of the ruler at the expense of the community.

(St Thomas Aquinas, op. cit., p. 161.)

CHAPTER 12

The Secular Reaction

The end of the thirteenth and the beginning of the fourteenth century is a period when a movement developed against the claims of the Church to the plenitude of power. The reaction had two main aspects: it was anti-clerical and it was pro-secular. The growth of anti-clerical feeling was mainly due to the condition of the Church at this time. As in the tenth century before the Cluniac reforms, simony and clerical un-chastity were prevalent. Even more important was the obvious disparity between the great wealth of the Church and its protestations of poverty. Another major charge levelled at the Church was that its greed for wealth and political power had led the papacy to interfere in the secular affairs of states, thereby contributing to the almost constant warfare which bedevilled Europe.

More positively, the cause of secularism was advanced by the contemporary intellectual revival. Areas of learning such as philosophy and science, which had formerly been studied in the context of theology, were now increasingly considered as subjects of speculation in their own right; moreover, the growing study of Roman Law led in the same direction, away from scholastic theology. Perhaps the most important factor of all was the growth of the national monarchies, particularly in England and France. In both countries, the kings were attempting to build up a centralized administrative system against the resistance of the feudal aristocracy. Naturally enough, there existed a royal resentment against the exercise of papal sovereignty in these countries and against the payment of money to the papal see.

In 1294, against this background of growing anti-clericalism, Boniface VIII became pope. Unfortunately for the Church, which would have been better served by a conciliatory pope, Boniface was an inflexible man with much the same view of the papal authority as Innocent III had possessed. Conflict with the secular powers was inevitable. Philip IV of France and Edward I of England, who were at war with each other, were financing their operations by raising taxes from the clergy as well as from the laity. In the bull *Clericis Laicos* (1296), Boniface prohibited lay taxation of the clergy without papal consent (Ex. 43a).

Both monarchs were offended and took instant reprisals. Edward threatened to place tax-evading priests outside the king's peace. Philip expelled the papal tax-collectors and cut off the export of gold and silver to the papal see. Although a compromise settlement was established in 1297, in 1301 hostility once more flared up and in the famous bull of 1302, *Unam Sanctam*, a complete statement was made of the papal position *vis-à-vis* the temporal power (Ex. 43b). It is perhaps the most forthright and extreme claim to temporal supremacy ever made by a pope: 'Both are in the power of the Church, the spiritual sword and the material.'

As with the investiture conflict of the eleventh century, this new regal-sacerdotal dispute stimulated a great deal of political literature from both sides. The outstanding difference between this and the earlier dispute, however, was that with few exceptions the most important political and philosophical works were on the side of the secular authority and against the spiritual.

Egidius Colonna (c. 1247–1316)

Egidius was one of the exceptional cases mentioned above. Ironically, for he had earlier written a political treatise for the future Philip IV of France, he was a firm supporter of the papal cause. His book, *De Ecclesiastica Potestate* (*Ecclesiastical Power*), written in 1301, was widely read and highly influential in its day, and was probably the inspiration for Boniface's *Unam Sanctam*. In the first extract quoted (Ex. 44a), there is a notable similarity of expression in the consideration of the relation of the two swords to each other. The Church possesses both swords, although the inferior secular sword is exercised by princes. The principle of hierarchy as expounded by Pseudo-Dionysius is invoked to show that there can be no true order unless the secular sword is under the control of the spiritual by which it is instituted. Any secular power not instituted by the priesthood is not a rightful power since it does not contain justice.

The most interesting, as well as the most extreme, part of *De Ecclesiastica Potestate* is the theory of *Dominium* or Lordship (Ex. 44b). Egidius states that there is no true justice except in that commonwealth founded and ruled by Christ. Furthermore, no one can justly hold true *dominium* over anything unless he holds it from the Church. The word *dominium* which derives from *dominus* (lord) expresses the relationship of superior to inferior. Hence the authority of one man over another, or the ownership of property, were only possible for those Christians spiritually 'reborn through the Church'. One implication of this theory was, of course, that any authority over persons or material things exercised by non-Christians was illegitimate. A further implication was that just as the Church with its 'universal and superior lordship' over temporal things could assign inferior lordships to the laity, so the Church by excommunication could deprive a person of all such authority.

John of Paris (1269-1306)

Like Thomas Aquinas, John of Paris was a Dominican friar who taught at the University of Paris. Moreover, his philosophical and political writings applied Thomist principles to the issues of the day. His book, *De Potestate Regia et Papali* (*On Royal and Papal Power*, 1302) was written in support of the royal authority and was a direct answer to the papalist arguments of Egidius Colonna and James of Viterbo.

In the Thomist tradition he accepts the place of the state and the Church as catering for man's natural and supernatural ends respectively. He accepts the notion of papal monarchy in the spiritual sphere, even accepting the superior dignity of *sacerdotium* to *regnum*. However, he rejects the position taken up by contemporary papal writers that the regal authority is derived from the Church. Both authorities, in fact, originate in the divine power of God and each is supreme in its own sphere (Ex. 45a).

In a later passage John summarizes the powers entrusted to the *sacerdotium* in order to discover whether they can lead to the exercise of temporal power (Ex. 45b). The difficulty arises when he considers the judicial power over spiritual offences. The ecclesiastical judge has authority only over spiritual cases and he may coerce unrepentant sinners only with spiritual penalties such as excommunication. However, should a prince be heretical and incorrigible, the pope, by excommunicating all who obey him, may cause the people to depose him.

In a similar manner, a pope who brings 'scandal on the Church' may be indirectly excommunicated and deposed by the prince acting through the cardinals and by preventing the people from obeying the pope. If these measures are insufficient, the cardinals may call upon the aid of the secular power; even the power of the emperor, if requested, may be used to depose an incorrigible pope.

In direct opposition to Egidius's statement that *dominium* issues from the pope, John considers that the pope has no rights of any kind over the goods of laymen (Ex. 45c). Such goods belong to individual persons who have acquired them by their own skill and labour. Each person has a true lordship over his goods and may dispose of them without reference to either pope or prince. John concedes, however, that the pope, as supreme head of 'the faithful', has the right to determine what goods should be given up to the community in the form of taxes should the Christian faith be endangered.

Pierre Dubois

Another royalist tract emanating from the France of Philip IV was *De Recuperatione Terre Sancte* (*The Recovery of the Holy Land*) written about 1306 by the middle-class lawyer, Pierre Dubois. Although the treatise had little influence in the course of political ideas, it is of interest as reflecting the purely secular arguments of the day. Dubois is not interested in the problem of the relationship between papacy and empire, nor has he anything but scorn for the use of biblical references to make political points. He is mainly concerned to outline the characteristics of a secular state in which the king is completely independent of any other authority. The ostensible subject of the book—the scheme for a crusade—is little more than a framework on which he hangs his ideas. These include the secularization of ecclesiastical property and the transference to the French king of the pope's temporal powers.

The extract quoted (Ex. 46), illustrates Dubois's contention that kings should not regard themselves as bound by any kind of absolute standard such as natural law.

Dante Alighieri (1265-1321)

Dante was born in Florence, took part in Florentine politics, and, although exiled for the last twenty years of his life, never ceased to think of Florence as the most 'agreeable place in the world'. As an associate of the *Ghibelline* (anti-clerical) faction, Dante from 1295 to 1301 was a member of the Florentine government, but in the latter years he was driven into permanent exile as the result of a coup inspired by the papacy. Like his compatriot Machiavelli two centuries later, Dante attributed the conflicts and factional dissension of contemporary Italy to the Church. His own political experience reinforced this view. His book, *Monarchy* (*De Monarchia*), written in 1312 or 1313, was inspired by the attempts of Emperor Henry VII to re-establish the authority of the Holy Roman Empire over Italy and thus restore peace.

Monarchy is essentially a plea for what Dante considered to be the only solution to the problem of political disunity: the establishment over the whole world of a temporal monarch who would be completely independent of the papacy. It is divided into three books.

Book One attempts to demonstrate the need for a universal monarchy. Dante's arguments here are avowedly Aristotelian with occasional references to Averroes. He begins by examining the goal of humanity. Man must have an end since nature creates nothing in vain. Man is a social and political animal naturally fitted for life in society. Hence the question must be: what is the goal or purpose of human society? Dante's answer is 'to fulfil the total capacity of the possible intellect . . . primarily by speculation and secondarily . . . by action'. In other words, rational man is capable of acquiring a certain amount of knowledge. But this knowledge is only a small part of that which potentially could be attained by the human race acting as a unified community. Humanity can achieve its goal only if it lives in conditions of peace and unity (Ex. 47a).

In order that such conditions may be achieved, the world must have a single temporal monarch to rule it. In the remainder of Book One, Dante presents a large number of arguments to 'prove' that such a government is necessary. Most of his arguments are derived from Aristotle or Aquinas. For example, his first argument is that direction by one is necessary when several things are directed towards a single end. The authority of the 'Philosopher' (Aristotle) is sufficient proof of the assertion although its truth can also be demonstrated by inductive reason. Further arguments recall Thomas's treatment of the case for monarchic government; for instance that monarchy is most like nature and God (Ex. 47b).

Book Two The middle book of *Monarchy* is devoted to proving the proposition that the Roman people acquired their imperial position lawfully. The Romans were the noblest of all people and their rule was not for their own good but for the good of the ruled. The fact that the Romans succeeded in establishing their empire when all others failed indicates the working of divine providence (Ex. 47c). Finally, an interesting argument is presented to show that if the Roman Empire had not been lawful, then Christ's crucifixion would not have been a proper punishment for the sins of mankind (Ex. 47d).

The second book of *Monarchy* clearly indicates Dante's immoderate respect for the Roman imperial tradition. His admiration for Rome stemmed partly from his studies in Roman law at Bologna and partly from his reading of Virgil, whose impact on Dante is best exhibited in the *Divine Comedy*, where the Roman poet is Dante's guide through hell and purgatory.

Book Three Having proved to his own satisfaction that the Roman Emperor (even in his contemporary German manifestation as Holy Roman Emperor) is the legitimate monarch over the human race, Dante now attempts to show that the imperial authority comes directly from God and does not depend upon the Church. In disposing of the claims of the Church, Dante examines and rejects all the papal arguments for supremacy. For example, the sun and moon allegory so frequently used by papalist writers to signify the superiority of the *sacerdotium* to the *regnum* is rejected on the grounds that the existence, powers, and operation of the moon are independent of the sun. The *Donation of Constantine*, although accepted by Dante as a genuine document, he regards as invalid since Constantine had no power to divide the empire nor had the Church the power to accept such a gift (Ex. 47e).

Later arguments demonstrate more positively that the emperor's power is independent of the Church. The empire flourished before the Church existed, hence imperial authority cannot be dependent upon the Church. Again the Church's power to confer authority upon the emperor must stem either from natural or from divine law. But the Church is not a product of nature and the scriptures contain no evidence that priests were given this power (Ex. 47f).

Dante's *Monarchy* ends with a statement of man's dual end: happiness in this life and happiness in the next. The universal monarch leads man to the first in accordance with rational philosophy; the pope leads man to the second in accordance with revelation (Ex. 47g). Rather oddly, in view of Dante's relentless attack on the papacy, the last sentences of the book imply a certain subordination of emperor to pope. The distinction drawn between reason and revelation or faith which Dante emphasized, was anti-scholastic and prepared the way for the more Erastian writers such as Marsilius of Padua.

Marsilius of Padua (c. 1275–1343)

Marsilius grew up in Padua, an Italian city state similar in many respects to Dante's Florence. Like Dante, contemporary political events turned Marsilius to an anti-clericalism which he never lost. His years in France, where he studied and taught at the University of Paris, were doubtless also instrumental in reinforcing his anti-papalism. In Paris he wrote in 1324, possibly in collaboration with the Averroist John of Jandun, his important political book *Defensor Pacis* (*Defender of Peace*). Not surprisingly in view of the secularist tone of the book, Marsilius and John were declared to be heretics and, in order to avoid a papal trial, they fled to the protection of the Emperor Louis of Bavaria. For most of the remainder of his life, Marsilius was obliged to stay within imperial protection.

Although the *Defensor Pacis* was written within a decade of Dante's *Monarchy*, its thought marks it out as belonging to another age. Whereas *Monarchy* is essentially a medieval work, the *Defensor Pacis* seems remarkably modern by contrast. Indeed, Marsilius rejects nearly all of the traditional assumptions of the later Middle Ages. Against the scholastic assumption that reason and faith reinforced one another, Marsilius (following Averroes) argues that they should be strictly demarcated, neither impinging upon the other. Against the principle that earthly law and justice are derived from the immutable law of nature, he maintains that the sole source of law is the community itself. To the problem of the relative positions of *sacerdotium* and *regnum* he presents the most radical of solutions: the complete subordination of the Church to the secular power in all earthly matters.

The *Defensor Pacis* is divided into three parts or 'discourses'. Discourse One is an examination of the objects and nature of the state. Discourse Two is an examination of the papal claims to spiritual supremacy. Discourse Three merely summarizes his conclusions.

The State and Justice

The first discourse begins by emphasizing the need for peace and tranquility as prerequisites of man's intellectual and moral perfection. It is the function of the state therefore to provide peace and this is achieved when each of the functional parts of the body politic plays its appointed role in co-operation with the others. Marsilius's account of the origin and nature of the state is closely modelled on Aristotle's *Politics*, although without the teleological implications of that work. The state is seen as an organic whole composed of functional members: 'the agricultural, the artisan, the military, the financial, the priestly and the judicial or deliberative.' All must co-operate for the common good. Marsilius's cynicism about religion is shown when he discusses the need for priests. They exist as a kind of supplementary law-enforcement agency by teaching people to abstain from those anti-social acts which cannot be prevented by the ordinary law. The truth or falsity of what they preach is irrelevant.

The late medieval theory of law was essentially that law had to be based upon justice and justice was a transcendental quality which could be known through human reason. Because the Church was traditionally the authoritative interpreter of the universal moral law, any secular theory was forced to arrive at a radically different conception of law. Marsilius's solution was to define law in terms of its form rather than its content (Ex. 48a). Law becomes a coercive command rather than an expression of reason and it is thus possible for a law to be unjust. To be perfect, however, a law should be just as well as coercive. Neither divine law nor natural law can be considered to be law in the proper sense, since neither have coercive force in this world.

Marsilius does not deny that objective norms of justice exist, only that these norms affect the laws of the state. Provided that legislation is effected in the proper way, the law of the state is likely to be just and hence to conform to the natural law. The proper legislature is the 'whole body of citizens, or the weightier part (*pars valentior*) thereof' (Ex. 48b). The democratic implications of this are modified by Marsilius's qualifications to the phrase 'weightier part': 'the quantity and quality of the persons . . .'. Hence, although law should be made by the people, Marsilius, like Aristotle, does not advocate a strict egalitarianism.

The Church and the Pope

In the second discourse Marsilius devotes himself to showing how the Church should be governed in a perfect state. The word 'Church' is commonly used to mean the clergy alone. The truest meaning of the word, however, is that which denotes the 'whole body of the faithful' (the *universitas fidelium*). (Ex. 48c). The pope's present authority in the Church is illegitimate, being founded upon a misinterpretation of scripture. Neither the pope nor the rest of the clergy have any right to be immune from temporal jurisdiction, to hold property nor to exercise coercive power. Heretics ought not to be punished by priests for a breach of the divine law (because this law is coercive only in the next world), but should the heresy have anti-social consequences, then the heretic may be punished for a breach of the civil law (Ex. 48d).

The body of the faithful (*universitas fidelium*) must, of course, be co-extensive with the body of the community (*universitas civium*). As the community in its latter form is responsible for governing the state, so, in its capacity as the ecclesiastical community, it is responsible for the government of the Church. Priests are retained as subordinate officials of the *universitas fidelium* and even the pope has a place as symbolic head of the Church (Ex. 48e). The function of declaring doctrine is to be taken from the pope and carried out by a general council composed of priests and laymen, to be convened by the various Christian communities (Ex. 48f).

One can detect in the writings of Marsilius many ideas which were to be seen in a more developed form in the sixteenth and seventeenth centuries. The suggestion that the law of the state was valid regardless of its conformity or otherwise to 'natural justice', or 'reason', or the views of the Church or any other authority, paved the way for the secularist and absolutist writings of Machiavelli and Hobbes. More immediately, however, his conception of a general council of the Church to carry out the traditionally papal functions, was one of the first hints of what later became the 'conciliar' theory of Church government.

Nicholas of Cusa (1401-1464) and Conciliarism

The conciliar movement began as an attempt to end the schism within the Church which stemmed from the election of an anti-pope in 1378. For thirty-nine years, Christian Europe was divided between the supporters of the pope in Avignon and those of his rival in Rome. Matters were made worse in 1409 by the action of the Council of Pisa which declared both popes deposed and elected a third. The schism was ended in 1417 by a new council, that of Constance. The leading theorist associated with the Council of Constance was John Gerson, whose ideas were influenced by Marsilius of Padua and his friend William of Ockham. The decree *Sacrosancta* puts succinctly the Council's view that its authority is supreme in the Church (Ex. 49).

In accordance with the rule agreed at Constance that a general council must be summoned every seven years, a council was convened at Basle in 1431. At this council the latent conflict between papal and conciliar authority came to a head. The attacks on the Council of Basle by the pope met with an interesting and important defence developed by Nicholas of Cusa in his work *Universal Harmony* (*De Concordantia Catholica*), submitted in 1433. In Book Two, Nicholas puts forward his view that government should be based upon the consent of the governed (Ex. 50). There is a kind of contract between king and society which is brought into operation by the free election of those who are naturally best fitted by reason and wisdom to rule. The argument used by Nicholas rests upon familiar assumptions. The notion of human equality under the natural law goes back to the Greek Stoics, and that of popular consent to government is a Roman legal concept. Thomas Aquinas and John of Paris had both declared that authority is conferred on the ruler by the people. But Nicholas goes further than his predecessors in applying such democratic ideas to an actual political situation.

The conciliar experiment did not survive the fifteenth century. The arguments for popular sovereignty were in advance of their time and were never accepted as a practical proposition. The Council of Basle was regarded as being more potentially schismatic than a return to papal government. Even Nicholas himself in time became a cardinal and a protagonist of the papal cause.

FURTHER READING

Texts
Dante: *De Monarchia*
Pierre Dubois: *The Recovery of the Holy Land*, part I, tr. W. I. Brandt (Columbia University Press 1956)
E. Lewis: *Medieval Political Ideas* (Routledge & Kegan Paul 1954)
Marsilius of Padua: *Defensor Pacis*, tr. A. Gewirth (Columbia University Press 1956)

Commentaries
R. W. and A. J. Carlyle: *History of Medieval Political Theory in the West*, vol. 5 (Blackwood 1962)
A. P. d'Entreves: *Dante as a Political Thinker* (Clarendon Press 1965)
A. P. d'Entreves: *Mediaeval Contributions to Political Thought* (Oxford University Press 1939)
A. Gewirth: *Marsilius of Padua*, vol. 1 (Columbia University Press 1951)
E. Gilson: *Dante the Philosopher* (Sheed & Ward 1948)

43a   POPE BONIFACE VIII: BULL: CLERICIS LAICOS

Boniface Bishop, servant of the servants of God, for the perpetual record of the matter. That laymen have been very hostile to the clergy antiquity relates; and it is clearly proved by the experiences of the present time. For not content with what is their own the laity strive for what is forbidden and loose the reins for things unlawful. Nor do they prudently realize that power over clerks or ecclesiastical persons or goods is forbidden them: they impose heavy burdens on the prelates of the churches and ecclesiastical persons regular and secular, and tax them, and impose collections: they exact and demand from the same the half, tithe, or twentieth, or any other portion or proportion of their revenues or goods; and in many ways they try to bring them into slavery, and subject them to their authority. And, we regret to say, some prelates of the churches and ecclesiastical persons, fearing where there should be no fear, seeking a temporary peace, fearing more to offend the temporal majesty than the eternal, acquiesce in such abuses, not so much rashly as improvidently, without obtaining authority or licence from the Apostolic See. We therefore, desirous of preventing such wicked actions, decree, with apostolic authority and on the advice of our brethren, that any prelates and ecclesiastical persons, religious or secular, of whatsoever orders, condition or standing, who shall pay or promise or agree to pay to lay persons collections or taxes for the tithe, twentieth, or hundredth of their own rents, or goods, or those of the churches . . . without the authority of the same see:

And also whatsoever emperors, kings, or princes . . . and all others of whatsoever rank, eminence or state, who shall impose, exact, or receive the things aforesaid, or arrest, seize, or presume to take possession of things anywhere deposited in holy buildings, or to command them to be arrested, seized, or taken, or receive them when taken, seized, or arrested, and also all who knowingly give aid, counsel, or support, openly or secretly, in the things aforesaid, by this same should incur sentence of excommunication.

(H. Bettenson, ed., *Documents of the Christian Church*, pp. 157-8, Oxford University Press 1967.)

43b   POPE BONIFACE VIII: BULL: UNAM SANCTAM

And we learn from the words of the Gospel that in this Church and in her power are two swords, the spiritual and the temporal. For when the apostles said, 'Behold, here' (that is, in the Church, since it was the apostles who spoke) 'are two swords'—the Lord did not reply, 'It is too much,' but 'It is enough.' Truly he who denies that the temporal sword is in the power of Peter, misunderstands the words of the Lord, 'Put up thy sword into the sheath.' Both are in the power of the Church, the spiritual sword and the material. But the latter is to be used for the Church, the former by her; the former by the priest, the latter by kings and captains but at the will and by the permission of the priest. The one sword, then, should be under the other, and temporal authority subject to spiritual. For when the apostle says 'there is no power but

of God, and the powers that be are ordained of God' they would not be so ordained were not one sword made subject to the other. . . .

Thus, concerning the Church and her power, is the prophecy of Jeremiah
fulfilled, 'See, I have this day set thee over the nations and over the kingdoms,'
etc. If, therefore, the earthly power err, it shall be judged by the spiritual
power; and if a lesser power err, it shall be judged by a greater. But if the supreme power err, it can only be judged by God, not by man; for the testimony
of the apostle is 'The spiritual man judgeth all things, yet he himself is judged
of no man.' For this authority, although given to a man and exercised by a
man, is not human, but rather divine, given at God's mouth to Peter and
established on a rock for him and his successors in Him whom he confessed,
the Lord saying to Peter himself, 'Whatsoever thou shalt bind,' etc. Whoever
therefore resists this power thus ordained of God, resists the ordinance of
God. . . . Furthermore we declare, state, define and pronounce that it is altogether necessary to salvation for every human creature to be subject to the
Roman pontiff.

(H. Bettenson, ed., op. cit., pp. 160-1.)

44a AEGIDIUS ROMANUS: THE RELATIONSHIP BETWEEN THE TWO SWORDS

. . . From the order of the universe we can clearly show that the church was
established over peoples and kingdoms. For, according to Dionysius [Pseudo-
Dionysius], *De Angelica Hierarchia*, [ch. 10], the law of divinity is to subdue
the lowest to the highest through the intermediate. . . . If, therefore, there are
two swords, the one spiritual and the other temporal (as is apparent from the
saying of the Gospel [Luke 22:38], 'Behold, here are two swords,' to which the
Lord at once adds, 'It is enough,' because these two swords suffice in the
church), these two swords, these two authorities and powers, are necessarily
from God; because, as has been said, there is no power except from God. It
follows, moreover, that they must needs be ordained; because, as we stated, the
powers that are from God must be ordained. Now they would not be ordained
unless one sword were subjected through the other and placed under the other;
because, as Dionysius said, the law of divinity which God gave to all created
things . . . requires this: that all be not immediately subjected to the supreme,
but the lowest through the intermediate, and the lower through the higher.
Therefore the temporal sword, as inferior, is to be subjected through the
spiritual sword as through the higher, and the one is to be subordinated to the
other as the lower to the higher.

But someone might say that kings and princes ought to be subjected in
spiritual and not temporal matters, and that therefore this doctrine ought to be
understood to mean that kings and princes are spiritually but not temporally
under the church. And he might also argue that the church has received temporals themselves from the temporal lordship, as in the case of the donation
and grant which Constantine made to the church. But anyone who says this
does not grasp the force of the argument. For if kings and princes were only

spiritually subject to the church, sword would not be under sword, temporals would not be under spirituals, there would be no order of powers, the lowest would not be subjected to the highest through the intermediate. Therefore, if these powers are ordained, the temporal sword must be under the spiritual, kingdoms must be under the vicar of Christ, and, as a matter of right—though some may act contrarily as a matter of fact—the vicar of Christ must have dominion over temporals themselves. . . .

Among the wise there can be no doubt that the sacerdotal power precedes the royal and earthly power in dignity and nobility. . . .

Therefore the royal power ought to recognize the superiority of the sacerdotal dignity, as that through which at God's command it was instituted. And if it be said that not every royal power was instituted through the priesthood, we shall say that any royal power not instituted through the priesthood either is not righteous, and therefore is brigandage rather than authority, or is united with the priesthood, or is successor to a power instituted through the priesthood. For when there were kingdoms of the gentiles, under the law of nature, all such kingdoms were obtained through invasion and usurpation. Thus Nimrod, who, as we read in Genesis 10:[8-10], was the first king, reigning in Babylon, made himself king through violence and usurpation. whence it is said there that he began to be mighty in the land; therefore he acquired the kingship through civil power and not through justice. But according to Augustine, *De Civitate Dei*, [bk. 4, ch. 4], kingdoms without justice are great bands of robbers. Moreover, although such rulers are called kings, they are not kings, but thieves and robbers. . . .

Therefore let kings recognize that they were instituted through the priesthood. And therefore, if we diligently examine the origin and institution of royal power, the fact that it was instituted through the priesthood leads to the conclusion that the royal power ought to be under the sacerdotal power and especially under the power of the highest priest. . . .

And even as in the universe itself every corporal substance is ruled through a spiritual substance, since the heavens themselves, which are supreme among corporal things, and which have influence over all bodies, are governed through spiritual substances, namely, through the intelligences that move them, so among believers all temporal lords and every earthly power ought to be ruled and governed through the spiritual and ecclesiastical power, and especially through the supreme pontiff, who holds the apex and the highest rank in the church and in the spiritual power. Moreover, the supreme pontiff is to be judged by God alone. For . . . it is he who judges all and is judged by no one: that is, by no mere man but by God alone. . . .

And if anyone should say that the whole earthly power ought to be under the spiritual in regard to the articles of faith but not in regard to temporal and earthly power, his argument would have no weight, because he who says this does not grasp the force of our reasoning, since bodies, as bodies, are under spirits, even as the movers of bodies, and especially the movers of the superior bodies, are themselves ruled through moving spirits and through the intelligences which move the spheres: so temporal powers, as temporal, and especially the supreme temporal powers, can be judged through the spiritual power and especially through the power of the supreme pontiff, who is the supreme and most sublime spiritual power in the church; inferior temporal lords, if they are at fault, can be judged through temporal lords, but those superior temporal lords can themselves be judged through the spiritual power, since among temporal lords they have no superiors. But the spiritual power, and especially the power of the supreme priest, can be judged by no one but God alone, since no man is superior to it.

(Aegidius Romanus, *De Ecclesiastica Potestate*, Bk 1, chs. 4, 5, in E. Lewis, *Medieval Political Ideas*, pp. 574-5, 577-9, Routledge and Kegan Paul, London 1954.)

44b AEGIDIUS ROMANUS: THEORY OF LORDSHIP

We intend . . . to show that there is no lordship with justice, either of temporal things or of lay persons or of anything whatever, except under the church and through the church: for example, a man cannot have with justice, unless he has it under and through the church, his field or his vineyard or anything else that he has.

For we say with Augustine in his *De Civitate Dei*, bk. 2, ch. 22, that true justice does not exist except in that commonwealth whose founder and ruler is Christ. For the Roman gentiles seemed to talk much of justice and to make much ado over their commonwealth. But that commonwealth, as Augustine says in the above-mentioned chapter, was not a living fact, but a painted picture. For . . . true justice could not exist in their commonwealth, where the true God was not worshipped; and since the passion of Christ no commonwealth can be a true commonwealth unless the holy mother church is cherished there and Christ is its founder and ruler. For this reason Augustine, *De Civitate Dei*, bk. 29, ch. 21, thinks that the commonwealth of the Romans was not a true commonwealth because true justice was never there.

And in case someone may not be satisfied with the citing of authorities, we wish to add arguments to show that no one can with justice hold lordship of anything unless he has been reborn through the church. For, as Augustine says in the aforesaid book and chapter, justice is the virtue which distributes to each his own. Therefore, there is no true justice unless to everyone is rendered what is his. Therefore, since you ought to be under God and under Christ, you are not just unless you are under Him; and because you are unjustly withdrawn from your Lord Christ, everything is justly withdrawn from your lordship. For he who is unwilling to be under His lordship cannot with justice have lordship of anything. For if a knight were unwilling to be under the king, it would be fitting that the subjects of the knight should not be under him. If, therefore, a knight unjustly withdraws himself from his lord, he is justly deprived of all his own lordship. But whoever is not reborn through the church is not under Christ his lord; fittingly, therefore, is he derived of all his own lordship, so that he cannot justly be lord of anything.

You see, therefore, that for a just and worthy possession of things spiritual regeneration through the church is more important than carnal generation through a father. . . . Carnally born, we are by nature sons of wrath, we were conceived in iniquities, and as a result we are not under our Lord, as we have said. It is fitting that he who was carnally born of a father should be deprived of all his lordship, nor can he justly succeed into the lordship of the paternal heritage unless he be reborn through the church; for by this regeneration he is brought under Christ his Lord, and thus he is not deprived of his lordship, but the lordship of his heritage is justly due him. . . .

It follows that you ought to recognize that your heritage, and all your lordship and all your possession, are yours from the church and through the church and because you are the son of the church, more than from your carnal father, or through him, or because you are his son. It follows also that if your father, in his lifetime, is more lord of the heritage than you, the church, which does not die, is more lord of your possessions than you.

Yet it should be noticed that, although we say that the church is mother and mistress of all possessions and all temporal things, yet we do not thereby deprive the faithful of their lordships and possessions, because . . . both the church and the faithful have lordship of a kind: but the church has universal and superior lordship, while the faithful have particular and inferior lordship. We therefore render unto Caesar the things that are Caesar's and unto God the things that are God's, because we assign the universal and superior lordship of temporal things to the church, distributing particular and inferior lordships among the faithful.

We wish, moreover, to show clearly that whoever is bound by the church, or excommunicated by her, can call nothing his own—or, if he can, it will be only by the indulgence of the church. And when this has been shown, it will be plainly revealed that the church has the superior lordship over all temporal things and over all possessions in such a way that nothing will remain as his own to him whom she binds, unless through her indulgence. . . .

If, therefore, the church can bring it about that someone is deprived of the communion of men or the communion of the faithful, she can bring it about that he is deprived of that foundation upon which all these things are built. Therefore, to a man so deprived, partitions, sales, grants, transfers, and laws of every kind avail nothing. Therefore, he cannot say that anything is his, since all the aforesaid conditions on the basis of which a man can call a thing his own are founded on the fact of communication.

(Aegidius Romanus, *De Ecclesiastica Potestate*, Bk 2, chs. 7, 12, in E. Lewis, op. cit., pp. 112-15.)

45a JOHN OF PARIS: KINGSHIP AND PRIESTHOOD

From what has just been said, one can easily see which is first in dignity, the kingship or the priesthood. For what is later in time is customarily first in dignity, as the perfect in comparison with the imperfect, and the end in comparison with the means. And therefore we say that the priestly power is greater than the royal power and excels it in dignity, since we always find that that to which belongs the ultimate end is more perfect than, and better than, and gives direction to that to which belongs the inferior end. Now the kingship is ordained for this purpose: that the associated multitude may live according to virtue. . . . And it is further ordained to a higher end, which is the enjoyment of God; and guidance to this end is the charge of Christ, Whose ministers and vicars are the priests. Therefore the priestly power is of greater dignity than the secular power. And this is commonly conceded. . . .

However, if the priest is, in an absolute sense, greater in dignity than the prince, it does not follow that he is the greater in all respects. For the lesser secular power is not related to the greater spiritual power as originating from it or being derived from it, as, for example, the power of a proconsul is related to the emperor, who is greater than he in all respects and from whom his power is derived. But it is like the power of the head of a household in comparison with the power of a commander of soldiers, neither one of which is derived from the other, but both of which are derived from some superior power. Therefore the secular power is greater than the spiritual in some respects: namely, in temporal affairs; and in regard to those affairs it is not subjected to the spiritual power in any way, since it does not owe its origin to the spiritual power, but both owe their origin immediately to one supreme power: namely, the divine; therefore the lower is not subjected completely to the higher but only in those respects in which the supreme power has subordinated it to the greater. For who would say that because a teacher of letters or instructor in morals ordains all the members of a household to a nobler end (namely, to the knowledge of truth), therefore a physician, who looks after the lower end (namely, the health of the body), should be subjected to him in the preparing of his medicines? For this is not fitting, since the head of the household, who established them both in the house, did not subordinate the physician to the tutor in this respect. Therefore the priest is greater than the prince in spiritual affairs and, conversely, the prince is greater than the priest in temporal affairs, although in an absolute sense the priest is the greater, inasmuch as the spiritual power is greater than the temporal. . . .

(John of Paris, *De Potestate Regia et Papali*, ch. 5, in E. Lewis, op. cit., pp. 585-6.)

45b   JOHN OF PARIS: THE TWO POWERS

Having explained, [in ch. 12, the powers involved in the nature of the priesthood], we should now discover what bishops and priests can do in temporals and over princes on the basis of the powers entrusted to them. And it seems that none of the aforesaid powers has given them direct power in temporals, nor temporal jurisdiction, except in so far as they have the right to take what is necessary to sustain their lives. And this can be demonstrated through analysis of the individual powers. . . .

In regard to the fourth power, which is judicial power in the external court, all the difficulty arises. Therefore it should be understood that this power has two subdivisions: namely, the authority to define or take cognizance . . . and the power to coerce . . . , for these are the two keys in the external court. In regard to the former, it should be realized that the ecclesiastical judge, as an ecclesiastic judging in the external court, has no regular cognizance except of spiritual cases, which are called ecclesiastical, and has no cognizance of temporals except by reason of fault. . . .

In regard to the power of correction, or ecclesiastical censure, it should be known that, directly, it is only spiritual, since it can impose no penalty in the external court except a spiritual penalty, unless conditionally and indirectly. For, although the ecclesiastical judge has the function of bringing men back to God, and withdrawing them from sin, and correcting them, yet he has this function only in accordance with the method given him by God, which is by cutting the sinner off from the sacraments and from the communion of believers, and penalties of this sort which are proper to ecclesiastical censure. I said that temporal penalties are not imposed 'unless conditionally': that is, on condition that the sinner wishes to repent and to accept a pecuniary penalty; for the ecclesiastical judge cannot, by reason of the fault, impose a corporal or pecuniary penalty as does a secular judge, but only if the sinner is willing to accept it. For, if he is not willing to accept it, the ecclesiastical judge coerces him through excommunication or some other spiritual penalty, which is the utmost that he can inflict; nor can he do anything further. I said also 'indirectly,' because if a prince were a heretic and incorrigible and contemptuous of the ecclesiastical censure, the pope could so influence the people that he would be deprived of his secular honour and be deposed by the people. And the pope could do this in the case of an ecclesiastical crime whose cognizance belonged to him, by excommunicating all who obeyed the sinner as a lord; and thus the people, and indirectly the pope, would depose him. Thus also, on the other hand, if the pope were criminous and brought scandal on the church, and were incorrigible, the prince could excommunicate him indirectly, and depose him indirectly: namely, by warning him through himself and through the cardinals. And if the pope were unwilling to yield, the prince could so influence the people that he would be compelled to yield or be deposed by the people; because the emperor could, by hypothecation of property or by bodily penalties, prevent each and everyone from obeying the pope. In this way each can depose the other. For both pope and emperor have jurisdiction universally and everywhere; but the one has spiritual, the other temporal jurisdiction.

Yet on this point a distinction ought to be made. When the king is at fault in spiritual matters, namely, in the faith, in marriage, and the like, the jurisdiction of which belongs to the ecclesiastical judge, the pope first warns him and then, if he is found to be pertinacious and incorrigible, can excommunicate him, but cannot go further except indirectly, . . . as was said. But when the king is at fault in temporal matters, the cognizance of which does not belong to an ecclesiastic, then not the pope but the barons and peers of the realm have in the first instance the function of correcting him; and if they cannot, or dare not, they can invoke the help of the church; and the church, having been requested by the peers to give aid to the right, can warn the prince and proceed against him in the aforesaid way.

Similarly, if the pope were at fault in temporal affairs, the cognizance of which belongs to the secular prince—for instance, if he should lend at usury or give protection to usurers—and especially when he is at fault in those things that are prohibited by the civil laws, then, if there were an emperor, he would have the primary right to correct him by admonishing him and punishing him; for to the prince belongs by primary right the correction of all malefactors. . . .

If, however, the pope were delinquent in spiritual matters, through conferring the benefices of the church simoniacally, destroying churches, depriving ecclesiastical persons and chapters of their rights, or even by teaching and pronouncing wrongly concerning those things that pertain to the faith and to good morals, then he ought first to be admonished by the cardinals, who act on behalf of the whole clergy; and if he were incorrigible and they could not of themselves remove the scandal from the church, then they would have the function of invoking the secular arm, by supplication, to give aid to the right; and then the emperor, at the request of the cardinals, ought as a member of the church to proceed against him to secure his deposition. For the church does not in any way have a secular sword, as Bernard said to Eugenius [*De Consideratione*, bk. 4, ch. 3, sec. 7]: 'not indeed by your hand, nor by your command, but by your suggestion and supplication'; the two swords are thus mutually bound to aid each other because of the common charity which unites the members of the church. . . .

(John of Paris, *De Potestate Regia et Papali*, ch. 13, in E. Lewis, op. cit., pp. 586-9.)

45c JOHN OF PARIS: LORDSHIP

. . . . The pope has a weaker lordship in the external goods of laymen [than in those of clerics], since in regard to these he is not an administrator, unless perhaps in the ultimate necessity of the church, and even in that case he is not an administrator but simply the declarer of right. To prove this, it should be considered that the external goods of men are not granted to the community as are the goods of the church but are acquired by individual persons, by their own skill, labour, and industry. And individuals, as individuals, have right and power in them, and true lordship; and each can ordain concerning his own, dispose, administer, retain or alienate them at his pleasure, without injury of another, since he is the lord; and therefore such goods have no relation or connection with each other, or with any one common head who might have a right to administer or dispose them, since each man at his pleasure is the ordainer of his own property. And therefore neither prince nor pope has lordship or administration in such goods.

But because it sometimes happens that on account of such external goods the common peace is disturbed, when someone usurps what belongs to another; and also because men who love their possessions too much sometimes do not share them as befits the necessity or utility of their fatherland; therefore the prince has been set up by the people to preside as judge in such cases, defining the just and the unjust, and as the punisher of injustices, and as the measurer who takes goods from individuals, in accordance with due proportion, for the common necessity or utility. But because the pope is the supreme head, not only of the clergy, but of all the faithful in general, as such, he has the right, as the general formulator of faith and morals, in the case of the supreme necessity of the faith and of morals—in which case all the goods of the faithful are common and to be shared, even the chalices of the churches—to dispense the goods of the faithful and to define what ought to be given up, as befits the common necessity of the faith, which otherwise might be overturned through an invasion of pagans or something of the sort. And the necessity might be so great and so evident that he could exact tithes or definite portions from the individual believers—in accordance with due proportion, however, lest some should without reason be more burdened than others in succouring the common necessity of the faith; and the ordaining of this by the pope is nothing except a declaration of right. And he could also compel those who were rebellious or refractory, through the censure of the church. And if the believers of some parish were recently multiplied to such an extent that the ancient returns of the parish were inadequate to the care of the parish because for the care of the parish the priest would need many new coadjutor chaplains, the pope could by similar means ordain that the believers of the parish should add more from their own goods, up to the sufficient amount: in which case, such an ordaining would be a declaration of right. But except in such cases of necessity, for the sake of the common spiritual good, the pope does not have the disposition of the goods of laymen, but each man disposes of his own in accordance with his will, and the prince, in case of necessity, disposes them for the sake of the common temporal good. In cases not of necessity, however, but of some spiritual utility, or where it is clear that the external goods of the laymen are not due for such utility or necessity, the pope does not have the right to compel anyone; but in this case he could give indulgences for aid brought by the faithful, and nothing else, I think, is allowed him.

(John of Paris, *De Potestate Regia et Papali*, ch. 7, in E. Lewis, op. cit., pp. 116-17.)

46 PIERRE DUBOIS

According to the civil law we ought not to have regard for 'what is being done at Rome nor what has been done, but what ought to be done and what ought to have been done.' We should not hesitate to adopt new methods when their usefulness is evident.

Does not Averroes say that the Arabs suffered many evils because they believed that their laws were to be universally obeyed and in no instance modified? Was not every law and stature of the civil code framed in accordance with what was good and expedient? Indeed, scarcely anything in this world can be found which would be good and expedient in every place, at every time, and for all persons. The laws and statutes of men therefore vary with place, time, and individuals. Many philosophers have taught that this should be so when expediency clearly demands it. The Lord and Master of all knowledge, who is master of the holy fathers and of the philosophers, changed in the New Testament many things He had commanded in the Old in order to teach us to do likewise, and to do it without misgivings. The apostolic canon proclaimed by the aforesaid holy fathers says this in so many words: 'It ought not to be considered reprehensible that human laws are sometimes changed with changing times; for even God Himself changed many things in the New Testament which He had commanded in the Old.' The rule of civil law puts it thus: 'In civil law every definition is dangerous; for what cannot be altered is inadequate.' And another rule says, 'In all our law a general principle is modified by an exception.'

Hence this was, is, and ought to be the way to establish laws: after a general law has been enacted for the common good, if it appears that anything unduly harsh or absurd or iniquitous results from applying that law strictly in a particular case under the rule, it has been and ought to be the custom in such a case to make a directly contrary decision, lest injustice arise from the general law. That is to say, a special law ought to be applied to a particular case and within limits, modifying the generally published law when a special situation arises.

(Pierre Dubois, *The Recovery of the Holy Land*, tr. W. I. Brandt, part I, pp. 106-7, Columbia University Press 1956.)

47a DANTE ALIGHIERI: THE NECESSITY FOR PEACE

The proper work of the human race, taken as a whole, is to set in action the whole capacity of that understanding which is capable of development: first in the way of speculation, and then, by its extension, in the way of action. And seeing that what is true of a part is true also of the whole, and that it is by rest and quiet that the individual man becomes perfect in wisdom and prudence; so the human race, by living in the calm and tranquillity of peace, applies itself most freely and easily to its proper work; a work which according to the saying, 'Thou has made him a little lower than the angels,' is almost divine. Whence it is manifest that of all things that are ordered to secure blessings to men, peace is the best. And hence the word which sounded to the shepherds from above was not riches, nor pleasure, nor honour, nor length of life, nor health, nor strength, nor beauty; but peace. For the heavenly host said: 'Glory to God in the highest, and on earth, peace to men of good will.' Therefore also, 'Peace be with you,' was the salutation of the Saviour of mankind. For it behoved Him, who was the greatest of saviours, to utter in His greeting the greatest of saving blessings. And this custom His disciples too chose to preserve; and Paul also did the same in his greetings, as may appear manifest to all.

Now that we have declared these matters, it is plain what is the better, nay the best, way in which mankind may attain to do its proper work. And consequently we have seen the readiest means by which to arrive at the point, for which all our works are ordered, as their ultimate end; namely, the universal peace, which is to be assumed as the first principle for our deductions. As we said, this assumption was necessary, for it is as a sign-post to us, that into it we may resolve all that has to be proved, as into a most manifest truth.

(Dante, *De Monarchia*, tr. F. C. Church, in R. W. Church, *Dante: An Essay*, Bk 1, ch. 4, pp. 184-5, Macmillan, London 1878.)

47b DANTE ALIGHIERI: ARGUMENTS FOR MONARCHY

The first question, then, is whether temporal Monarchy is necessary for the welfare of the world; and that it is necessary can, I think, be shown by the strongest and most manifest arguments; for nothing, either of reason or of authority, opposes me. Let us first take the authority of the Philosopher in his *Politics*. There, on his venerable authority, it is said that where a number of things are arranged to attain an end, it behoves one of them to regulate or govern the others, and the others to submit. And it is not only the authority of his illustrious name which makes this worthy of belief, but also reason, instancing particulars.

If we take the case of a single man, we shall see the same rule manifested in him: all his powers are ordered to gain happiness; but his understanding is what regulates and governs all the others; and otherwise he would never attain to happiness. Again, take a single household: its end is to fit the members thereof to live well; but there must be one to regulate and rule it, who is called the father of the family, or, it may be, one who holds his office. As the Philosopher says: 'Every house is ruled by the oldest.' . . .

If, again, we take a single city: its end is to secure a good and sufficient life to the citizens; but one man must be ruler in imperfect as well as in good forms of the state. If it is otherwise, not only is the end of civil life lost, but the city too ceases to be what it was. Lastly, if we take any one kingdom, of which the end is the same as that of a city, only with greater security for its tranquillity, there must be one king to rule and govern. For if this is not so, not only do his subjects miss their end, but the kingdom itself falls to destruction, according to that word of the infallible truth: 'Every kingdom divided against itself shall be brought to desolation.' If then this holds good in these cases, and in each individual thing which is ordered to one certain end, what we have laid down is true.

Now it is plain that the whole human race is ordered to gain some end, as has been before shown. There must, therefore, be one to guide and govern, and the proper title for this office is Monarch or Emperor. And so it is plain that Monarchy or the Empire is necessary for the welfare of the world.

And all is well and at its best which exists according to the will of the first agent, who is God. This is self-evident, except to those who deny that the divine goodness attains to absolute perfection. Now, it is the intention of God that all created things should represent the likeness of God, so far as their proper nature will admit. Therefore was it said: 'Let us make man in our image, after our likeness.' And though it could not be said that the lower part of creation was made in the image of God, yet all things may be said to be after His likeness, for what is the whole universe but the footprint of the divine goodness? The human race, therefore, is well, nay at its best state, when, so far as can be, it is made like unto God. But the human race is then most made like unto God when most it is one; for the true principle of oneness is in Him alone. Wherefore it is written: 'Hear, O Israel; the Lord thy God is one God.' But the race of man is most one when it is united wholly in one body, and it is evident that this cannot be, except when it is subject to one prince. Therefore in this subjection mankind is most made like unto God, and, in consequence, such a subjection is in accordance with the divine intention, and it is indeed well and best for man when this is so, as we showed at the beginning of this chapter.

Again, things are well and at their best with every son when he follows, so far as by his proper nature he can, the footsteps of a perfect father. Mankind is the son of heaven, which is most perfect in all its works; for it is 'man and the sun which produce man,' according to the second book on Natural Learning. The human race, therefore, is at its best when it imitates the movements of heaven, so far as human nature allows. And since the whole heaven is regulated with one motion, to wit, that of the *primum mobile*, and by one mover, who is God, in all its parts, movements, and movers (and this human reason readily seizes from science); therefore, if our argument be correct, the human race is at its best state when, both in its movements, and in regard to those who move it, it is regulated by a single Prince, as by the single movement of heaven, and by one law, as by the single motion. Therefore it is evidently necessary for the welfare of the world for there to be a Monarchy, or single Princedom, which men call the Empire.

(Dante, *De Monarchia*, op. cit., Bk 1, chs. 5, 8, 9, pp. 185–91.)

47c   DANTE ALIGHIERI: THE PROVIDENTIAL GOVERNMENT OF ROME

My answer then to the question is, that it was by right, and not by usurpation, that the Roman people assumed to itself the office of Monarchy, or, as men call it, the Empire, over all mankind. For in the first place it is fitting that the noblest people should be preferred to all others; the Roman people was the noblest; therefore it is fitting that it should be preferred to all others. By this reasoning I make my proof; for since honour is the reward of goodness, and since to be preferred is always honour, therefore to be preferred is always the reward of goodness. It is plain that men are ennobled for their virtues; that is, for their own virtues or for those of their ancestors. . . .

That people then, which conquered when all were striving hard for the Empire of the world, conquered by the will of God. For God cares more to settle a universal strife than a particular one; and even in particular contests the athletes sometimes throw themselves on the judgment of God, according to the common proverb: 'To whom God makes the grant, him let Peter also bless.' It cannot, then, be doubted that the victory in the strife for the Empire of the world followed the judgment of God. The Roman people, when all were striving for the Empire of the world, conquered; it will be plain that so it was, if we consider the prize or goal, and those who strove for it. The prize or goal was the supremacy over all men; for it is this that we call the Empire. None reached this but the Roman people. Not only were they the first, they were the only ones to reach the goal. . . .

(Dante, *De Monarchia*, op. cit., Bk 2, ch. 3, p. 216, ch. 9, pp. 239–40.)

47d   DANTE ALIGHIERI: ROMAN JUSTICE

I say, then, that if the Roman empire did not exist by right, Christ in being born presupposed and sanctioned an unjust thing. . . .

I prove the consequence thus: wherever a man of his own free choice carries out a public order, he countenances and persuades by his act the justice of that order; and seeing that acts are more forcible to persuade than words . . . therefore by this he persuades us more than if it were merely an approval in words. But Christ, as Luke who writes His story, says, willed to be born of the Virgin Mary under an edict of Roman authority, so that in that unexampled census of mankind, the Son of God, made man, might be counted as man: and this was to carry out that edict. Perhaps it is even more religious to suppose that it was of God that the decree issued through Caesar, so that He who had been such long years expected among men should Himself enroll himself with mortal man.

Therefore Christ, by His action, enforced the justice of the edict of Augustus, who then wielded the Roman power. And since to issue a just edict implies jurisdiction, it necessarily follows that He who showed that He thought an edict just, must also have showed that He thought the jurisdiction under which it was issued just; but unless it existed by right it were unjust. . . .

And if the Roman empire did not exist by right, the sin of Adam was not punished in Christ. This is false, therefore its contradictory is true. The falsehood of the consequent is seen thus. Since by the sin of Adam we were all sinners, as the Apostle says:—'Wherefore, as by one man sin entered into the world, and death by sin, and so death passed upon all men, for that all have sinned,'—then, if Christ had not made satisfaction for Adam's sin by his death, we should still by our depraved nature be the children of wrath. But this is not so. . . .

It is convenient that it should be understood that punishment is not merely penalty inflicted on him who has done wrong, but that penalty inflicted by one who has penal jurisdiction. And therefore a penalty should not be called punishment, but rather injury, except where it is inflicted by the sentence of a regular judge. Therefore the Israelites said unto Moses: 'Who made thee a judge over us?'

If, therefore, Christ had not suffered by the sentence of a regular judge, the penalty would not properly have been punishment; and none could be a regular judge who had not jurisdiction over all mankind; for all mankind was punished in the flesh of Christ, who 'hath borne our griefs and carried our sorrows,' as saith the Prophet Isaiah. And if the Roman empire had not existed by right, Tiberius Caesar, whose vicar was Pontius Pilate, would not have had jurisdiction over all mankind. It was for this reason that Herod, not knowing what he did, like Caiaphas, when he spoke truly of the decree of heaven, sent Christ to Pilate to be judged, as Luke relates in his gospel. For Herod was not the vicegerent of Tiberius, under the standard of the eagle, or the standard of the Senate; but only a king, with one particular kingdom given him by Tiberius, and ruling the kingdom committed to his charge under Tiberius.

Let them cease, then, to insult the Roman empire, who pretend that they are the sons of the Church; when they see that Christ, the bridegroom of the Church, sanctioned the Roman empire at the beginning and at the end of His warfare on earth. And now I think that I have made it sufficiently clear that it was by right that the Romans acquired to themselves the empire of the world.

(Dante, *De Monarchia*, op. cit., Bk 2, chs. 12, 13, pp. 251-5.)

47e DANTE ALIGHIERI: REFUTATION OF PAPAL ARGUMENTS

Those men to whom all our subsequent reasoning is addressed, when they assert that the authority of the Empire depends on the authority of the Church, as the inferior workman depends on the architect, are moved to take this view by many arguments, some of which they draw from Holy Scripture, and some also from the acts of the Supreme Pontiff and of the Emperor himself. Moreover, they strive to have some proof of reason.

For in the first place they say that God, according to the book of Genesis, made two great lights, the greater light to rule the day, and the lesser light to rule the night; this they understand to be an allegory, for that the lights are the two powers, the spiritual and the temporal. And then they maintain that as the moon, which is the lesser light, only has light so far as she receives it from the sun, so the temporal power only has authority as it receives authority from the spiritual power. . . .

I say then that, although the moon has not light of its own abundantly, unless it receives it from the sun, yet it does not therefore follow that the moon is from the sun. Therefore be it known that the being, and the power, and the working of the moon are all different things. For its being, the moon in no way depends on the sun, nor for its power, nor for its working, considered in itself. Its motion comes from its proper mover, its influence is from its own rays. For it has a certain light of its own, which is manifest at the time of an eclipse; though for its better and more powerful working it receives from the sun an abundant light, which enables it to work more powerfully.

Therefore I say that the temporal power does not receive its being from the spiritual power, nor its power which is its authority, nor its working considered in itself. Yet it is good that the temporal power should receive from the spiritual the means of working more effectively by the light of the grace which the benediction of the Supreme Pontiff bestows on it both in heaven and on earth. . . .

Again, from the first book of Kings they take the election and the deposition of Saul; and they say that Saul, an enthroned king, was deposed by Samuel, who, by God's command, acted in the stead of God, as appears from the text of Scripture. From this they argue that, as that Vicar of God had authority to give temporal power, and to take it away and bestow it on another, so now the Vicar of God, the bishop of the universal Church, has authority to give the sceptre of temporal power, and to take it away, and even to give it to another. And if this were so, it would follow without doubt that the authority of the Empire is dependent on the Church, as they say.

But we may answer and destroy this argument, by which they say that

Samuel was the Vicar of God: for it was not as Vicar of God that he acted, but as a special delegate for this purpose, or as a messenger bearing the express command of his Lord. For it is clear that what God commanded him, that only he did, and that only he said.·

Therefore we must recognise that it is one thing to be another's vicar, and that it is another to be his messenger or minister, just as it is one thing to be a doctor, and another to be an interpreter. For a vicar is one to whom is committed jurisdiction with law or with arbitrary power, and therefore within the bounds of the jurisdiction which is committed to him, he may act by law or by his arbitrary power without the knowledge of his lord. It is not so with a mere messenger, in so far as he is a messenger; but as the mallet acts only by the strength of the smith, so the messenger acts only by the authority of him that sent him. Although, then, God did this by His messenger Samuel, it does not follow that the Vicar of God may do the same. For there are many things which God has done and still does, and yet will do through angels, which the Vicar of God, the successor of Peter, might not do.

Certain persons say further that the Emperor Constantine, having been cleansed from leprosy by the intercession of Sylvester, then the Supreme Pontiff, gave unto the Church the seat of Empire which was Rome, together with many other dignities belonging to the Empire. Hence they argue that no man can take unto himself these dignities unless he receive them from the Church, whose they are said to be. From this it would rightly follow, that one authority depends on the other, as they maintain. . . .

This premiss then will I destroy; and as for their proof, I say that it proves nothing. For the dignity of the Empire was what Constantine could not alienate, nor the Church receive. And when they insist, I prove my words as follows: No man on the strength of the office which is committed to him, may do aught that is contrary to that office; for so one and the same man, viewed as one man, would be contrary to himself, which is impossible. But to divide the Empire is contrary to the office committed to the Emperor; for his office is to hold mankind in all things subject to one will: as may be easily seen from the first book of this treatise. Therefore it is not permitted to the Emperor to divide the Empire.

(Dante, *De Monarchia*, op. cit., Bk 3, ch. 4, pp. 264-5, ch. 6, pp. 269-70, ch. 10, pp. 271-3.)

47f DANTE ALIGHIERI: SECULAR AUTHORITY NOT CONFERRED BY THE CHURCH

We prove that the authority of the Church is not the cause of the authority of the Empire in the following manner. Nothing can be the cause of power in another thing when that other thing has all its power, while the first either does not exist, or else has no power of action. But the Empire had its power while the Church was either not existing at all, or else had no power of action. Therefore the Church is not the cause of the power of the Empire, and therefore not of its authority either, for power and authority mean the same thing. . . .

Again, if the Church had power to bestow authority on the Roman Prince, she would have it either from God, or from herself, or from some Emperor, or from the universal consent of mankind, or at least of the majority of mankind. There is no other crevice by which this power could flow down to the Church. But she has it not from any of these sources; therefore she has it not at all.

It is manifest that she has it from none of these sources; for if she had received it from God, she would have received it either by the divine or by the natural law: because what is received from nature is received from God; though the converse of this is not true. But this power is not received by the natural law; for nature lays down no law, save for the effects of nature, for God cannot fail in power, where he brings anything into being without the aid of secondary agents. Since therefore the Church is not an effect of nature, but of God who said: 'Upon this rock I will build my Church,' and elsewhere: 'I have finished the work which Thou gavest me to do,' it is manifest that nature did not give the Church this law.

Nor was this power bestowed by the divine law; for the whole of the divine law is contained in the bosom of the Old or of the New Testament, and I cannot find therein that any thought or care for worldly matters was commanded, either to the early or to the latter priesthood. Nay, I find rather such care taken away from the priests of the Old Testament by the express command of God to Moses, and from the priests of the New Testament by the express command of Christ to His disciples. But it could not be that this care was taken away from them, if the authority of the temporal power flowed from the priesthood; for at least in giving the authority there would be an anxious watchfulness of forethought, and afterwards continued precaution, lest he to whom authority had been given should leave the straight way.

Then it is quite plain that the Church did not receive this power from herself; for nothing can give what it has not. Therefore all that does anything, must be such in its doing, as that which it intends to do, as is stated in the book 'of Simple Being.' But it is plain that if the Church gave to herself this power, she had it not before she gave it. Thus she would have given what she had not, which is impossible.

But it is sufficiently manifest from what we have previously made evident that the Church has received not this power from any Emperor.

And further, that she had it not from the consent of all, or even of the greater part of mankind, who can doubt? seeing that not only all the inhabitants of Asia and Africa, but even the greater number of Europeans, hold the thought in abhorrence.

(Dante, *De Monarchia*, op. cit., Bk 3, chs. 13, 14, pp. 292-7.)

47g   DANTE ALIGHIERI: MAN'S TWO ENDS

Two ends, therefore, have been laid down by the ineffable providence of God for man to aim at: the blessedness of this life, which consists in the exercise of his natural powers, and which is prefigured in the earthly Paradise; and next, the blessedness of the life eternal, which consists in the fruition of the sight of

God's countenance, and to which man by his own natural powers cannot rise, if he be not aided by the divine light; and this blessedness is understood by the heavenly Paradise.

But to these different kinds of blessedness, as to different conclusions, we must come by different means. For at the first we may arrive by the lessons of philosophy, if only we will follow them, by acting in accordance with the moral and intellectual virtues. But at the second we can only arrive by spiritual lessons, transcending human reason, so that we follow them in accordance with the theological virtues, faith, hope, and charity. . . .

Therefore man had need of two guides for his life, as he had a twofold end in life; whereof one is the Supreme Pontiff, to lead mankind to eternal life, according to the things revealed to us; and the other is the Emperor, to guide mankind to happiness in this world, in accordance with the teaching of philosophy. . . .

And now, methinks, I have reached the goal which I set before me. I have unravelled the truth of the questions which I asked: whether the office of Monarchy was necessary to the welfare of the world; whether it was by right that the Roman people assumed to themselves the office of Monarchy; and, further, that last question, whether the authority of the Monarch springs immediately from God, or from some other. Yet the truth of this latter question must not be received so narrowly as to deny that in certain matters the Roman Prince is subject to the Roman Pontiff. For that happiness, which is subject to mortality, in a sense is ordered with a view to the happiness which shall not taste of death. Let, therefore, Caesar be reverent to Peter, as the first-born son should be reverent to his father, that he may be illuminated with the light of his father's grace, and so may be stronger to lighten the world over which he has been placed by Him alone, who is the ruler of all things spiritual as well as temporal.

(Dante, *De Monarchia*, op. cit., Bk 3, ch. 16, pp. 301-2, 304.)

48a MARSILIUS OF PADUA: DEFINITION OF LAW

Law may be considered in two ways. In one way it may be considered in itself, as it only shows what is just or unjust, beneficial or harmful; and as such it is called the science or doctrine of right (*juris*). In another way it may be considered according as with regard to its observance there is given a command coercive through punishment or reward to be distributed in the present world, or according as it is handed down by way of such a command; and considered in this way it most properly is called, and is, a law. It was in this sense that Aristotle also defined it in the last book of the *Ethics*, Chapter 8, when he said: 'Law has coercive force, for it is discourse emerging from prudence and understanding.' Law, then, is a 'discourse' or statement 'emerging from prudence and' political 'understanding,' that is, it is an ordinance made by political prudence, concerning matters of justice and benefit and their opposites, and having 'coercive force,' that is, concerning whose observance there is given a command which one is compelled to observe, or which is made by way of such a command.

Hence not all true cognitions of matters of civil justice and benefit are laws unless a coercive command has been given concerning their observance, or they have been made by way of a command, although such true cognition is necessarily required for a perfect law. Indeed, sometimes false cognitions of the just and the beneficial become laws, when there is given a command to observe them, or they are made by way of a command. An example of this is found in the regions of certain barbarians, who cause it to be observed as just that a murderer be absolved of civil guilt and punishment on payment of a fine. This, however, is absolutely unjust, and consequently the laws of such barbarians are not absolutely perfect. For although they have the proper form, that is, a coercive command of observance, they lack a proper condition, that is, the proper and true ordering of justice.

(Marsilius of Padua, *Defensor Pacis*, tr. A. Gewirth, in A. Gewirth, *Marsilius of Padua*, vol. II, ch. 10, p. 36, Columbia University Press 1956.)

48b MARSILIUS OF PADUA: THE LEGISLATOR

We must next discuss that efficient cause of the laws which is capable of demonstration. For I do not intend to deal here with that method of establishing laws which can be effected by the immediate act or oracle of God apart from the human will, or which has been so effected in the past. It was by this latter method, as we have said, that the Mosaic law was established; but I shall not deal with it here even insofar as it contains commands with regard to civil acts for the status of the present world. I shall discuss the establishment of only those laws and governments which emerge immediately from the decision of the human mind.

Let us say, to begin with, that it can pertain to any citizen to discover the law taken materially and in its third sense, as the science of civil justice and benefit. Such inquiry, however, can be carried on more appropriately and be completed better by those men who are able to have leisure, who are older and experienced in practical affairs, and who are called 'prudent men,' than by the mechanics who must bend all their efforts to acquiring the necessities of life. But it must be remembered that the true knowledge or discovery of the just and the beneficial, and of their opposites, is not law taken in its last and most proper sense, whereby it is the measure of human civil acts, unless there is given a coercive command as to its observance, or it is made by way of such a command, by someone through whose authority its transgressors must and can be punished. Hence, we must now say to whom belongs the authority to make such a command and to punish its transgressors. This, indeed, is to inquire into the legislator or the maker of the law.

Let us say, then, in accordance with the truth and the counsel of Aristotle in the *Politics*, Book III, Chapter 6, that the legislator, or the primary and proper efficient cause of the law, is the people or the whole body of citizens, or the weightier part thereof, through its election or will expressed by words in the general assembly of the citizens, commanding or determining that something be done or omitted with regard to human civil acts, under a temporal pain or punishment. By the 'weightier part' I mean to take into consideration the quantity and the quality of the persons in that community over which the law is made. The aforesaid whole body of citizens or the weightier part thereof is the legislator regardless of whether it makes the law directly by itself or entrusts the making of it to some person or persons, who are not and cannot be the legislator in the absolute sense, but only in a relative sense and for a particular time and in accordance with the authority of the primary legislator. And I say further that the laws and anything else established through election must receive their necessary approval by that same primary authority and no other, whatever be the case with regard to certain ceremonies or solemnities, which are required not for the being of the matters elected but for their well-being, since the election would be no less valid even if these ceremonies were not performed. Moreover, by the same authority must the laws and other things established through election undergo addition, subtraction, complete change, interpretation, or suspension, insofar as the exigencies of time or place or other circumstances make any such action opportune for the common benefit. And by the same authority, also, must the laws be promulgated or proclaimed after their enactment, so that no citizen or alien who is delinquent in observing them may be excused because of ignorance.

(Marsilius of Padua, *Defensor Pacis*, op. cit., Discourse 1, ch. 12, pp. 144-5.)

48c MARSILIUS OF PADUA: DEFINITION OF 'CHURCH'

In another sense this word 'church' means all the priests or bishops, deacons, and others who minister in the temple or the church taken in the preceding sense. And according to this meaning, only clergymen or ministers are commonly called persons of the church or churchmen.

Again in another sense, and especially among the moderns, this word 'church' means those ministers, priests or bishops and deacons, who minister in and preside over the metropolitan or principal church. This usage was long since brought about by the church of the city of Rome, whose ministers and overseers are the Roman pope and his cardinals. Through custom they have brought it about that they are called the 'church' and that one says the 'church' has done or received something when it is these men who have done or received or otherwise ordained something.

But the word 'church' has also another meaning which is the truest and the most fitting one of all, according to the first imposition of the word and the intention of these first imposers, even though this meaning is not so familiar nor in accord with modern usage. According to this signification, the 'church' means the whole body of the faithful who believe in and invoke the name of Christ, and all the parts of this whole body in any community, even the household. And this was the first imposition of this term and the sense in which it was customarily used among the apostles and in the primitive church. Hence the Apostle, in the first epistle to the Corinthians, Chapter 1, wrote: 'To the church of God that is at Corinth, to them that are sanctified in Christ Jesus, called to be saints, with all that invoke the name of our Lord Jesus

Christ.' Whereon the gloss according to Ambrose: 'Sanctified in baptism, and this in Christ Jesus.' And it was in accordance with this meaning that the Apostle spoke in the twentieth chapter of the Acts, to the Ephesian priests, when he said: 'Take heed to yourselves and to the whole flock, wherein the Holy Ghost hath placed you bishops, to rule the church of God which he hath purchased with his own blood.' And therefore all the Christian faithful, both priests and non-priests , are and should be called churchmen according to this truest and most proper signification, because Christ purchased and redeemed all men with his blood.

(Marsilius of Padua, *Defensor Pacis,* op. cit., Discourse 2, ch. 2, pp. 102–3.)

48d   MARSILIUS OF PADUA: HUMAN LAW AND DIVINE LAW

A bishop must hold fast the faithful word as he hath been taught, that he may be able by sound doctrine both to exhort and to convince the gainsayers. For there are many deceivers, whose mouths must be stopped.' With respect to the second question, as to whether or not such an act is prohibited by law, the ruler ought to ascertain this from the law, taken in its last and proper sense, in accordance with which he has to rule by authority of the legislator. And as for the third thing which must be known, as to whether or not the heretical word or deed has been spoken or done by the person accused of such crime, this can be judged by both the learned and the unlearned who are usually called 'witnesses,' through their external and internal senses. And then, after these matters have been ascertained, the ruler must deliver the judgment or sentence of conviction or acquittal, and exact or remit the penalty of the person who had been accused of the crime.

For a person is not punished by the ruler solely for sinning against divine law. For there are many mortal sins even against divine law, such as fornication, which the human legislator knowingly permits, and which the bishop or priest does not, cannot, and should not prohibit by coercive force. But if the heretic's sin against divine law is such as human law also prohibits, then he is punished in this world as a sinner against human law. For this latter sin is the precise or primary essential cause why a person is punished in this life, for where this is given, the effect is given, and where it is removed, so is the effect. And conversely, he who sins against human law will be punished in the other world as sinning aginst divine law, not as sinning against human law. For many things prohibited by human law are nevertheless permitted by divine law; for example, if a person does not repay a loan at the established date because of inability due to accident, illness, forgetfulness, or some other obstacle, he will not be punished for this in the other world by the coercive judge of divine law, and yet he is justly punished for it in this world by the coercive judge of human law. But if any person has sinned against divine law, he will be punished in the other world regardless of whether or not his act, such as fornication, is permitted by human law; and hence sinning against divine law is the primary essential cause, which in philosophy is usually called the cause 'as such,' of the punishment which is inflicted for and in the status of the future world; since where this cause is given, the effect is given, and where it is removed, so is the effect.

(Marsilius of Padua, *Defensor Pacis*, op. cit., Discourse 2, ch. 10, pp. 176-7.)

48e MARSILIUS OF PADUA: THE POPE AND THE GENERAL COUNCIL (i)

There is another, and proper, sense in which a bishop or church can be understood to be or to have been made the head and leader of the other bishops and churches. This proper headship is derived from the authority of the general council or the faithful legislator, and is of the following kind: It is the duty of the head bishop, although together with his college of priests (whom the faithful human legislator or the general council has willed to associate with him for this purpose), to notify the faithful legislator lacking a superior if any emergency of the faith, or clear need of the believers, is brought to his attention which, after due deliberation, seems absolutely to require the calling of a general council. The general council must then be assembled by the coercive command of the legislator, in the way we have said. It is also the head bishop's duty to hold the leading seat or position among all the bishops and clergymen at the general council, to propose questions for deliberation, to review the discussions in the presence of the whole council, to have the proceedings recorded in writing under authentic seals and notarial stamps, to communicate and publish these proceedings to all churches which so request, to know and teach these results and answer questions about them; and also, if any persons transgress the council's decisions with regard both to the faith and to church ritual or divine worship, as well as the other ordinances for the peace and unity of the believers, the head bishop has to punish such transgressors by some ecclesiastic censure, like excommunication or interdict or other similar penalty, but in accordance with the determination of the council and by its authority, and not by any coercive power inflicting punishment in person or in property in and for the status of the present world. It is also the duty of the head bishop, acting together with the weightier part or majority of the college which has been assigned to him by the legislator, to sit in judgment over bishops and churches (not subordinated to one another) with respect to spiritual controversies properly so called, according to the second and third senses of the term 'spiritual,' as indicated in Chapter II of this discourse, in which class fall the ordinances concerning church ritual which the council has made and ordered to be observed. However, if the other churches with comparative unanimity clearly feel that it is likely that this duty is being abused or neglected by the head church's bishop or college, then these other churches may lawfully appeal to the faithful human legislator, if the legislator, or the ruler by its authority, can conveniently correct such abuse or neglect; or else the other churches may request a general council, if, in the eyes of a majority of the other churches and in the judgment of the legislator, the case requires the calling of such a council.

We now come to the questions of what bishop and church it is most proper to choose as head of the others, and from which province or diocese this head ought to be chosen. Discussing first the qualities of the head bishop, let us say, in accordance with the truth, that he ought to be the one who excels all others in the goodness of his life and in sacred doctrine, although the former qualification should be given more weight. As to which place or province should have its church put over the others, it must be said that the headship should be given to that church whose college of priests or clergymen includes the most men who are most honorable in their lives and most pure in their sacred doctrine. But other things being equal, or not much different, it seems that the bishop and church of Rome (so long as that place remains habitable) deserves such headship for several reasons: first, because of the surpassing faith, love, and renown of the first bishop of Rome, who was St Peter or St Paul or both, and the great reverence paid to them by the other apostles; also, because of the venerable tradition of the city of Rome, its long leadership over the other cities, the great number of illustrious men, saints, and teachers of the Christian faith who lived at Rome in most periods from the very beginning of the established church, and the diligent care and assiduous labor which they exerted on behalf of the other churches to spread the faith and to preserve its unity; and again, because of the general monarchy and coercive authority which the people and ruler of Rome once exercised over all the rulers and peoples in the world, so that they alone had the power to make coercive commands binding on all men with respect to the observance of the faith and of the decisions of general councils, and to punish transgressors of these commands wherever they might be; and besides this, they greatly increased the size of the church, even though later on some of the Romans sometimes persecuted the Christians because of the malice of certain priests. And a final reason why it is appropriate that the bishop and church of Rome have the leadership is custom, inasmuch as all the believers have learned, or have become accustomed, to honor the bishop and church of Rome above all the rest, and to be stirred to virtuous living and the worship of God by their exhortations and admonitions, and to be recalled from vices and crimes by their reproofs, censures, and threats of eternal damnation.

As for the question of who has the authority to establish this leadership, the answer must be that this authority belongs to the general council or the faithful human legislator lacking a superior, to whom it also pertains to designate the clerical college or group which shall hold this leadership; and in accordance with this procedure, the city of Rome, so long as it endures and its people do not object, will lawfully and rightfully continue to hold the episcopal and ecclesiastic leadership, because of men's reverence for Saints Peter and Paul, and for the other reasons given above.

(Marsilius of Padua, *Defensor Pacis*, op. cit., Discourse 2, ch. 22, pp. 302-5.)

48f MARSILIUS OF PADUA: THE POPE AND THE GENERAL COUNCIL (ii)

Furthermore, that this authority to establish the headship belongs to the faithful human legislator or to the ruler by its authority, in accordance with the advice and decision of the general council, can be proved by the same reasonings and authorities whereby we showed in Chapter XXI of this discourse that to the legislator or the ruler belongs the authority to call a general council and to punish by coercive force all those, whether priests or laymen, who refuse to come to the council and who transgress the council's ordinances. All that has to be done is to change the minor term of the reasonings. And from these propositions it necessarily follows that it pertains to the same authority lawfully to correct the head bishop and his church or college, to suspend him from office, and to deprive or depose him therefrom if such action seems reasonable and expedient. . . .

At whose call shall the council of priests and of other suitable believers be assembled? This is a question which may well be asked, since no one of the priests or other believers is made leader of the rest, in the senses discussed above, by divine or by human law, because the human legislator is assumed to be everywhere infidel. We reply, in accordance with the sense of Scripture, that the general council is to be called or assembled by no bishop or priest having authority over the other priests and bishops, unless perhaps such authority may chance to have been granted to a priest by the above-mentioned majority of the believers. Suppose then, that no one priest has thus been put at the head of all the rest by the multitude of priests and other believers, but that it is nevertheless expedient to choose such a head or to make some other regulation with regard to the faith or to church ritual. In such case I say that either the call for this council will come from all the priests, if by chance every one of them is of such great love as to wish to arouse the others for the sake of the preservation and growth of the faith, so that they will all unhesitatingly and readily agree and consent to assemble in a council; or else, if by chance they are not all so loving as to wish to induce the others to assemble with them in a council, then the call will come from those who are more fervent in divine love than the rest, whereupon the other priests or laymen will heed their words and recognize the rightness of their counsels.

(Marsilius of Padua, *Defensor Pacis,* op. cit., Discourse 2, ch. 22, pp. 306-7.)

49 THE COUNCIL OF CONSTANCE

This holy Council of Constance. . . . declares, first that it is lawfully assembled in the Holy Spirit, that it constitutes a General Council, re-presenting the Catholic Church, and that therefore it has its authority immediately from Christ; and that all men, of every rank and condition, including the Pope himself, is bound to obey it in matters concerning the Faith, the abolition of the schism, and the reformation of the Church of God in its head and its members. Secondly it declares that any one, of any rank and condition, who shall contumaciously refuse to obey the orders, decrees, statutes or instructions, made or to be made by this holy Council, or by any other lawfully assembled general council . . . shall, unless he comes to a right frame of mind, be subjected to fitting penance and punished appropriately:

and, if need be, recourse shall be had to the other sanctions of the law. . . .

(Council of Constance, Decree: *Sacrosancta,* in H. Bettenson, ed., *Documents of the Christian Church,* p. 189, Oxford University Press, 1967.)

50 NICHOLAS OF CUSA

Every decree is rooted in natural law, and if a decree contradicts it it cannot be valid *(Decretum,* di.9, *Dicta Gratiani, 'cum ergo'* and *'constitutiones').* Whence, since natural law is naturally in the reason, every law is know to man in its root. The wiser and more eminent are chosen rulers of others for this reason: that they, being endowed with their natural clear reason, wisdom, and foresight, may discover just laws and through them rule others and settle disputes, that peace may be preserved (c.5, di.2). Whence it follows that those who are vigorous in reason are naturally lords and rulers of others, but not through coercive law or judgment rendered against the unwilling. Whence, since by nature all are free, every government—whether it consists in written law or in a living law in the prince— through which the subjects are coerced from evil deeds and their liberty is regulated to good by fear of punishment is based on agreement alone and the consent of the subjects. For if by nature men are equally powerful and equally free, the valid and ordained authority of one man naturally equal in power with the others cannot be established except by the choice and consent of the others, even as law also is established by consent (c.1, di.2; c.2, di.8, where it is said that 'there is a general compact of human society to obey its kings'). Now, since by a general compact human society has agreed to obey its kings, it follows that in a true order of government there should be an election to choose the ruler himself, through which election he is constituted ruler and judge of those who elect him; thus ordained and righteous lordships and presidencies are constituted through election.

(Nicholas of Cusa, *De Concordantia Catholica,* Bk 2, ch. 14, in E. Lewis, *Medieval Political Ideas,* p. 192, Routledge and Kegan Paul, London 1954.)

PART THREE

Modern Political Ideas

CHAPTER 13

Machiavelli

By the beginning of the sixteenth century the medieval order had been well-nigh destroyed. Although the papacy had recovered some of its prestige after the failure of the conciliar experiment, it was unable to exercise any substantial sovereignty in the states of western Europe. The medieval theory of the unity of Christendom had been eroded by the rise of national monarchies based on force, such as those in England, France and Spain. In these countries the political power of the nobility was declining and was being replaced by the power of the rising middle classes who saw their welfare best ensured by the protection of the king. In Italy, however, the medieval city state was still the prevailing political unit. At the time when Machiavelli wrote the important independent cities of Italy were: Milan, Venice, Florence, the Papal States and Naples.

Niccolo Machiavelli (1469-1527) was born in Florence in the same year that Lorenzo de Medici became the chief magistrate or dictator, ushering in a period of tyrannical government that lasted until 1494. In that year Lorenzo's successor, Piero, was expelled by the invading French armies of Charles VIII. As a consequence, the rule of the Medici family was replaced by that of Savonarola, a demagogic friar who attempted to impose on the Florentines his own version of the divine law. His end came in 1498 when he lost popular support and was burned at the stake. Machiavelli, for a time, had been impressed by Savonarola, but the latter's fall from power confirmed him in his view that the 'unarmed prophet' was ineffective and that political power rests upon force and fraud.

After the episode of Savonarola, the republic was restored and Machiavelli was elected to the post of Secretary to the Council of Ten, the 'foreign office' of Florence. He served the republic faithfully until its collapse in 1512 when the Medici tyranny was restored and Machiavelli driven into exile. During his fourteen years of political activity, Machiavelli was sent on many political and military missions from which he absorbed a great deal of knowledge about contemporary statecraft. In 1502 he met Cesare Borgia, the son of the most notorious of Renaissance popes, Alexander VI. Cesare's tactics in the campaign to subdue the rebellious aristocracy in the Romagna are recorded in *The Prince* where Machiavelli implies that only a leader with Cesare's qualities could raise Italy from its degradation and restore peace.

While in exile, Machiavelli found time to write a number of books, including two specifically concerned with politics: *The Prince* and *The Discourses on the First Ten Books of Titus Livius*. Both works were probably begun in 1513 although *The Discourses* took several years longer than the *Prince* to complete. Both are concerned with the establishment and maintenance of government, but whereas the *Discourses* is concerned with republican government, applicable to a relatively uncorrupted people, the *Prince* is concerned with the one-man rule of a principality, applicable to a corrupt people such as the Italians. In addition, both books are purportedly inductive in their method of argument; that is, Machiavelli bases his conclusions upon observations of facts—especially historical facts. Machiavelli believed that history tends to repeat itself in cycles, so that examples of political behaviour taken from the past would have current validity. Ancient Rome provided the best source of such examples since it had the longest and noblest history of all former states.

If history is cyclical, the degeneration of even the best state is inevitable. This fact indicates the limitations on even the most efficient ruler to control political events. Machiavelli uses the term *virtu* or prowess to signify the ability of a person to impose his will upon events. Even the most intelligent and resourceful ruler cannot expect to succeed more than about half the time. The other half is dominated by *fortuna* or chance, the element which cannot be predicted nor overcome by *virtu* (Ex. 51a).

The Prince

The *Prince* is by far the best known of Machiavelli's writings. It was written partly in order to impress Lorenzo de Medici with the author's qualities so that he might be brought back from exile to political office. Unfortunately for Machiavelli, there is no evidence that Lorenzo even saw the book dedicated to him, and it was not until 1532, well after Machiavelli's death, that the book was published. A more profound reason for its composition is expressed in the last chapter of the book where Machiavelli, in unusually emotional language, exhorts the Medici ruler to lead a unified Italy against the foreign invaders who had enslaved and degraded the Italian people (Ex. 51b).

The *Prince* has been rightly called a practical handbook of statecraft for rulers. It purports to show how political power may be achieved and maintained. The political techniques which it describes are by no means original; not only had Aristotle depicted in the *Politics* how tyrants maintain themselves in power, but most contemporary European rulers used such methods as a matter of course. What made Machiavelli's book so shocking to its readers was its frank unhypocritical acceptance that these methods were essential to the efficient Prince.

There are two implicit assumptions underlying the main theme of the *Prince*. The first is the ancient Greek view that the state is the highest form of human association, providing all that is necessary for human welfare. It follows from this assumption that reasons of state outweigh any other kind of moral obligation and that a settled political order must precede anything else, such as culture and the conventional virtues. The second basic assumpion is that of egoism. Of all the factors underlying human motivation, self-interest—particularly material self-interest—is by far the strongest. It therefore follows that princely *virtu* will involve assessment of the elements of self-interest in a political situation and act accordingly.

Politics and Ethics

In the fifteenth chapter of the *Prince*, Machiavelli explicitly declares his intention to examine political realities rather than imaginary ideals (Ex. 51c). He points to the undeniable fact that actual states are governed by non-virtuous men, and therefore a prince who wishes to maintain himself in power must 'learn how not to be virtuous'. A prince who always practises virtue will be at a total disadvantage in his dealings with other rulers who are likely to use evil means to gain their ends. Furthermore, the virtuous prince will bring about the downfall of his people as well as that of himself.

It was this reasoning which led Machiavelli to his concept of a double standard of ethics. The ordinary citizen can afford to act according to the canons of conventional morality; indeed he must do so if he is to live with others in society. For the prince, however, this luxury is impossible. His actions must always be governed by considerations of expediency. As an egoist, his self-interest is paramount, and it is satisfied if he maintains himself in power. Thus in Chapters 16 to 18, Machiavelli counsels the prince to be parsimonious rather than generous, cruel rather than compassionate (Ex. 51d), dishonest rather than honest (Ex. 51e). It is the apparently cynical advice given in these chapters which is responsible for Machiavelli's reputation as an immoral flatterer of tyrants.

The *Prince* was placed on the Index of Prohibited Books in 1557. In view of its anti-clerical sentiments it is surprising that this act was so belated. The Papal States were regarded by Machiavelli as largely responsible for the disunity of Italy, and there is an implication (more definitely stated in the *Discourses)* that Christian virtues such as humility and meekness have weakened the resolve of Italian armies. His most fundamental ethical theme, that the end justifies the means, was clearly inconsistent with Christian morality which must always hold that nothing can justify evil actions. As we have seen, Machiavelli was convinced that for a ruler to bind himself with the constraints of Christian virtue would be the quickest way to the destruction of the state and the ruin of its inhabitants. He considered that where the people were as corrupt and degraded as the Italians were, it was not immoral to suggest the means whereby law, order, decency and the conventional virtues might be re-established.

Machiavelli's works may be regarded as continuing the same line of secular thought which we have earlier noted in the writings of Pierre Dubois and Marsilius of Padua. There is nothing in the *Prince* about divine law or natural law, or indeed, any source of law other than the will of the prince himself. For the first time since the Greek city state, politics was seen as a science which was concerned with the state alone and the forces within it; it had nothing whatsoever to do with the systematic philosophies which were so typical of political speculation in the later Middle Ages. It is in that sense, as well as in his admiration for ancient Greece and Rome, that Machiavelli is a man of the Renaissance. One feature of the intellectual Renaissance was the tendency to compartmentalize areas of knowledge. Physics and chemistry, for instance, were beginning to be studied without reference to the authority of the Bible or the theologians. Machiavelli's writings about politics seem to conform to this trend. Politics is concerned with the conflict of men and social forces. It is only indirectly concerned with questions of morality, religion and legitimacy.

FURTHER READING

Text

N. Machiavelli: The *Prince*

Commentaries

J. Allen: *Political Thought in the Sixteenth Century* (Methuen 1960)

S. Anglo: *Machiavelli: A Dissection* (Gollancz 1969)

H. Butterfield: *The Statecraft of Machiavelli* (Bell 1940)

F. Chabod: *Machiavelli and the Renaissance* (Harper Torchbooks 1965)

D. L. Jensen (ed): *Machiavelli* (D. C. Heath, Lexington, Mass., 1960)

51a NICCOLO MACHIAVELLI: WHAT FORTUNE CAN EFFECT IN HUMAN AFFAIRS, AND HOW TO WITHSTAND HER

It is not unknown to me how many men have had, and still have, the opinion that the affairs of the world are in such wise governed by fortune and by God that men with their wisdom cannot direct them and that no one can even help them; and because of this they would have us believe that it is not necessary to labour much in affairs, but to let chance govern them. This opinion has been more credited in our times because of the great changes in affairs which have been seen, and may still be seen, every day, beyond all human conjecture. Sometimes pondering over this, I am in some degree inclined to their opinion. Nevertheless, not to extinguish our free will, I hold it to be true that fortune is the arbiter of one half of our actions, but that she still leaves us to direct the other half, or perhaps a little less. . . .

But confining myself more to the particular, I say that a prince may be seen happy to-day and ruined to-morrow without having shown any change of disposition or character. This, I believe, arises firstly from causes that have already been discussed at length, namely, that the prince who relies entirely upon fortune is lost when it changes. I believe also that he will be successful who directs his actions according to the spirit of the times, and that he whose actions do not accord with the times will not be successful. Because men are seen, in affairs that lead to the end which every man has before him, namely, glory and riches, to get there by various methods; one with caution, another with haste; one by force, another by skill; one by patience, another by its opposite; and each one succeeds in reaching the goal by a different method. . . .

I conclude therefore that, fortune being changeful and mankind steadfast in their ways, so long as the two are in agreement men are successful, but unsuccessful when they fall out, For my part I consider that it is better to be adventurous than cautious, because fortune is a woman, and if you wish to keep her under it is necessary to beat and ill-use her; and it is seen that she allows herself to be mastered by the adventurous rather than by those who go to work more coldly. She is, therefore, always, woman-like, a lover of young men, because they are less cautious, more violent, and with more audacity command her.

(Niccolo Machiavelli, *The Prince*, tr. W. K. Marriott, ch. 25, pp. 203–5, Everyman Library Edition, Dent, London, and E. P. Dutton, New York, 1908.)

51b NICCOLO MACHIAVELLI: AN EXHORTATION TO LIBERATE ITALY FROM THE BARBARIANS

Having carefully considered the subject of the above discourses, and wondering within myself whether the present times were propitious to a new prince, and whether there were the elements that would give an opportunity to a wise and virtuous one to introduce a new order of things which would do honour to him and good to the people of this country, it appears to me that so many things concur to favour a new prince that I never knew a time more fit than the present. . . .

Although lately some spark may have been shown by one, which made us think he was ordained by God for our redemption, nevertheless it was afterwards seen, in the height of his career, that fortune rejected him; so that Italy, left as without life, waits for him who shall yet heal her wounds and put an end to the ravaging and plundering of Lombardy, to the swindling and taxing of the Kingdom and of Tuscany, and cleanse those sores that for long have festered. It is seen how she entreats God to send some one who shall deliver her from these wrongs and barbarous insolencies. It is seen also that she is ready and willing to follow a banner if only someone will raise it.

Nor is there to be seen at present one in whom she can place more hope than in your illustrious house, with its valour and fortune, favoured by God and by the Church of which it is now the chief, and which could be made the head of this redemption. This will not be difficult if you will recall to yourself the actions and lives of the men I have named. And although they were great and wonderful men, yet they were men, and each one of them had no more opportunity than the present offers, for their enterprises were neither more just nor easier than this, nor was God more their friend than He is yours. . . .

This opportunity, therefore, ought not to be allowed to pass for letting Italy at last see her liberator appear. Nor can one express the love with which he would be received in all those provinces which have suffered so much from these foreign scourings, with what thirst for revenge, with what stubborn faith, with what devotion, with what tears. What door would be closed to him? Who would refuse obedience to him? What envy would hinder him? What Italian would refuse him homage? To all of us this barbarous dominion stinks. Let, therefore, your illustrious house take up this charge with that courage and hope with which all just enterprises are undertaken, so that under its standard our native country may be ennobled.

(Niccolo Machiavelli, op. cit., ch. 26, pp. 211-13, 216.)

51c NICCOLO MACHIAVELLI: CONCERNING THINGS FOR WHICH MEN, AND ESPECIALLY PRINCES, ARE PRAISED OR BLAMED

It remains now to see what ought to be the rules of conduct for a prince towards subject and friends. And as I know that many have written on this point, I expect I shall be considered presumptuous in mentioning it again, especially as in discussing it I shall depart from the methods of other people. But, it being my intention to write a thing which shall be useful to him who apprehends it, it appears to me more appropriate to follow up the real truth of a matter than the imagination of it; for many have pictured republics and principalities which in fact have never been known or seen, because how one lives is so far distant from how one ought to live, that he who neglects what is done for what ought to be done, sooner effects his ruin than his preservation; for a man who wishes to act entirely up to his professions of virtue soon meets with what destroys him among so much that is evil.

Hence it is necessary for a prince wishing to hold his own to know how to do wrong, and to make use of it or not according to necessity. Therefore, putting on one side imaginary things concerning a prince, and discussing those which are real, I say that all men when they are spoken of, and chiefly princes for being more highly placed, are remarkable for some of those qualities which bring them either blame or praise; and thus it is that one is reputed liberal, another miserly; . . . one is reputed generous, one rapacious; one cruel, one compassionate; one faithless, another faithful; one effeminate and cowardly, another bold and brave; one affable, another haughty; one lascivious, another chaste; one sincere, another cunning; one hard, another easy; one grave, another frivolous; one religious, another unbelieving, and the like. And I know that every one will confess that it would be most praiseworthy in a prince to exhibit all the above qualities that are considered good; but because they can neither be entirely possessed nor observed, for human conditions do not permit it, it is necessary for him to be sufficiently prudent that he may know how to avoid the reproach of those vices which would lose him his state; and also to keep himself, if it be possible, from those which would not lose him it; but this not being possible, he may with less hesitation abandon himself to them. And again, he need not make himself uneasy at incurring a reproach for those vices without which the state can only be saved with difficulty, for if everything is considered carefully, it will be found that something which looks like virtue, if followed, would be his ruin; whilst something else, which looks like vice, yet followed brings him security and prosperity.

(Niccolo Machiavelli, op. cit., ch. 15, pp. 121-3.)

51d NICCOLO MACHIAVELLI: CONCERNING LIBERALITY AND MEANNESS

Commencing then with the first of the above-named characteristics, I say that it would be well to be reputed liberal. Nevertheless, liberality exercised in a way that does not bring you the reputation for it, injures you; for if one exercises it honestly and as it should be exercised, it may not become known, and you will not avoid the reproach of its opposite. Therefore, any one wishing to maintain among men the name of liberal is obliged to avoid no attribute of magnificence; so that a prince thus inclined will consume in such acts all his property, and will be compelled in the end, if he wish to maintain the name of liberal, to unduly weigh down his people, and tax them, and do everything he can to get money. This will soon make him odious to his subjects, and becoming poor he will be little valued by any one; thus, with his liberality, having offended many and rewarded few, he is affected by the very first trouble and imperilled by whatever may be the first danger; recognising this himself, and wishing to draw back from it, he runs at once into the reproach of being miserly.

Therefore, a prince, not being able to exercise this virtue of liberality in such a way that it is recognised, except to his cost, if he is wise he ought not to fear the reputation of being mean, for in time he will come to be more considered than if liberal, seeing that with his economy his revenues are enough, that he can defend himself against all attacks, and is able to engage in enterprises without burdening his people; thus it comes to pass that he exercises liberality towards all from whom he does not take, who are numberless, and meanness towards those to whom he does not give, who are few.

Concerning Cruelty and Clemency, and whether it is better to be Loved than Feared

Coming now to the other qualities mentioned above, I say that every prince ought to desire to be considered clement and not cruel. Nevertheless he ought to take care not to misuse this clemency. Cesare Borgia was considered cruel; notwithstanding, his cruelty reconciled the Romagna, unified it, and restored it to peace and loyalty. And if this be rightly considered, he will be seen to have been much more merciful than the Florentine people, who, to avoid a reputation for cruelty, permitted Pistoia to be destroyed. Therefore a prince, so long as he keeps his subjects united and loyal, ought not to mind the reproach of cruelty; because with a few examples he will be more merciful than those who, through too much mercy, allow disorders to arise, from which follow murder or robbery; for these are wont to injure the whole people, whilst those executions which originate with a prince offend the individual only.

And of all princes, it is impossible for the new prince to avoid the imputation of cruelty, owing to new states being full of dangers. . . .

Upon this a question arises: whether it be better to be loved than feared or feared than loved? It may be answered that one should wish to be both, but, because it is difficult to unite them in one person, it is much safer to be feared than loved, when, of the two, either must be dispensed with. Because this is to be asserted in general of men, that they are ungrateful, fickle, false, cowards, coveteous, and as long as you succeed they are yours entirely; they will offer you their blood, property, life, and children, as is said above, when the need is far distant; but when it approaches they turn against you. And that prince who, relying entirely on their promises, has neglected other precautions, is ruined; because friendships that are obtained by payments, and not by greatness or nobility of mind, may indeed be earned, but they are not secured, and in time of need cannot be relied upon; and men have less scruple in offending one who is beloved than one who is feared, for love is preserved by the link of obligation which, owing to the baseness of men, is broken at every opportunity for their advantage; but fear preserves you by a dread of punishment which never fails.

Nevertheless a prince ought to inspire fear in such a way that, if he does not win love, he avoids hatred; because he can endure very well being feared whilst he is not hated, which will always be as long as he abstains from the property of his citizens and subjects and from their women. But when it is necessary for him to proceed against the life of some one, he must do it on proper justification and for manifest cause, but above all things he must keep his hands off the property of others, because men more quickly forget the death of their father than the loss of their patrimony. Besides, pretexts for taking away the property are never wanting; for he who has once begun to live by robbery will always find pretexts for seizing what belongs to others; but reasons for taking life, on the contrary, are more difficult to find and sooner lapse.

(Niccolo Machiavelli, op. cit., ch. 16, pp. 127-8, ch. 17, pp. 133-5.)

51e NICCOLO MACHIAVELLI: CONCERNING THE WAY IN WHICH PRINCES SHOULD KEEP FAITH

Every one admits how praiseworthy it is in a prince to keep faith, and to live with integrity and not with craft. Nevertheless our experience has been that those princes who have done great things have held good faith of little account, and have known how to circumvent the intellect of men by craft, and in the end have overcome those who have relied on their word. You must know there are two ways of contesting, the one by the law, the other by force; the first method is proper to men, the second to beasts; but because the first is frequently not sufficient, it is necessary to have recourse to the second. Therefore it is necessary for a prince to understand how to avail himself of the beast and the man. . . . A prince, therefore, being compelled knowingly to adopt the beast, ought to choose the fox and the lion; because the lion cannot defend himself against snares and the fox cannot defend himself against wolves. Therefore, it is necessary to be a fox to discover the snares and a lion to terrify the wolves. Those who rely simply on the lion do not understand what they are about. Therefore a wise lord cannot, nor ought he to keep faith when such observance may be turned against him, and when the reasons that caused him to pledge it exist no longer. If men were entirely good this precept would not hold, but because they are bad, and will not keep faith with you, you too are not bound to observe it with them. Nor will there ever be wanting to a prince legitimate reasons to excuse this non-observance. Of this endless modern examples could be given, showing how many treaties and engagements have been made void and of no effect through the faithlessness of princes; and he who has known best how to employ the fox has succeeded best.

But it is necessary to know well how to disguise this characteristic, and to be a great pretender and dissembler; and men are so simple, and so subject to present necessities, that he who seeks to deceive will always find some one who will allow himself to be deceived. One recent example I cannot pass over in silence. Alexander the Sixth did nothing else but deceive men, nor ever thought of doing otherwise, and he always found victims; for there never was a man who had greater power in asserting, or who with greater oaths would affirm a thing, yet would observe it less; nevertheless his deceits always succeeded according to his wishes, because he well understood this side of mankind.

Therefore it is unnecessary for a prince to have all the good qualities I have enumerated, but it is very necessary to appear to have them. And I shall dare to say this also, that to have them and always to observe them is injurious, and that to appear to have them is useful; to appear merciful, faithful, humane, religious, upright, and to be so, but with a mind so framed that should you

require not to be so, you may be able and know how to change to the opposite.
And you have to understand this, that a prince, especially a new one, cannot
observe all those things for which men are esteemed, being often forced, in
order to maintain the state, to act contrary to fidelity, friendship, humanity,
and religion. Therefore it is necessary for him to have a mind ready to turn itself accordingly as the winds and variations of fortune force it, yet, as I have
said above, not to diverge from the good if he can avoid doing so, but, if compelled, then to know how to set about it.

(Niccolo Machiavelli, op. cit., ch. 18, pp. 141-4.)

CHAPTER 14

The Reformation

Although Machiavelli's works were not without influence, they had little significance in the mainstream of sixteenth-century political thought. It is not until the seventeenth century in the writings of Hobbes that we find another major political work so little concerned with medieval notions of legitimacy. Most political ideas in the sixteenth century were offshoots from the religious struggles of the Protestant Reformation. In so far as political speculation derived from religion and the assumptions underlying such speculation were medieval in origin, it can be appreciated that, at least as far as political theory was concerned, the sixteenth century belongs rather more with the Middle Ages than with modern times.

Martin Luther (1483–1546)

The inspirer of the Reformation was not a political theorist but a theologian. Nevertheless, as a result of his involvement in sixteenth-century politics, Luther was driven into a position where he could not avoid making political statements. Luther's theological stance led him to reject the sacramental claims of the Church and the notion that the priesthood was necessary for salvation. His view was similar to that of St Paul and St Augustine: that man is saved through faith alone, and true faith is a gift to men from God. Man is so corrupted through original sin that no amount of good works could possibly lead to the acquisition of the merit necessary for the soul's salvation.

Luther's political utterances also show his links with St Augustine and the early Christian tradition. He conceives of government as a divinely ordained consequence of human sin, not as part of the natural order. It exists because most men are evil and can be restrained from sin only by force. Luther's doctrine of the 'two kingdoms' also has obvious similarities with Augustine's two cities. In his treatise on *Secular Authority*, Luther states that the members of the kingdom of God—the 'true believers in Christ'—need no secular government since they will act virtuously in any case. However, as the number of true Christians is small, God has ordained secular government to restrain the vast majority of wicked people. Even the true Christians must submit to the secular sword because their submission increases the prestige, and hence the value, of law and government (Ex. 52a).

It followed for Luther, as it had for the early Christians, that as secular authority was ordained by God to repress sin, then it must be unquestioningly obeyed at all times except when it commanded a man to sin. In his open letter to the rebellious peasants in Swabia, *An Admonition to Peace* (Ex. 52b), Luther quotes the usual passages from Paul and Peter and declares that even the wickedness and injustice of rulers cannot excuse rebellion. His consistent emphasis upon the subject's duty of obedience was perhaps motivated by his belief that rebellion endangers the social order, the basis of every man's security, and increases the opportunity for the wicked to sin.

Luther was less consistent in his views on the relation of the secular ruler to religious beliefs. Before the German peasants' revolt of 1525, his attitude was one of toleration. He did not consider it desirable that questions of belief should be decided nor orthodoxy defended by the secular authorities. 'Heresy', he wrote in 1523, 'can never be contained by force.' In the year 1525, however, he urged the suppression of the doctrines of the Anabaptists, a religious sect associated with the peasants' revolt. In later years Luther's intolerance developed to the point that in 1533 he declared it the duty of the secular ruler to suppress by force all false doctrines.

Jean Calvin (1509–1564)

Whereas Luther's political views were expounded in a series of tracts responding to particular political circumstances, Calvin's theological and political ideas were represented as a coherent whole in his *Institutes of the Christian Religion*. This book, first published in 1536, went into seven subsequent editions with the final one in 1559, thus reflecting the development of this thought. His theology, like Luther's, has its roots in early Christianity, especially in the thought of St Augustine. He stresses original sin to an even greater extent than does Luther, conceiving it as the defect in man which condemns him to eternal damnation. Only if God mercifully predestines some men to salvation can hell be avoided. For those not elected—the 'reprobate'—such a destiny is inevitable as they are specifically predestined for damnation.

This harsh doctrine of predestination is little different from that of Augustine. Man is predestined to be saved not because he is good but in order that he might be good. A person who, through divine grace, has received the gift of true faith from God is made individually aware of his election. It is this awareness which relieves him from anxiety and renders him capable of living a morally good life. The elect form a group bound together by the realization of their moral superiority and as such must provide leadership and a model for the rest of society. Calvin, as well as Luther, conceived of the Church as the community of all Christians. Its function is to provide spiritual guidance for its members in accordance with the will of God as revealed in the Scriptures. Where Calvinistic churches were established, as in Geneva, the officers of the Church were elected, examined and nominated by the pastors, and approved by the Church community.

Calvin saw the state and government as performing an important role in his scheme. Unlike Luther, who only gradually came to accept that the state should support the true religion, Calvin always recognized the need for co-operation between secular and spiritual authorities. In the passage quoted from his *Institutes of the Christian Religion* (Ex. 53), he points out that government is necessary as long as the temporal life exists. Its function is primarily to promote the true religion and to defend the Church. The theocratic implications of this statement, which subordinates the state to the Church, were exemplified in the constitution of Geneva in the latter half of the sixteenth century.

Calvin's view of the origin of the state again reflects his Augustinian outlook. It is a divinely ordained remedy for sin and is the agency through which men are made to conform as far as possible to the divine will. A tyrannical ruler could well be part of God's punishment for human sin and thus must not be resisted, although where his commands conflict with those of God, he must be passively disobeyed.

Unlike Luther, who seems never to have even hinted that rebellion against the government could ever be possible, Calvin does seem to have modified his apparent defence of absolutism. He declares that where special officers exist, whose function it is to protect the liberty of the people, they may restrain kings from acting oppressively. He instances the ephors of Sparta and the tribunes of Rome from the past, and the assembled Estates of the Realm as a contemporary example. This remarkable exception to his theory of obedience is not developed by him, but it could be argued that where Calvinists found themselves in a position where resistance to the government was advantageous, it was these few statements of their founder which provided them with the basis of their justifications for rebellion.

Theories of Rebellion

The first deviation from the Reformers' doctrines of passive obedience was, unexpectedly, made by the Lutherans in the German city of Magdeburg. The *Bekenntnis* (*Confession*) which appeared in 1550 was a treatise attempting to justify the resistance of the Magdeburg Lutherans to the Interim of Charles V. After 1555, however, Lutheranism was so firmly established in Germany that it no longer needed a theory of rebellion.

Calvinists found themselves in quite a different situation. In Scotland and France they were confronted by Catholic monarchs who were hostile to their religion. Consequently in both countries there developed crude theories of resistance bearing a distinct resemblance to the theory of the Magdeburg Treatise. For example, John Knox in Scotland and Christopher Goodman, an English Calvinist exile in Geneva, both produced tracts in 1558 which argued that impious and unjust rulers should be forcibly resisted. All of these early theories based their claim to resist the king on the grounds that the authority of the ruler, which is derived from God, is limited to acting for the common good. It is the duty of the people and particularly of the nobility to prevent a ruler from acting evilly by overthrowing him if necessary.

Such theories were clearly in the late medieval tradition of Aquinas and his successors and the same may be said of their later development into the theory of contract. Possibly the first important example of the anti-monarchical argument to incorporate the contract theory of government was that of George Buchanan whose *De Jure Regni apud Scotos (The Law of Rulership as it pertains to the Scots)* was written about 1570 in order to justify the deposition of Mary Stuart. This was followed by two anonymous Huguenot tracts: *Du Droit des Magistrats sur les Sujets (The Right of Magistrates over their Subjects)*, almost certainly written by Calvin's friend Theodore Beza in 1574, and the *Vindiciae Contra Tyrannos (A Defence of Liberty against Tyrants)*, probably written by Hubert Languet in 1579. This latter book became the most famous of all the Huguenot political writings and contains the most interesting example of the theory of contract of government in the sixteenth century.

The Vindiciae Contra Tyrannos

The book is divided into four parts, each concerned with the answer to a different question. The first question asks whether subjects are required to obey a ruler who commands them to act against God. The answer to this is obviously a negative since no Christian writer could ever have argued that one should obey an order to sin.

The second question is more controversial. It asks whether it is lawful to resist a prince who infringes the law of God or ruins the Church (Ex. 54a). The answer involves the discussion of a contract which is presumed to exist between God on the one side, and the king and the people jointly on the other. The purpose of the covenant (or contract) was that the worship of God should be maintained. As the king and the people are jointly responsible for the maintenance of religion, should either be negligent, God may inflict the penalty of damnation on the innocent party as much as on the guilty. Hence each of the co-contractors has an interest in ensuring that the other performs his duty. It follows that should an impious king neglect or oppress the Church, the people are authorized to restrain or punish him.

The third question asks whether it is lawful to resist a prince who oppresses or ruins the state, and if so, how far resistance may be extended (Ex. 54b). The answer is that such a prince may lawfully be resisted and indeed killed. Justification for resistance is provided by the existence of a second contract: between the ruler and the people. A king is instituted by God acting through the people who actually establish him in power. He contracts unconditionally to rule justly for the sake of the people. The people, on the other hand, contract conditionally to obey the ruler so long as he fulfils the contract to reign justly. Should the ruler break his agreement and become tyrannical the people are absolved from allegiance to him.

The theory that the people have a right to resist a tyrant is reminiscent of the similar theory held by Aquinas, particularly as both are hedged about with qualifications. Armed resistance should not be attempted until every other means has failed. Only a usurper may be killed by a citizen since he is not a party to any contract and has no right to rule. When a tyrant has been elected lawfully, only the people as a corporate body may resist and their collective action can only take place if it is instigated by their natural leaders: the magistrates, nobles or estates. It is important to note that the *Vindiciae* was not a theory of popular resistance to oppression. The individual was subject to the rule of passive obedience that Calvin had emphasized. In spirit the book was aristocratic and medieval, emphasizing the rights of corporate bodies against the king.

The fourth question asks whether neighbouring princes are bound to help the oppressed subjects of another prince. This question, again answered affirmatively, was designed to justify the aid given to the French Protestants by the princes of Germany. The answer contains no important theoretical implications.

Althusius (1557-1638)

The *Politica Methodica Digesta* (the *Politics*) of Johannes Althusius, first published in 1603, continues the sequence of Calvinist anti-royalist contractual theories. At the same time it can be regarded as an early example of a 'social contract' theory of society which prefigured the better known theories of Hobbes and Locke in the later seventeenth century.

However, this latter parallel cannot be drawn too closely. The typical social contract theory of the seventeenth century postulated an agreement between individual men to escape from an unsatisfactory natural state. Althusius regards men as naturally social and political animals whose association with other men, although implicitly contractual, is not artificial. Moreover, the basic unit which associates with others is not the individual but the family, and this is only one of a large number of natural associations such as the local community, the province and the state (Ex. 55a). The state, therefore, comes into being by a contract not between individuals but between associations.

Like Bodin (q. v.), Althusius considered sovereignty to be the hallmark of the state. Unlike Bodin, however, he considered that sovereignty remained with the corporate community and could not be alienated. Government, therefore, is established by a second contract and its authority is regulated by the law of the state (Ex. 55b). Should the ruler act in such a way as to frustrate the purpose for which he was installed—the common good—he may be resisted and, if necessary, deposed. The right of resistance is given not to the people individually, but to the magistrates who guard the interests of the community (Ex.55c). Clearly Althusius has in mind Calvin's 'inferior magistrates' who alone are given the right to instigate rebellion against tyranny.

The Jesuits

The Society of Jesus was the main agency of the Counter-Reformation. Its ultimate aim was to restore, as far as possible, the spiritual supremacy of the pope over Christendom. The Jesuits' more immediate aim, therefore, was to stop the spread of Protestantism, and one way to accomplish this was to provide theoretical justifications for the overthrow of Protestant rulers. The Jesuit theories of rebellion which were produced in the late sixteenth and early seventeenth centuries were, at least in one respect, very similar to those of their Protestant opponents: both used the idea of a contract as justification for resisting tyranny. In several respects, however, the Jesuit theories have a more modern ring to them: the origin of society as well as of government is examined, the authority of the king is from the people and not from God, and the right of resistance is given to the subjects, in some cases to individuals.

The most well-known Jesuit writers of the period were Robert Bellarmine, Juan de Mariana and Francisco Suarez. Bellarmine in the *Disputations* (1586) emphasizes the right of the pope to depose a tyrant along the same theoretical lines as Thomas Aquinas. Mariana in *De Rege et Regis Institutione (On Rulership and the Royal Institution, 1598)* has an interesting account of a pre-social state of nature from which government eventually arose, and advocates tyrannicide by individual citizens.

Perhaps the most well-formulated of the Jesuit theories was that of Francisco Suarez in his *Tractatus de Legibus ac Deo Legislatore (On*

Laws and God the Lawgiver, 1611*).* Suarez was mainly concerned to construct a philosophy of law closely based on Aquinas, and his political ideas were a by-product of this task. He conceives of the state as conforming to the natural need of man for society and originating in agreement between heads of families who sacrificed their freedom for the sake of the common good (Ex. 56). The organized community thus brought into existence possesses an inherent authority to rule itself. Political authority, therefore, is derived from the community and not from God, but as government can hardly be performed by the whole community it must be transferred by the consent of the community to a ruler. There is a virtual contract between the community and the ruler by which the king undertakes to rule for the benefit of all according to the natural law, and the people undertake to obey him. If he becomes a tyrant he may be deposed by the community to whom governmental authority has reverted.

FURTHER READING

Texts
M. Luther: *Concerning Secular Authority*
       An Admonition to Peace
J. Calvin: *The Institutes of the Christian Religion*
Junius Brutus (H. Languet): *Vindiciae Contra Tyrannos*, tr. H. J. Laski
    (Bell 1924)
J. Althusius: *The Politics*, tr. F. S. Carney (Eyre & Spottiswoode 1965)
F. Suarez: *On Laws and God the Lawgiver* (Clarendon Press 1944)

Commentaries
J. Allen: *A History of Political Thought in the Sixteenth Century*
    (Methuen 1960)
J. N. Figgis: *Political Thought from Gerson to Grotius* (Harper
    Torchbooks, NY, 1960)
F. J. C. Hearnshaw (ed): *The Social and Political Ideas of Some Great
    Thinkers of the Renaissance and the Reformation* (Dawsons 1967)
S. S. Wolin: *Politics and Vision* (Allen & Unwin 1961)

52a MARTIN LUTHER: SECULAR AUTHORITY

III. We must divide all the children of Adam into two classes; the first belong to the kingdom of God, the second to the kingdom of the world. Those belonging to the kingdom of God are all true believers in Christ and are subject to Christ. For Christ is the King and Lord in the kingdom of God, as the second Psalm and all the Scriptures say. For this reason He came into the world, that He might begin God's kingdom and establish it in the world. Therefore He says before Pilate, 'My kingdom is not of the world but whoever is of the truth hears My voice'; and continually in the Gospel He refers to the kingdom of God and says, 'Amend your ways, the kingdom of God is at hand.' Likewise, 'Seek first the kingdom of God and His righteousness.' He also calls the Gospel a Gospel of the kingdom, for the reason that it teaches, governs, and contains God's kingdom.

Now observe, these people need no secular sword or law. And if all the world were composed of real Christians, that is, true believers, no prince, king, lord, sword, or law would be needed. For what were the use of them, since Christians have in their hearts the Holy Spirit, who instructs them and causes them to wrong no one, to love every one, willingly and cheerfully to suffer injustice and even death from every one. Where every wrong is suffered and every right is done, no quarrel, strife, trial, judge, penalty, law, or sword is needed. Therefore, it is not possible for the secular sword and law to find any work to do among Christians, since of themselves they do much more than its laws and doctrines can demand. Just as Paul says in I Timothy i, 'The law is not given for the righteous, but for the unrighteous.'. . .

IV. All who are not Christians belong to the kingdom of the world and are under the law. Since few believe and still fewer live a Christian life, do not resist the evil, and themselves do no evil, God has provided for non-Christians a different government outside the Christian estate and God's kingdom, and has subjected them to the sword, so that, even though they would do so, they cannot practice their wickedness, and that, if they do, they may not do it without fear nor in peace and prosperity. Even so a wild, savage beast is fastened with chains and bands, so that it cannot bite and tear as is its wont, although it gladly would do so; whereas a tame and gentle beast does not require this, but without any chains and bands is nevertheless harmless. If it were not so, seeing that the whole world is evil and that among thousands there is scarcely one true Christian, men would devour one another, and no one could preserve wife and child, support himself and serve God; and thus the world would be reduced to chaos. For this reason God has ordained the two governments; the spiritual, which by the Holy Spirit under Christ makes Christians and pious people, and the secular, which restrains the unchristian and wicked so that they must needs keep the peace outwardly, even against their will. So Paul interprets the secular sword, Romans xiii, and says it is not a terror to good works, but to the evil. And Peter says it is for the punishment of evil doers. . . .

V. But perhaps you will say, Since Christians do not need the secular sword and the law, why does Paul say to all Christians, in Romans xiii, 'Let all souls be subject to power and authority'? And St Peter says, 'Be subject to every human ordinance,' etc, as quoted above. I answer, as I have said, that Christians, among themselves and by and for themselves, need no law or sword, since it is neither necessary nor profitable for them. Since, however, a true Christian lives and labors on earth not for himself, but for his neighbor, therefore, the whole spirit of his life impels him to do even that which he need not do, but which is profitable and necessary for his neighbor. Because the sword is a very great benefit and necessary to the whole world, to preserve peace, to punish sin and to prevent evil. he submits most willingly to the rule of the sword, pays tax, honors those in authority, serves, helps, and does all he can to further the government, that it may be sustained and held in honor and fear. Although he needs none of these things for himself and it is not necessary for him to do them, yet he considers what is for the good and profit of others, as Paul teaches in Ephesians v. . . .

(Martin Luther, *Of Secular Authority*, in *The Works of Martin Luther*, Fortress Press, Philadelphia 1930.)

52b MARTIN LUTHER: OBEDIENCE TO AUTHORITY

For here stands God's Word, and says through the mouth of Christ, 'He who takes the sword shall perish by the sword.' That means nothing else than that no one, by his own violence shall arrogate authority to himself; but as Paul says, 'Let every soul be subject to the higher powers with fear and reverence.'

How can you get over these sayings and laws of God, when you boast that you are acting according to divine law, and yet take the sword in your own hands, and revolt against the 'higher powers' that are ordained of God? Do you not think that Paul's judgment in Romans xiii will strike you, 'He that withstands the ordinance of God shall receive condemnation'? That is 'bearing God's name in vain'; alleging God's law and withstanding God's law, under His name. O have a care, dear sirs! It will not turn out that way in the end.

In the third place, you say that the rulers are wicked and intolerable, for they will not allow us the Gospel, and they oppress us too hard by the burdens they lay on our temporal goods, and they are ruining us body and soul. I answer: The fact that the rulers are wicked and unjust does not excuse tumult and rebellion, for to punish wickedness does not belong to everybody, but to the worldly rulers who bear the sword. Thus Paul says in Romans xiii, and Peter in I Peter iii, that they are ordained of God for the punishment of the wicked. Then, too, there is the natural law of all the world, which says that no one may be judge in his own cause or take his own revenge. The proverb is true, 'He who resists is wrong,' and the other proverb, 'He who resists makes strife.' The divine law agrees with this, and says, in Deuteronomy xxxii, 'Vengeance is mine, I will repay, saith the Lord.' Now you cannot deny that your rebellion proceeds in such a way that you make yourselves your own judges, and avenge yourselves, and are unwilling to suffer any wrong. That is contrary not only to Christian law and the Gospel, but also to natural law and all equity.

(Martin Luther, *An Admonition to Peace: Reply to the Twelve Articles of the Peasants*, op. cit.)

53 JEAN CALVIN

Having already stated that man is the subject of two kinds of government, and having sufficiently discussed that which is situated in the soul, or the inner man, and relates to eternal life, we shall now say something of the other kind which relates to civil justice and the regulation of the external conduct. . . . In the first place, before we enter on the subject itself, it is necessary for us to recur to the distinction which we have already established. lest we fall into an error very common in the world, and injudiciously confound together these two things the nature of which is altogether different.

For some men, when they hear that the Gospel promises a liberty which acknowledges no king or magistrate among them, but submits to Christ alone, think they can enjoy no advantage of their liberty while they see any power exalted above them. They imagine, therefore, that nothing will prosper unless the whole world be modeled in a new form, without any tribunals or laws, or magistrates, or anything of a similar kind which they consider injurious to their liberty. But he who knows how to distinguish between the body and the soul, between this present transitory life and the future eternal one, will find no difficulty in understanding that the spiritual kingdom of Christ and civil government are things very different and remote from each other. . . .

Yet this distinction does not lead us to consider the whole system of civil government as a polluted thing which has nothing to do with Christian men. But as we have just suggested that this kind of government is distinct from that spiritual and internal reign of Christ, so it ought to be known that they are in no respect at variance with each other. For that spiritual reign, even now upon earth, commences within us some preludes of the heavenly kingdom, and in this mortal and transitory life affords us some prelibations of immortal and incorruptible blessedness; but this civil government is designed, as long as we live in this world, to cherish and support the external worship of God, to preserve the pure doctrine of religion, to defend the constitution of the Church, to regulate our lives in a manner requisite for the society of men, to form our manners to civil justice, to promote our concord with each other, and to establish general peace and tranquillity—all of which I confess to be superfluous if the kingdom of God, as it now exists in us, extinguishes the present life. But if it is the will of God that while we are aspiring toward our true country, we be pilgrims on the earth, and if such aids are necessary to our pilgrimage, they who take them from man deprive him of his human nature.

Nor let anyone think it strange that I now refer to human policy the charge of the due maintenance of religion, which I may appear to have placed beyond the jurisdiction of men. For I do not allow men to make laws respecting religion and the worship of God now any more than I did before, though I approve of civil government which provides that the true religion contained in the law of God be not violated and polluted by public blasphemies with impunity. . . . Let us, therefore, examine, first, the function of a magistrate, whether it be a legitimate calling and approved by God, the nature of the duty, and the extent of the power; secondly, by what laws Christian government ought to be regulated; and lastly, what advantage the people derive from the laws, and what obedience they owe to the magistrate. . . .

Here it is necessary to state in a brief manner the nature of the office of magistracy, as described in the word of God, and wherein it consists. If the Scripture did not teach that this office extends to both tables of the law, we might learn it from heathen writers; for not one of them has treated of the office of magistrates, of legislation, and civil government, without beginning with religion and Divine worship. And thus they have all confessed that no government can be happily constituted unless its first object be the promotion of piety, and that all laws are preposterous which neglect the claims of God and merely provide for the interests of men. Therefore, as religion holds the first place among all the philosophers, and as this has always been regarded by the universal consent of all nations, Christian princes and magistrates ought to be ashamed of their indolence if they do not make it the object of their most serious care. We have already shown that this duty is particularly enjoined upon them by God; for it is reasonable that they should employ their utmost efforts in asserting and defending the honor of Him whose vicegerents they are and by whose favor they govern. And the principal commendations given in the Scripture to the good kings are for having restored the worship of God when it had been corrupted or abolished, or for having devoted their attention to religion, that it might flourish in purity and safety under their reigns. On the contrary, the sacred history represents it as one of the evils arising from anarchy, or a want of good government, that when 'there was no king in Israel, every man did that which was right in his own eyes.' These things evince the folly of those who would wish magistrates to neglect all thoughts of God, and to confine themselves entirely to the administration of justice among men, as though God appointed governors in his name to decide secular controversies, and disregarded that which is of far greater importance—the pure worship of himself according to the rule of his law.

The first duty of subjects toward their magistrates is to entertain the most honorable sentiments of their function, which they know to be a jurisdiction delegated to them from God, and on that account to esteem and reverence them as God's ministers and vicegerents. For there are some persons to be found who show themselves very obedient to their magistrates and have not the least wish that there were no magistrates for them to obey, because they know them to be so necessary to the public good, but who, nevertheless, consider the magistrates themselves as no other than necessary evils. But something more than this is required of us by Peter when he commands us to 'honor the king'; and by Solomon, when he says, 'Fear thou the Lord and the king'; for Peter, under the term 'honor,' comprehends a sincere and candid esteem; and Solomon, by connecting the king with the Lord, attributes to him a kind of sacred veneration and dignity. . . .

Now, as we have hitherto described a magistrate who truly answers to his title—who is the father of his country and, as the poet calls him, the pastor of his people, the guardian of peace, the protector of justice, the avenger of innocence; he would justly be deemed insane who disapproved of such a government. But, as it has happened, in almost all ages, that some princes, regardless of everything to which they ought to have directed their attention and provision, give themselves up to their pleasures in indolent exemption from every care; others absorbed in their own interest, expose to sale all laws, privileges, rights, and judgments; others plunder the public wealth which they afterwards lavish in mad prodigality; others commit flagrant outrages, pillaging houses, violating virgins and matrons, and murdering infants; many persons cannot be persuaded that such ought to be acknowledged as princes whom, as far as possible, they ought to obey. . . . And certainly the minds of men have always been naturally disposed to hate and execrate tyrants as much as to love and reverence legitimate kings.

But, if we direct our attention to the word of God, it will carry us much farther; even to submit to the government, not only of those princes who discharge their duty to us with becoming integrity and fidelity, but of all who possess the sovereignty, even though they perform none of the duties of their function. For, though the Lord testifies that the magistrate is an eminent gift of his liberality to preserve the safety of men, and prescribes to magistrates themselves the extent of their duty, yet he at the same time declares that whatever be their characters, they have their government only from him; that those who govern for the public good are true specimens and mirrors of his beneficence; and that those who rule in an unjust and tyrannical manner are raised up by him to punish the iniquity of the people; that all equally possess that sacred majesty with which he has invested legitimate authority.

But whatever opinion be formed of the acts of men, yet the Lord equally executed his work by them when he broke the sanguinary scepters of insolent kings and overturned tyrannical governments. Let princes hear and fear. But, in the meanwhile, it behooves us to use the greatest caution, that we do not despise or violate that authority of magistrates which is entitled to the greatest veneration, which God has established by the most solemn commands, even though it reside in those who are most unworthy of it, and who, as far as in them lies, pollute it by their iniquity. For though the correction of tyrannical domination is the vengeance of God, we are not, therefore, to conclude that it is committed to us who have received no other command than to obey and suffer. This observation I always apply to private persons. For if there be, in the present day, any magistrates appointed for the protection of the people and the moderation of the power of kings, such as were, in ancient times, the Ephori, who were a check upon the kings among the Lacedaemonians, or the the popular tribunes upon the consuls among the Romans, or the Demarchi upon the senate among the Athenians; or with power such as perhaps is now possessed by the three estates in every kingdom when they are assembled; I am so far from prohibiting them, in the discharge of their duty, to oppose the violence or cruelty of kings that I affirm that if they connive at kings in their oppression of their people, such forbearance involves the most nefarious perfidy because they fraudulently betray the liberty of the people, of which they know that they have been appointed protectors by the ordination of God.

(Jean Calvin, *Institutes of the Christian Religion,* tr. J. Allen, Bk 4, ch. 20, pp. 515-19, 525-6, 541-4, 550-1, London 1813.)

54a JUNIUS BRUTUS (HUBERT LANGUET): THE SECOND QUESTION

Whether it be lawful to resist a prince who doth infringe the law of God, or ruin His Church: by whom, how, and how far it is lawful

. . . We have formerly said at the inaugurating of kings, there was a double covenant treated of, to wit 'between God and the king'; and 'between God and the people.' The agreement was first passed between 'God, the king, and the people.' Or between the 'high priest, the people' (which is named in the first place in the twenty-third chapter of the second book of the Chronicles) 'and the king.' The intention of this was, that the 'people should be the people of God' (which is as much as to say) 'that the people should be the church of God.' We have shewed before to what end God contracted covenants with the king.

Let us now consider wherefore also He allies Himself with the people. It is a most certain thing, that God has not done this in vain, and if the people had not 'authority to promise, and to keep promise,' it were vainly lost time to contract or covenant with them. It may seem then that God has done like those creditors, which having to deal with not very sufficient borrowers, take divers jointly bound for one and the same sum, insomuch as two or more being bound one for another and each of them apart, for the entire payment of the total sum, he may demand his whole debt of which of them he pleases. There was much danger to commit the custody of the church to one man alone, and therefore God did recommend, and put it in trust 'to all the people.' The king being raised to so slippery a place might easily be corrupted: for fear lest the church should stumble with him, God would have the people also to be respondents for it. In the convenant of which we speak, God, or (in His place) the High Priest are stipulators, the king and all the people, to wit, Israel, do jointly and voluntarily assume, promise and oblige themselves for one and the same thing. The High Priest demands if they promise, that the people shall be the people of God, that God shall always have His temple, His church amongst them, where He shall be purely served. The king is respondent, so also are the people (the whole body of the people representing, as it were, the office and place of one man) not severally, but jointly, as the words themselves make clear, being incontinent, and not by intermission or distance of time, the one after the other. . . .

If either of them be negligent of their covenant, God may justly demand the whole of which of the two He pleases, and the more probably of the people than of the king, and for that many cannot so easily slip away as one, and have better means to discharge the debts than one alone. . . .

Furthermore, in so much as it is the duty of a good magistrate rather to endeavour to hinder and prevent a mischief than to chastise the delinquents after the offence is committed, as good physicians who prescribe a diet to allay and prevent diseases, as well as medicines to cure them, in like manner a people truly affected to true religion, will not simply consent themselves to reprove and repress a prince who would abolish the law of God, but also will have special regard, that through malice and wickedness he innovate nothing that may hurt the same, or that in tract of time may corrupt the pure service of God; and instead of supporting public offences committed against the Divine Majesty, they will take away all occasions wherewith the offenders might cover their faults. . . .

It is then lawful for Israel to resist the king, who would overthrow the law of God and abolish His church; and not only so, but also they ought to know that in neglecting to perform this duty, they make themselves culpable of the same crime, and shall bear the like punishment with their king.

If their assaults be verbal, their defence must be likewise verbal; if the sword be drawn against them, they may also take arms, and fight either with tongue or hand, as occasion is. . . .

But I see well, here will be an objection made. What will you say? That a whole people, that beast of many heads, must they run in a mutinous disorder, to order the business of the commonwealth? What address or direction is there in an unruly and unbridled multitude? What counsel or wisdom, to manage the affairs of state?

When we speak of all the people, we understand by that, only those who hold their authority from the people, to wit, the magistrates, who are inferior to the king, and whom the people have substituted, or established, as it were, consorts in the empire, and with a kind of tribunitial authority, to restrain the encroachments of sovereignty, and to represent the whole body of the people. We understand also, the assembly of the estates, which is nothing else but an epitome, or brief collection of the kingdom, to whom all public affairs have special and absolute reference.

(Junius Brutus, *Vindiciae Contra Tyrannos,* tr. H. J. Laski, pp. 87, 89-91, 96-7, G. Bell, London 1924.)

54b JUNIUS BRUTUS (HUBERT LANGUET): THE THIRD QUESTION

Whether it be lawful to resist a prince who doth oppress or ruin a public state, and how far such resistance may be extended: by whom, how, and by what right or law it is permitted

. . . We have shewed already, that in the establishing of the king, there were two alliances or covenants contracted: the first between God, the king, and the people, of which we have formerly treated; the second, between the king and the people, of which we must now say somewhat. . . .

In all the before-remembered places of the holy story, it is ever said, 'that a covenant was made with all the people, with all the multitude, with all the elders, with all the men of Judah': to the end that we might know, as it is also fully expressed, that not only the principals of the tribes, but also all the milleniers, centurions, and subaltern magistrates should meet together, each of them in the name, and for the towns and communalties, to covenant and contract with the king. In this assembly was the creating of the king determined of, for it was the people who made the king, and not the king the people.

It is certain, then, that the people by way of stipulation, require a performance of covenants. The king promises it. Now the condition of a stipulator is in terms of law more worthy than of a promiser. The people ask the king, whether he will govern justly and according to the laws? He promises he will. Then the people answer, and not before, that whilst he governs uprightly, they will obey faithfully. The king therefore promises simply and absolutely, the people upon condition: the which failing to be accomplished, the people rest according to equity and reason, quit from their promise.

In the first covenant or contract there is only an obligation to piety: in the second, to justice. In that the king promises to serve God religiously: in this, to rule the people justly. By the one he is obliged with the utmost of his endeavours to procure the glory of God: by the other, the profit of the people. In the first, there is a condition expressed, 'if thou keep my commandments': in the second, 'if thou distribute justice equally to every man.' God is the proper revenger of deficiency in the former, and the whole people the lawful punisher of delinquency in the latter, or the estates, the representative body thereof, who have assumed to themselves the protection of the people. This has been always practised in all well-governed estates. . . .

If we take into our consideration the condition of the empires, kingdoms, and states of times, there is not any of them worthy of those names, where there is not some such covenant or confederacy between the people and the prince. It is not long since, that in the empire of Germany, the king of the Romans being ready to be crowned emperor, was bound to do homage, and make oath of fealty to the empire, no more nor less than as the vassal is bound to do to his lord when he is invested with his fee. . . .

Finally, . . . princes are chosen by God, and established by the people. As all particulars considered one by one, are inferior to the prince; so the whole body of the people and officers of state, who represent that body, are the princes' superiors. In the receiving and inauguration of a prince, there are covenants and contracts passed between him and the people, which are tacit and expressed, natural or civil; to wit, to obey him faithfully whilst he commands justly, that he serving the commonwealth, all men shall serve him, that whilst he governs according to law, all shall be submitted to his government, etc. The officers of the kingdom are the guardians and protectors of these covenants and contracts. He who maliciously or wilfully violates these conditions, is questionless a tyrant by practice. And therefore the officers of state may judge him according to the laws. And if he support his tyranny by strong hands, their duty binds them, when by no other means it can be effected by force of arms to suppress him.

Of these officers there be two kinds, those who have generally undertaken the protection of the kingdom; as the constable, marshals, peers, palatines, and the rest, every one of whom, although all the rest do either connive or consort with the tyranny, are bound to oppose and repress the tyrant; and those who have undertaken the government of any province, city, or part of the kingdom, as dukes, marquesses, earls, consuls, mayors, sheriffs, etc., they may according to right, expel and drive tyranny and tyrants from their cities, confines, and governments.

But particular and private persons may not unsheathe the sword against tyrants by practice, because they were not established by particulars, but by the whole body of the people. But for tyrants, who, without title intrude themselves for so much as there is no contract or agreement between them and the people, it is indifferently permitted all to oppose and depose them; and in this rank of tyrants may those be ranged, who, abusing the weakness and sloth of a lawful prince, tyrannously insult over his subjects.

(Junius Brutus, op. cit., pp. 117, 174-7, 212-13.)

55a   JOHANNES ALTHUSIUS: THE FORMATION OF THE STATE

We will discuss, first, the members of a realm and, then, its right. The members of a realm, or of this universal symbiotic association, are not, I say, individual men, families, or collegia, as in a private or a particular public association. Instead, members are many cities, provinces, and regions agreeing among themselves on a single body constituted by mutual union and communication. Individual persons from these group members are called natives, inhabitants of the realm, and sons and daughters of the realm. They are to be distinguished from foreigners and strangers, who have no claim upon the right or the realm. It can be said that individual citizens, families, and collegia are not members of a realm, just as boards, rails, and pegs are not considered parts of a ship, nor rocks, beams, and cement parts of a house. On the other hand, cities, urban communities, and provinces are members of a realm, just as prow, stern, and keel are members of a ship, and roof, walls, and floor are essential parts of a house. . . .

The bond of this body and association is consensus, together with trust extended and accepted among the members of the commonwealth. The bond is, in other words, a tacit or expressed promise to communicate things, mutual services, aid, counsel, and the same common laws *(jura)* to the extent that the utility and necessity of universal social life in a realm shall require. Even the reluctant are compelled to comply with this communication. However, this does not prevent separate provinces of the same realm from using different special laws. Plato rightly said that this trust is the foundation of human society, while lack of trust is its plague, and that trust is the bond of concord among the different members of a commonwealth. For the promise of so many different men and orders has as its purpose that the diverse actions of the individual parts be referred to the utility and communion of one commonwealth, and that inferiors be held together with superiors by a certain fairness in the law *(jus)*. . . .

(Johannes Althusius, *Politica Methodice Digesta (The Politics)*, tr. F. S. Carney, ch. 9, p. 62, Eyre and Spottiswoode, London 1965.)

55b   JOHANNES ALTHUSIUS: THE FORMATION OF THE GOVERNMENT

There is no doubt that this covenant, or contractual mandate *(contractum mandati)* entered into with the supreme magistrate, obligates both of the contracting parties, so much so that it is permitted to neither magistrate nor subjects to revoke or dishonour it. However, in this reciprocal contract between the supreme magistrate as the mandatory, or promisor, and the universal association as the mandator, the obligation of the magistrate comes first, as is customary in a contractual mandate. By it he binds himself to the body of the universal association to administer the realm or commonwealth according to laws prescribed by God, right reason, and the body of the commonwealth. According to the nature of a mandate, the obligation of the people, or members of the realm, follows. By it the people in turn binds itself in obedience and compliance to the supreme magistrate who administers the commonwealth according to the prescribed laws.

The supreme magistrate exercises as much authority *(jus)* as has been explicitly conceded to him by the associated members or bodies of the realm. And what has not been given to him must be considered to have been left under the control of the people or universal association. Such is the nature of the contractual mandate. The less the power of those who rule, the more secure and stable the imperium remains. For power is secure that places a control upon force, that rules willing subjects, and that is circumscribed by laws, so that it does not become haughty and engage in excesses to the ruin of the subjects, nor degenerate into tyranny. . . . Absolute power, or what is called the plentitude of power, cannot be given to the supreme magistrate. For first, he who employs a plentitude of power breaks through the restraints by which human society has been contained. Secondly, by absolute power justice is destroyed, and when justice is taken away realms become bands of robbers, as Augustine says. Thirdly, such absolute power regards not the utility and welfare of subjects, but private pleasure. Power, however, is established for the utility of those who are ruled, not of those who rule, and the utility of the people or subjects does not in the least require unlimited power. Adequate provision has been made for them by laws.

(Johannes Althusius, op. cit., ch. 19, pp. 116-17.)

55c   JOHANNES ALTHUSIUS: RESISTANCE TO TYRANNY

This tyranny, or tyrannical administration of a commonwealth, is twofold. One type of it is concerned with the overthrow and destruction of the fundamental laws of the realm. The other consists in the administration of functions and things of the associated body in a manner that is contrary to piety and justice. . . .

Having become acquainted with the nature of tyranny, we are now to look for the remedy by which it may be opportunely removed. This consists in resistance to and deposition of the tyrant, which remedy has been entrusted to the optimates alone. This resistance is the process by which the ephors impede the tyranny of the supreme magistrate by word and deed. And when he is incurable, or the rights of the associated body cannot otherwise be kept sound, well-protected, and in good condition, or the commonwealth free from evil, they depose him and cast him out of their midst. . . .

In order that the ephors may rightly exercise this right of resistance to a tyrant, it is necessary that they pay attention to the following matters: (1) what optimates or ephors can resist a tyrant and are responsible for doing so, (2) when, (3) in what manner, and (4) how long and how far?

Concerning the first matter, the optimates of the realm both collectively and individually can and should resist tyranny to the best of their ability. For since they have the right of creating the magistrate by the consent and command of the people, they also receive the power of judging and deposing him. . . . Subjects and citizens who love their country and resist a tyrant, and want the commonwealth and its rights to be safe and sound, should join themselves to a resisting ephor or optimate. Those who refuse to help the resisting ephor with their strength, money, and counsel are considered enemies and deserters.

(Johannes Althusius, op. cit., ch. 38, pp. 186-7.)

56 FRANCISCO SUAREZ

We infer, then, that by the nature of things, men as individuals possess to a partial extent (so to speak) the faculty for establishing, or creating, a perfect community; and, by virtue of the very fact that they establish it, the power in question does come to exist in this community as a whole. Nevertheless, natural law does not require either that the power should be exercised directly by the agency of the whole community, or that it should always continue to reside therein. On the contrary, it would be most difficult, from a practical point of view, to satisfy such requirements, for infinite confusion and trouble would result if laws were established by the vote of every person; and therefore, men straightway determine the said power by vesting it in one of the above-mentioned forms of government, since no other form can be conceived, as is easily evident to one who gives the matter consideration.

2. The second inference [to be drawn from the preceding Chapter] is as follows: civil power, whenever it resides—in the right and ordinary course of law—in the person of one individual, or prince, has flowed from the people as a community, either directly or indirectly; nor could it otherwise be justly held. . . .

A reason for this view, supplied by what we have said above, is the fact that such power, in the nature of things, resides immediately in the community; and therefore, in order that it may justly come to reside in a given individual, as in a sovereign prince, it must necessarily be bestowed upon him by the consent of the community. . . .

For this governing power, regarded from a political viewpoint and in its essence, is undoubtedly derived from God, as I have said; yet the fact that it resides in a particular individual results—as has been demonstrated—from a grant on the part of the state itself; and therefore, in this sense, the said power pertains to human law. Moreover, the monarchical nature of the government of such a state or province is brought about by human disposition, as has already been shown; therefore, the principate itself is derived from men.

Another proof of this derivation is the fact that the power of the king is greater or less, according to the pact or agreement, between him and the kingdom; therefore, absolutely speaking that power is drawn from men.

6. The passages cited from Holy Scripture, however, are to be interpreted as having two meanings. One is as follows: the power in question, viewed in itself, is derived from God; and it is just and in conformity with the divine will. The other meaning is this: assuming that the said power has been transferred to the king, he is now the vicar of God, and natural law makes it obligatory that he be obeyed. The case is similar to that of a private individual who surrenders himself by sale to be the slave of another; so that the resulting power of *dominium* has, in an absolute sense, a human derivation, yet the slave is. [also] bound by divine and natural law—once we assume that the contract has been made—to render obedience to his master.

Thus the reply to the confirmation [of the opposing view] consists clearly in a general denial of the [second] deduction [and its corollary]. For, once the power has been transferred to the king, he is through that power rendered superior even to the kingdom which bestowed it; since by this bestowal the kingdom has subjected itself and has deprived itself of its former liberty, just as is, in due proportion, clearly true in the case of the slave, which we have mentioned by way of illustration. Moreover, in accordance with the same reasoning, the king cannot be deprived of this power, since he has acquired a true ownership of it; unless perchance he lapses into tyranny, on which ground the kingdom may wage a just war against him.

(Francisco Suarez, *Tractatus de Legibus ac Deo Legislatore (On Laws and God the Lawgiver),* tr. G. Williams, A. Brown, J. Waldron, Bk 3, ch. 4, pp. 383-4, 386-7, Clarendon Press, Oxford 1944.)

CHAPTER 15

The Royalist Reaction

The theories of resistance to secular authority propounded by the Huguenots and the Jesuits were opposed by writers who believed that only by submission to strong central authority could the evils of civil conflict be ended. Two groups of exponents of royal power can be distinguished. First, those such as Jean Bodin and the *Politiques*, who saw the only chance of saving France in religious toleration and the rule of a strong king. Secondly the exponents of the theory of the Divine Right of Kings who attached a religious significance to monarchy and conceived of resistance to it as rebellion against God Himself.

Jean Bodin (1530–1596)

Bodin's work, *Six Books of the Republic* (1576), is arguably the greatest systematic treatise on politics that was produced in the sixteenth century. Nevertheless, its arrangement is so formless and confused that it is one of the least read of the great works of political philosophy. Bodin's intention in his book was to show rationally the origin and nature of political authority and to demonstrate that such authority was inevitable if the state was to survive.

The *Republic* opens with a definition of the Commonwealth which he conceives of as an aggregation of families governed by a sovereign power (Ex. 57a). The patriarchal family is important not only because it is the primary human association, but also because its structure is an image of the structure of authority in the good state. Furthermore, the state can only be healthy when families are regulated on the proper authoritarian lines. To this end he advocates a return to the Roman practice whereby fathers had the power of life and death over their children.

Sovereignty

It is in his theory of sovereignty that Bodin is most original. He defines sovereignty as 'absolute and perpetual power vested in a commonwealth' and it is the 'distinguishing mark of a commonwealth' (Ex. 57b). The fact that sovereignty is necessarily a 'perpetual' power excludes from the category of sovereign any person who holds power for a limited term or who rules by consent, since in the latter case consent may be withdrawn and his power will cease. The typical sovereign is therefore a king to whom has been unconditionally given absolute power for the term of his natural life.

Because sovereignty is defined as 'absolute' power, a person who exercises a conditional authority or who is bound by the laws of the state is not truly sovereign. A sovereign cannot be bound by the laws of his predecessors nor by the laws which he makes himself.

Despite Bodin's insistence on the absolute nature of sovereignty, it turns out that the sovereign is subject to certain extra-legal limitations. He must obey the law of God and nature. If he does not, and he cannot rightfully be compelled to by any human force, he must answer for his actions to God. He must honour agreements made by his predecessors with other rulers if he promises to do so, and similarly he must honour his promises to his subjects, although these are only moral obligations.

Because of the importance of the family in the establishment of the state, the sovereign must respect this institution and the paternal rights of the father. A law which infringed the father's right to decide how his children were to be brought up would be regarded by Bodin as a danger not only to the family but to the state itself. The institution of private property is seen as of comparable significance to that of the family. Hence the sovereign's power to take away a subject's property is limited to his authority to tax with the subject's consent and then only as a last resort (Ex. 57c).

Yet a further limitation to the sovereign's authority stems from the inviolability of certain long-established fundamental principles of the constitution. A French sovereign, for example, may not alter or repeal the Salic law (which excluded females from the throne) and the law prohibiting the alienation of domain.

It is clear that the exercise of sovereign power is not totally unrestricted. Although the sovereign is free of legal limitations to his power, this is only meaningful while the commonwealth is maintained in being. If the sovereign should act in such a way as to destroy the state or to frustrate the ends for which it was formed then he cannot rationally be regarded as acting in a sovereign capacity.

The Divine Right of Kings

Bodin's theory of sovereignty was firmly rooted in expediency. In an age of near anarchy it was clear to him that order must rest upon authority. Although monarchy was the best form of government it was not the only form approved by God, and for some states other kinds of government might be more appropriate. The royalist theories which followed and continued into the seventeenth century claimed that monarchical authority was divinely ordained.

The notion that government is ordained by God has a long ancestry—at least as far back as St Paul. The Christian tradition, until the time of the investiture controversy in the eleventh century, was to regard the ruler as God's appointed agent against whom rebellion would be a sin. As we have seen in Chapter 14, this traditional view of government was revived by Luther and Calvin in the early sixteenth century.

The view that monarchy is specially favoured by God does not appear until the theory of papal monarchy in the twelfth and thirteenth centuries. With the decline of the papacy in the fourteenth century a similar theory emerges in the writings of Dante and others, although this time it is the secular monarchy which is given its justification. In Dante's *Monarchy* nearly all the elements of the modern divine right of kings' theory may be found. Monarchy is the form of government ordained by God; the power of kings is legally unlimited and their actions may be judged by God alone; resistance to a king is the equivalent of resistance to God and will incur damnation.

Divine Right in France

The exponents of the divine right of kings theory in sixteenth-century France can be divided into two groups: first, the Huguenot supporters of Henry of Navarre who, after the latter's assumption of the French throne, changed their political attitude from the support of rebellion to the support of absolutism; secondly, the 'Gallican' Catholics who were able to reconcile support of an absolute king with their religion by espousing a religious nationalism which reduced papal authority to a negligible quantity.

One of the first fully-formulated theories of divine right in France emanated from the pen of the lawyer Pierre de Belloy whose *De L'Autorité du Roi (Royal Authority, 1587)* is a typical expression of subservience to monarchical power little different except in detail to the theories of the early Christians regarding the duties of obedience to the ruler. More interesting because less dogmatic is William Barclay's *De Regno et Regale Potestate (The Kingdom and the Royal Power,* 1600). Barclay repeats with approval most earlier arguments for divine right, but unlike his predecessors he does admit that there are rare exceptions to the general rule of passive obedience to the king.

Bossuet (1627-1704)

Jacques Bossuet, Bishop of Meaux, was arguably the most talented of the very few French political writers of the seventeenth century. Although primarily a theologian, he was encouraged to write a number of political works for the edification of the Dauphin, whose tutor he became in 1670. His principal work was *La Politique tirée des propres paroles de l'Ecriture sainte (Politics Drawn from the Words of Holy Scripture)* written in 1667-68 although not published until 1709. As one might expect of a book emanating from the court of Louis XIV, it is a defence of the theory of the divine right of kings, although Bossuet emphasizes, with copious references to the Bible, that monarchs also have duties.

Bossuet quotes Augustine and the Christian Fathers to show that government became necessary to suppress the sins of man. He postulates a state of nature similar to that portrayed by Hobbes but in which original sin rather than egoism is the source of conflict. The only escape from war and anarchy is for each individual to give up his power to a sovereign ruler, who is normally a monarch. Bossuet attempts to show that monarchy is specially favoured by God. His argument here is somewhat similar to that of Filmer *(q.v.)* in using the patriarchal monarchy of Adam as the model for human government to follow. He has to accept, however, that many governments are not monarchical and argues that 'each people ought to accept as divinely ordained the form of government established in its country'.

The extract quoted from Bossuet's *Politics* (Ex. 58) presents his conception of royal authority as sacred, paternal, absolute and rational. It may stand as a typical illustration of the views of divine right theorists about the qualities of kings.

Divine Right in England

In sixteenth-century England the theory of divine right of kings was less important than in France. The break with the papacy in the reigns of Henry VIII and Elizabeth caused comparatively little religious discord although the excommunication of Elizabeth in 1570 did lead to the theory being propounded by a number of writers of minor importance.

King James I (1566-1625)

In his *Trew Law of Free Monarchies* published anonymously in 1598, five years before he assumed the English crown, James set down his ideas about kingship. Although his ideas do not add up to a coherent political philosophy, they are interesting as an expression of royalist views at the end of the sixteenth century. The extract quoted (Ex. 59) gives the flavour of his argument. Kings care for their people as a father cares for his children; rebellion against tyranny can never be justified because the sword belongs to the ruler alone and rebellion always makes matters worse; furthermore, kings can never be so wicked as completely to destroy justice and order in the state.

Sir Robert Filmer (c. 1588-1653)

Filmer was a supporter of the royalist cause at the time of the English Civil War. His book *Patriarcha,* written in the 1640s, was not published until 1680 when the time for the expression of such views was more propitious. It acquired a good deal of fame, not so much for its own merits as because it was the subject of a scathing refutation in Locke's *First Treatise of Government.*

Patriarcha, subtitled *A Defence of the Natural Power of Kings Against the Unnatural Liberty of the People,* is an attack on the contractual theories of the Calvinists and Jesuits: 'Cardinal Bellarmine and Mr Calvin both look asquint this way' (Ex. 60a). The view that men are free to choose their form of government is regarded by Filmer as contrary to Scripture and natural law. Kingly authority is rooted in the natural authority of the father over his family and such patriarchal authority is the only kind which God has ordained.

This attempt to show that the king's absolute authority was natural was quite logical, bearing in mind that contemporary society conformed more in practice to Filmer's conception of patriarchal authority than to the theoretical notion of consent. However, his argument to show that kings have inherited the patriarchal power given by God to Adam leads him into absurdities (Ex. 60b). He states that all nations of the world are descended from the three sons of Noah and implies that patriarchal authority is descended in the same way. He admits that it is not possible to trace the descent of existing kings from the biblical patriarchs and accepts that the genealogical line must have been broken by usurpations, but argues that this does not invalidate the true natural authority which present kings possess.

FURTHER READING

Texts
J. Bodin: *Six Books of the Commonwealth*
J. Bossuet: *Politics Drawn from the Very Words of Holy Scripture*
James I: *The Trew Law of Free Monarchies*
R. Filmer: *Patriarcha*

Commentaries
J. Allen: *A History of Political Thought in the Sixteenth Century* (Methuen 1960)
J. N. Figgis: *The Divine Right of Kings* (Cambridge University Press 1914)
F. J. C. Hearnshaw (ed): *The Social and Political Ideas of Some Great Thinkers of the Sixteenth and Seventeenth Centuries* (Dawsons 1967)
J. Plamenatz: *Man and Society*, Vol. 1 (Longmans 1963)

57a JEAN BODIN: DEFINITION OF THE COMMONWEALTH

A Commonwealth may be defined as the rightly ordered government of a number of families, and of those things which are their common concern, by a sovereign power. We must start in this way with a definition because the final end of any subject must first be understood before the means of attaining it can profitably be considered, and the definition indicates what that end is. If then the definition is not exact and true, all that is deduced from it is valueless. . . .

Let us consider more particularly the terms of this definition. We say in the first place *right* ordering to distinguish a commonwealth from a band of thieves or pirates. With them one should have neither intercourse, commerce, nor alliance. . . . The law has always distinguished robbers and pirates from those who are recognized to be enemies legitimately at war, in that they are members of some commonwealth founded upon that principle of justice that brigands and pirates seek to subvert. For this reason brigands cannot claim that the conventions of war, recognized by all peoples, should be observed in their case, nor are they entitled to those guarantees that the victors normally accord to the vanquished. . . .

A family may be defined as the right ordering of a group of persons owing obedience to a head of a household, and of those interests which are his proper concern. The second term of our definition of the commonwealth refers to the family because it is not only the true source and origin of the commonwealth, but also its principal constituent. . . . I understand by domestic government the right ordering of family matters, together with the authority which the head of the family has over his dependants, and the obedience due from them to him, things which Aristotle and Xenophon neglect. Thus the well-ordered family is a true image of the commonwealth, and domestic comparable with sovereign authority. It follows that the household is the model of right order in the commonwealth. And just as the whole body enjoys health when every particular member performs its proper function, so all will be well with the commonwealth when families are properly regulated.

(Jean Bodin, *Six Books of the Commonwealth*, Bk 1, ch. 1, p. 1, ch. 2, pp. 6-7, Blackwell, Oxford 1955.)

57b JEAN BODIN: DEFINITION OF SOVEREIGNTY

Sovereignty is that absolute and perpetual power vested in a commonwealth which in Latin is termed *majestas*. . . .The term needs careful definition, because although it is the distinguishing mark of a commonwealth, and an understanding of its nature fundamental to any treatment of politics, no jurist or political philosopher has in fact attempted to define it. . . .

I have described it as *perpetual* because one can give absolute power to a person or group of persons for a period of time, but that time expired they become subjects once more. Therefore even while they enjoy power, they cannot properly be regarded as sovereign rulers, but only as the lieutenants and agents of the sovereign ruler, till the moment comes when it pleases the prince or the people to revoke the gift. The true sovereign remains always seized of his power. Just as a feudal lord who grants lands to another retains his eminent domain over them, so the ruler who delegates authority to judge and command, whether it be for a short period, or during pleasure, remains seized of those rights of jurisdiction actually exercised by another in the form of a revocable grant, or precarious tenancy. For this reason the law requires the governor of a province, or the prince's lieutenant, to make a formal surrender of the authority committed to him, at the expiration of his term of office. In this respect there is no difference between the highest officer of state and his humblest subordinate. If it were otherwise, and the absolute authority delegated by the prince to a lieutenant was regarded as itself sovereign power, the latter could use it against his prince who would thereby forfeit his eminence, and the subject could command his lord, the servant his master. This is a manifest absurdity, considering that the sovereign is always excepted personally, as a matter of right, in all delegations of authority, however extensive. However much he gives there always remains a reserve of right in his own person, whereby he may command, or intervene by way of prevention, confirmation, evocation, or any other way he thinks fit, in all matters delegated to a subject, whether in virtue of an office or a commission. Any authority exercised in virtue of an office or a commission can be revoked, or made tenable for as long or short a period as the sovereign wills. . . .

A perpetual authority therefore must be understood to mean one that lasts for the lifetime of him who exercises it. If a sovereign magistrate is given office for one year, or for any other predetermined period, and continues to exercise the authority bestowed on him after the conclusion of his term, he does so either by consent or by force and violence. If he does so by force, it is manifest tyranny. The tyrant is a true sovereign for all that. The robber's possession by violence is true and natural possession although contrary to the law, for those who were formerly in possession have been disseized. But if the magistrate continues in office by consent, he is not a sovereign prince, seeing that he only exercises power on sufferance. Still less is he a sovereign if the term of his office is not fixed, for in that case he has no more than a precarious commission. . . .

What bearing have these considerations on the case of the man to whom the people has given absolute power for the term of his natural life? One must distinguish. If such absolute power is given him simply and unconditionally, and not in virtue of some office or commission, nor in the form of a revocable grant, the recipient certainly is, and should be acknowledged to be, a sovereign. The people has renounced and alienated its sovereign power in order to invest him with it and put him in possession, and it thereby transfers to him all its powers, authority, and sovereign rights, just as does the man who gives to another possessory and proprietary rights over what he formerly owned. . . .

Let us now turn to the other term of our definition and consider the force of the word *absolute*. The people or the magnates of a commonwealth can bestow simply and unconditionally upon someone of their choice a sovereign and perpetual power to dispose of their property and persons, to govern the state as he thinks fit, and to order the succession, in the same way that any proprietor, out of his liberality, can freely and unconditionally make a gift of his property to another. Such a form of gift, not being qualified in any way, is the only true gift, being at once unconditional and irrevocable. Gifts burdened with obligations and hedged with conditions are not true gifts. Similarly sovereign power given to a prince charged with conditions is neither properly sovereign, nor absolute, unless the conditions of appointment are only such as are inherent in the laws of God and of nature. . . .

If we insist however that absolute power means exemption from all law whatsoever, there is no prince in the world who can be regarded as sovereign, since all the princes of the earth are subject to the laws of God and of nature, and even to certain human laws common to all nations. . . .

On the other hand it is the distinguishing mark of the sovereign that he cannot in any way be subject to the commands of another, for it is he who makes law for the subject, abrogates law already made, and amends obsolete law. . . .

For all laws, ordinances, letters patent, privileges, and grants whatsoever issued by the prince, have force only during his own lifetime, and must be expressly, or at least tacitly confirmed by the reigning prince who has cognizance of them . . . In proof of which, it is the custom of this realm for all corporations and corporate bodies to ask for the confirmation of their privileges, rights, and jurisdictions, on the accession of a new king. Even Parlements and high courts do this, as well as individual officers of the crown.

If the prince is not bound by the laws of his predecessors, still less can he be bound by his own laws. One may be subject to laws made by another, but it is impossible to bind oneself in any matter which is the subject of one's own free exercise of will. As the law says, 'there can be no obligation in any matter which proceeds from the free will of the undertaker'. It follows of necessity that the king cannot be subject to his own laws. Just as, according to the canonists, the Pope can never tie his own hands, so the sovereign prince cannot bind himself, even if he wishes. For this reason edicts and ordinances conclude with the formula 'for such is our good pleasure', thus intimating that the laws of a sovereign prince, even when founded on truth and right reason, proceed simply from his own free will.

It is far otherwise with divine and natural laws. All the princes of the earth are subject to them, and cannot contravene them without treason and rebellion against God. His yoke is upon them, and they must bow their heads in fear and reverence before His divine majesty. The absolute power of princes and sovereign lords does not extend to the laws of God and of nature. He who best understood the meaning of absolute power, and made kings and emperors submit to his will, defined his sovereignty as a power to override positive law; he did not claim power to set aside divine and natural law.

But supposing the prince should swear to keep the laws and customs of his country, is he not bound by that oath? One must distinguish. If a prince promises in his own heart to obey his own laws, he is nevertheless not bound to do so, any more than anyone is bound by an oath taken to himself. Even private citizens are not bound by private oaths to keep agreements. The law permits them to cancel them, even if the agreements are in themselves reasonable and good. But if one sovereign prince promises another sovereign prince to keep the agreements entered into by his predecessors, he is bound to do so even if not under oath, if that other prince's interests are involved. If they are not, he is not bound either by a promise, or even by an oath.

The same holds good of promises made by the sovereign to the subject, even if the promises were made prior to his election (for this does not make the difference that many suppose). It is not that the prince is bound either by his own laws or those of his predecessors. But he is bound by the just covenants and promises he has made, whether under oath to do so or not, to exactly the same extent that a private individual is bound in like case.

(Jean Bodin, op. cit., Bk 1, ch. 8, pp. 25-9.)

57c JEAN BODIN: RESTRICTIONS ON TAXATION

The last method of raising revenue is to tax the subject. One should never have recourse to it till all other measures have failed, and only then because urgent necessity compels one to make some provision for the commonwealth. In such a case, seeing that the security and defence of each private citizen depends on the preservation of the common good, each individual must be prepared to assist in the matter. In such a crisis, taxes and impositions are most just, for nothing is more just than that which is necessary, as a Roman senator once observed. Nevertheless, in order to secure that an extraordinary tax, imposed in time of war, should not be continued in peace time, it is better to impose it in the form of a forced loan. Moreover the money comes in more readily when the payer hopes both to receive his money back again sometime, and to enjoy the distinction of having made a contribution. . . .

It was declared by the estates of this realm, in the presence of King Philip of Valois in the year 1338, that he could not levy any tax on his people without their consent . . . This rule has always been observed, and is also a well established custom in Spain, England, and Germany. At the Estates of Tours, assembled in the time of Charles VIII, Philippe de Comines declared that there was nowhere a prince who had power to levy taxes on his subjects, nor could he acquire such a right by prescription, without their consent. . . .

(Jean Bodin, op. cit., Bk 6, ch. 2, pp. 188-9.)

58 JACQUES BOSSUET: ROYAL AUTHORITY

Royal authority has four characteristics or essential qualities

First, royal authority is sacred; second, it is paternal; third, it is absolute; fourth, it is subject to reason. . . .

Princes therefore act as the agents of God and his lieutenants upon earth. It is through them that he wields his power of command. . . . This is why we have seen that the royal throne is not the throne of a man but the throne of God himself. . . .

The respect which we pay to the prince therefore has within it something of religion. The service of God and respect for kings are things united; and Saint Peter joins these two duties together: 'Fear God; honor the king.' (I Peter 2: 17)

God has therefore put something of divinity in princes. 'I have said: You are gods, and all of you are the sons of the most High.' (Psalm LXXXI: 6) . . .

Kings should respect their own power and employ it only for the public welfare

Since their power comes from on high, as we have said, they should not believe that they are its masters, having a right to use it however they wish. They should use it with fear and restraint as a thing which comes to them from God and for which God will call them to account. . . .

Kings should therefore tremble when using the power which God gives them, and keep in mind how horrible is the sacrilege of misusing a power which comes from God. . . .

Royal authority is absolute

There are some who pretend that they cannot find any difference between absolute and arbitrary government, in order to make the name of 'absolute government' odious and insufferable. But there is no greater difference than this between them. . . .

Without this absolute authority, he [the king] can neither do good nor repress evil; his power must be such that no one can hope to escape him, and finally, the only defense of individuals against the public power must be their innocence. . . .

Only God can judge their judgments and their persons. . . .

The prince, as prince, is not to be considered a private person; he is a public figure, the whole state is in him, the will of the whole people is contained in his. Just as all the perfections and virtues are joined in God, so is the power of all private persons joined in the prince's person. What greatness that one man should have so much power!

God's power is felt in an instant from one end of the world to the other; royal power takes the same time to act throughout the kingdom. It preserves the order of the whole kingdom, as does God with the whole world. Let God take away his hand and the world will fall back into nothingness; let authority fail in the kingdom, and total confusion will result.

Consider the king in his work-chamber. From it go forth the orders which make magistrates and captains, citizens and soldiers, provinces, navies and armies, act in unison. He is the image of God, who from his throne in highest heaven makes all the world go. . . .

Something of divinity adheres to the prince and inspires the people's fear. Let not the king therefore forget what he is himself. 'I have said (it is God who speaks): You are gods and all of you the sons of the most High. But like men you shall die: and shall fall like one of the great.' (Psalms LXXXI: 6-7) I have said that you are gods, that is, that you possess within your authority and carry upon your brow the character of divinity. You are the sons of the most High; it was he who established your power for the good of the human race. But, O gods of flesh and blood, O gods of mud and dust, you will die like men, you will fall as the great have fallen. For a little time greatness sets men apart; in the end a common fall makes them all equal.

Therefore, O kings, be bold in your use of power, for it is divine and beneficial to the human race, but use it with humility. It is set upon you from without. In the end it leaves you weak, it leaves you mortal, it leaves you sinful, and it places upon you the burden of answering to God for so much more.

(J. Bossuet, *Politics Drawn from the Very Words of Holy Scripture,* quoted in H. H. Rowen, ed, *From Absolutism to Revolution, 1648-1848,* pp. 31-2, Collier-Macmillan, New York 1968.)

59 KING JAMES I

Since I have so clearly proved then out of the fundamental laws and practice of this country what right and power a king has over his subjects, it is easy to be understood what allegiance and obedience his lieges owe unto him. . . . If it be not lawful to any particular lords, tenants or vassals, upon whatsoever pretext, to control and displace their master and overlord, how much less may the subjects and vassals of the great overlord, the king, control or displace him? And since in all inferior judgments in the land, the people may not upon any respect displace their magistrates, although but subaltern: for the people of a borough cannot displace their provost before the time of their election, nor in ecclesiastical policy the flock can upon any pretence displace the pastor nor judge of him, yea even the poor schoolmaster cannot be displaced by his scholars: if these, I say . . . cannot be displaced for any occasion or pretext by them that are ruled of them, how much less is it lawful upon any pretext to displace or control the great provost and great schoolmaster of the whole land, except by inverting the order of all law and reason. . . .

The king towards his people is rightly compared to a father of his children, and to a head of a body composed of divers members. For as fathers the good princes and magistrates of the people of God acknowledged themselves to their subjects. And for all other well-ruled commonwealths, the style of *pater patriae* was ever and is commonly used to kings. And the proper office of a king towards his subjects agrees very well with the office of the head towards the body and all members thereof. For from the head, being the seat of judgment, proceeds the care and foresight of guiding and preventing every evil that may come to the body or any part thereof. The head cares for the body; so does the king for his people. As the discourse and direction flows from the head, and the execution thereunto belongs to the rest of the members, everyone according to their office, so it is betwixt a wise prince and his people. . . .

It is cast up by divers that employ their pens upon apologies for rebellions and treasons that every man is born to carry such a natural zeal and duty to his commonwealth as to his mother; that seeing it so rent and deadly wounded, as whiles it will be by wicked and tyrannous kings, good citizens will be forced, for the natural zeal and duty they owe their own native country, to put their hand to work for freeing their commonwealth from such a pest.

Whereunto I give two answers. First, it is a sure axiom in theology that evil should not be done that good may come of it. The wickedness, therefore, of the king can never make them that are ordained to be judged by him to become his judges. And if it be not lawful to a private man to revenge his private injury upon his private adversary (since God has only given the sword to the magistrate), how much less is it lawful to the people, or any part of them (who are all private men, the authority being always with the magistrate, as I have already proved) to take upon them the use of the sword, whom to it belongs not, against the public magistrate whom to only it belongs. Next, in place of relieving the commonwealth out of distress (which is their only excuse and color), they shall heap double distress and desolation upon it; and so their rebellion shall procure the contrary effects that they pretend it for. For a king cannot be imagined to be so unruly and tyrannous but the commonwealth will be kept in better order, notwithstanding thereof, by him than it can be by his away-taking.

. . . All sudden mutations are perilous in commonwealths, hope being thereby given to all bare men to set up themselves and fly with other men's feathers, the reins being loosed to all the insolencies that disordered people can commit by hope of impunity, because of the looseness of all things. And next it is certain that a king can never be so monstrously vicious but he will generally favor justice and maintain some order, except in the particulars wherein his inordinate lusts and passions carry him away; where by the contrary, no king being, nothing is unlawful to none. . . .

(James I, *Trew Law of Free Monarchies,* in James I, *Political Works,* ed C. H. McIlwain, pp. 64-6.)

60a   SIR ROBERT FILMER: LIBERTY IS AGAINST SCRIPTURE AND NATURE

I   The Natural Freedom of Mankind, a New, Plausible and Dangerous Opinion

Within the last hundred years many of the Schoolmen and other Divines have published and maintained an opinion that:

'Mankind is naturally endowed and born with freedom from all subjection, and at liberty to choose what form of government it please, and that the power which any one man hath over others was at the first by human right bestowed according to the discretion of the multitude.'

This tenet was first hatched in the Schools for good Divinity, and hath been fostered by succeeding Papists. The Divines of the Reformed Churches have entertained it, and the common people everywhere tenderly embrace it as being most plausible to flesh and blood, for that it prodigally distributes a portion of liberty to the meanest of the multitude, who magnify liberty as if the height of human felicity were only to be found in it, never remembering that the desire of liberty was the cause of the fall of Adam.

But howsoever this opinion hath of late obtained great reputation, yet it is not to be found in the ancient fathers and doctors of the primitive Church. It contradicts the doctrine and history of the Holy Scriptures, the constant practice of all ancient monarchies, and the very principles of the law of nature. It is hard to say whether it be more erroneous in Divinity or dangerous in policy.

Upon the grounds of this doctrine, both Jesuits and some zealous favourers of the Geneva discipline have built a perilous conclusion, which is, 'that the people or multitude have power to punish or deprive the Prince if he transgress the laws of the kingdom'. Witness Parsons and Buchanan. The first, under the name of Dolman, in the third chapter of his first book, labours to prove that Kings have been lawfully chastised by their commonwealths. The latter, in his book *De Jure Regni apud Scotos*, maintained a liberty of the people to depose their Prince. Cardinal Bellarmine and Mr. Calvin both look asquint this way.

(Sir Robert Filmer, *Patriarcha*, ed. P. Laslett, ch. 1, pp. 53-4, Blackwell, Oxford 1949.)

60b SIR ROBERT FILMER: ROYAL AUTHORITY DESCENDED FROM ADAM

III The Argument of Bellarmine Answered out of Bellarmine himself: and of the Regal Authority of the Patriarchs before the Flood

I come now to examine that argument which is used by Bellarmine, and is the one and only argument I can find produced by any author for the proof of the natural liberty of the people. It is thus framed: That God hath given or ordained power, is evident by Scripture; but God hath given it to no particular man, because by nature all men are equal; therefore he hath given power to the people or multitude.

To answer this reason, drawn from the equality of mankind by nature, I will first use the help of Bellarmine himself, whose words are these: 'If many men had been created out of the earth, all they ought to have been Princes over their posterity.' In these words we have an evident confession, that creation made man Prince of his posterity. And indeed not only Adam, but the succeeding Patriarchs had, by right of fatherhood, royal authority over their children. Nor dares Bellarmine deny this also. 'That the patriarchs' (saith he) 'were endowed with Kingly power, their deeds do testify.' For as Adam was lord of his children, so his children under him had a command over their own children, but still with subordination to the first parent, who is lord paramount over his children's children to all generations, as being the grandfather of his people.

I see not then how the children of Adam, or of any man else, can be free from subjection to their parents. And this subordination of children is the fountain of all regal authority, by the ordination of God himself. From whence it follows, that civil power, not only in general is by Divine institution, but even the assigning of it specifically to the eldest parent. Which quite takes away that new and common distinction which refers only power universal or absolute to God, but power respective in regard of the special form of government to the choice of the people. Nor leaves it any place for such imaginary pactions between Kings and their people as many dream of. . . .

This lordship which Adam by creation had over the whole world, and by right descending from him the Patriarchs did enjoy, was as large and ample as the absolutest dominion of any monarch which hath been since the creation.

Not only until the Flood, but after it, this patriarchal power did continue, as the very name of Patriarch doth in part prove.

IV   The Dispersion of Nations after the Flood was by Entire Families over which the Fathers were Kings, and from those Kings, all Kings are Descended

The three sons of Noah had the whole world divided amongst them by their Father; for of them was the whole world overspread, according to the benediction given to him and his sons: 'Be fruitful and multiply and replenish the earth.' Most of the civilest nations of the world labour to fetch their original from some one of the sons or nephews of Noah, which were scattered abroad after the confusion of Babel. In this dispersion we must certainly find the establishment of regal power throughout the kingdoms of the world. . . .

V   Kings are either Fathers of their People, or Heirs of such Fathers, or the Usurpers of the Rights of such Fathers

It may seem absurd to maintain that Kings now are the fathers of their people, since experience shows the contrary. It is true, all Kings be not the natural parents of their subjects, yet they all either are, or are to be reputed, as the next heirs of those progenitors who were at first the natural parents of the whole people, and in their right succeed to the exercise of supreme jurisdiction. And such heirs are not only lords of their own children, but also of their brethren, and all others that were subject to their Fathers. . . .

VI   Of the Escheating of Kingdoms

It may be demanded what becomes of the right of fatherhood in case the Crown does escheat for want of an heir, whether it doth not then devolve to the people. The answer is:

First, it is but the negligence or ignorance of the people to lose the knowledge of the true heir, for an heir there always is. If Adam himself were still living, and now ready to die, it is certain that there is one man, and but one in the world, who is next heir, although the knowledge who should be that one man be quite lost. . . .

In all kingdoms or commonwealths in the world, whether the Prince be the supreme Father of the people or but the true heir of such a Father, or whether he come to the Crown by usurpation, or by election of the nobles or of the people, or by any other way whatsoever, or whether some few or a multitude govern the commonwealth, yet still the authority that is in any one, or in many, or in all of these, is the only right and natural authority of a supreme Father. There is, and always shall be continued to the end of the world, a natural right of a supreme Father over every multitude, although, by the secret will of God, many at first do most unjustly obtain the exercise of it.

Sir Robert Filmer, op. cit., chs 3-6, pp. 57-62.)

CHAPTER 16

The English Civil War and Commonwealth

The reigns of James I (1603-1625) and Charles I (1625-1649) stimulated surprisingly little anti-monarchical writings. The main theme of political thought in the first forty years of the seventeenth century was the limitation rather than the overthrow of monarchy.

Francis Bacon

The most outstanding political figure on the royalist side during these years was James I's intellectual ally and attorney-general, Francis Bacon. Bacon was not a believer in the divine right of kings—in fact before the civil war there were very few exponents of that theory outside the ranks of the Anglican clergy; he was, however, conservatively inclined, defending the use of the royal prerogative in the interests of the state and the unqualified allegiance of subjects to the king. This is emphasized in his essay *Of Judicature* (Ex. 61a) in which he argues that judges only interpret and do not make law. They are to remember the maxim, *Salus populi suprema lex* (the welfare of the people is the highest law) and must therefore not interfere with the sovereignty of the king.

In his essay *Of Seditions* (Ex. 61b), Bacon argues that poverty and discontent are the great causes of sedition. The state must therefore involve itself in economic life by regulating industry and prices and ensuring that extremes of wealth and poverty are eliminated. In a passage reminiscent of Machiavelli's *Prince* he points to the danger of allowing a focus of disaffection to be built up around an important rival and advocates the military suppression of potential seditions before they develop.

Edward Coke

Opposition to the practice of government by prerogative came first of all from the lawyers, led by Edward Coke, and later from the Puritans. Coke claimed that the law and not the king was the true ruler of England, but his ultra-conservative temperament led him to view parliament's function not as that of making laws but of declaring principles which already existed in the ancestral common law.

Coke's principle of the supremacy of common law over parliamentary statute was best illustrated in Bonham's Case (1610). The court denied the right of the Royal College of Physicians to act under authority given to it by parliamentary statute on the grounds that its action was forbidden by common law. The Petition of Right drafted by Coke in 1628 and which Charles I was forced to sign may be regarded as epitomizing the struggle to limit the king's prerogative powers.

The Levellers

The anti-royalist side in the English Civil War was a heterogeneous alliance of quite distinct political and religious groups. It embraced those who wished only to limit what they regarded as the unconstitutional excesses of Stuart monarchy and those who were prepared to change the whole balance of king and parliament. In the religious field it included those who merely wished to eradicate the 'popish' elements introduced by Archbishop Laud and Charles I and those who desired to change the whole establishment in a Calvinist direction. The Levellers and Diggers represented the 'left wing' in that they demanded radical democratic reforms in the political and economic structure.

Most of the New Model Army was independent in religion. But whereas the officers tended to be middle class and cautious in their proposals for reform, many of the other ranks, having less to lose, were in favour of a radical change in the constitution. These men constituted the Leveller party. Most of them, including their leader John Lilburne, had been solidly behind Parliament in its resistance to the king at the beginning of the war. They considered that the king had broken his implied contract with the people and should therefore be overthrown. The negotiations of 1647 between Charles I, Parliament and Cromwell led to fears among the army rank and file that a settlement would be reached which would leave things substantially as they were. It seemed to them that the best that could be hoped for was the replacement of Episcopalianism by Presbyterianism as the established religion and the replacement of an oppressive king by an oppressive parliament.

The Levellers considered that their struggle against royal absolutism should lead to a transference of sovereignty from the monarchy to the people. This democratic sentiment was manifested in many documents including *The Agreement of the People* which was presented to the army council in 1647 (Ex. 62). The *Agreement*, which owed a great deal to the ideas of John Lilburne, contained a number of radical proposals. Parliament was to be dissolved in a year's time; future parliaments were to be chosen by 'the people' every two years: the power of such parliaments was to be inferior to no one save the people; the 'native rights' of liberty and equality were to be maintained 'against all opposition'.

The proposals in the *Agreement* were discussed by the members of the army council at Putney where the Leveller representatives were faced by the opposition of Oliver Cromwell and his formidable son-in-law, Ireton.

In the debate the ideological division between the two parties became more clear-cut. The Levellers stood for guaranteed natural rights and popular sovereignty to be exercised through a fully representative parliament; the army chiefs considered natural rights to be a subversive doctrine and maintained that sovereignty should lie with a parliament representing the interests of men of property—those men who have, as Ireton said, 'a permanent fixed interest in this kingdom'.

In his attack on the principle of natural rights, Ireton affected to believe that such a doctrine should lead to anarchy. It would, he thought, allow each individual the right to decide according to conscience whether or not he would obey the law, and furthermore it would make private property insecure. This was an unfair argument. The Levellers never proposed such an extreme individualism. They merely pointed out that it was unjust to enforce obedience to all laws on men who had no opportunity to consent to the machinery whereby the laws were made. In the words of Colonel Rainborough: 'Every man who is to live under a government ought first by his own consent to put himself under that government; and I do think the poorest man in England is not strictly bound to that government that he had not a voice to put himself under.'

The Levellers were ahead of their time. The proposals in *The Agreement of the People* made no headway against the entrenched opposition of the 'Independent Grandees' who emasculated the document before presenting it to an unyielding parliament. A final version of the *Agreement* made its appearance in 1649, in which the implied manhood suffrage of the 1647 document was made explicit. All men were to be allowed to vote provided that they had not fought for the king or were not servants or in receipt of alms.

The Leveller movement declined after rank and file mutinies in the army had been put down with great severity. It was never resurrected. No comparable English theory of popular democracy was to emerge again until the nineteenth century.

The Diggers

Although the Levellers were accused by many of being in favour of the redistribution of wealth, this was never their objective. They demanded a political rather than an economic democracy. On the other hand, one contemporary group imbued with the ideas of their leader,

Gerrard Winstanley, did advocate a thorough-going communism. This group called itself the True Levellers or Diggers, the latter name being applied to it as a result of its action in 1649 of settling on and cultivating a stretch of common land on St George's Hill in Surrey. The intention of the Diggers in their communist experiment was to provide an example of peaceful communal living which it was hoped would eventually recommend the practice to everybody. As Christians and pacifists they disclaimed any intention of forcibly overthrowing the existing economic order and expropriating the landlords, although in the pamphlet, *The True Levellers' Standard Advanced* (April 1649), the implication is that the oppressed poor will in time rise up against the property system.

In a letter written to Lord Fairfax and his Council of War just after Fairfax had visited the Digger settlement, Winstanley explains that common ownership of the earth is justified by the law of nature (Ex. 63a). Oppressive laws are rooted in greed which is inseparable from private ownership. In a series of questions addressed to the lawyers he argues that as the English people were dispossessed by William the Conqueror and their lands held by William's successors, the defeat of the king in the civil war ought to lead to the restoration of the land to the people and the replacement of unjust laws by laws based upon equality.

The Law of Freedom written by Gerrard Winstanley in 1652 is a description of a communist society comparable with those of More (*Utopia*) and Campanella (*City of the Sun*). The 'true commonwealth' has its basis in 'true freedom' which stems from the common use of the earth (Ex. 63b). Private ownership of land is responsible for all the human evils. Kingly government differs from 'commonwealth's government' as bondage, oppression and ignorance differ from freedom and knowledge.

In addition to private property, wages and money are to be abolished. There is to be universal adult suffrage, retirement from work at the age of forty, and the substitution of communal discussion of current affairs and the natural sciences for organized religious worship.

Unfortunately the times were not propitious for the establishment of Winstanley's dream. His settlement in Surrey aroused the resentment of the local gentry, who had no trouble in obtaining military help to disperse it. Although the Diggers were only a small and transitory community, they were an interesting manifestation of a traditional political notion which stretched from the Stoics to the Marxists—that most of man's troubles can be attributed to the institution of private property.

John Milton (1608–1674)

Milton's justly famous statement of the right of free expression in the *Areopagitica* (1644) has overshadowed his more specifically political writings. These are interesting and occasionally original but rarely profound. *The Tenure of Kings and Magistrates* (1649) appeared a fortnight after the execution of Charles I and was a defence of regicide based upon a contract theory of government (Ex. 64a). Men are naturally free but prone to wrong-doing. Hence they agreed by a form of social contract to refrain from mutual injury and set up political society. Realizing that governmental authority was necessary to keep the peace, kings and magistrates were elected who undertook to rule according to law and justice. Kings therefore have only a derived power which comes from the people, and it follows that the people may renounce their allegiance should the king act contrary to trust. Indeed, the people may depose him at any time and for any reason they think fit, 'though no tyrant'. Milton's theory, which in some respects bears a strong resemblance to that of John Locke, surprisingly does not argue for republican government.

In his *Ready and Easy Way to Establish a Free Commonwealth* (1660) written just before the restoration of the monarchy, Milton elaborates his republican ideas, which had been developing since the establishment of the Commonwealth (Ex. 64b). In this, his last political tract, he proposes that a perpetual council of the ablest men should be elected to govern an English republic. Such an aristocracy he conceived as the only alternative to a restored monarchy. In this unrealistic proposal Milton exhibits the same paradox as that later held by some of the *Philosophes* of the French enlightenment: a passionate love of individual liberty combined with a Platonic contempt for the abilities of the masses.

James Harrington (1611–1677)

Harrington has claims to be considered the most eminent and influential of the republican political theorists. His book, *Oceana*, published in 1656, is in the Utopian tradition. The commonwealth of Oceana (a disguised England) is a country that has replaced its former monarchy by a republican constitution in which the various social, political and economic forces are properly balanced. This balance, argues Harrington, comes from ensuring that land holdings are widely distributed since political and economic power tend to go together in the long run. Thus, absolute monarchy occurs where one man owns all or most of the land; a mixed monarchy where the few own most of the land; and commonwealth where the whole people are landlords (Ex. 65a). The theory reminds one forcibly of the Marxist conception of the relationship of the social and political superstructure to the economic substructure of society.

Should the economic structure change, political arrangements must change accordingly. If they do not, tensions and conflicts develop and civil war, such as that experienced by Oceana, takes place. The parallel with England is clear. Harrington argues that since the reign of Henry VIII economic power had been passing from the nobles to the people. The English civil war was therefore a conflict rooted in the erosion of the economic power supporting the monarch. The new distribution of wealth indicates that a commonwealth or republic is the appropriate form of constitution.

In Oceana the balance of the commonwealth is to be preserved by the agrarian laws which limit the amount of land held by any man to a value of £2,000 per year (£500 per year in Marpesia, or Scotland) (Ex. 65b). These laws ensure a permanent broad base for the common-wealth. Further proposals made by Harrington include rotation in office, voting by ballot, a wide franchise excluding only employees, and a government comprising an aristocratic senate and popular assembly. Executive magistrates are to be elected by the senate.

Harrington's constitutional theories were an amalgam of Aristotle's belief in the stability of the middle-class 'polity', and Machiavelli's reliance upon the satisfaction of material self-interest as a pre-requisite of political order. His influence was great. The constitutions of several New England states reflected some of the actual ideas of *Oceana*, although a petition asking for the formation of an English government on Oceanic lines was turned down by parliament.

FURTHER READING

Texts
F. Bacon: *Essays*
D. M. Wolfe (ed.): *Leveller Manifestoes of the Puritan Revolution* (Cass 1967)
G. Winstanley: *The Law of Freedom*
J. Milton: *The Tenure of Kings and Magistrates*
        Ready and Easy Way to Establish a Free Commonwealth
J. Harrington: *Oceana*

Commentaries
L. H. Berens: *The Digger Movement in the Days of the Commonwealth* (Simpkin Marshall 1906)
G. P. Gooch: *English Democratic Ideas in the Seventeenth Century* (Harper and Row, N.Y. 1959)
C. Hill: *The World Turned Upside Down* (Temple Smith 1972)
P. Zagorin: *A History of Political Thought in the English Revolution* (Routledge & Kegan Paul 1954)

61a FRANCIS BACON: OF JUDICATURE

Judges ought, above all, to remember the conclusion of the Roman Twelve Tables, *The welfare of the people is the supreme law*; and to know that laws, except they be in order to that end, are but things captious, and oracles not well inspired; therefore it is a happy thing in a state, when kings and states do often consult with judges; and again, when judges do often consult with the king and state: the one, when there is matter of law intervenient in business of state; the other, when there is some consideration of state intervenient in matter of law; for many times the things deduced to judgment may be *meum* and *tuum*, when the reason and consequence thereof may trench to point of estate. I call matter of estate, not only the parts of sovereignty, but whatsoever introduceth any great alteration, or dangerous precedent, or concerneth manifestly any great portion of people; and let no man weakly conceive that just laws and true policy have any antipathy, for they are like the spirits and sinews, that one moves with the other. Let judges also remember that Solomon's throne was supported by lions on both sides; let them be lions, but yet lions under the throne, being circumspect that they do not check or oppose any points of sovereignty. Let not judges also be so ignorant of their own right, as to think there is not left to them, as a principal part of their office, a wise use and application of laws; for they may remember what the apostle saith of a greater law than theirs: *We know that the law is good if a man use it lawfully*.

(Francis Bacon, *Of Judicature*, in *Essays and New Atlantis*, ed. G. S. Haight, pp. 230-1, Walter J. Black Inc., New York 1942.)

61b FRANCIS BACON: OF SEDITIONS AND TROUBLES

The causes and motives of seditions are, innovation in religion, taxes, alteration of laws and customs, breaking of privileges, general oppression, advancement of unworthy persons, strangers, dearths, disbanded soldiers, factions grown desperate, and whatsoever in offending people joineth and knitteth them in a common cause. . . .

The first remedy, or prevention, is to remove, by all means possible, that material cause of sedition whereof we spake, which is, want and poverty in the estate; to which purpose serveth the opening and well-balancing of trade; the cherishing of manufactures; the banishing of idleness; the repressing of waste and excess by sumptuary laws; the improvement and husbanding of the soil; the regulating of prices of things vendible; the moderating of taxes and tributes, and the like. Generally, it is to be foreseen that the population of a kingdom (especially if it be not mown down by wars) do not exceed the stock of the kingdom which should maintain them; neither is the population to be reckoned only by number; for a smaller number, that spend more and earn less, do wear out an estate sooner than a greater number that live lower and gather more. Therefore the multiplying of nobility and other degrees of quality, in an overproportion to the common people, doth speedily bring a state to necessity; and so doth likewise an overgrown clergy, for they bring nothing to the stock; and in like manner, when more are bred scholars than preferments can take off. . . .

Above all things, good policy is to be used, that the treasure and moneys in a state be not gathered into few hands; for, otherwise, a state may have a great stock, and yet starve. And money is like muck, not good except it be spread. This is done chiefly by suppressing, or, at the least, keeping a strait hand upon the devouring trades of usury, engrossing, great pasturages, and the like. . . .

Certainly the politic and artificial nourishing and entertaining of hopes, and carrying men from hopes to hopes, is one of the best antidotes against the poison of discontentments; and it is a certain sign of a wise government and proceeding, when it can hold men's hearts by hopes, when it cannot by satisfaction; and when it can handle things in such manner as no evil shall appear so peremptory, but that it hath some outlet of hope; which is the less hard to do, because both particular persons and factions are apt enough to flatter themselves, or at least to brave that which they believe not.

Also the foresight and prevention, that there be no likely or fit head whereunto discontented persons may resort, and under whom they may join, is a known but an excellent point of caution. I understand a fit head to be one that hath greatness and reputation, that hath confidence with the discontented party, and upon whom they turn their eyes, and that is thought discontented in his own particular: which kind of persons are either to be won and reconciled to the state, and that in a fast and true manner; or to be fronted with some other of the same party that may oppose them, and so divide the reputation. Generally, the dividing and breaking of all factions and combinations that are adverse to the state, and setting them at distance, or at least distrust amongst themselves, is not one of the worst remedies; for it is a desperate case, if those that hold with the proceeding of the state be full of discord and faction, and those that are against it be entire and united. . . .

Lastly, let princes, against all events, not be without some great person, one or rather more, of military valor, near unto them, for the repressing of seditions in their beginnings; for without that, there useth to be more trepidation in court upon the first breaking out of troubles than were fit, and the state runneth the danger of that which Tacitus saith: *And such was the state of mind that a few dared to commit the worst crime, many more would have liked to do so, and all acquiesced*; but let such military persons be assured, and well reputed of, rather than factious and popular; holding also good correspondence with the other great men in the state, or else the remedy is worse than the disease.

(Francis Bacon, *Of Seditions and Troubles*, op. cit., pp. 60-5.)

62   THE LEVELLERS: AN AGREEMENT OF THE PEOPLE, FOR A FIRME AND PRESENT PEACE, UPON GROUNDS OF COMMON-RIGHT

Having by our late labours and hazards made it appeare to the world at how high a rate wee value our just freedome, and God having so far owned our cause, as to deliver the Enemies thereof into our hands: We do now hold our selves bound in mutual duty to each other, to take the best care we can for the future, to avoid both the danger of returning into a slavish condition, and the chargable remedy of another war: for as it cannot be imagined that so many of our Country-men would have opposed us in this quarrel, if they had understood their owne good; so may we safely promise to our selves, that when our Common Rights and liberties shall be cleared, their endeavours will be disappointed, that seek to make themselves our Masters: since therefore our former oppressions, and scarce yet ended troubles have beene occasioned, either by want of frequent Nationall meetings in Councell, or by rendring those meetings ineffectuall; We are fully agreed and resolved, to provide that hereafter our Representatives be neither left to an uncertainty for the time, nor made uselesse to the ends for which they are intended: In order whereunto we declare,

I

That the People of England being at this day very unequally distributed by Counties, Cities, & Burroughs, for the election of their Deputies in Parliament, ought to be more indifferently proportioned, according to the number of the Inhabitants: the circumstances whereof, for number, place, and manner, are to be set down before the end of this present Parliament.

II

That to prevent the many inconveniences apparently arising from the long continuance of the same persons in authority, this present Parliament be dissolved upon the last day of September, which shall be in the year of our Lord, 1648.

III

That the People do of course chuse themselves a Parliament once in two yeares, viz. upon the first Thursday in every 2d. March, after the manner as shall be prescribed before the end of this Parliament, to begin to sit upon the first Thursday in Aprill following at Westminster, or such other place as shall bee appointed from time to time by the preceding Representatives; and to continue till the last day of September, then next ensuing, and no longer.

IV

That the power of this, and all future Representatives of this Nation, is inferiour only to theirs who chuse them, and doth extend, without the consent or concurrence of any other person or persons; to the enacting, altering, and repealing of Lawes; to the erecting and abolishing of Offices and Courts; to the appointing, removing, and calling to account Magistrates, and Officers of all degrees; to the making War and peace, to the treating with forraign States:

And generally, to whatsoever is not expresly, or implyedly reserved by the represented to themselves.

Which are as followeth,

1. That matters of Religion, and the wayes of Gods Worship, are not at all intrusted by us to any humane power, because therein wee cannot remit or exceed a tittle of what our Consciences dictate to be the mind of God, without wilfull sinne: neverthelesse the publike way of instructing the Nation (so it be not compulsive) is referred to their discretion.
2. That the matter of impresting and constraining any of us to serve in the warres, is against our freedome; and therefore we do not allow it in our Representatives; the rather, because money (the sinews of war) being alwayes at their disposall, they can never want numbers of men, apt enough to engage in any just cause.
3. That after the dissolution of this present Parliament, no person be at any time questioned for anything said or done, in reference to the late publike differences, otherwise then in execution of the Judgments of the present Representatives, or House of Commons.
4. That in all Laws made, or to be made, every person may be bound alike, and that no Tenure, Estate, Charter, Degree, Birth, or place, do confer any exemption from the ordinary Course of Legall proceedings, whereunto others are subjected.
5. That as the Laws ought to be equall, so they must be good, and not evidently destructive to the safety and well-being of the people.

These things we declare to be our native Rights, *and therefore are agreed and resolved to maintain them with our utmost possibilities, against all opposition whatsoever, being compelled thereunto, not only by the examples of our Ancestors, whose bloud was often spent in vain for the recovery of their Freedomes, suffering themselves,* through fradulent accommodations, *to be still deluded of the fruit of their Victories, but also by our own wofull experience, who having long expected, & dearly earned the establishment of these certain rules of Government are yet made to depend for the settlement of our Peace and Freedome, upon him that intended our bondage, and brought a cruell Warre upon us.*

(*An Agreement of the People*, in D. M. Wolfe, ed., *Leveller Manifestoes of the Puritan Revolution*, pp. 226-8, Frank Cass, London 1967.)

63a GERRARD WINSTANLEY: A LETTER TO LORD FAIRFAX AND HIS COUNCIL OF WAR:

With divers questions to the Lawyers and Ministers:Proving it an undeniable equity that the Common People ought to dig, plow, plant and dwell upon the Commons without hiring them or paying Rent to any.
    Delivered to the General and his Chief Officers, June 9th, 1649, by Gerrard Winstanley in the behalf of those who have begun to dig upon George Hill in Surrey.

Our digging and ploughing upon George Hill in Surrey is not unknown to you, since you have seen some of our persons, and heard us speak in defence thereof; and we did receive kindness and moderation from you and your Council of War, both when some of us were at Whitehall before you, and when you came in person to George Hill to view our works. We endeavour to lay open the bottom and intent of our business as much as can be, that none may be troubled with doubtful imaginations about us, but may be satisfied in the sincerity and universal righteousness of the work.

We understand that our digging upon that Common is the talk of the whole Land, some approving, some disowning; some are friends filled with love, and see that the work intends good to the Nation, the peace whereof is that which we seek after; others are enemies filled with fury, who falsely report of us that we have intent to fortify ourselves, and afterwards to fight against others and take away their goods from them, which is a thing we abhor. And many other slanders we rejoice over, because we know ourselves clear, our endeavour being no otherwise but to improve the Commons and to call off that oppression and outward bondage which the Creation groans under, as much as in us lies, and to lift up and preserve the purity thereof. . . .

We told you, upon a question you put to us, that we were not against any that would have Magistrates and Laws to govern, as the Nations of the World are governed, but that, for our own parts, we shall need neither the one nor the other in that nature of government. For as our land is common, so our cattle is to be common, and our corn and fruits of the earth common, and are not to be bought and sold among us, but to remain a standing portion of livelihood to us and our children, without that cheating entanglement of buying and selling; and we shall not arrest one another. And then what need have we of imprisoning, whipping or hanging laws to bring one another into bondage? And we know that none of those that are subject to this righteous law dares arrest or enslave his brother for or about the objects of the Earth, because the Earth is made by our Creator to be a Common Treasury of Livelihood to one equal with another, without respect of persons . . . What need have we of any outward, selfish, confused laws, made to uphold the Power of Covetousness, when we have the Righteous Law written in our hearts, teaching us to walk purely in the Creation.

We desire that your Lawyers may consider these questions, which we affirm to be truths, and which give good assurance, by the law of the land, that we that are the younger brothers, or common people, have a true right to dig, plow up and dwell upon the Commons, as we have declared.

Questions to the Lawyers

1. Did not William the Conqueror dispossess the English, and thus cause them to be servants to him?

2. Was not King Charles the direct successor of William the First?

3. Whether Lords of the Manor were not the successors of the chief officers of William the First, holding their rights to the Commons by the power of the sword?

4. Whether Lords of the Manor have not lost their royalty to the common lånd by the recent victories?

5. Whether any laws since the coming in of kings have been made in the light of the righteous law of our Creation, *respecting all alike,* or have not been grounded upon selfish principles in fear or flattery of their king, to uphold freedom in the gentry and clergy, and to hold the common people under bondage still, and so respecting persons?

6. Whether all laws that are not grounded upon equity and reason, not giving an universal freedom to all, but respecting persons, ought not to be cut off with the king's head? We affirm they ought. If all laws be grounded upon equity and reason, then the whole land of England is to be a Common Treasury to everyone born in the Land.

7. Whether everyone without exception, by the Law of Contract, ought not to have liberty to enjoy the earth for his livelihood, and to settle his dwelling in any part of the Commons of England, without buying or renting land of any, seeing that everyone by agreement and covenant among themselves have paid taxes, given free-quarter and adventured their lives to recover England out of bondage? We affirm they ought.

8. Whether the laws that were made in the days of the king do give freedom to any but the gentry and clergy?

(Quoted in L. H. Berens, *The Digger Movement in the Days of the Commonwealth,* pp. 100-3, Simpkin, Marshall and Co, London 1906.)

63b   GERRARD WINSTANLEY: THE LAW OF FREEDOM

TRUE COMMONWEALTH'S FREEDOM LIES IN THE FREE ENJOYMENT OF THE EARTH

True Freedom lies where a man receives his nourishment and preservation, and that is in the use of the Earth. . . .All that a man labours for, saith Solomon, is this, That he may enjoy the free use of the Earth with the fruits thereof (Eccles. 2:24). Do not the Ministers preach for maintenance in the Earth? The Lawyers plead causes to get the possessions of the Earth? Doth not the Soldier fight for the Earth? And doth not the Land Lord require Rent that he may live in the fullness of the Earth by the labour of his Tenants? And so from the Thief upon the Highway to the King who sits upon the Throne, does not everyone strive, either by force of Arms or secret Cheats, to get the possessions of the Earth one from another, because they see their Freedom lies in plenty, and their Bondage lies in Poverty?

Surely, then, oppressing Lords of Manors, exacting Landlords and Tythe-takers, may as well say their Bretheren shall not breathe in the air, nor enjoy warmth in their bodies, nor have the moist waters to fall upon them in showers, unless they will pay them rent for it, as to say their Bretheren shall not work upon Earth, nor eat the fruits thereof, unless they will hire that liberty of them. For he that takes upon him to restrain his Brother from the liberty of the one, may upon the same ground restrain him from the liberty of all four viz, Fire, Water, Earth and Air.

A man had better to have had no body than to have no food for it.

Therefore this restraining of the Earth from Bretheren by Bretheren is oppression and bondage; but the free enjoyment thereof is true Freedom.

INWARD AND OUTWARD BONDAGE

I speak now in relation between the Oppressor and the Oppressed, the Inward Bondages I meddle not with in this place, though I am assured that if it be rightly searched into, the inward bondages of the mind, as covetousness, pride, hypocrisy, envy, sorrow, fears, desperation and madness, are all occasioned by the outward bondage that one sort of people lay upon another. And thus far natural experience makes it good, THAT TRUE FREEDOM LIES IN THE FREE ENJOYMENT OF THE EARTH.

WHAT IS GOVERNMENT IN GENERAL?

Government is a wise and free ordering of the Earth and of the Manners of Mankind by observation of particular Laws or Rules, so that all the inhabitants may live peaceably in plenty and freedom in the Land where they are born and bred.

WHAT IS KINGLY GOVERNMENT?

There is a twofold Government: a Kingly Government and a Commonwealth's Government.

Kingly Government governs the Earth by that cheating art of buying and selling, and thereby becomes a man of contention, his hand is against every man, and every man's hand against him . . . and if it had not a Club Law to support it, there would be no order in it, because it is but the covetous and proud will of a Conqueror enslaving a conquered people. . . . Indeed, this Government may well be called the Government of Highwaymen, who hath stolen the Earth from the Younger Bretheren by force and holds it from them by force. . . . The great Lawgiver of this Kingly Government is Covetousness, ruling in the hearts of mankind, making one Brother to covet a full possession of the Earth, and a Lordly Rule over another Brother. . . . The Rise of Kingly Government is attributable to a politic wit in drawing the people out of Common Freedom into a way of Common Bondage: FOR SO LONG AS THE EARTH IS A COMMON TREASURY TO ALL MEN, KINGLY COVETOUSNESS CAN NEVER REIGN AS KING.

WHAT IS COMMONWEALTH'S GOVERNMENT?

Commonwealth's Government governs the Earth without buying and selling, and thereby becomes a man of peace, and the Restorer of Ancient Peace and Freedom. He makes provision for the oppressed, the weak and the simple, as well as for the rich, the wise and the strong. . . . All slavery and Oppressions . . . are cast out by this Government, *if it be right in power as well as in name*. . . . IF ONCE COMMONWEALTH'S GOVERNMENT BE SET UPON THE THRONE, THEN NO TYRANNY OR OPPRESSION CAN LOOK HIM IN THE FACE AND LIVE.

(Quoted in L. H. Berens, op. cit., pp. 180–2.)

64a JOHN MILTON: THE TENURE OF KINGS AND MAGISTRATES

No man who knows aught, can be so stupid to deny that all men naturally were born free, being the image and resemblance of God himself, and were, by privilege above all the creatures, born to command, and not to obey; and that they lived so, till from the root of Adam's transgression falling among themselves to do wrong and violence, and foreseeing that such courses must needs tend to the destruction of them all, they agreed by common league to bind each other from mutual injury; and jointly to defend themselves against any that gave disturbance or opposition to such agreement. Hence came cities, towns, and commonwealths. And because no faith in all was found sufficiently binding, they saw it needful to ordain some authority that might restrain by force and punishment what was violated against peace and common right.

This authority and power of self-defence and preservation being originally and naturally in every one of them, and unitedly in them all, for ease, for order, and lest each man should be his own partial judge, they communicated and derived either to one whom for the eminence of his wisdom and integrity they chose above the rest, or to more than one whom they thought of equal deserving. The first was called a king, the other, magistrates: not to be their lords and masters (though afterwards those names in some places were given voluntarily to such as had been authors of inestimable good to the people), but to be their deputies and commissioners, to execute, by virtue of their intrusted power, that justice which else every man by the bond of nature and of covenant must have executed for himself, and for one another. And to him that shall consider well why among free persons one man by civil right should bear authority and jurisdiction over another, no other end or reason can be imaginable.

These for a while governed well and with much equity decided all things at their own arbitrement, till the temptation of such a power, left absolute in their hands, perverted them at length to injustice and partiality. Then did they who now by trial had found the danger and inconveniences of committing arbitrary power to any, invent laws, either framed or consented to by all, that should confine and limit the authority of whom they chose to govern them: that so man, of whose failing they had proof, might no more rule over them, but law and reason, abstracted as much as might be from personal errors and frailties: while, as the magistrate was set above the people, so the law was set above the magistrate. When this would not serve, but that the law was either not executed, or misapplied, they were constrained from that time, the only remedy left them, to put conditions and take oaths from all kings and magistrates at their first instalment to do impartial justice by law: who, upon those terms and no other, received allegiance from the people, that is to say, bond or covenant to obey them in execution of those laws which they, the people, had themselves made or assented to. And this oft-times with express warning, that if the king or magistrate proved unfaithful to his trust, the people would be disengaged.

They added also counsellors and parliaments, not to be only at his beck, but, with him or without him, at set times, or at all times when any danger threatened, to have care of the public safety. .. . .

It being thus manifest that the power of kings and magistrates is nothing else but what is only derivative, transferred, and committed to them in trust from the people to the common good of them all, in whom the power yet remains fundamentally and cannot be taken from them without a violation of their natural birthright, and seeing that from hence Aristotle, and the best of political writers, have defined a king, 'him who governs to the good and profit of his people, and not for his own ends'—it follows from necessary causes that the titles of sovereign lord, natural lord, and the like, are either arrogancies or flatteries, not admitted by emperors and kings of best note, and disliked by the church. . .

It follows, lastly, that since the king or magistrate holds his authority of the people, both originally and naturally for their good in the first place, and not his own, then may the people, as oft as they shall judge it for the best, either choose him or reject him, retain him or depose him, though no tyrant, merely by the liberty and right of freeborn men to be governed as seems to them best. This, though it cannot but stand with plain reason, shall be made good also by Scripture (Deut xvii.14): 'When thou art come into the land which the Lord thy God giveth thee, and shalt say, I will set a king over me, like as all the nations about me.' These words confirm us that the right of choosing, yea of changing their own government, is by the grant of·God himself in the people.

(Milton, *Prose Writing*, pp. 191-5, Everyman Library Edition, Dent, London and E. P. Dutton, New York, 1958.)

64b JOHN MILTON: THE READY AND EASY WAY TO ESTABLISH A FREE COMMONWEALTH

I doubt not but all ingenuous and knowing men will easily agree with me, that a free commonwealth without single person or house of lords is by far the best government, if it can be had; but we have all this while, say they, been expecting it, and cannot yet attain it. It is true, indeed, when monarchy was dissolved, the form of a commonwealth should have forthwith been framed, and the practice thereof immediately begun; that the people might have soon been satisfied and delighted with the decent order, ease, and benefit thereof; we had been then by this time firmly rooted, past fear of commotions or mutations, and now flourishing; this care of timely settling a new government instead of the old, too much neglected, hath been our mischief. Yet the cause thereof may be ascribed with most reason to the frequent disturbances, interruptions, and dissolutions, which the parliament hath had, partly from the impatient or disaffected people, partly from some ambitious leaders in the army; much contrary, I believe, to the mind and approbation of the army itself, and their other commanders, once undeceived, or in their own power.

Now is the opportunity, now the very season, wherein we may obtain a free commonwealth, and establish it for ever in the land, without difficulty or much delay. Writs are sent out for elections, and, which is worth observing; in the name, not of any king, but of the keepers of our liberty, to summon a free parliament: which then only will indeed be free; and deserve the true honour of that supreme title, if they preserve us a free people. Which never parliament was more free to do, being now called not as heretofore, by the summons of a king, but by the voice of liberty. And if the people, laying aside prejudice and impatience, will seriously and calmly now consider their own good, both religious and civil, their own liberty and the only means thereof, as shall be here laid down before them, and will elect their knights and burgesses able men, and according to the just and necessary qualifications (which, for aught I hear, remain yet in force unrepealed, as they were formerly decreed in parliament), men not addicted to a single person or house of lords, the work is done; at least the foundation firmly laid of a free commonwealth, and good part also erected of the main structure. For the ground and basis of every just and free government (since men have smarted so oft for committing all to one person), is a general council of ablest men, chosen by the people to consult of public affairs from time to time for the common good. In this grand council must the sovereignty, not transferred, but delegated only, and as it were desposited, reside; with this caution, they must have the forces by sea and land committed to them for preservation of the common peace and liberty; must raise and manage the public revenue, at least with some inspectors deputed for satisfaction of the people, how it is employed; must make or propose, as more expressly shall be said anon, civil laws, treat of commerce, peace or war with foreign nations; and, for the carrying on some particular affairs with more secrecy and expedition, must elect, as they have already out of their own number and others, a council of state.

And, although it may seem strange at first hearing, by reason that men's minds are prepossessed with the notion of successive parliaments, I affirm, that the grand or general council, being well chosen, should be perpetual: for so their business is or may be, and ofttimes urgent; the opportunity of affairs gained or lost in a moment. The day of council cannot be set as the day of a festival; but must be ready always to prevent or answer all occasions. By this continuance they will become every way skilfullest, best provided of intelligence from abroad, best acquainted with the people at home, and the people with them. The ship of the commonwealth is always under sail; they sit at the stern, and if they steer well, what need is there to change them, it being rather dangerous?

(Milton, op. cit., pp. 228-9.)

65a JAMES HARRINGTON: RELATION OF POLITICAL AND ECONOMIC POWER

Empire is of two kinds: domestic and national, or foreign and provincial.

Domestic empire is founded upon dominion.

Dominion is property, real or personal; that is to say, in lands or in money and goods.

Lands, or the parts and parcels of a territory, are held by the proprietor or proprietors, lord or lords of it, in some proportion; and such (except it be in a city that has little or no land and whose revenue is in trade) as is the proportion or balance of dominion or property in land, such is the nature of the empire.

If one man be sole landlord of a territory, or overbalance the people, for example, three parts in four, he is *Grand Signior:* for so the Turk is called from his property; and his empire is absolute monarchy.

If the few or a nobility, or a nobility with the clergy be landlords, or overbalance the people unto the like proportion, it makes the Gothic balance (to be shown at large in the second part of this Discourse), and the empire is mixed monarchy, as that of Spain, Poland, and late of Oceana.

And if the whole people be landlords, or hold the lands so divided among them that no one man or number of men within the compass of the few or aristocracy overbalance them, the empire (without the interposition of force) is a commonwealth.

If force be interposed in any of these three cases, it must either frame the government to the foundation, or the foundation to the government; or, holding the government not according to the balance, it is not natural but violent; and therefore, if it be at the devotion of a prince, it is tyranny; if at the devotion of the few, oligarchy; or if in the power of the people, anarchy. Each of which confusions, the balance standing otherwise, is but of short continuance, because against the nature of the balance which, not destroyed, destroys that which opposes it.

But there be certain other confusions which, being rooted in the balance, are of longer continuance and of greater horror. As first, where a nobility holds half the property, or about that proportion, and the people the other half; in which case, without altering the balance, there is no remedy but the one must eat out the other, as the people did the nobility in Athens, and the nobility the people in Rome. Secondly, when a prince holds about half the dominion and the people the other half, which was the case of the Roman emperors, planted partly upon their military colonies and partly upon the Senate and the people, the government becomes a very shambles both of the princes and the people. Somewhat of this nature are certain governments at this day which are said to subsist by confusion. In this case, to fix the balance is to entail misery; but, in the three former, not to fix it is to lose the government.

(James Harrington, *Oceana,* part I, pp. 18-19, Routledge and Kegan Paul, London 1887.)

65b   JAMES HARRINGTON: THE AGRARIAN LAWS

Wherefore the fundamental laws of Oceana, or the centre of this commonwealth, are the Agrarian and the ballot: the Agrarian by the balance of dominion preserving equality in the root; and the ballot by an equal rotation conveying it into the branch, or exercise of sovereign power, as, to being with the former, appears by

The thirteenth order, 'Constituting the Agrarian laws of Oceana, Marpesia, and Panopea, whereby it is ordained, first, for all such lands as are lying and being within the proper territories of Oceana, that every man who is at present possessed, or shall hereafter be possessed, of an estate in land exceeding the revenue of £2000 a year, and having more than one son, shall leave his lands either equally divided among them, in case the lands amount to above £2000 a year to each, or so near equally in case they come under, that the greater part or portion of the same remaining to the eldest exceed not the value of £2000 revenue. And no man, not in present possession of lands above the value of £2000 by the year, shall receive, enjoy (except by lawful inheritance), acquire, or purchase to himself lands within the said territories, amounting, with those already in his possession, above the said revenue. And if a man has a daughter, or daughters, except she be an heiress, or they be heiresses, he shall not leave or give to any one of them in marriage, or otherwise, for her portion, above the value of £1500 in lands, goods, and moneys. Nor shall any friend, kinsman, or kinswoman, add to her or their portion or portions that are so provided for, to make any one of them greater. Nor shall any man demand or have more in marriage with any woman. Nevertheless an heiress shall enjoy her lawful inheritance, and a widow, whatsoever the bounty or affection of her husband shall bequeath to her, to be divided in the first generation, wherein it is divisible according as has been shown.

'Secondly, For lands lying and being within the territories of Marpesia, the Agrarian shall hold in all parts as it is established in Oceana, except only in the standard or proportion of estates in land, which shall be set for Marpesia, at five hundred pounds. And,

'Thirdly, For Panopea, the Agrarian shall hold in all parts as in Oceana. And whosoever possessing above the proportion allowed by these laws, shall be lawfully convicted of the same, shall forfeit the overplus to the use of the State.'

(James Harrington, op. cit., part III, pp. 104-5.)

CHAPTER 17

Hobbes and the Social Contract

The foremost theory of political obligation in the seventeenth century was the theory of the social contract. The contractual idea was not devised in the seventeenth century; it had existed in a rather different form since the later Middle Ages and had played a very significant role in the theories stimulated by the French wars of religion. In its sixteenth-century form it is usually referred to as the 'contract of government'; that is, it sought to show that government rested upon a contract which the ruler had made with the people as a whole.

The theory of the 'social contract', on the other hand, if we except rather similar theories held by the Sophists and Epicurus, is a product of the seventeenth century. It is the distinctive mark of the political theory of individualism. It is also closely associated with the rationalist conception of natural law.

Rationalism and Individualism

Seventeenth-century rationalism can best be explained by reference to the modernized theory of natural law. Since the time of the Stoics there had been a rationalist element in the concept of the law of nature. Almost every natural law philosopher had emphasized the working of 'natural reason' in human attempts to discover what the law commanded or prohibited. But in both the Middle Ages and the sixteenth century, the law of nature, although rational, had to be confirmed by other evidence—notably divine revelation and faith.

The devising of a purely rationalist theory of natural law is normally attributed to the Dutch jurist, Hugo Grotius, who stated that the law of nature would remain just as valid if, by hypothesis, God did not exist. He argues that God forbids or commands an act as a consequence of the intrinsic baseness or necessity of that act (Ex. 66). God cannot change the law of nature because he cannot do that which contradicts reality, such as making twice two not equal four. The comparison of the spheres of ethics and mathematics—the most obviously rational of all sciences—is typical of rationalist thinking from Plato onwards. Although much of Grotius's argument was only a continuation of scholastic views about natural law, it did provide a base on which later writers such as Pufendorf could construct a purely secular ethical theory.

The other outstanding new element in seventeenth-century political philosophy was individualism. This can be regarded as the doctrine that each human being should be regarded as a discrete unit, valuable in himself, rather than as a part of a greater whole. It implies, therefore, that each man should be treated as an equal, and normally, although not always, the doctrine implies that he should be allowed private property and a large measure of individual liberty.

As a political concept individualism had flourished among the Stoics of both Greece and Rome. It had declined somewhat in importance during the Middle Ages as a result of the tendency to see men as essentially part of larger corporate bodies, such as the Church, the nobility and the commons. The importance of individualism grew during the sixteenth century partly as a consequence of the Reformation with its emphasis upon the direct communication between God and individual man, and partly as a consequence of the new science which replaced the authority of the Bible and the Church with that of the individual scientist.

Once the notion of the individual equality of all men was generally accepted and human reason was generally recognized as providing an absolute moral standard, the theory of the social contract was seen to be the only logical way of explaining the existence and nature of states and governments. All social contract theories in the seventeenth century contained certain similar elements:

1. All men are born free and equal.
2. Men at some time in the past lived in a 'state of nature' without political organization or laws.
3. The natural condition was imperfect because of the harm done by some men against others.
4. Reason taught men that if they agreed to refrain from harming each other, life would be better.
5. This agreement or 'contract' between individuals brought into existence a politically organized society.
6. In most theories the formation of the state was followed by the establishment of coercive government to enforce the law.

Thomas Hobbes (1588-1679)

The writings which best exemplified the rationalism and individualism of seventeenth-century political philosophy were those of Hobbes. As a moderate royalist who had written in favour of the royal prerogative, Hobbes considered it wise on the outbreak of the civil war to flee to France where he remained in exile for eleven years. His great book *Leviathan*, written during his exile and published in England in 1651, was not well received by the royalist émigrés because of its secularism, and Hobbes thought it advisable to return to London. Cromwell allowed him to remain in England, doubtless because he considered *Leviathan* to be a justification of his own position.

The *Leviathan* is divided into four parts of which the latter two are concerned with the Church and religion and are of relatively minor political importance. The first part, entitled 'Of Man', deals first with human psychology and then with man's natural condition.

Psychology

Hobbes was in his forties when, in the course of a number of visits to Europe, he became converted to the doctrines of rationalism and materialism. His rationalism was derived from his love of geometry and he came to regard the geometrical method as the only means of obtaining true knowledge. His materialism, derived from the French philosopher Gassendi, led him to view the universe as a machine made up of parts moving according to discoverable laws. Man he saw as a microcosm of the universe also made up of predictably moving parts. In his introduction to *Leviathan* he compares living creatures not only to machines, but to the state itself—the Leviathan or artificial man (Ex. 67a).

Although Hobbes was a rationalist he denied that innate ideas exist in the mind. All mental conceptions come originally from sense experience and every idea is the result of the effect produced on the senses by the motion of an external object. Moral concepts are therefore derived from the phenomena of matter and motion and are not innate in man.

All human passions spring from the two basic emotions of desire and aversion. Desire or appetite refers to a potential movement towards an object; aversion is a potential movement away from an object (Ex. 67b). 'Good' is simply a description of something which stimulates appetite; 'evil' is what one feels an aversion towards. It is quite clear that for Hobbes there are no moral absolutes. Each person is impelled solely by his own assessment of self-interest. Not since the Sophists had there been such a forcible expression of naked egoism. On this assumption of a completely subjectivist ethical system, it is easy to see why Hobbes was led to advocate an absolute sovereign power as the only alternative to chaos and conflict.

The State of Nature

Like other contractualists of the period, Hobbes postulates a natural condition of mankind in order to explain the origin and nature of the state (Ex. 67c). The outstanding characteristic of this condition is war, 'where every man is enemy to every man'. Men compete with each other for the same things: food, clothing and so on, but as they have a rough equality of power to attain their ends the inevitable result is conflict. Furthermore, men are vainglorious creatures who crave the admiration and deference of others and this makes matters worse. The result is that man's life is 'solitary, poor, nasty, brutish, and short'.

In the state of nature each man possesses the natural right to do whatever he thinks fit to preserve his life (Ex. 67d). He is also bound by the law of nature which forbids a man to do anything which does not favour the preservation of his life. By the law of nature which he discovers through his reason, man should attempt to find peace and he can only do so if he renounces his natural right to all things. It is the equal natural rights of all men which make life in the state of nature so insecure. It is the apprehension of the rational principles of the law of nature which leads men to abandon their intolerable existence. Later Hobbes argues that these principles ought not to be called 'laws' but 'conclusions' or 'theorems' since 'law, properly, is the word of him that by right hath command over others'. The 'conclusions' of nature are followed not because they are morally binding on men, but because reason tells them that it is expedient to do so.

The Establishment of the State

The second part of *Leviathan* is concerned with the contractual origin of the state and the characteristics of the sovereign. The 'conclusions' of nature being rational and contrary to man's irrational egoism, demand force to coerce man into following them—'covenants without the sword are but words' (Ex. 67e). The problem was to devise a formula which would enable each man to renounce his unrestricted natural right against others, free from the fear that others would not keep to the agreement. The formula produced by Hobbes is ingenious. Each man contracts to renounce his natural right on a reciprocal basis and, at the same time, contracts to give his right to a sovereign power who will use the will and strength of each person for the peace and security of all. By this means the self-interest of each person is attained, since the illusory 'natural liberty' of the state of war has been exchanged for security of life and possessions.

The Sovereign

Unlike Bodin who imposed specific limitations on the actions of his sovereign, Hobbes argues that an unlimited governmental authority is the only alternative to the intolerable conditions of nature. There can thus be no grounds on which to base rebellion against the sovereign (Ex. 67f). A minority may not rebel on the grounds that they did not choose the sovereign because it is an article of the contract that in that respect the minority is bound by the wishes of the majority. Nor can the subjects legitimately depose the sovereign for any other reason, such as the pretence of a covenant with God. More importantly, bearing in mind the implications of other contract theories, the sovereign cannot be legitimately deposed for breach of contract since he alone is not a party to the contract which established him in power.

Hobbes goes on to declare that whatever the sovereign does cannot injure his subjects because it is done with the authority of all. He cannot therefore be accused of injustice. Moreover, Hobbes has earlier stated that justice is 'that men perform their covenants made'. As the sovereign has made no covenant it is clear that his actions cannot be regarded as either just or unjust; such standards are applicable only to the subject in so far as he obeys or disobeys the sovereign's law.

Although no legitimate rebellion against the sovereign is ever possible, illegal rebellion may nevertheless take place if the sovereign acts so tyrannically that a continuation of his rule is intolerable. If the rebellion fails, the sovereign will have vindicated his position. If it succeeds, then, paradoxically, it justifies itself since its success has proved that the government was not capable of providing peace and security and was therefore not truly sovereign.

Liberty

Superficially it might appear that Hobbesian man in the *Leviathan* had sacrificed his freedom for security. In fact this is not entirely true since Hobbes himself points to a number of areas where a man retains freedom in the state. First, he may act freely in spheres where the sovereign has not legislated, and secondly he retains a freedom to disobey the sovereign or his agents when they command the subject to do that which would jeopardize his life (Ex. 67g). Neither of these can be regarded as a particularly important freedom. The first allows a man a free choice in those aspects of life where control is rarely thought necessary; the second, rationalized by Hobbes on the grounds that destruction of life would frustrate the intention of the contract, is simply an acceptance of the fact that one cannot renounce one's right to act according to the instinct of self-preservation.

It seems curious that Hobbes does not lay greater emphasis upon the important freedom that is created by security. In the hostile state of nature man's natural freedom, although theoretically absolute, is in practice limited by the restraints imposed upon his capacity to achieve his ends. In the civil state his theoretical freedom is curtailed by the 'artificial chains called civil laws', but his ability to pursue and achieve his ends is enhanced by the security provided by the laws. As John

Locke was to say: 'The end of law is not to abolish or restrain but to preserve and enlarge freedom.'

Spinoza (1632-1677)

Benedict de Spinoza, whose *Tractatus Theologico-Politicus (Treatise on Theology and Politics)* was published anonymously in 1670, was the author of a theory of contract somewhat similar to that of Hobbes in that it is used to justify absolutism rather than rebellion. The extract quoted is from Chapter 16 of the *Tractatus* which examines the foundations of the state (Ex. 68).

In discussing natural right and natural law, Spinoza differs markedly from Hobbes. Whereas Hobbes had qualified man's natural right by relating it to self-preservation and had equated the laws of nature with rational rules of expediency, Spinoza argues that men have a natural right to do whatever they will, regardless of whether their actions are dictated by reason. As men will always pursue what seems to them to be in their self-interest, it follows that nature forbids only what no one can do. It would therefore seem that nothing and nobody can ever break the law of nature.

Spinoza depicts a state of nature which is wretched and insecure. In order to escape from this condition and to achieve security, self-interest prescribes that men follow reason rather than emotion and make a contract (of the Hobbesian type) to renounce the unrestricted exercise of natural right. But because men will only act if it benefits them, the contract must be validated by utility. As soon as it ceases to be expedient it becomes void. Hence, obedience to the law must be enforced by the recipient of each individual's natural right so that each man is obliged through self-interest to maintain the original agreement.

It is at this point that Spinoza makes his most significant deviation from the theory of Hobbes. Instead of the transference of their natural right to one man or an assembly, Spinoza considers that men transfer their powers to society as a whole, thus creating a democracy. He is led to this conclusion by his view that an absolute monarchy is likely to be more oppressive and inefficient than government by the majority of the people.

Nevertheless, his conclusion is much the same as that of Hobbes. Although a popular one, his sovereign is above the law and cannot be disobeyed in anything which it commands. Obedience to the sovereign is even less firmly based than in Hobbes upon the moral obligation to uphold the original contract. The keeping of one's covenants is not rooted in any law of nature, but in self-interest; in other words men obey the government solely because they will be punished if they do not. Therefore, if obedience to the sovereign ceases to be expedient, rebellion will take place.

Pufendorf (1632-1694)

As we have seen, the theory of the social contract in the seventeenth century was used for a variety of purposes. Althusius, Milton and, later in the century, Locke, used it as the basis for justifying resistance to rulers; Hobbes and Spinoza used it to stress the absolute nature of the ruler's authority. The German writer on international law, Samuel Pufendorf, in his book *De Jure Naturae et Gentium (On the Law of Nature and Nations,* 1672), stresses neither resistance nor absolute authority but uses the contract theory to show that the ruler's authority is limited by moral restraints.

In the state of nature, man is governed by the law of nature which enjoins peace (Ex. 69a). But men are sometimes governed by their passions instead of by their reason and peace is therefore somewhat uncertain. To escape from such uncertainty men agree by voluntary compact to form civil society. The agreement must be unanimous; any person who does not agree 'continues in his natural liberty' and makes his own arrangement for his security (Ex. 69b).

We have noted above that Hobbes and Spinoza were able to defend absolutism by arguing that the sovereign was not established by a contract between himself and the people, the latter being unable to contract as a corporate group. Pufendorf overcomes this objection by the device of using two contracts. The first establishes an organized civil society; the second allows this organized body to establish a government which will provide security for the community who bind themselves to obedience. It is here that the moral limitations on the sovereign are imposed. The government, which may be democratic or monarchic, must govern according to natural law and custom. More-over, Pufendorf argues in another treatise, *Duties of Men and States* (1673), that when the government is installed, the people may expressly agree to restrict its control over certain matters.

Pufendorf's theory of contract, although emphasizing the duties of rulers and subjects, could be of little use in restraining the actions of a tyrannical sovereign. It was left to John Locke a few years later to devise a theory that met this objection and provided a justification for enforcing constitutional restraints on the actions of governments.

FURTHER READING

Texts
H. Grotius: *On the Law of War and Peace*
T. Hobbes: *Leviathan*
B. de Spinoza: *Treatise on Theology and Politics*

S. Pufendorf: *On the Law of Nature and Nations*

Commentaries
A. P. d'Entreves: *Natural Law* (Hutchinson 1951)
K. C. Brown (ed): *Hobbes Studies* (Basil Blackwell 1965)
D. P Gauthier: *The Logic of Leviathan* (Clarendon Press 1969)
M. M. Goldsmith: *Hobbe's Science of Politics* (Columbia University Press 1966)
C. B. Macpherson: *The Political Theory of Possessive Individualism* (Oxford University Press 1964)
L. Strauss: *The Political Philosophy of Hobbes* (University of Chicago Press 1963)
H. Warrender: *The Political Philosophy of Hobbes* (Clarendon Press 1957)

66 HUGO GROTIUS: THE LAW OF NATURE

1. The law of nature is a dictate of right reason, which points out that an act, according as it is or is not in conformity with rational nature, has in it a quality of moral baseness or moral necessity; and that, in consequence, such an act is either forbidden or enjoined by the author of nature, God.
2. The acts in regard to which such a dictate exists are, in themselves, either obligatory or not permissible, and so it is understood that necessarily they are enjoined or forbidden by God. In this characteristic the law of nature differs not only from human law, but also from volitional divine law; for volitional divine law does not enjoin or forbid those things which in themselves and by their own nature are obligatory or not permissible, but by forbidding things it makes them unlawful, and by commanding things it makes them obligatory.
5. The law of nature, again, is unchangeable—even in the sense that it cannot be changed by God. Measureless as is the power of God, nevertheless it can be said that there are certain things over which that power does not extend; for things of which this is said are spoken only, having no sense corresponding with reality and being mutually contradictory. Just as even God, then, cannot cause that two times two should not make four, so He cannot cause that that which is intrinsically evil be not evil.

This is what Aristotle means when he says: 'Some things are thought of as bad the moment they are named.' For just as the being of things, from the time that they begin to exist, and in the manner in which they exist, is not dependent on anything else, so also the properties, which of necessity characterize that being; such a property is the badness of certain acts, when judged by the standard of a nature endowed with sound reason. Thus God Himself suffers Himself to be judged according to this standard, as may be seen by referring to *Genesis*, xviii. 25; *Isaiah*, v. 3; *Ezekiel*, xviii. 25; *Jeremiah*, ii. 9; *Micah*, vi. 2; *Romans*, ii. 6, iii. 6.

(Hugo Grotius, *On the Law of War and Peace*, tr. F. W. Kelsey, Bk 1, ch. 1, sect. 10, pp. 38-40, Clarendon Press, Oxford 1925.)

67a   THOMAS HOBBES: LEVIATHAN, THE ARTIFICIAL MAN

Nature, the art whereby God hath made and governs the world, is by the *art* of man, as in many other things, so in this also imitated, that it can make an artificial animal. For seeing life is but a motion of limbs, the beginning whereof is in some principal part within; why may we not say, that all *automata* (engines that move themselves by springs and wheels as doth a watch) have an artificial life? For what is the *heart*, but a *spring*; and the *nerves*, but so many *strings*; and the *joints*, but so many *wheels*, giving motion to the whole body, such as was intended by the artificer? *Art* goes yet further, imitating that rational and most excellent work of nature, *man*. For by art is created the great LEVIATHAN called a COMMONWEALTH, or STATE, in Latin CIVITAS, which is but an artificial man; though of greater stature and strength than the natural, for whose protection and defence it was intended; and in which the *sovereignty* is an artificial *soul*, as giving life and motion to the whole body; the *magistrates*, and other *officers* of judicature and execution, artificial *joints; reward* and *punishment*, by which fastened to the seat of the sovereignty every joint and member is moved to perform his duty, are the *nerves*, that do the same in the body natural; the *wealth* and *riches* of all the particular members, are the *strength*; *salus populi*, the *people's safety*, its *business*; *counsellors*, by whom all things needful for it to know are suggested unto it, are the *memory*; *equity*, and *laws*, an artificial *reason* and *will*; *concord*, *health*; *sedition*, *sickness*; and *civil war*, *death*. Lastly, the *pacts* and *covenants*, by which the parts of this body politic were at first made, set together, and united, resemble that *fiat*, or the *let us make man*, pronounced by God in the creation.

(Thomas Hobbes, *Leviathan*, ed. M. Oakeshott, Introduction, p. 5, Blackwell, Oxford 1946.)

67b   THOMAS HOBBES: EGOISTIC MORALITY

There be in animals, two sorts of *motions* peculiar to them: one called *vital*; begun in generation, and continued without interruption through their whole life; such as are the *course* of the *blood*, the *pulse*, the *breathing*, the *concoction, nutrition, excretion, &c.*, to which motions there needs no help of imagination: the other is *animal motion*, otherwise called *voluntary motion*; as to *go*, to *speak*, to *move* any of our limbs, in such manner as is first fancied in our minds. That sense is motion in the organs and interior parts of man's body, caused by the action of the things we see, hear, &c.; and that fancy is but the relics of the same motion, remaining after sense, has been already said in the first and second chapters. And because *going, speaking*, and the like voluntary motions, depend always upon a precedent thought of *whither, which way*, and *what*; it is evident, that the imagination is the first internal beginning of all voluntary motion. And although unstudied men do not conceive any motion at all to be there, where the thing moved is invisible; or the space it is moved in is, for the shortness of it, insensible; yet that doth not hinder, but that such motions are. For let a space be never so little, that which is moved over a greater space, whereof that little one is part, must first be moved over that. These small beginnings of motion, within the body of man, before they appear in walking, speaking, striking, and other visible actions, are commonly called ENDEAVOUR.

This endeavour, when it is toward something which causes it, is called APPETITE, or DESIRE; the latter, being the general name; and the other oftentimes restrained to signify the desire of food, namely *hunger* and *thirst*. And when the endeavour is fromward something, it is generally called AVERSION. . . .

That which men desire, they are also said to LOVE: and to HATE those things for which they have aversion. So that desire and love are the same thing; save that by desire, we always signify the absence of the object; by love, most commonly the presence of the same. So also by aversion, we signify the absence; and by hate, the presence of the object.

Of appetites and aversions, some are born with men; as appetite of food, appetite of excretion, and exoneration, which may also and more properly be called aversions, from somewhat they feel in their bodies; and some other appetites, not many. The rest, which are appetites of particular things, proceed from experience, and trial of their effects upon themselves or other men. For of things we know not at all, or believe not to be, we can have no further desire, than to taste and try. But aversion we have for things, not only which we know have hurt us, but also that we do not know whether they will hurt us, or not.

Those things which we neither desire, nor hate, we are said to *contemn*; CONTEMPT being nothing else but an immobility, or contumacy of the heart, in resisting the action of certain things; and proceeding from that the heart is already moved otherwise, by other more potent objects; or from want of experience of them.

And because the constitution of a man's body is in continual mutation, it is impossible that all the same things should always cause in him the same appetites, and aversions: much less can all men consent, in the desire of almost any one and the same object.

But whatsoever is the object of any man's appetite or desire, that is it which he for his part calleth *good*: and the object of his hate and aversion, *evil*; and of his contempt, *vile* and *inconsiderable*. For these words of good, evil, and contemptible, are ever used with relation to the person that useth them: there being nothing simply and absolutely so; nor any common rule of good and evil, to be taken from the nature of the objects themselves; but from the person of the man, where there is no commonwealth; or, in a commonwealth, from the person that representeth it; or from an arbitrator or judge, whom men disagreeing shall by consent set up, and make his sentence the rule thereof. . . .

As, in sense, that which is really within us, is, as I have said before, only motion, caused by the action of external objects, but in appearance; to the sight, light and colour; to the ear, sound; to the nostril, odour, &c.: so, when the action of the same object is continued from the eyes, ears, and other organs to the heart, the real effect there is nothing but motion, or endeavour; which consisteth in appetite, or aversion, to or from the object moving. But the appearence, or sense of that motion, is that we either call *delight*, or *trouble of mind.*

This motion, which is called appetite, and for the appearence of it *delight*, and *pleasure*, seemeth to be a corroboration of vital motion, and a help thereunto; and therefore such things as caused delight, were not improperly called *jucunda*, *à juvando*, from helping or fortifying; and the contrary, *molesta*, *offensive*, from hindering, and troubling the motion vital.

Pleasure therefore, or *delight*, is the appearance, or sense of good; and *molestation*, or *displeasure*, the appearance, or sense of evil. And consequently all appetite, desire, and love, is accompanied with some delight more or less; and all hatred and aversion, with more or less displeasure and offence.

(Thomas Hobbes, op. cit., part 1, ch. 6, pp. 31-3.)

67c THOMAS HOBBES: THE STATE OF NATURE

Nature hath made men so equal, in the faculties of the body, and mind; as that though there be found one man sometimes manifestly stronger in body, or of quicker mind than another; yet when all is reckoned together, the difference between man, and man, is not so considerable, as that one man can thereupon claim to himself any benefit, to which another may not pretend, as well as he. For as to the strength of body, the weakest has strength enough to kill the strongest, either by secret machination, or by confederacy with others, that are in the same danger with himself. . . .

From this equality of ability, ariseth equality of hope in the attaining of our ends. And therefore if any two men desire the same thing, which nevertheless they cannot both enjoy, they become enemies; and in the way to their end, which is principally their own conservation, and sometimes their delectation only, endeavour to destroy, or subdue one another. And from hence it comes to pass, that where an invader hath no more to fear, than another man's single power; if one plant, sow, build, or possess a convenient seat, others may probably be expected to come prepared with forces united, to dispossess, and deprive him, not only of the fruit of his labour, but also of his life, or liberty. And the invader again is in the like danger of another. . . .

So that in the nature of man, we find three principal causes of quarrel. First, competition; secondly, diffidence; thirdly, glory.

The first, maketh men invade for gain; the second, for safety; and the third, for reputation. The first use violence, to make themselves masters of other men's persons, wives, children, and cattle; the second, to defend them; the third, for trifles, as a word, a smile, a different opinion, and any other sign of undervalue, either direct in their persons, or by reflection in their kindred, their friends, their nation, their profession, or their name.

Hereby it is manifest, that during the time men live without a common power to keep them all in awe, they are in that condition which is called war; and such a war, as is of every man, against every man. . . .

Whatsoever therefore is consequent to a time of war, where every man is enemy to every man; the same is consequent to the time, wherein men live without other security, than what their own strength, and their own invention shall furnish them withal. In such condition, there is no place for industry; because the fruit thereof is uncertain: and consequently no culture of the earth; no navigation, nor use of the commodities that may be imported by sea; no commodious building; no instruments of moving, and removing, such things as require much force; no knowledge of the face of the earth; no account of time; no arts; no letters; no society; and which is worst of all, continual fear, and danger of violent death; and the life of man, solitary, poor, nasty, brutish, and short. . . .

To this war of every man, against every man, this also is consequent; that nothing can be unjust. The notions of right and wrong, justice and injustice have there no place. Where there is no common power, there is no law: where no law, no injustice. Force, and fraud, are in war the two cardinal virtues. Justice, and injustice are none of the faculties neither of the body, nor mind. If they were, they might be in a man that were alone in the world, as well as his senses, and passions. They are qualities, that relate to men in society, not in solitude. It is consequent also to the same condition, that there be no propriety, no dominion, no *mine* and *thine* distinct; but only that to be every man's, that he can get: and for so long, as he can keep it. And thus much for the ill condition, which man by mere nature is actually placed in; though with a possibility to come out of it, consisting partly in the passions, partly in his reason.

The passions that incline men to peace, are fear of death; desire of such things as are necessary to commodious living; and a hope by their industry to obtain them. And reason suggesteth convenient articles of peace, upon which men may be drawn to agreement. These articles, are they, which otherwise are called the Laws of Nature: whereof I shall speak more particularly, in the two following chapters.

(Thomas Hobbes, op. cit., part 1, ch. 13, pp. 80-4.)

67d THOMAS HOBBES: NATURAL RIGHT AND NATURAL LAW

The RIGHT OF NATURE, which writers commonly call *jus naturale,* is the liberty each man hath, to use his own power, as he will himself, for the preservation of his own nature; that is to say, of his own life; and consequently, of doing any thing, which in his own judgment, and reason, he shall conceive to be the aptest means thereunto.

By LIBERTY, is understood, according to the proper signification of the word, the absence of external impediments: which impediments, may oft take away part of a man's power to do what he would; but cannot hinder him from using the power left him, according as his judgment, and reason shall dictate to him.

A LAW OF NATURE, *lex naturalis,* is a precept or general rule, found out by reason, by which a man is forbidden to do that, which is destructive of his life, or taketh away the means of preserving the same; and to omit that, by which he thinketh it may be best preserved. For though they that speak of this subject, use to confound *jus,* and *lex, right* and *law*: yet they ought to be distinguished; because RIGHT, consisteth in liberty to do, or to forbear: whereas LAW, determineth, and bindeth to one of them: so that law, and right, differ as much, as obligation, and liberty; which in one and the same matter are inconsistent.

And because the condition of man, as hath been declared in the precedent chapter, is a condition of war of every one against every one; in which case every one is governed by his own reason; and there is nothing he can make use of, that may not be a help unto him, in preserving his life against his enemies; it followeth, that in such a condition, every man has a right to every thing; even to one another's body. And therefore, as long as this natural right of every man to every thing endureth, there can be no security to any man, how strong or wise soever he be, of living out the time, which nature ordinarily alloweth men to live. And consequently it is a precept, or general rule of reason, *that every man, ought to endeavour peace, as far as he has hope of obtaining it; and when he cannot obtain it, that he may seek, and use, all helps, and advantages of war.* The first branch of which rule, containeth the first, and fundamental law of nature; which is, *to seek peace, and follow it.* The second, the sum of the right of nature; which is, *by all means we can, to defend ourselves.*

From this fundamental law of nature, by which men are commanded to endeavour peace, is derived this second law; *that a man be willing, when others are so too, as far-forth, as for peace, and defence of himself he shall think it necessary, to lay down this right to all things; and be contented with so much liberty against other men, as he would allow other men against himself.* For as long as every man holdeth this right, of doing any thing he liketh; so long are all men in the condition of war. But if other men will not lay down their right, as well as he; then there is no reason for any one, to divest himself of his: for that were to expose himself to prey, which no man is bound to, rather than to dispose himself to peace. This is that law of the Gospel; *whatsoever you require that others should do to you, that do ye to them.*

(Thomas Hobbes, op. cit., part 1, ch. 14, pp. 84-5.)

67e   THOMAS HOBBES: THE SOCIAL CONTRACT

The final cause, end, or design of men, who naturally love liberty, and dominion over others, in the introduction of that restraint upon themselves, in which we see them live in commonwealths, is the foresight of their own preservation, and of a more contented life thereby; that is to say, of getting themselves out from that miserable condition of war, which is necessarily consequent, as hath been shown (chapter XIII), to the natural passions of men, when there is no visible power to keep them in awe, and tie them by fear of punishment to the performance of their covenants, and observation of those laws of nature set down in the fourteenth and fifteenth chapters.

For the laws of nature, as *justice, equity, modesty, mercy,* and, in sum, *doing to others, as we would be done to,* of themselves, without the terror of some power, to cause them to be observed, are contrary to our natural passions, that carry us to partiality, pride, revenge, and the like. And covenants, without the sword, are but words, and of no strength to secure a man at all. Therefore notwithstanding the laws of nature (which every one hath then kept, when he has the will to keep them, when he can do it safely) if there be no power erected, or not great enough for our security; every man will, and may lawfully rely on his own strength and art, for caution against all other men. . . .

The only way to erect such a common power, as may be able to defend them from the invasion of foreigners, and the injuries of one another, and thereby to secure them in such sort, as that by their own industry, and by the fruits of the earth, they may nourish themselves and live contentedly; is, to confer all their power and strength upon one man, or upon one assembly of men, that may reduce all their wills, by plurality of voices, unto one will: which is as much to say, to appoint one man, or assembly of men, to bear their person; and every one to own, and acknowledge himself to be author of whatsoever he that so beareth their person, shall act, or cause to be acted, in those things which concern the common peace and safety; and therein to submit their wills, every one to his will, and their judgments, to his judgment. This is more than consent, or concord; it is a real unity of them all, in one and the same person, made by covenant of every man with every man, in such manner, as if every man should say to every man, *I authorize and give up my right of governing myself, to this man, or to this assembly of men, on this condition, that thou give up thy right to him, and authorize all his actions in like manner.* This done, the multitude so united in one person, is called a COMMONWEALTH, in Latin CIVITAS. This is the generation of that great LEVIATHAN, or rather, to speak more reverently, of that *mortal god, to which we owe under the immortal God,* our peace and defence. For by this authority, given him by every particular man in the commonwealth, he hath the use of so much power and strength conferred on him, that by terror thereof, he is enabled to form the wills of them all, to peace at home, and mutual aid against their enemies abroad. And in him consisteth the essence of the commonwealth; which, to define it, is *one person, of whose acts a great multitude, by mutual covenants one with another, have made themselves every one the author, to the end he may use the strength and means of them all, as he shall think expedient, for their peace and common defence.*

(Thomas Hobbes, op. cit., part 2, ch. 17, pp. 109, 112.)

67f THOMAS HOBBES: THE SOVEREIGN

A *commonwealth* is said to be *instituted,* when a *multitude* of men do agree, and *covenant, every one, with every one,* that to whatsoever *man,* or *assembly of men,* shall be given by the major part, the *right* to *present* the person of them all, that is to say, to be their *representative;* every one, as well he that *voted for it,* as he that *voted against it,* shall *authorize* all the actions and judgments, of that man, or assembly of men, in the same manner, as if they were his own, to the end, to live peaceably amongst themselves, and be protected against other men.

From this institution of a commonwealth are derived all the *rights*, and *faculties* of him, or them, on whom the sovereign power is conferred by the consent of the people assembled.

First, because they covenant, it is to be understood, they are not obliged by former covenant to any thing repugnant hereunto. And consequently they that have already instituted a commonwealth, being thereby bound by covenant, to own the actions, and judgments of one, cannot lawfully make a new covenant, amongst themselves, to be obedient to any other, in any thing whatsoever, without his permission. And therefore, they that are subjects to a monarch, cannot without his leave cast off monarchy, and return to the confusion of a disunited multitude; nor transfer their person from him that beareth it, to another man, or other assembly of men: for they are bound, every man to every man, to own, and be reputed author of all that he that already is their sovereign shall do, and judge fit to be done: so that any one man dissenting, all the rest should break their covenant made to that man, which is injustice: and they have also every man given the sovereignty to him that beareth their person; and therefore if they depose him, they take from him that which is his own, and so again it is injustice. Besides, if he that attempteth to depose his sovereign, be killed, or punished by him for such attempt, he is author of his own punishment, as being by the institution, author of all his sovereign shall do: and because it is injustice for a man to do any thing, for which he may be punished by his own authority, he is also upon that title, unjust. And whereas some men have pretended for their disobedience to their sovereign, a new covenant, made, not with men, but with God; this also is unjust: for there is no covenant with God, but by mediation of somebody that representeth God's person; which none doth but God's lieutenant, who hath the sovereignty under God. But this pretence of covenant with God, is so evident a lie, even in the pretenders' own consciences, that it is not only an act of an unjust, but also of a vile, and unmanly disposition.

Secondly, because the right of bearing the person of them all, is given to him they make sovereign, by covenant only of one to another, and not of him to any of them; there can happen no breach of covenant on the part of the sovereign; and consequently none of his subjects, by any pretence of forfeiture, can be freed from his subjection.

(Thomas Hobbes, op. cit., part 2, ch. 18, pp. 113-14.)

67g   THOMAS HOBBES: LIBERTY

LIBERTY, or FREEDOM, signifieth, properly, the absence of opposition; by opposition, I mean external impediments of motion; and may be applied no less to irrational, and inanimate creatures, than to rational. For whatsoever is so tied, or environed, as it cannot move but within a certain space, which space is determined by the opposition of some external body, we say it hath not liberty to go further. And so of all living creatures, whilst they are imprisoned, or restrained, with walls, or chains; and of the water whilst it is kept in by banks, or vessels, that otherwise would spread itself into a larger space, we use to say, they are not at liberty, to move in such manner, as without those external impediments they would. But when the impediment of motion, is in the constitution of the thing itself, we use not to say; it wants the liberty; but the power to move: as when a stone lieth still, or a man is fastened to his bed by sickness. . . .

But as men, for the attaining of peace, and conservation of themselves thereby, have made an artificial man, which we call a commonwealth; so also have they made artificial chains, called *civil laws,* which they themselves, by mutual covenants, have fastened at one end, to the lips of that man, or assembly, to whom they have given the sovereign power; and at the other end to their own ears. These bonds, in their own nature but weak, may nevertheless be made to hold, by the danger, though not by the difficulty of breaking them.

In relation to these bonds only it is, that I am to speak now, of the *liberty of subjects.* For seeing there is no commonwealth in the world, wherein there be rules enough set down, for the regulating of all the actions, and words of men; as being a thing impossible: it followeth necessarily, that in all kinds of actions by the laws praetermitted, men have the liberty, of doing what their own reasons shall suggest for the most profitable to themselves. For if we take liberty in the proper sense, for corporal liberty; that is to say, freedom from chains and prison; it were very absurd for men to clamour as they do, for the liberty they so manifestly enjoy. Again, if we take liberty, for an exemption from laws, it is no less absurd, for men to demand as they do, that liberty, by which all other men may be masters of their lives. And yet, as absurd as it is, this is it they demand; not knowing that the laws are of no power to protect them, without a sword in the hands of a man, or men, to cause those laws to be put in execution. The liberty of a subject, lieth therefore only in those things, which in regulating their actions, the sovereign hath praetermitted: such as is the liberty to buy, and sell, and otherwise contract with one another; to choose their own abode, their own diet, their own trade of life, and institute their children as they themselves think fit; and the like. . . .

If the sovereign command a man, though justly condemned, to kill, wound, or maim himself; or not to resist those that assault him; or to abstain from the use of food, air, medicine, or any other thing, without which he cannot live; yet hath that man the liberty to disobey.

If a man be interrogated by the sovereign, or his authority, concerning a crime done by himself, he is not bound, without assurance of pardon, to confess it; because no man, as I have shown in the same chapter, can be obliged by covenant to accuse himself.

Again, the consent of a subject to sovereign power, is contained in these words, *I authorize, or take upon me, all his actions*; in which there is no restriction at all, of his own former natural liberty: for by allowing him to *kill me*, I am not bound to kill myself when he commands me. It is one thing to say, *kill me, or my fellow, if you please;* another thing to say, *I will kill myself, or my fellow.* It followeth therefore, that

No man is bound by the words themselves, either to kill himself, or any other man; and consequently, that the obligation a man may sometimes have, upon the command of the sovereign to execute any dangerous or dishonourable office, dependeth not on the words of our submission; but on the intention, which is to be understood by the end thereof. When therefore our refusal to obey, frustrates the end for which the sovereignty was ordained; then there is no liberty to refuse: otherwise there is.

(Thomas Hobbes, op. cit., part 2, ch. 21, pp. 136-9, 142.)

68 BENEDICT DE SPINOZA

By the right and law of nature I simply mean the rules of each individual thing's nature, the rules whereby we conceive it as naturally determined to exist and act in a definite way. Fish, for example, are determined by nature to swim, and the large to eat the smaller; so fish occupy the water, and the large eat the smaller, with perfect natural right. For there is no doubt that nature in the absolute sense has a perfect right to do everything in its power, i.e., that the right of nature extends as far as its power; the power of nature being nothing but the power of God, who has a perfect right to do everything. But the universal power of nature as a whole is simply the power of all individual things combined; hence each individual thing has a perfect right to do everything it can, in other words, its right extends to the limit of its power. And since the supreme law of nature is that everything does its utmost to preserve its own condition, and this without regard to anything but itself, everything has a perfect right to do this, i.e. (as I said) to exist and act as nature has determined it to do. Nor do I recognize any diference in this respect between men and other individual things in nature, or between men endowed with reason and others to whom true reason is unknown, or between the foolish, the mad, and the sane: for whatever anything does by the laws of its nature it does with perfect right, simply because it acts as it has been determined by nature to act, and can do nothing else. Hence as long as men are regarded as living under the sway of nature alone, he who is still blind to reason, or has still to acquire a virtuous disposition, lives wholly by the laws of appetite with as perfect a right as he who guides his life by the laws of reason. In other words, just as an enlightened man has a perfect right to do everything which reason dictates, or to live by the laws of reason, so too an unenlightened and weak-minded man has a perfect right to do everything that appetite suggests, or to live by the laws of appetite. . . .

It follows that the right and law of nature, under which all are born and for the most part live, forbids nothing save what nobody desires and nobody can do: it forbids neither strife, nor hatred, no anger, nor deceit; in short, it is opposed to nothing that appetite can suggest. . . .

Still, nobody can doubt that it is much more advantageous for men to live by the laws and sure dictates of our reason, which, as I said, aim at nothing but the true interest of men. Moreover everyone desires to enjoy the maximum safety and security (which is impossible as long as each may do anything he pleases, and reason is allowed no more influence than hatred and anger); for everyone lives a life of anxiety when surrounded by hostility, hatred, anger, and treachery, and so does his utmost to escape such things. If we also reflect on what was shown in Chapter V, that without mutual help men live in utter wretchedness, and are inevitably debarred from the cultivation of reason, we shall see very clearly that to live safely and well men had necessarily to join together. They therefore arranged that the right to do everything which each had by nature should be held collectively, and should be determined no longer by the force and appetite of each but by the power and will of all together. But they would not have succeeded in this had they been willing to follow nothing but the prompting of appetite (for by the laws of appetite individuals are drawn in different ways); so each must have firmly resolved and contracted to direct everything by the dictate of reason alone (which no one dares to oppose openly lest he appear to lack understanding), to bridle his appetite when it suggested anything harmful to another, to do to nobody what he would not wish done to himself, and, finally, to defend his neighbour's right as if it were his own.

But we must now inquire how this contract must be made if it is to be permanently binding: for it is a universal law of human nature, that no one forgoes anything he thinks good save from hope of a greater good or fear of a greater loss, or tolerates any evil save to avoid a greater, or from hope of a greater good.

From this I conclude that a contract can have no binding force but utility; when that disappears it at once becomes null and void. Hence it is foolish to require a man to keep faith with you for ever unless you also try to ensure that breach of the contract will bring him more loss than gain. Now this precaution must be given pride of place in the formation of the state. No doubt if it were easy for everyone to be guided by reason alone, and to grasp the supreme utility and necessity of the state, all men would regard perfidy with utter detestation, and, in their desire for this supreme good, the preservation of the state, would abide most faithfully by their contracts and cherish good faith, the chief bulwark of the state, above all else. But for everyone always to be guided by reason alone is far from easy; for each is seduced by his own pleasure, and it is very common for greed, pride, envy, anger, etc. to take such a hold upon the mind that no place is left for reason. Hence even although men give sure signs of honest intentions in promising and contracting to keep faith, no one can be certain of the good faith of another unless his promise is guaranteed by something else, since everyone can make counterfeit promises by the right of nature, and is not bound to abide by his contracts save by hope of a greater good or fear of a greater evil. But since everyone's natural right is determined solely by his power (as I have already shown), it follows that in so far as he transfers his power to another—whether voluntarily or by compulsion does not matter—he necessarily surrenders to the other his right as well; and that the man who has supreme power to coerce all, and to restrain them by the threat of a supreme penalty which is universally feared, has also supreme right over all. Of course he will only retain this right as long as he preserves the power to do everything he wishes; otherwise he will govern by courtesy, and no one stronger will be bound to obey him unless he wants to do so.

In this way then, a society can be formed without any opposition from natural law, and every contract can always be kept with the greatest good faith; if, that is, everyone transfers all his power to the society. Thus it alone will have a perfect natural right to do everything, i.e. sovereign power, and everyone will be bound to obey it either in freedom of spirit or from fear of the supreme penalty. Now when the right belongs to a society so formed the state is called a democracy; which is accordingly defined as a general assembly of men that possesses in its corporate capacity the supreme right to do everything it can. It follows that the sovereign is bound by no law, and that all citizens must obey it in all things, since they must all have contracted to do so, either tacitly or expressly, when they transferred to it all their power to defend themselves, i.e. all their right. For had they wished to retain any part of their right, they would also have had to provide themselves with some safe way of defending it; but they did not do so, and could not have done so without dividing and hence destroying the state. They therefore submitted unreservedly to the jurisdiction of the sovereign: and this complete submission was (as I have just shown) both forced on them by necessity and advised by reason itself. It follows that, unless we wish to be enemies of the state and to contravene reason's advice to do our utmost to defend it, we are bound to perform all the commands of the sovereign without exception; for no matter how foolish they may be, reason still bids us perform them so as to choose the lesser evil.

(Benedict de Spinoza, *Treatise on Theology and Politics*, ch. 16, in Benedict de Spinoza, *The Political Works*, tr. A. G. Wernham, pp. 125-33, Clarendon Press, Oxford 1958.)

69a SAMUEL PUFENDORF: THE STATE OF NATURE

The natural state of men, even when considered apart from commonwealths, is not one of war, but of peace; a peace founded on the following laws: A man shall not harm one who is not injuring him; he shall allow every one to enjoy his own possessions; he shall faithfully perform whatever has been agreed upon; and he shall willingly advance the interests of others, so far as he is not bound by more pressing obligations. For since a natural state presupposes the use of reason, any obligation which reason points out cannot, and must not, be separated from it; and since every man is able of himself to appreciate that it is for his advantage to conduct himself in such a way as to profit from the friendly attitude of men rather than incur their anger, he can easily judge, from the similarity of nature, that other men feel the same way. And so it is quite wrong for a person in his description of this state to suppose that the majority of men, at least, neglect the guidance of reason, which nature has set up as the final director of men's actions; and equally wrong is it to designate as natural a state which is in the main produced by the neglect and misuse of a natural principle. . . .

Therefore, the real and principal reason why the fathers of families left their natural liberty and undertook to establish states, was in order that they could surround themselves with defences against the evils which threaten man from his fellow man. For just as nothing, next to most Good and Great God, can be so helpful to man as man himself, so nothing can do him greater harm, as is shown at large by Cicero, *On Duties*, Bk. II [v ff.]. Although mankind is exposed to various ills, his ingenuity has found for each of them some sort of remedy. Against the onslaughts of diseases have been discovered the arts of physicians; the rigours of the atmosphere are resisted by dwellings, clothing, and fire. The earth has been cultivated by men's industry and banishes famine. Arms or traps curb the ferocity of wild beasts. But against those ills with which man in his baseness delights to threaten his own kind, the most efficient cure had to be sought from man himself, by men joining into states and establishing sovereignty.

(Samuel Pufendorf, *De Jure Naturae et Gentium*, tr. C. H. and W. A. Oldfather, Bk 2, ch. 2, pp. 172–3, Bk 7, ch. 1, p. 959, Clarendon Press, Oxford 1934.)

69b SAMUEL PUFENDORF: THE TWO CONTRACTS

For a multitude, or many men, to become one person, to whom one action can be attributed and certain rights belong, in so far as this one person is distinct from individuals, and the rights be such as the individuals cannot attribute to themselves, it is necessary for them to have united their wills and strength by intervening pacts, without which a union of several persons equal by nature is impossible of comprehension.

The number and the nature of those pacts by the intervention of which a state is built up are discovered in the following manner. If we imagine to ourselves a multitude of men endowed with natural liberty and equality, who voluntarily set about to establish a new state, it is necessary for the future citizens, as the first step, to enter into an agreement, every individual with every other one, that they are desirous of entering into a single and perpetual group, and of administrating the considerations of their safety and security by common council and leadership. (Although in such a pact the individuals usually reserve to themselves the privilege of emigration.)

Such a pact is entered into either absolutely or conditionally. Absolutely, when a man pledges himself to remain with the group, whatever form of government the majority may finally decide upon. Conditionally, when he stipulates that the form of government be such as he approves of. Furthermore, when this pact is entered into, it is necessary for each and all to give their consent. Whoever does not do so, for so long as he continues in the same place with the rest, remains outside the future state, nor is he required by the agreement of the rest, however numerous they be, to join their group at all; but he continues in his natural liberty, wherein he will be permitted to decide matters of his safety according to his own judgement.

But after such a group, already taking on the rudiments and beginnings of a state, has been formed by the pact mentioned, it is yet further necessary for a decree to be passed upon the form of government that shall be introduced. For until this decision is reached, it will be impossible to take consistent action on matters concerning the common safety. At this step those who have joined themselves to the group absolutely, will be forced by the agreement of the majority to consent to that form of government, which these latter have agreed upon, although they might have preferred another, if, indeed, they wish to remain in the spot where the group is fixed. For in making no exception to the pact, they are understood to have submitted themselves to the will of the majority, at least in that point, for they can have no grounds for demanding that all the others prefer the judgement of a few to their own. But he who has joined the group conditionally will not become a member of the future state, nor be obligated by the agreement of the majority, unless he has expressly agreed to the form of government to be introduced.

After the decree upon the form of government, a new pact will be necessary when the individual or body is constituted that receives the government of the group, by which pact the rulers bind themselves to the care of the common security and safety, and the rest to render them obedience, and in which there is that subjection and union of wills, by reason of which a state is looked upon as a single person. From this pact there finally comes a finished state. . . .

It should be carefully noted that this method of forming a state by the intervention of two pacts and one decree is in the highest accord with nature, and common to all forms of states. Yet it is possible for a monarchy to be established by a single pact, in case many men, before any preceding agreement between them, have, each of them for himself, put themselves under one person, whether all at one time, or at different times, practically in the same way as armies are gathered together which are composed of strangers and mercenaries. And, in the same way, those who join a state which is already established, have need of but a single agreement, whereby they ask to be received into the state, while those who represent the state receive the same after requiring of them obedience.

Now we would not have it thought that these remarks on the pacts which give rise to a state, are a creation of our imagination, because the origins of most states are unknown, or at least it is not entirely certain that they were established in that manner. For one thing is sure, namely, that every state had at some time its beginning. And yet it was necessary that those who compose a state be not held together before its establishment by the same bond as they are afterwards; and that they be not subject to the same persons to whom they are afterwards. Yet since it is impossible to understand that union and subjection without the above-mentioned pacts, they must have interposed, tacitly at least, in the formation of states. Nor is there anything to prevent men from being able to reason out the origin of a thing, despite the fact that there remain no written records upon them.

(Samuel Pufendorf, op. cit., Bk 7, ch. 2, pp. 974-5, 977.)

CHAPTER 18

Locke and Natural Rights

The ideas of rationalism and individualism in the seventeenth century led thinkers to espouse not only the social contract theory but also its corollary, the concept of the natural rights of man. The rationalist ancestry of this concept lay with the doctrine of natural law, modified by an emphasis upon moral rights rather than moral duties. Its individualist ancestry could be seen in the ideas of human equality and liberty that had been developing since the Reformation. As Immanuel Kant was later to point out: 'the contract theory was the only means whereby the natural rights of the individual could be set within the framework of the state.'

The theory of natural rights was expressed most coherently and influentially in the works of John Locke, who used it to justify the 'glorious revolution' of 1688. The argument that government and the state exist solely to protect the natural rights of individuals is rooted in the late medieval doctrine of Aquinas and his successors, who considered that the ruler's aim should be the common good. The link between Locke and the Middle Ages is best represented by Richard Hooker (1554-1600), the Anglican clergyman whose *Laws of Ecclesiastical Polity* was a source of much that Locke admired.

The 'judicious' Hooker, although a Protestant, was firmly within the scholastic tradition. He regarded political society as natural to man, but, as it does not occur spontaneously, it must be formed by mutual agreement (Ex. 70a). Law he sees as the rule of natural reason reflected in the collective will of the community: 'the very soul of a politic body.'

The consent of the community is therefore necessary both for the establishment of political society and for the authority of the laws. A law which has not received 'public approbation' is not a law, but such approbation may be given indirectly through representatives or may even be tacit (Ex. 70b). As Hooker wrote his *Laws of Ecclesiastical Polity* to show why the Puritans should obey the laws of Elizabethan England, it is not surprising to discover that it admits no right of rebellion even against tyrants.

Locke's debt to Hooker was more apparent than real. Although, superficially, Hooker's theory seems to explain political obligation in terms of popular individual consent, in fact individualism is almost entirely absent. Hooker's conception of society was in the medieval organic tradition in which consent was given to the institutions of government by corporate bodies and not by individuals.

John Locke (1632-1704)

The restoration of the Stuart monarchy in 1660 signified the failure of the Puritan revolution and the success of the alliance between the monarchy and the Anglican church. The political theory held by the Royalists was that of the divine right of kings, of which the late Sir Robert Filmer had been one of the most important exponents. Filmer's *Patriarcha,* hitherto unpublished, was resurrected in 1680 in order to provide ammunition against what was seen as a potential threat to the king's prerogative following the 'popish plot'. Within a few months of the publication of *Patriarcha,* Locke was working on his *Two Treatises of Government* designed, in part, as a refutation of Filmer's theory.

Locke was the son of a Roundhead soldier but, although a Puritan like his father, was a supporter of the restored monarchy. His introduction to politics and his conversion to Whiggism came as a result of his association with the Earl of Shaftesbury, whom he met in 1666. As Shaftesbury's importance in the government increased, so did Locke's standing. By 1680 Locke was widely regarded as one of the ablest of the Whig theoreticians and therefore a fit person to provide the justification for the cause of parliamentary supremacy.

The *First Treatise* is a detailed refutation of Filmer's *Patriarcha* in which Locke, while experiencing little difficulty in exposing the absurdities in the historical part of the theory, is less convincing in his attack on the argument that political authority is natural. The *Second Treatise,* published in 1690 but probably written a decade earlier, is entitled 'An Essay concerning the True, Original, Extent and End of Civil Government.' It was an attempt to construct a theory of political obligation in place of the one that he had purportedly destroyed in the *First Treatise.*

The theory is firmly within the individualist and rationalist traditions of the seventeenth century. It is a curious paradox that whereas Locke's theory of knowledge is empiricist (that is, that knowledge is derived ultimately from sense-experience), his political philosophy is rationalist, so much so that he has been referred to as the founder of the 'age of reason'.

The State of Nature

The beginning of the *Second Treatise of Government* reflects Locke's reliance upon reason. He assumes as a rational axiom that men once inhabited a 'state of nature' where they lived in freedom and equality according to the law of nature (Ex. 71a). Unlike the Hobbesian picture of man's natural condition, which was a state of perpetual warfare, Locke depicts the natural state as one of peace in which most men respect the lives, liberty and property of each other. These are the 'natural rights' of man, given to him by the law of nature which commands that 'no one ought to harm another in his life, health, liberty, or possessions'.

It may be observed that Locke's theory of the natural law, compared to that of Hobbes, was much more in the normal tradition; whereas Hobbes had declared that men were bound by no moral obligation other than their own self-interest, Locke argued that the law of nature was a moral precept absolutely binding upon man at all times. In this he was close to the late medieval (and Hooker's) conception of natural law, although Locke's theory was much more individualistic than the Thomist version which had stressed duty to the community rather than individual rights.

Property

Of the natural rights of man, none is regarded by Locke as more important than the right to property. Such is its pre-eminence that at times Locke implies that the preservation of private property is the main reason for entering into political association. As we would expect from his friendship with the wealthy Whig leaders, Locke was no economic leveller. His defence of the individual's right to possess property turns out, in fact, to be a defence of contemporary social and economic inequality since he considered that only a minority of the population could exercise this right in any meaningful sense.

Originally, men possessed the earth and its fruits in common; private ownership is derived from the mixing of a person's labour with land or anything else that is in the original common state. As one's person is indisputably one's own, anything with which it is blended becomes equally one's own property (Ex. 71b). At first, property appropriated in this way was limited to the amount that a person could use. Anything taken from the common stock beyond that amount belonged to others. Moreover, the right of appropriation was limited by the necessity of leaving enough for other men to use.

Such limitations were hardly consistent with the facts of property distribution in England at that time. Large accumulations of wealth existed in the hands of a few while the majority possessed little or nothing. Locke manages to overcome this difficulty by arguing that the development of money allowed men to accumulate property beyond their immediate needs without spoiling.

Most commentators agree that Locke's theory of property is highly unsatisfactory and amounts to little more than a justification of the economic *status quo*. J. Plamenatz in his *Man and Society* (Longman, 1963), argues, for example, that the right to bequeath property does not derive from a person's supposed right to the exclusive use of it after he has mixed his labour with it. He points out also the illogicality in Locke's assumption that it is the *first* man to mix his labour with a good who has the exclusive use of it, even to the exclusion of those who later mix their labour with the same property because the common stock has run out. C. B. Macpherson in *The Political Theory of Possessive Individualism* considers that Locke's views on property reflect his predominant concern with the 'industrious and rational' part of the population who alone possess property.

The Contract

In the state of nature men have a further right, which is to judge and punish transgressors of the natural law. As there is no formal judicial system, each man must protect his own life, liberty and property. This procedure entails several obvious disadvantages: men are 'judges in their own cases' and hence their reactions to crimes against themselves or their property are likely to be extreme and inconsistent (Ex. 71c). Although Locke admits that the establishment of government is the 'remedy for the inconveniences of the state of nature', he points out that the arbitrary government of an absolute monarch is more intolerable than the natural state. If government is to be set up to improve man's condition it must be based upon the consent of the governed.

Locke, in common with most other political philosophers of his time, cannot conceive of the 'people' as a contracting party to set up government in the late medieval sense. The 'people' or 'community' as a political entity must first be established by a social contract (Ex. 71d). Each individual contracts with each other to form a political community by agreeing to give up to the community as a whole his right to execute the law of nature. The agreement also involves obedience to the majority will which is taken to represent the will of the whole community. Such a contract is the only kind which will eventually produce lawful government. To those who deny that such a contract ever took place because there are no records of man in the state of nature, Locke argues that although 'government is everywhere antecedent to records', reason tells us that men are naturally free and therefore the first political unions must have been matters of voluntary agreement.

Having established the state, men's first task is to erect the law-making body—'the supreme power of the Commonwealth' (Ex. 71e). The legislature is established in order to interpret and enact the natural law, or, in other words, to protect the life, liberty and property of each member of the community. It must follow that the government cannot act in an arbitrary manner since its power to act is so narrowly limited. Locke is somewhat ambiguous in describing how the legislature is established. Some commentators have considered that a second contract is implied: between the government and the community. Others believe that Locke does not mean that government is contracted into existence, but that government is *entrusted* with authority by the community on whose behalf as beneficiary of the trust the authority must be used. Certainly Locke never uses the term 'contract' in this connection but he does on several occasions use the language of trusteeship.

Rebellion
There is no doubt that however the government is established, it must be based upon the consent of the people. Consent to it will be forthcoming so long as the government remains in the form in which it was set up and acts according to natural law. In the final chapter of the *Second Treatise* Locke explains in what ways a government may be invalidated or 'dissolved from within' (Ex. 71f). The dissolution of government is carefully distinguished from the dissolution of society. Civil society can normally be dissolved only by conquest by outside forces and, should this happen, government too is overthrown. But governments are more likely to be dissolved because of an alteration in the legislature. This can happen in four ways. First, when the executive sets up his own will in place of the will of the legislature. Secondly, 'when the prince hinders the legislative from assembling in its due time, or from acting freely'. Thirdly, when the executive power alters without consent the electoral regulations contrary to the public good. Fourthly, when the people are made subject to a foreign power.

Furthermore, a government is dissolved when the executive power neglects or abandons its duty to put the laws into operation. Finally, and most importantly, dissolution of government is deemed to have taken place when either the legislative or the executive powers acts contrary to its trust.

There is little doubt that Locke considered the Stuart monarchy to be guilty of several of these dissolving actions, thereby opening the way to popular rebellion. Although the people are likely to suffer a tyrannical and thus illegitimate government for a considerable time, eventually they will find the burden intolerable, their consent will be withdrawn and the tyranny will be forcibly overthrown.

Popular withdrawal of consent presents certain problems. Although Locke argues that a majority of the whole community originally entrusts government with its authority, consent to the continuation of government must be tacit only for the vast majority of the people since Locke certainly did not envisage a representative parliament elected on a universal suffrage. As there is no practicable way of expressing disapproval of the government's actions other than active resistance, it seems that that is the only alternative to consent. A further problem arises from the question of deciding when the government is dissolved. Locke states that 'the people shall be judge' (Ex. 71g). But as 'every man is judge for himself' there is a difficulty in reconciling the individual decisions to rebel with the requirement that only the 'body of the people' may lawfully rebel, since there exists no machinery whereby individuals may discover whether they are a part of a majority or a minority of the community. Any attempt to influence a person's decision would contravene that person's right to consult only God and his conscience in arriving at a decision.

It is now fairly widely accepted that the *Second Treatise* although published in 1690 was written and circulated in manuscript several years before the 'glorious revolution' of 1688. This makes the work a revolutionary manifesto rather than, as had formerly been maintained, a *post-hoc* justification of the Whig revolt. Nevertheless, the revolutionary aspect of Locke's book was probably less influential than its doctrine of individual rights. The notion that government and the state existed solely to protect the natural rights of man, particularly the right to private property, was an important intellectual influence not only on the American and French revolutionaries, but also in the *laissez-faire* theory underlying Britain's industrial revolution. In that important sense the individualist tradition of western capitalist democracy rests upon the theoretical foundations constructed by Locke.

FURTHER READING

Texts
R. Hooker: *Works* (Clarendon Press 1890)
J. Locke: *Two Treatises of Government*

Commentaries:
M. Cranston: *John Locke* (Longmans 1957)
J. W. Gough: *John Locke's Political Philosophy* (Clarendon Press 1950)
C. B. Macpherson: *The Political Theory of Possessive Individualism* (Oxford University Press 1964)
M. Seliger: *The Liberal Politics of John Locke* (Allen and Unwin 1968)

J. W. Yolton (ed): *John Locke: Problems and Perspectives* (Cambridge University Press 1969)

70a RICHARD HOOKER: STATES FORMED BY AGREEMENT

We see then how nature itself teacheth laws and statutes to live by. The laws which have been hitherto mentioned do bind men absolutely even as they are men, although they have never any settled fellowship, never any solemn agreement amongst themselves what to do or not to do. But forasmuch as we are not by ourselves sufficient to furnish ourselves with competent store of things needful for such a life as our nature doth desire, a life fit for the dignity of man; therefore to supply those defects and imperfections which are in us living single and solely by ourselves, we are naturally induced to seek communion and fellowship with others. This was the cause of men's uniting themselves at the first in politic Societies, which societies could not be without Government, nor Government without a distinct kind of Law from that which hath been already declared. Two foundations there are which bear up public societies; the one, a natural inclination, whereby all men desire sociable life and fellowship; the other, an order expressly or secretly agreed upon touching the manner of their union in living together. The latter is that which we call the Law of a Commonwealth, the very soul of a politic body, the parts whereof are by law animated, held together, and set on work in such actions, as the common good requireth. Laws politic, ordained for external order and regiment amongst men, are never framed as they should be, unless presuming the will of man to be inwardly obstinate, rebellious, and averse from all obedience unto the sacred laws of his nature; in a word, unless presuming man to be in regard of his depraved mind little better than a wild beast, they do accordingly provide notwithstanding so to frame his outward actions, that they be no hindrance unto the common good for which societies are instituted: unless they do this, they are not perfect.

(Richard Hooker, *Laws of Ecclesiastical Polity*, Bk 1, ch. 10, in Richard Hooker, *Works*, pp. 184-5, Clarendon Press, Oxford 1890.)

70b RICHARD HOOKER: CONSENT NECESSARY FOR LAW

Howbeit laws do not take their constraining force from the quality of such as devise them, but from that power which doth give them the strength of laws. That which we spake before concerning the power of government must here be applied unto the power of making laws whereby to govern; which power God hath over all: and by the natural law, whereunto he hath made all subject, the lawful power of making laws to command whole politic societies of men belongeth so properly unto the same entire societies, that for any prince or potentate of what kind soever upon earth to exercise the same of himself, and not either by express commission immediately and personally received from God, or else by authority derived at the first from their consent upon whose persons they impose laws, it is no better than mere tyranny.

Laws they are not therefore which public approbation hath not made so. But approbation not only they give who personally declare their assent by voice sign or act, but also when others do it in their names by right originally at the least derived from them. As in parliaments, councils, and the like assemblies, although we be not personally ourselves present, notwithstanding our assent is by reason of other agents there in our behalf. And what we do by others, no reason but that it should stand as our deed, no less effectually to bind us than if ourselves had done it in person. In many things assent is given, they that give it not imagining they do so, because the manner of their assenting is not apparent. As for example, when an absolute monarch commandeth his subjects that which seemeth good in his own discretion, hath not his edict the force of a law whether they approve or dislike it? Again, that which hath been received long sithence and is by custom now established, we keep as a law which we may not transgress; yet what consent was ever thereunto sought or required at our hands?

Of this point therefore we are to note, that sith men naturally have no full and perfect power to command whole politic multitudes of men, therefore utterly without our consent we could in such sort be at no man's commandment living. And to be commanded we do consent, when that society whereof we are part hath at any time before consented, without revoking the same after by the like universal agreement.

(Richard Hooker, *Laws of Ecclesiastical Polity*, Bk 1, ch. 10, op. cit., pp. 190-1.)

71a   JOHN LOCKE: THE STATE OF NATURE

4. To understand political power aright, and derive it from its original, we must consider what state all men are naturally in, and that is a state of perfect freedom to order their actions and dispose of their possessions and persons as they think fit, within the bounds of the law of nature, without asking leave, or depending upon the will of any other man.

A state also of equality, wherein all the power and jurisdiction is reciprocal, no one having more than another; there being nothing more evident than that creatures of the same species and rank, promiscuously born to all the same advantages of nature, and the use of the same faculties, should also be equal one amongst another without subordination or subjection, unless the Lord and Master of them all should by any manifest declaration of his will set one above another, and confer on him by an evident and clear appointment an undoubted right to dominion and sovereignty.

5. This equality of men by nature the judicious Hooker looks upon as so evident in itself and beyond all question, that he makes it the foundation of that obligation to mutual love amongst men on which he builds the duties they owe one another, and from whence he derives the great maxims of justice and charity. . . .

6. But though this be a state of liberty, yet it is not a state of licence; though man in that state have an uncontrollable liberty to dispose of his person or

possessions, yet he has not liberty to destroy himself, or so much as any creature in his possession, but where some nobler use than its bare preservation calls for it. The state of nature has a law of nature to govern it, which obliges every one; and reason, which is that law, teaches all mankind who will but consult it, that, being all equal and independent, no one ought to harm another in his life, health, liberty, or possessions. For men being all the workmanship of one omnipotent and infinitely wise Maker—all the servants of one sovereign Master, sent into the world by his order, and about his business—they are his property, whose workmanship they are, made to last during his, not one another's pleasure; and being furnished with like faculties, sharing all in one community of nature, there cannot be supposed any such subordination among us, that may authorise us to destroy one another, as if we were made for one another's uses, as the inferior ranks of creatures are for ours. Every one, as he is bound to preserve himself, and not to quit his station wilfully, so, by the like reason, when his own preservation comes not in competition, ought he, as much as he can, to preserve the rest of mankind, and not, unless it be to do justice on an offender, take away or impair the life, or what tends to the preservation of the life, the liberty, health, limb, or goods of another.

7. And that all men may be restrained from invading others' rights, and from doing hurt to one another, and the law of nature be observed, which willeth the peace and preservation of all mankind, the execution of the law of nature is in that state put into every man's hand, whereby every one has a right to punish the transgressors of that law to such a degree as may hinder its violation. For the law of nature would, as all other laws that concern men in this world, be in vain if there were nobody that, in the state of nature, had a power to execute that law, and thereby preserve the innocent and restrain offenders. And if any one in the state of nature may punish another for any evil he has done, every one may do so. For in that state of perfect equality, where naturally there is no superiority or jurisdiction of one over another, what any may do in prosecution of that law, every one must needs have a right to do.

8. And thus in the state of nature one man comes by a power over another; but yet no absolute or arbitrary power, to use a criminal, when he has got him in his hands, according to the passionate heats or boundless extravagance of his own will; but only to retribute to him so far as calm reason and conscience dictate what is proportionate to his transgression, which is so much as may serve for reparation and restraint. For these two are the only reasons why one man may lawfully do harm to another, which is that we call punishment. In transgressing the law of nature, the offender declares himself to live by another rule than that of common reason and equity, which is that measure God has set to the actions of men, for their mutual security; and so he becomes dangerous to mankind, the tie which is to secure them from injury and violence being slighted and broken by him. Which, being a trespass against the whole species, and the peace and safety of it, provided for by the law of nature, every man upon this score, by the right he hath to preserve mankind in general, may restrain, or, where it is necessary, destroy things noxious to them, and so may bring such evil on any one who hath transgressed that law,

as may make him repent the doing of it, and thereby deter him, and by his example others, from doing the like mischief. And in this case, and upon this ground, every man hath a right to punish the offender, and be executioner of the law of nature.

(John Locke, *Second Treatise of Civil Government*, ed. J. W. Gough, ch. 2, sects 4-8, pp. 4-6, Blackwell, Oxford 1949.)

71b   JOHN LOCKE: PROPERTY

26. God, who hath given the world to men in common, hath also given them reason to make use of it to the best advantage of life and convenience. The earth and all that is therein is given to men for the support and comfort of their being. And though all the fruits it naturally produces, and beasts it feeds, belong to mankind in common, as they are produced by the spontaneous hand of nature; and nobody has originally a private dominion exclusive of the rest of mankind in any of them as they are thus in their natural state; yet being given for the use of men, there must of necessity be a means to appropriate them some way or other before they can be of any use or at all beneficial to any particular man. . . .

27. Though the earth and all inferior creatures be common to all men, yet every man has a property in his own person; this nobody has any right to but himself. The labour of his body and the work of his hands we may say are properly his. Whatsoever, then, he removes out of the state that nature hath provided and left it in, he hath mixed his labour with, and joined to it something that is his own, and thereby makes it his property. It being by him removed from the common state nature placed it in, it hath by this labour something annexed to it that excludes the common right of other men. For this labour being the unquestionable property of the labourer, no man but he can have a right to what that is once joined to, at least where there is enough and as good left in common for others. . . .

31. It will perhaps be objected to this, that if gathering the acorns, or other fruits of the earth, etc., makes a right to them, then any one may engross as much as he will. To which I answer, Not so. The same law of nature that does by this means give us property, does also bound that property too. 'God has given us all things richly' (1 Tim. vi. 17), is the voice of reason confirmed by inspiration. But how far has he given it us? To enjoy. As much as any one can make use of to any advantage of life before it spoils, so much he may by his labour fix a property in; whatever is beyond this is more than his share, and belongs to others. Nothing was made by God for man to spoil or destroy. And thus considering the plenty of natural provisions there was a long time in the world, and the few spenders, and to how small a part of that provision the industry of one man could extend itself, and engross it to the prejudice of others—especially keeping within the bounds, set by reason, of what might serve for his use—there could be then little room for quarrels or contentions about property so established.

32. But the chief matter of property being now not the fruits of the earth, and the beasts that subsist on it, but the earth itself, as that which takes in and carries with it all the rest, I think it is plain that property in that, too, is

acquired as the former. As much land as a man tills, plants, improves, cultivates, and can use the product of, so much is his property. He by his labour does as it were enclose it from the common. . . .

33. Nor was this appropriation of any parcel of land, by improving it, any prejudice to any other man, since there was still enough and as good left; and more than the yet unprovided could use. So that in effect there was never the less left for others because of his enclosure for himself. For he that leaves as much as another can make use of, does as good as take nothing at all. Nobody could think himself injured by the drinking of another man, though he took a good draught, who had a whole river of the same water left him to quench his thirst; and the case of land and water, where there is enough of both, is perfectly the same.

34. God gave the world to men in common; but since he gave it them for their benefit, and the greatest conveniences of life they were capable to draw from it, it cannot be supposed he meant it should always remain common and uncultivated. He gave it to the use of the industrious and rational (and labour was to be his title to it), not to the fancy or covetousness of the quarrelsome and contentious. He that had as good left for his improvement as was already taken up, needed not complain, ought not to meddle with what was already improved by another's labour; if he did, it is plain he desired the benefit of another's pains, which he had no right to, and not the ground which God had given him in common with others to labour on, and whereof there was as good left as that already possessed, and more than he knew what to do with, or his industry could reach to. . . .

46. . . . He that gathered a hundred bushels of acorns or apples had thereby a property in them; they were his goods as soon as gathered. He was only to look that he used them before they spoiled, else he took more than his share, and robbed others; and, indeed, it was foolish thing, as well as dishonest, to hoard up more than he could make use of. If he gave away part to anybody else, so that it perished not uselessly in his possession, these he also made use of; and if he also bartered away plums that would have rotted in a week, for nuts that would last good for his eating a whole year, he did no injury; he wasted not the common stock, destroyed no part of the portion of goods that belonged to others, so long as nothing perished uselessly in his hands. Again, if he would give his nuts for a piece of metal, pleased with its colour, or exchange his sheep for shells, or wool for a sparkling pebble or a diamond, and keep those by him all his life, he invaded not the right of others; he might heap up as much of these durable things as he pleased, the exceeding of the bounds of his just property not lying in the largeness of his possessions, but the perishing of anything uselessly in it.

47. And thus came in the use of money—some lasting thing that men might keep without spoiling, and that, by mutual consent, men would take in exchange for the truly useful but perishable supports of life.

48. And as different degrees of industry were apt to give men possessions in different proportions, so this invention of money gave them the opportunity to continue and enlarge them. . . .

(John Locke, op. cit., ch. 5, pp. 15, 17–18, 24-5.)

71c JOHN LOCKE: DISADVANTAGES OF THE STATE OF NATURE

13. To this strange doctrine—*viz.*, That in the state of nature every one has the executive power of the law of nature—I doubt not but it will be objected that it is unreasonable for men to be judges in their own cases, that self-love will make men partial to themselves and their friends: and on the other side, that ill-nature, passion, and revenge will carry them too far in punishing others; and hence nothing but confusion and disorder will follow; and that therefore God hath certainly appointed government to restrain the partiality and violence of men. I easily grant that civil government is the proper remedy for the inconveniences of the state of nature, which must certainly be great where men may be judges in their own case, since 'tis easy to be imagined that he who was so unjust as to do his brother an injury, will scarce be so just as to condemn himself for it. But I shall desire those who make this objection, to remember that absolute monarchs are but men, and if government is to be the remedy of those evils which necessarily follow from men's being judges in their own cases, and the state of nature is therefore not to be endured, I desire to know what kind of government that is, and how much better it is than the state of nature, where one man commanding a multitude has the liberty to be judge in his own case, and may do to all his subjects whatever he pleases, without the least question or control of those who execute his pleasure; and in whatsoever he doth, whether led by reason, mistake, or passion, must be submitted to? Much better it is in the state of nature, wherein men are not bound to submit to the unjust will of another: and if he that judges, judges amiss in his own or any other case, he is answerable for it to the rest of mankind.

(John Locke, op. cit., ch. 2, sect. 13, pp. 8-9.)

71d JOHN LOCKE: THE SOCIAL CONTRACT

95. Men being, as has been said, by nature all free, equal, and independent, no one can be put out of this estate, and subjected to the political power of another, without his own consent. The only way by which any one divests himself of his natural liberty and puts on the bonds of civil society is by agreeing with other men to join and unite into a community for their comfortable, safe, and peaceable living one amongst another, in a secure enjoyment of their properties, and a greater security against any that are not of it. This any number of men may do, because it injures not the freedom of the rest; they are left as they were in the liberty of the state of nature. When any number of men have so consented to make one community or government, they are thereby presently incorporated, and make one body politic, wherein the majority have a right to act and conclude the rest.
96. For when any number of men have, by the consent of every individual, made a community, they have thereby made that community one body, with a power to act as one body, which is only by the will and determination of the majority. For that which acts any community being only the consent of the in-

dividuals of it, and it being necessary to that which is one body to move one way, it is necessary the body should move that way whither the greater force carries it, which is the consent of the majority; or else it is impossible it should act or continue one body, one community, which the consent of every individual that united into it agreed that it should; and so every one is bound by that consent to be concluded by the majority. And therefore we see that in assemblies empowered to act by positive laws, where no number is set by that positive law which empowers them, the act of the majority passes for the act of the whole, and of course determines, as having by the law of nature and reason the power of the whole.

97. And thus every man, by consenting with others to make one body politic under one government, puts himself under an obligation to every one of that society, to submit to the determination of the majority, and to be concluded by it; or else this original compact, whereby he with others incorporates into one society, would signify nothing, and be no compact, if he be left free and under no other ties than he was in before in the state of nature. For what appearance would there be of any compact? What new engagement if he were no farther tied by any decrees of the society, than he himself thought fit, and did actually consent to? This would be still as great a liberty as he himself had before his compact, or any one else in the state of nature hath, who may submit himself and consent to any acts of it if he thinks fit. . . .

99. Whosoever therefore out of a state of nature unite into a community must be understood to give up all the power necessary to the ends for which they unite into society, to the majority of the community, unless they expressly agreed in any number greater than the majority. And this is done by barely agreeing to unite into one political society, which is all the compact that is, or needs be, between the individuals that enter into or make up a commonwealth. And thus that which begins and actually constitutes any political society is nothing but the consent of any number of freemen capable of a majority to unite and incorporate into such a society. And this is that, and that only, which did or could give beginning to any lawful government in the world.

(John Locke, op. cit., ch. 8, sects 95-9, pp. 48-50.)

71e   JOHN LOCKE: THE LEGISLATIVE POWER

134. The great end of men's entering into society being the enjoyment of their properties in peace and safety, and the great instrument and means of that being the laws established in that society: the first and fundamental positive law of all commonwealths, is the establishing of the legislative power; as the first and fundamental natural law, which is to govern even the legislative itself, is the preservation of the society, and (as far as will consist with the public good) of every person in it. This legislative is not only the supreme power of the commonweath, but sacred and unalterable in the hands where the community have once placed it; nor can any edict of anybody else, in what form soever conceived, or by what power soever backed, have the force and obligation of a law, which has not its sanction from that legislative which the public

has chosen and appointed. For without this the law could not have that, which is absolutely necessary to its being a law, the consent of the society over whom nobody can have a power to make laws; but by their own consent, and by authority received from them; and therefore all the obedience, which by the most solemn ties any one can be obliged to pay, ultimately terminates in this supreme power, and is directed by those laws which it enacts; nor can any oaths to any foreign power whatsoever, or any domestic subordinate power discharge any member of the society from his obedience to the legislative, acting pursuant to their trust, nor oblige him to any obedience contrary to the laws so enacted, or farther than they do allow; it being ridiculous to imagine one can be tied ultimately to obey any power in the society which is not the supreme.

135. Though the legislative, whether placed in one or more, whether it be always in being, or only by intervals, though it be the supreme power in every commonwealth, yet,

It is not nor can possibly be absolutely arbitrary over the lives and fortunes of the people. For it being but the joint power of every member of the society given up to that person, or assembly, which is legislator; it can be no more than those persons had in a state of nature before they entered into society, and gave it up to the community. For nobody can transfer to another more power than he has in himself; and nobody has an absolute arbitrary power over himself, or over any other to destroy his own life, or take away the life or property of another. A man, as has been proved, cannot subject himself to the arbitrary power of another; and having in the state of nature no arbitrary power over the life, liberty, of possession of another, but only so much as the law of nature gave him for the preservation of himself, and the rest of mankind; this is all he doth, or can give up to the commonwealth, and by it to the legislative power, so that the legislative can have no more than this. Their power in the utmost bounds of it, is limited to the public good of the society. It is a power that hath no other end but preservation, and therefore can never have a right to destroy, enslave, or designedly to impoverish the subjects.

(John Locke, op. cit., ch. 11, sects 134-5, pp. 66-7.)

71f   JOHN LOCKE: THE DISSOLUTION OF GOVERNMENT

211. He that will with any clearness speak of the dissolution of government ought, in the first place, to distinguish between the dissolution of the society and the dissolution of the government. That which makes the community, and brings men out of the loose state of nature into one politic society, is the agreement which every one has with the rest to incorporate and act as one body, and so be one distinct commonwealth. The usual and almost only way whereby this union is dissolved, is the inroad of foreign force making a conquest upon them. For in that case (not being able to maintain and support themselves as one entire and independent body) the union belonging to that body which consisted therein must necessarily cease, and so every one return to the state he was in before, with a liberty to shift for himself and provide for his own safety

as he thinks fit in some other society. Whenever the society is dissolved, it is certain the government of that society cannot remain. . . .

212. Besides this overturning from without, governments are dissolved from within.

First, When the legislative is altered. . . .

When any one or more shall take upon them to make laws, whom the people have not appointed so to do, they make laws without authority, which the people are not therefore bound to obey; by which means they come again to be out of subjection, and may constitute to themselves a new legislative, as they think best, being in full liberty to resist the force of those who without authority would impose anything upon them. Every one is at the disposure of his own will when those, who had by the delegation of the society the declaring of the public will, are excluded from it, and others usurp the place who have no such authority or delegation. . . .

219. There is one way more whereby such a government may be dissolved, and that is, when he who has the supreme executive power neglects and abandons that charge, so that the laws already made can no longer be put in execution. This is demonstratively to reduce all to anarchy, and so effectually to dissolve the government. For laws not being made for themselves, but to be by their execution the bonds of the society, to keep every part of the body politic in its due place and function, when that totally ceases, the government visibly ceases, and the people become a confused multitude without order or connection. . . .

220. In these and the like cases, when the government is dissolved, the people are at liberty to provide for themselves by erecting a new legislative, differing from the other, by the change of persons, or form, or both, as they shall find it most for their safety and good. For the society can never, by the fault of another, lose the native and original right it has to preserve itself, which can only be done by a settled legislative, and a fair and impartial execution of the laws made by it. But the state of mankind is not so miserable that they are not capable of using this remedy, till it be too late to look for any. To tell people they may provide for themselves by erecting a new legislative, when by oppression, artifice, or being delivered over to a foreign power, their old one is gone, is only to tell them they may expect relief when it is too late, and the evil is past cure. This is in effect no more than to bid them first be slaves, and then to take care of their liberty; and when their chains are on tell them they may act like free men. This, if barely so, is rather mockery than relief; and men can never be secure from tyranny if there be no means to escape it till they are perfectly under it. And therefore it is that they have not only a right to get out of it, but to prevent it.

221. There is therefore, secondly, another way whereby governments are dissolved, and that is when the legislative or the prince, either of them, act contrary to their trust.

(John Locke, op. cit., ch. 19, sects 211, 212, 219-21, pp. 103-7.)

71g JOHN LOCKE: REBELLION

240. Here, 'tis like, the common question will be made: Who shall be judge whether the prince or legislative act contrary to their trust? This, perhaps ill-affected and factious men may spread amongst the people when the prince only makes use of his due prerogative. To this I reply: The people shall be judge; for who shall be judge whether the trustee or deputy acts well and according to the trust reposed in him, but he who deputes him, and must, by having deputed him, have still the power to discard him when he fails in his trust? If this be reasonable in particular cases of private men, why should it be otherwise in that of the greatest moment, where the welfare of millions is concerned, and also where the evil, if not prevented, is greater, and the redress very difficult, dear, and dangerous?

241. But farther, this question, who shall be judge, cannot mean that there is no judge at all; for where there is no judicature on earth to decide controversies amongst men, God in heaven is Judge. He alone, it is true, is Judge of the right; but every man is judge for himself, as in all other cases, so in this, whether another hath put himself into a state of war with him, and whether he should appeal to the Supreme Judge as Jephtha did.

242. If a controversy arise betwixt a prince and some of the people in a matter where the law is silent or doubtful, and the thing be of great consequence, I should think the proper umpire in such a case should be the body of the people; for in cases where the prince hath a trust reposed in him, and is dispensed from the common ordinary rules of the law; there, if any men find themselves aggrieved, and think the prince acts contrary to or beyond that trust, who so proper to judge as the body of the people (who at first lodged that trust in him) how far they meant it should extend? But if the prince or whoever they be in the administration decline that way of determination, the appeal then lies nowhere but to heaven; force between either persons who have no known superior on earth, or which permits no appeal to a judge on earth, being properly a state of war, wherein the appeal lies only to heaven, and in that state the injured party must judge for himself when he will think fit to make use of that appeal and put himself upon it.

243. To conclude, the power that every individual gave the society when he entered into it, can never revert to the individuals again as long as the society lasts, but will always remain in the community, because without this there can be no community, no commonwealth, which is contrary to the original agreement; so also when the society hath placed the legislative in any assembly of men to continue in them and their successors, with direction and authority for providing such successors, the legislative can never revert to the people whilst that government lasts, because having provided a legislative with power to continue for ever, they have given up their political power to the legislative and cannot resume it. But if they have set limits to the duration of their legislative, and made this supreme power in any person or assembly only temporary; or else when by the miscarriages of those in authority it is forfeited; upon the forfeiture, or at the determination of the time set, it reverts to the society, and the people have a right to act as supreme, and continue the legislative in themselves: or place it in a new form, or new hands as they think good.

(John Locke, op. cit., ch. 19, sects 240-3, pp. 118-20.)

CHAPTER 19

Rousseau and Burke

Just as the political thought of the seventeenth century was dominated by England, the eighteenth century was pre-eminently French. French eighteenth-century society was dominated by an absolute monarchy, an arrogant aristocracy and an obscurantist church. The ideas of the philosophers of the French enlightenment, Voltaire, Montesquieu, Diderot, and the Physiocrats, developed as a reaction against these institutions. The remedy that they proposed for the ills of society was liberty, for if men had freedom to act and to speak as they wished, the rule of reason would be free to emerge. The sovereignty of reason would usher in a regenerated society, free from privilege, religious superstition and secular persecution. From Locke the French *philosophes* borrowed the ideas of natural rights, natural law and toleration; from Isaac Newton, the English scientist, they borrowed the notion of an orderly and rational universe; from Pierre Bayle, the seventeenth-century French philosopher, they borrowed their scepticism for religious faith.

With their emphasis upon Lockean natural rights, most of the *philosophes* found it difficult to reconcile their ideas with popular democracy since they suspected that the masses would have little sympathy with, for example, the right to private property. Hence they tended to favour the kind of government practised by the so-called 'enlightened despots'. Although the 'rights of man' became a rallying cry in both the American and the French revolutions, the *philosophes* were never conscious revolutionists.

Montesquieu (1689–1755)

If one were to select a work of political philosophy to represent the French enlightenment, *De l'Esprit des Lois* (*The Spirit of the Laws*), written in 1748 by the Baron de Montesquieu, would be an obvious choice. It reflects admirably the optimistic emphases upon reason and liberty which pervaded French thought in the eighteenth century.

The declared purpose of the book is to examine different societies in order to discover the fundamental principle which underlies the laws and government of those societies. His first sentence states: 'Laws, in their most general signification, are the necessary relations arising from the nature of things.' Although Montesquieu is by no means clear about the nature of law,' he seems to think that there are certain rules which were followed by men prior to civil society and which are maintained after the state has been founded. These rules correspond closely to the rational laws of nature. Additionally, each society possesses laws which, although rational, are unique to it. These laws bear a distinctive relation to the varying characteristics of that society such as the type of government, climate, soil, situation, economic structure, religion and degree of liberty. 'These relations . . . together constitute what I call the Spirit of Laws.'

No part of this brilliant and erudite but long and rambling work was to have greater influence than the eleventh book in which Montesquieu discusses the English constitution. His analysis, based upon observation of the English system of government during his visit there from 1729 to 1731, led him to declare that liberty in England depended upon the separation of the legislative, executive and judicial powers, and upon the existence of devices whereby the legislative and executive powers may check the actions of each other (Ex. 72).

A great deal of modern criticism has been directed at Montesquieu for his apparent failure to recognize that the king's ministers were drawn from parliament and that therefore no separation between executive and legislative in fact existed. It is most unlikely that Montesquieu, who moved in the highest political circles, could have overlooked this. No doubt, in common with most English observers, he considered that ministers as the king's appointees were primarily responsible to him, and thus it would seem quite sensible to conceive of the executive power as separate from the legislative.

Whatever doubts there may be about the relevance of Montesquieu's analysis to the British constitution there can be no dispute about his influence upon the constitution makers of other countries. Both the United States Constitution and the French Declaration of the Rights of Man embody Montesquieu's principles regarding the separation and balancing of constitutional powers.

Jean-Jacques Rousseau (1712-1778)

Although Rousseau cannot be regarded as representative of the Age of Reason, he was a contemporary of the rationalist French *philosophes* and his political philosophy was in large measure stimulated by reaction against them. He was born in the city state of Geneva where he lived until he was abandoned by his father. Taking up residence in France, his literary and musical talents and his natural charm enabled him to live comfortably if precariously, largely on the generosity of women friends. In 1742 he travelled to Paris hoping to be accepted as an equal by the Parisian intellectuals. He was, however, treated very coldly by many of them who saw him as an arrogant and irresponsible interloper, and he found solace in withdrawing from society and embarking upon a long relationship with the uneducated servant, Thérèse Levasseur, in the course of which she bore him five children.

It has been thought highly probable that Rousseau's extreme anti-rationalism and his quarrels with the *philosophes* stemmed from his unstable personality and his sense of rejection by those whom he originally sought as allies. Furthermore, his democratic sentiments made him a convinced opponent of the French monarchy and of the church. He was therefore very much a lone figure in the eighteenth-century intellectual world.

Rousseau's career as a literary celebrity began with his prize-winning essay, the *Discourse on the Arts and Sciences* (1749). The sponsors of the essay contest, the Academy of Dijon, no doubt expected a typically 'enlightened' or progressive set of essays arguing that the arts and sciences had contributed to the purification of morals. Rousseau, however, in his essay concluded that, on the contrary, morality had been corrupted by the so-called benefits of civilization.

The romantic idealization of the 'noble savage' first hinted at in the *Discourse on the Arts and Sciences* was developed in Rousseau's second discourse, the *Discourse on the Origin of Inequality* (1755). In order to discover the true nature of man, Rousseau, in common with his great predecessors Hobbes and Locke, examines him in a 'state of nature' living without any of the appurtenances of civilization. Natural man is seen as solitary, carefree, ignorant, innocent and capable of instinctively satisfying his few desires. Because he lives alone and has no human contact other than the momentary satisfaction of sexual desire, he cannot be said to possess virtue. He is neither good nor bad, because morality has meaning only in the context of man's relationships with others.

Natural man possesses two motivating forces both of which are prior to reason. They are self-preservation, the chief concern of man, and compassion, which inclines him to help others who are in distress. 'From this quality alone are derived all man's social virtues.' In this natural state man is both free and equal. He is under no authority save that of his free will and although there exist natural inequalities of strength, intelligence, etc, there are none of the institutionalized inequalities which occur in civilization.

It is implicit in the *Second Discourse* that man is morally incomplete in the state of nature. Although he is content, man is not positively happy and therefore although civil society in its actual contemporary form is corrupting, nevertheless man needs the state in order to achieve the happiness which accompanies moral fulfilment. Society and the state develop largely as a result of co-operation between men which is itself a consequence of the development of agriculture and industry. The innocent spontaneity of natural man is replaced by the manipulation of some men by others and the introduction of private property. From this comes class division and the evils of greed and ambition. As a remedy, government and laws are introduced by the strong and the rich to protect their privileges and their property. The poor and the weak are tricked into agreeing to the establishment of these institutions: 'all ran headlong to their chains.' Government begins by being equitable, but sooner or later, inequalities of wealth and power are legitimized and despotism is established. At this stage, man's noblest faculty of freedom is lost and he is enslaved.

Rousseau's greatest political work, the *Social Contract* (1762), is concerned with man in civil society and in that sense can be regarded as a kind of sequel to the *Second Discourse*. The first chapter opens with the famous sentence: 'Man is born free; and everywhere he is in chains' (Ex. 73a). The problem with which Rousseau is faced is that of reconciling man's original and natural freedom with the binding laws (or chains) of civil society. His solution (the main theme of the *Social Contract*) is to show that in a properly organized state, the laws are not restrictive 'chains' at all but, besides being necessary for security, are perfectly compatible with human freedom and equality. If there was any implicit nostalgia for man's natural condition in the earlier discourses, there is certainly none now. Society and state are not only inevitable but positively desirable provided that they conform to certain democratic conditions. Unfortunately no existing contemporary states do so conform; hence they are corrupt and tyrannical.

The Contract

The solution to the problem of reconciling freedom and authority is found in the well-tried device of the social contract (Ex. 73b). Life in the state of nature becomes intolerable, although no details are given of why this is so. The origin of civil association must be by the individual agreement of all men since all are naturally free and equal. So far there is nothing novel compared with earlier contract theorists. However, Rousseau considers that freedom and equality can be preserved only if each man gives up all his natural rights to the community as a whole, which thereupon becomes a 'moral and collective body'. Equality is maintained since every person without exception alienates all his rights to the whole and not to a part. Liberty is maintained because each in obeying the will of the whole community—the 'general will'—is obeying himself.

The General Will

Unlike the theories of Hobbes and Locke where the complete individuality of each participant is retained, in Rousseau's theory the individual becomes a part of an organic whole. As a moral body, the organic state possesses a will which is the sovereign authority over the whole community. This is the 'general will, which tends always to the preservation and welfare of the whole and of every part, and is the source of the laws, (and) constitutes for all the members of the state, in their relations to one another and to it, the rule of what is just or unjust' (*Discourse on Political Economy*). Rousseau seems to consider that while each person's actions are governed by self-interest, part of this self-interest is specific to the individual and is represented by that person's 'selfish' or 'particular' will, and part is common to the whole community and is represented by his 'real' will. Given the right conditions for the process to develop, the divergent individual wills cancel out and the 'general will', being the corporate identical real will of each individual, is allowed to emerge.

Because of the identification of the general will of society with the real will of the individual, Rousseau does not feel it necessary to provide guarantees for the subjects. Guaranteed rights in the Lockean sense are a feature of a theory which seeks to impose restrictions on legislative authority. They have no place in Rousseau's theory, which cannot conceive of the general will acting against anyone's real interests (Ex. 73c). Although an individual may possess a dominant particular will that opposes the general will and therefore predisposes him to disobey it, he is to be 'forced to be free'. That is, in being forced to obey the law a person is constrained into obedience to his own real will: what he would wish to do if he had full knowledge of all the facts and was able to view his interest objectively as a member of the community. This is true freedom or 'positive' freedom, as T. H. Green over a century later was to call his own similar concept.

This point is re-emphasized in a later passage where the method used to express the general will is explained (Ex. 73d). Citizens meet together in a legislative assembly where they must decide whether a proposed law conforms to the general will. When the votes are counted the majority decision binds the whole group. Any individual who finds himself in the minority must realize that he was mistaken, and that had his particular will carried the day, he would not have been free.

The characteristics of the general will are summed up in Book II of the *Social Contract* in a series of three propositions: that sovereignty is inalienable, indivisible and infallible (Ex. 73e). Sovereignty cannot be alienated since the general will must always be the will of the whole community. Government can be established with power to execute the general will but the sovereign legislative function cannot be delegated to it because ultimately the individual wills of members of the government are bound to diverge from the general will. Sovereignty cannot be divided because the will of a part of the people is particular and not general. It is infallible because by definition it always tends to the public advantage. Nevertheless, it might happen that where public deliberations take place in less than perfect conditions, instead of the general will the 'will of all' emerges, and this is fallible, being merely 'the sum of particular wills'.

The Executive

Once the state has been established by contract, the executive government must be set up. This body, 'the means of communication between the state and the sovereign', although necessary, is a constant danger to the well-being of the state since it has an inevitable tendency towards tyranny. Hence it cannot be established by contract because that would lead to the absurd situation where the sovereign would be under a superior authority (Ex. 73f). The only possibility is for government to be given delegated powers by the community, which may withdraw them if the general will so desires.

Because Rousseau was a firm believer in popular sovereignty, it might have seemed consistent if he had advocated a democratic executive. But such a form of government he regards as impracticable, since it would demand the continuous session of the majority of the citizens, and dangerous, since as all government corrupts, government by all would corrupt the whole body of the people. Democratic government would be perhaps appropriate for very small states, but it is too weak for large ones. Monarchy, on the other hand, is strong but more prone to corruption. An elective aristocracy, he concludes, is likely to be the best compromise because it is more practicable than democracy and less liable to corruption than monarchy.

The Legislator

Although the general will is the expression of the sovereign will of each citizen, not all men are capable of knowing or expressing this will. No doubt in time, as the state becomes established on the right lines, the emergence of the general will becomes inevitable but in its early stages the people's will must be guided. Rousseau here introduces the curious figure of the 'legislator' (Ex. 73g). He is a person similar to the ancient semi-mythical legislators such as Lycurgus, who reputedly gave Sparta its laws. The legislator's function apparently is to propose laws to the sovereign people who then approve or disapprove them according to the general will. Rousseau does not inform us from where this remarkable genius is to come, although intellectually he has an obvious kinship with Plato's philosopher rulers.

Rousseau concludes the *Social Contract* with his famous chapter on civil religion. He regards the message of the Gospels as admirable but lacking in the social morality which was a good feature of the Roman pagan cults. Roman Catholicism, on the other hand, is a dangerous corruption of Christianity which impairs social unity by emphasizing the dual allegiance of man to the state and to the Church. What is therefore needed is a 'civil profession of faith' which incorporates certain basic moral rules laid down by the sovereign itself. Beyond these few dogmas a man may believe what he wishes, although an exception is made for creeds like Roman Catholicism which are theologically intolerant since such intolerance inevitably leads to the usurpation of power by priests (Ex. 73h).

Rousseau's political theory is a curious mixture. On the one hand, his emphasis upon inalienable popular sovereignty makes him the main ancestor of modern democracy, although he would have had little liking for the practice of legislating through representatives. Despite the fact that there is no express theory of revolution in the *Social Contract* the democratic theme of the book is itself an incitement to rebel against tyrannical and arbitrary government wherever it appears. Robespierre and the Jacobins of the French Revolution used the arguments of Rousseau in much the same way as the ideas of Karl Marx were used by the Russian revolutionaries.

On the other hand, Rousseau's theory contains elements which are totalitarian in their implications. His suppression of the individual in the collective body of the community, his denial of guarantees of rights, his view of freedom as acting according to one's real will; all of these are familiar elements in contemporary 'totalitarian democracies'. Whereas John Locke's bourgeois theory of inalienable natural rights leads to western liberal democracy with its emphasis upon freedom from state interference, Rousseau's metaphysical theory of the sovereignty of the general will leads to Marx and Lenin and to the kind of democracy associated with Communist states.

The Declaration of the Rights of Man and the Citizen

To some extent the ideas of Rousseau are reflected in this statement adopted by the French National Assembly in August 1789. The emphasis upon man's original freedom and equality, and upon law as an expression of the common will are recognizably Rousseauistic (Ex. 74). However, the frequent references to natural rights including that of property are more reminiscent of John Locke and the philosophers of the enlightenment.

The American Declaration of Independence

For purposes of comparison an extract from the *Declaration of*

316 MODERN POLITICAL IDEAS

Independence is included (Ex. 75). Unlike the French *Declaration*, this statement shows little influence of any political theorist other than Locke whose final chapter of the *Second Treatise* has clearly provided a closely followed model.

Edmund Burke (1720–1797)

The anti-intellectualism and collectivism espoused by Rousseau in France, was paralleled in England by Burke's attack on abstract reason and his assertion of the organic national community. The intellectual similarities between the two writers make the divergences all the more remarkable. Whereas Rousseau was led by his admiration for the national community to a theory of democracy, Burke is rightly regarded as the father of English conservatism.

Burke was not a philosopher in the sense that Hobbes and Locke were. His political philosophy emerges from speeches and pamphlets inspired by contemporary political events. For example, some of his most notable early utterances were produced in response to the revolt of the American colonies. In this case, Burke was morally on the side of the revolutionists who, as the descendants of Englishmen, were entitled to better treatment in government and taxation than they were receiving.

The conservatism of Burke's thought is best shown in his book *Reflections on the Revolution in France* published in 1790. The first extract illustrates his admiration for the continuity and traditional spirit of the British constitution (Ex. 76a). It is inheritance and not innovation that is responsible for our admirable social and political structure. Reform is not excluded; improvements are possible, but they must come about slowly and must remain consistent with custom and tradition.

His attack on the abstract doctrines which inspired the French Revolution is illustrated in the second extract (Ex. 76b). He does not deny the existence of natural rights but he does deny that government can be affected by them. Rational abstractions such as natural law and rights, the social contract, etc., are too simple to explain the facts of society and government. Institutions are not rational creations to be constructed or destroyed according to theory. They are to be regarded as living growing organisms developed by centuries of customary wisdom. It is the criminal folly of the revolutionists to have imposed their fanaticism for theory upon the actuality of the French constitution.

FURTHER READING

Texts
J. J. Rousseau: *The Social Contract*
T. Paine: *The Rights of Man*

E. Burke: *Reflections on the Revolution in France*

Commentaries

D. Cameron: *The Social Thought of Rousseau and Burke* (Weidenfeld and Nicolson, London 1973)

A. Cobban: *Rousseau and the Modern State* (Allen and Unwin 1964)

G. H. Dodge (ed): *Jean Jacques Rousseau: Authoritarian Libertarian?* (D. C. Heath & Co. Lexington 1971)

J. C. Hall: *Rousseau: An Introduction to his Political Philosophy* (Macmillan 1973)

J. McDonald: *Rousseau and the French Revolution* (Athlone Press 1965)

R. D. Masters: *The Political Philosophy of Rousseau* (Princeton University Press 1968)

F. O'Gorman: *Edmund Burke* (Unwin, London 1973)

K. F. Roche: *Rousseau, Stoic and Romantic* (Methuen, London 1974)

---

72 MONTESQUIEU: THE ENGLISH CONSTITUTION

In every government there are three sorts of power: the legislative; the executive in respect to things dependent on the law of nations; and the executive in regard to matters that depend on the civil law.

By virtue of the first, the prince or magistrate enacts temporary or perpetual laws, and amends or abrogates those that have been already enacted. By the second, he makes peace or war, sends or receives embassies, establishes the public security, and provides against invasions. By the third, he punishes criminals, or determines the disputes that arise between individuals. The latter we shall call the judiciary power, and the other simply the executive power of the state.

The political liberty of the subject is a tranquillity of mind arising from the opinion each person has of his safety. In order to have this liberty, it is requisite the government be so constituted as one man need not be afraid of another.

When the legislative and executive powers are united in the same person, or in the same body of magistrates, there can be no liberty; because apprehensions may arise, lest the same monarch or senate should enact tyrannical laws, to execute them in a tyrannical manner.

Again, there is no liberty, if the judiciary power be not separated from the legislative and executive. Were it joined with the legislative, the life and liberty of the subject would be exposed to arbitrary control; for the judge would be then the legislator. Were it joined to the executive power, the judge might behave with violence and oppression.

There would be an end of everything, were the same man or the same body, whether of the nobles or of the people, to exercise those three powers, that of enacting laws, that of executing the public resolutions, and of trying the causes of individuals. . . .

As in a country of liberty, every man who is supposed a free agent ought to be his own governor; the legislative power should reside in the whole body of the people. But since this is impossible in large states, and in small ones, is subject to many inconveniences, it is fit the people should transact by their representatives what they cannot transact by themselves.

The inhabitants of a particular town are much better acquainted with its wants and interests than with those of other places; and are better judges of the capacity of their neighbours than of that of the rest of their countrymen. The members, therefore, of the legislature should not be chosen from the general body of the nation; but it is proper that in every considerable place a representative should be elected by the inhabitants.

The great advantage of representatives is, their capacity of discussing public affairs. For this the people collectively are extremely unfit, which is one of the chief inconveniences of a democracy. . . .

The body of the nobility ought to be hereditary. In the first place it is so in its own nature; and in the next there must be a considerable interest to preserve its privileges—privileges that in themselves are obnoxious to popular envy, and of course in a free state are always in danger.

But as a hereditary power might be tempted to pursue its own particular interests, and forget those of the people, it is proper that where a singular advantage may be gained by corrupting the nobility, as in the laws relating to the supplies, they should have no other share in the legislation than the power of rejecting, and not that of resolving. . . .

The executive power ought to be in the hands of a monarch, because this branch of government, having need of despatch, is better administered by one than by many: on the other hand, whatever depends on the legislative power is oftentimes better regulated by many than by a single person.

But if there were no monarch, and the executive power should be committed to a certain number of persons selected from the legislative body, there would be an end then of liberty; by reason the two powers would be united, as the same persons would sometimes possess, and would be always able to possess, a share in both. . . .

The executive power, pursuant of what has been already said, ought to have a share in the legislature by the power of rejecting; otherwise it would soon be stripped of its prerogative. But should the legislative power usurp a share of the executive, the latter would be equally undone.

If the prince were to have a part in the legislature by the power of resolving, liberty would be lost. But as it is necessary he should have a share in the legislature for the support of his own prerogative, this share must consist in the power of rejecting. . . .

Here, then, is the fundamental constitution of the government we are treating of. The legislative body being composed of two parts, they check one another by the mutual privilege of rejecting. They are both restrained by the executive power, as the executive is by the legislative.

(Montesquieu, *The Spirit of Laws*, tr. T. Nugent, Rev. J. V. Prichard, Bk 11, sect. 6, pp. 151-2, 154, 156, 159-60, G. Bell, London 1914.)

73a JEAN-JACQUES ROUSSEAU: MAN NATURALLY FREE

Man is born free; and everywhere he is in chains. One thinks himself the master of others, and still remains a greater slave than they. How did this change come about? I do not know. What can make it legitimate? That question I think I can answer.

If I took into account only force, and the effects derived from it, I should say: 'As long as a people is compelled to obey, and obeys, it does well; as soon as it can shake off the yoke, and shakes it off, it does still better; for, regaining its liberty by the same right as took it away, either it is justified in resuming it, or there was no justification for those who took it away.' But the social order is a sacred right which is the basis of all other rights. Nevertheless, this right does not come from nature, and must therefore be founded on conventions. Before coming to that, I have to prove what I have just asserted.

(Jean-Jacques Rousseau, *The Social Contract*, tr. G. D. H. Cole, Bk 1, ch. 1, pp. 3-4, Everyman Library Edition, Dent, London and E. P. Dutton, New York 1913.)

73b JEAN-JACQUES ROUSSEAU: THE SOCIAL CONTRACT

I suppose men to have reached the point at which the obstacles in the way of their preservation in the state of nature show their power of resistance to be greater than the resources at the disposal of each individual for his maintenance in that state. That primitive condition can then subsist no longer; and the human race would perish unless it changed its manner of existence.

But, as men cannot engender new forces, but only unite and direct existing ones, they have no other means of preserving themselves than the formation, by aggregation, of a sum of forces great enough to overcome the resistance. These they have to bring into play by means of a single motive power, and cause to act in concert.

This sum of forces can arise only where several persons come together: but, as the force and liberty of each man are the chief instruments of his self-preservation, how can he pledge them without harming his own interests, and neglecting the care he owes to himself? This difficulty, in its bearing on my present subject, may be stated in the following terms:

'The problem is to find a form of association which will defend and protect with the whole common force the person and goods of each associate, and in which each, while uniting himself with all, may still obey himself alone, and remain as free as before.' This is the fundamental problem of which the *Social Contract* provides the solution.

The clauses of this contract are so determined by the nature of the act that the slightest modification would make them vain and ineffective; so that, although they have perhaps never been formally set forth, they are everywhere the same and everywhere tacitly admitted and recognized, until, on the violation of the social compact, each regains his original rights and resumes his natural liberty, while losing the conventional liberty in favour of which he renounced it.

These clauses, properly understood, may be reduced to one—the total alienation of each associate, together with all his rights, to the whole community; for, in the first place, as each gives himself absolutely, the conditions are the same for all; and, this being so, no one has any interest in making them burdensome to others.

Moreover, the alienation being without reserve, the union is as perfect as it can be, and no associate has anything more to demand: for, if the individuals retained certain rights, as there would be no common superior to decide between them and the public, each, being on one point his own judge, would ask to be so on all; the state of nature would thus continue, and the association would necessarily become inoperative or tyrannical.

Finally, each man, in giving himself to all, gives himself to nobody; and as there is no associate over which he does not acquire the same right as he yields others over himself, he gains an equivalent for everything he loses, and an increase of force for the preservation of what he has.

If then we discard from the social compact what is not of its essence, we shall find that it reduces itself to the following terms:

"Each of us puts his person and all his power in common under the supreme direction of the general will, and, in our corporate capacity, we receive each member as an indivisible part of the whole.'

At once, in place of the individual personality of each contracting party, this act of association creates a moral and collective body, composed of as many members as the assembly contains voters, and receiving from this act its unity, its common identity, its life, and its will. This public person, so formed by the union of all other persons, formerly took the name of *city*, and now takes that of *Republic* or *body politic*; it is called by its members *State* when passive, *Sovereign* when active, and *Power* when compared with others like itself. Those who are associated in it take collectively the name of *people*, and severally are called *citizens*, as sharing in the sovereign power, and *subjects*, as being under the laws of the State. But these terms are often confused and taken one for another: it is enough to know how to distinguish them when they are being used with precision.

(Jean-Jacques Rousseau, op. cit., Bk 1, ch. 6, pp. 11-13.)

73c JEAN-JACQUES ROUSSEAU: THE SOVEREIGN

The Sovereign, being formed wholly of the individuals who compose it, neither has nor can have any interest contrary to theirs; and consequently the sovereign power need give no guarantee to its subjects, because it is impossible for the body to wish to hurt all its members. We shall also see later on that it cannot hurt any in particular. The Sovereign, merely by virtue of what it is, is always what it should be.

This, however, is not the case with the relation of the subjects to the Sovereign, which, despite the common interest, would have no security that they would fulfil their undertakings, unless it found means to assure itself of their fidelity.

In fact, each individual, as a man, may have a particular will contrary or dissimilar to the general will which he has as a citizen. His particular interest may speak to him quite differently from the common interest: his absolute and naturally independent existence may make him look upon what he owes to the common cause as a gratuitous contribution, the loss of which will do less harm to others than the payment of it is burdensome to himself; and regarding the moral person which constitutes the State as a *persona ficta*, because not a man, he may wish to enjoy the rights of citizenship without being ready to fulfil the duties of a subject. The continuance of such an injustice could not but prove the undoing of the body politic.

In order then that the social compact may not be an empty formula, it tacitly includes the undertaking, which alone can give force to the rest, that whoever refuses to obey the general will shall be compelled to do so by the whole body. This means nothing less than that he will be forced to be free; for this is the condition which, by giving each citizen to his country, secures him against all personal dependence. In this lies the key to the working of the political machine; this alone legitimizes civil undertakings, which, without it, would be absurd, tyrannical and liable to the most frightful abuses.

(Jean-Jacques Rousseau, op. cit., Bk 1, ch. 7, pp. 14-15.)

73d JEAN-JACQUES ROUSSEAU: FREEDOM AND THE GENERAL WILL

If then there are opponents when the social compact is made, their opposition does not invalidate the contract, but merely prevents them from being included in it. They are foreigners among citizens. When the State is instituted, residence constitutes consent; to dwell within its territory is to submit to the Sovereign.

Apart from this primitive contract, the vote of the majority always binds all the rest. This follows from the contract itself. But it is asked how a man can be both free and forced to conform to wills that are not his own. How are the opponents at once free and subject to laws they have not agreed to?

I retort that the question is wrongly put. The citizen gives his consent to all the laws, including those which are passed in spite of his opposition, and even those which punish him when he dares to break any of them. The constant will of all the members of the State is the general will; by virtue of it they are citizens and free. When in the popular assembly a law is proposed what the people is asked is not exactly whether it approves or rejects the proposal, but whether it is in conformity with the general will, which is their will. Each man, in giving his vote, states his opinion on that point; and the general will is found by counting votes. When therefore the opinion that is contrary to my own prevails, this proves neither more nor less than that I was mistaken, and that what I thought to be the general will was not so. If my particular opinion had carried the day I should have achieved the opposite of what was my will; and it is in that case that I should not have been free.

(Jean-Jacques Rousseau, op. cit., Bk 4, ch. 2, p. 88.)

73e JEAN-JACQUES ROUSSEAU: CHARACTERISTICS OF THE GENERAL WILL

The first and most important deduction from the principles we have so far laid down is that the general will alone can direct the State according to the object for which it was instituted, i.e. the common good: for if the clashing of particular interests made the establishment of societies necessary, the agreement of these very interests made it possible. The common element in these different interests is what forms the social tie; and, were there no point of agreement between them all, no society could exist. It is solely on the basis of this common interest that every society should be governed.

I hold then that Sovereignty, being nothing less than the exercise of the general will, can never be alienated, and that the Sovereign, who is no less than a collective being, cannot be represented except by himself: the power indeed may be transmitted, but not the will.

In reality, if it is not impossible for a particular will to agree on some point with the general will, it is at least impossible for the agreement to be lasting and constant; for the particular will tends, by its very nature, to partiality, while the general will tends to equality. . . .

Sovereignty, for the same reason as makes it inalienable, is indivisible; for will either is, or is not, general; it is the will either of the body of the people, or only of a part of it. In the first case, the will, when declared, is an act of Sovereignty and constitutes law: in the second, it is merely a particular will, or act of magistracy—at the most a decree. . . .

It follows from what has gone before that the general will is always right and tends to the public advantage; but it does not follow that the deliberations of the people are always equally correct. Our will is always for our own good, but we do not always see what that is; the people is never corrupted, but it is often deceived, and on such occasions only does it seem to will what is bad.

There is often a great deal of difference between the will of all and the general will; the latter considers only the common interest, while the former takes private interest into account, and is no more than a sum of particular wills: but take away from these same wills the pluses and minuses that cancel one another, and the general will remains as the sum of the differences.

If, when the people, being furnished with adequate information, held its deliberations, the citizens had no communication one with another, the grand total of the small differences would always give the general will, and the decision would always be good. But when factions arise, and partial associations are formed at the expense of the great association, the will of each of these associations becomes general in relation to its members, while it remains particular in relation to the State: it may then be said that there are no longer as many votes as there are men, but only as many as there are associations. The differences become less numerous and give a less general result. Lastly, when one of these associations is so great as to prevail over all the rest, the result is no longer a sum of small differences, but a single difference; in this case there is no longer a general will, and the opinion which prevails is purely particular.

(Jean-Jacques Rousseau, op. cit., Bk 2, chs 1-3, pp. 20-3.)

73f JEAN-JACQUES ROUSSEAU: ESTABLISHMENT OF THE EXECUTIVE

The legislative power once well established, the next thing is to establish similarly the executive power; for this latter, which operates only by particular acts, not being of the essence of the former, is naturally separate from it. Were it possible for the Sovereign, as such, to possess the executive power, right and fact would be so confounded that no one could tell what was law and what was not; and the body politic, thus disfigured, would soon fall a prey to the violence it was instituted to prevent.

As the citizens, by the social contract, are all equal, all can prescribe what all should do, but no one has a right to demand that another shall do what he does not do himself. It is strictly this right, which is indispensable for giving the body politic life and movement, that the Sovereign, in instituting the government, confers upon the prince.

It has been held that this act of establishment was a contract between the people and the rulers it sets over itself—a contract in which conditions were laid down between the two parties binding the one to command and the other to obey. It will be admitted, I am sure, that this is an odd kind of contract to enter into. But let us see if this view can be upheld.

First, the supreme authority can no more be modified than it can be alienated; to limit it is to destroy it. It is absurd and contradictory for the Sovereign to set a superior over itself; to bind itself to obey a master would be to return to absolute liberty.

Moreover, it is clear that this contract between the people and such and such persons would be a particular act; and from this it follows that it can be neither a law nor an act of Sovereignty, and that consequently it would be illegitimate. . . .

There is only one contract in the State, and that is the act of association, which in itself excludes the existence of a second. It is impossible to conceive of any public contract that would not be a violation of the first.

(Jean-Jacques Rousseau, op. cit., Bk 3, ch. 16, pp. 80-1.)

73g JEAN-JACQUES ROUSSEAU: THE LEGISLATOR

In order to discover the rules of society best suited to nations, a superior intelligence beholding all the passions of men without experiencing any of them would be needed. This intelligence would have to be wholly unrelated to our nature, while knowing it through and through; its happiness would have to be independent of us, and yet ready to occupy itself with ours; and lastly, it would have, in the march of time, to look forward to a distant glory, and, working in one century, to be able to enjoy in the next. It would take gods to give men laws. . . .

The legislator occupies in every respect an extraordinary position in the State. If he should do so by reason of his genius, he does so no less by reason of his office, which is neither magistracy, nor Sovereignty. This office, which sets up the Republic, nowhere enters into its constitution; it is an individual and superior function, which has nothing in common with human empire; for if he who holds cdmmand over men ought not to have command over the laws, he who has command over the laws ought not any more to have it over men; or else his laws would be the ministers of his passions and would often merely serve to perpetuate his injustices: his private aims would inevitably mar the sanctity of his work. . . .

He, therefore, who draws up the laws has, or should have, no right of legislation, and the people cannot, even if it wishes, deprive itself of this incommunicable right, because according to the fundamental compact, only the general will can bind the individuals, and there can be no assurance that a particular will is in conformity with the general will, until it has been put to the free vote of the people.

(Jean-Jacques Rousseau, op. cit., Bk 2, ch. 7, pp. 32-3.)

73h   JEAN-JACQUES ROUSSEAU: CIVIL RELIGION

There is therefore a purely civil profession of faith of which the Sovereign should fix the articles, not exactly as religious dogmas, but as social sentiments without which a man cannot be a good citizen or a faithful subject. While it can compel no one to believe them, it can banish from the State whoever does not believe them—it can banish him, not for impiety, but as an anti-social being, incapable of truly loving the laws and justice, and of sacrificing, at need, his life to his duty. If any one, after publicly recognizing these dogmas, behaves as if he does not believe them, let him be punished by death: he has committed the worst of all crimes, that of lying before the law.

The dogmas of civil religion ought to be few, simple, and exactly worded, without explanation or commentary. The existence of a mighty, intelligent, and beneficent Divinity, possessed of foresight and providence, the life to come, the happiness of the just, the punishment of the wicked, the sanctity of the social contract and the laws: these are its positive dogmas. Its negative dogmas I confine to one, intolerance, which is a part of the cults we have rejected.

Those who distinguish civil from theological intolerance are, to my mind, mistaken. The two forms are inseparable. It is impossible to live at peace with those we regard as damned; to love them would be to hate God who punishes them: we positively must either reclaim or torment them. Wherever theological intolerance is admitted, it must inevitably have some civil effect; and as soon as it has such an effect the Sovereign is no longer Sovereign even in the temporal sphere: thenceforth priests are the real masters, and kings only their ministers.

(Jean-Jacques Rousseau, op. cit., Bk 4, ch. 8, pp. 114-15.)

74 DECLARATION OF THE RIGHTS OF MAN AND OF CITIZENS: BY THE NATIONAL ASSEMBLY OF FRANCE

The representatives of the people of France, formed into a National Assembly, considering that ignorance, neglect, or contempt of human rights, are the sole causes of public misfortunes and corruptions of Government, have resolved to set forth in a solemn declaration, these natural, imprescriptible, and inalienable rights; that this declaration being constantly present to the minds of the members of the body social, they may be ever kept attentive to their rights and their duties; that the acts of the legislative and executive powers of Government, being capable of being every moment compared with the end of political institutions, may be more respected; and also, that the future claims of the citizens, being directed by simple and incontestable principles, may always tend to the maintenance of the Constitution, and the general happiness.

For these reasons the National Assembly doth recognise and declare, in the presence of the Supreme Being, and with the hope of his blessing and favour, the following *sacred* rights of men and of citizens:

I. Men are born, and always continue, free and equal in respect of their rights. Civil distinctions, therefore, can be founded only on public utility.

II. The end of all political associations is the preservation of the natural and imprescriptible rights of man; and these rights are Liberty, Property, Security, and Resistance of Oppression.

III. The Nation is essentially the source of all sovereignty; nor can any individual, or any body of men, be entitled to any authority which is not expressly derived from it.

IV. Political Liberty consists in the power of doing whatever does not injure another. The exercise of the natural rights of every man, has no other limits than those which are necessary to secure to every *other* man the free exercise of the same rights; and these limits are determinable only by the law.

V. The law ought to prohibit only actions hurtful to society. What is not prohibited by the law should not be hindered; nor should any one be compelled to that which the law does not require.

VI. The law is an expression of the will of the community. All citizens have a right to concur, either personally, or by their representatives, in its formation. It should be the same to all, whether it protects or punishes; and all being equal in its sight, are equally eligible to all honours, places, and employments, according to their different abilities, without any other distinction than that created by their virtues and talents.

VII. No man should be accused, arrested, or held in confinement, except in cases determined by the law, and according to the forms which it has prescribed. . . .

VIII. The law ought to impose no other penalties but such as are absolutely and evidently necessary; and no one ought to be punished, but in virtue of a law promulgated before the offence, and legally applied.

IX. Every man being presumed innocent till he has been convicted, whenever his detention becomes indispensable, all rigour to him, more than is necessary to secure his person, ought to be provided against by the law.

X. No man ought to be molested on account of his opinions, not even on account of his *religious* opinions, provided his avowal of them does not disturb the public order established by the law.

XI. The unrestrained communication of . . . opinions being one of the most precious rights of man, every citizen may speak, write, and publish, freely, provided he is reponsible for the abuse of this liberty, in cases determined by the law.

XII. A public force being necessary to give security to the rights of men and of citizens, that force is instituted for the benefit of the community and not for the particular benefit of the persons to whom it is intrusted.

XIII. A common contribution being necessary for the support of the public force, and for defraying the other expenses of government, it ought to be divided equally among the members of the community, according to their abilities.

XIV. Every citizen has a right, either by himself or his representative, to a free voice in determining the necessity of public contributions, the appropriation of them, and their amount, mode of assessment, and duration.

XV. Every community has a right to demand of all its agents an account of their conduct.

XVI. Every community in which a separation of powers and a security of rights is not provided for, wants a constitution.

XVII. The right to property being inviolable and sacred, no one ought to be deprived of it, except in cases of evident public necessity, legally ascertained, and on condition of a previous just indemnity.

(Thomas Paine, *The Rights of Man,* pp. 94-7, Everyman Library Edition, Dent, London and E. P. Dutton, New York, 1915.)

75 THE AMERICAN DECLARATION OF INDEPENDENCE

When in the Course of human events, it becomes necessary for one people to dissolve the political bands which have connected them with another, and to assume among the Powers of the earth, the separate and equal station to which the Laws of Nature and of Nature's God entitle them, a decent respect to the opinions of mankind requires that they should declare the causes which impel them to the separation.

We hold these truths to be self-evident, that all men are created equal, that they are endowed by their Creator with certain unalienable Rights, that among these are Life, Liberty and the pursuit of Happiness. That to secure these rights, Governments are instituted among Men, deriving their just powers from the consent of the governed, That whenever any Form of Government becomes destructive of these ends, it is the Right of the People to alter or to abolish it, and to institute new Government, laying its foundation on such principles and organizing its powers in such form, as to them shall seem most likely to effect their Safety and Happiness. Prudence, indeed, will dictate that Governments long established should not be changed for light and transient causes; and accordingly all experience hath shown, that mankind are more disposed to suffer, while evils are sufferable, than to right themselves by abolishing the forms to which they are accustomed. But when a long train of abuses and usurpations, pursuing invariably the same Object evinces a design to reduce them under absolute Despotism, it is their right, it is their duty, to throw off such Government, and to provide new Guards for their future security.—Such has been the patient sufferance of these Colonies; and such is now the necessity which constrains them to alter their former Systems of Government. The history of the present King of Great Britain is a history of repeated injuries and usurpations, all having in direct object the establishment of an absolute Tyranny over these States. . . .

We, therefore, the Representatives of the united States of America, in General Congress, Assembled, appealing to the Supreme Judge of the world for the rectitude of our intentions, do, in the Name, and by authority of the good People of these Colonies, solemnly publish and declare, That these United Colonies are, and of Right ought to be Free and Independent States; that they are Absolved from all Allegiance to the British Crown, and that all political connection between them and the State of Great Britian, is and ought to be totally dissolved; and that as Free and Independent States, they have full power to levy War, conclude Peace, contract Alliances, establish Commerce, and to do all other Acts and Things which Independent States may of right do. And for the support of this Declaration, with a firm reliance on the Protection of Divine Providence, we mutually pledge to each other our lives, our Fortunes and our sacred Honor.

76a EDMUND BURKE: TRADITION AND THE BRITISH CONSTITUTION

You will observe, that from Magna Charta to the Declaration of Right, it has been the uniform policy of our constitution, to claim and assert our liberties, as an *entailed inheritance* derived to us from our forefathers, and to be transmitted to our posterity; as an estate specially belonging to the people of this kingdom, without any reference whatever to any other more general or prior right. By this means our constitution preserves an unity in so great a diversity of its parts. We have an inheritable crown; an inheritable peerage; and an house of commons and a people inheriting privileges, franchises, and liberties, from a long line of ancestors.

This policy appears to me to be the result of profound reflection; or rather the happy effect of following nature, which is wisdom without reflection, and above it. A spirit of innovation is generally the result of a selfish temper and confined views. People will not look forward to posterity, who never look backward to their ancestors. Besides, the people of England well know, that the idea of inheritance furnishes a sure principle of conservation, and a sure principle of transmission; without at all excluding a principle of improvement. It leaves acquisition free; but it secures what it acquires. Whatever advantages are obtained by a state proceeding on these maxims, are locked fast as in a sort of family settlement; grasped as in a kind of mortmain forever. By a constitutional policy, working after the pattern of nature, we receive, we hold, we transmit, our government and our privileges, in the same manner in which we enjoy and transmit our property and our lives. The institutions of policy, the goods of fortune, the gifts of Providence, are handed down, to us and from us, in the same course and order. Our political system is placed in a just correspondence and symmetry with the order of the world, and with the mode of existence decreed to a permanent body composed of transitory parts; wherein, by the disposition of a stupendous wisdom, moulding together the great mysterious incorporation of the human race, the whole, at one time, is never old, or middle-aged, or young, but in a condition of unchangeable constancy, moves on through the various tenour of perpetual decay, fall, renovation, and progression. Thus, by preserving the method of nature in the conduct of the state, in what we improve we are never wholly new; in what we retain we are never wholly obsolete. By adhering in this manner and on those principles to our forefathers, we are guided not by the superstition of antiquarians, but by the spirit of philosophic analogy. In this choice of inheritance we have given to our frame of polity the image of a relation in blood; binding up the constitution of our country with our dearest domestic ties; adopting our fundamental laws into the bosom of our family affections; keeping inseparable, and cherishing with the warmth of all their combined and mutually reflected charities, our state, our hearths, our sepulchres, and our altars.

(Edmund Burke, *Reflections on the Revolution in France,* pp. 35-7, Oxford University Press, 1907.)

76b EDMUND BURKE: THE RIGHTS OF MAN

Government is not made in virtue of natural rights, which may and do exist in total independence of it; and exist in much greater clearness, and in a much greater degree of abstract perfection: but their abstract perfection is their practical defeat. By having a right to every thing, they want every thing. Government is a contrivance of human wisdom to provide for human *wants.* Men have a right that these wants should be provided for by this wisdom. Among these wants is to be reckoned the want, out of civil society, of a sufficient restraint upon their passions. Society requires not only that the passions of individuals should be subjected, but that even in the mass and body as well as in the individuals, the inclinations of men should frequently be thwarted, their will controlled, and their passions brought into subjection. This can only be done *by a power out of themselves;* and not, in the exercise of its function, subject to that will and to those passions which it is its office to bridle and subdue. In this sense the restraints on men, as well as their liberties, are to be reckoned among their rights. But as the liberties and the restrictions vary with times and circumstances, and admit of infinite modifications, they cannot be settled upon any abstract rule; and nothing is so foolish as to discuss them upon that principle. . . .

The pretended rights of these theorists are all extremes; and in proportion as they are metaphysically true, they are morally and politically false. The rights of men are in a sort of *middle,* incapable of definition, but not impossible to be discerned. The rights of men in governments are their advantages; and these are often in balances between differences of good and evil, and sometimes, between evil and evil. Political reason is a computing principle; adding, subtracting, multiplying, and dividing, morally and not metaphysically or mathematically, true moral denominations. . . .

(Edmund Burke, op. cit., pp. 65, 67-8.)

CHAPTER 20

The Development of English Liberalism

Modern liberalism has several roots in political theory. The notion that the powers of government should be restricted to what is for the common good may be traced back to Thomas Aquinas. John Locke was responsible for the clear enunciation of the principles of popular sovereignty and consent to government, although earlier expressions of the same principles can be found in Marsilius of Padua. Lockean ideas of natural rights are enshrined in the constitutions of the United States and of France, and are still appealed to, albeit vaguely, by citizens of Great Britian. The collectivist strain in modern liberalism has its source in Rousseau and Idealist philosophers such as Hegel and T. H. Green. However, throughout most of the nineteenth century, the prevailing liberal philosophy was that based upon the ethical theory of 'utilitarianism'.

The doctrine of 'utilitarianism' was yet another reaction against the abstract concepts of eighteenth-century rationalism. In place of the absolute standards of good and evil which were rooted in the concept of natural law, the utilitarians substituted a relative ethical standard rooted in utility—the satisfaction of the individual. The guiding principle for legislation ought therefore to be the maximizing of such satisfactions: the 'Greatest happiness of the greatest number'. It followed, likewise, that the obligation of the citizen to the government stemmed entirely from expediency and had nothing to do with contract. Similarly the concept of absolute natural rights had to be abandoned since it was inconsistent with utilitarian relativity.

David Hume (1711-1776)
Hume, the Scottish Tory, was the founder of utilitarian ethics, although, of course, the doctrine that each man is impelled by considerations of self-interest had been held by Hobbes and Locke among many others. In his *Treatise of Human Nature* (1739-40), Hume, the empiricist, cannot accept any rational determination of morality; good and evil are judged in terms of sensations of pleasure and pain (Ex. 77a). Hobbes, the 'egoistic hedonist' had argued that men will only

approve actions which benefit themselves and that so-called altruistic actions are fundamentally disguised egoistic actions. Hume, on the other hand, considered that men will follow pleasure or the means to pleasure even when this involves a benevolent act towards others rather than to themselves, although selfishness is normally the stronger emotion.

In his essay *Of the Original Contract* (1748), Hume succinctly demolishes the popular theory that states always originated in a social contract. In some particular cases this may have been an approximation of the truth, but the contractual theory of consent implies a wisdom and a concern for justice that cannot be attained by men. In fact all the evidence points to force or political guile rather than consent as the basis of government and the state (Ex. 77b).

As consent does not make for legitimacy in government, Hume is led to the conclusion that the obligation of the citizen to the state rests upon utility. Regardless of the origin of political rule, men soon get used to it and appreciate the advantages which it brings—particularly the maintenance of justice, equated by Hume with respect for private property. In reply to Locke's statement in the *Second Treatise* that each man gives a tacit consent to authority by choosing to remain within a country and accept its laws, Hume realistically points out that for most men in practice such a choice does not exist.

Jeremy Bentham (1748-1832)

Bentham was the most influential of the English utilitarians and the man who did most to develop and popularize the legal, moral and political tenets of utilitarian philosophy. The intellectual influences on his thought included Helvetius, the utilitarian philosopher of the French enlightenment, and David Hume, whose demolition of the 'chimeras' of rationalist political philosophy, made a deep impression upon his mind.

Like Hume, Bentham considered that political obligation is based not upon contract but upon utility. In his *Fragment on Government* (1776) he writes: 'they (the subjects) should obey so long as the probable mischiefs of obedience are less than the probable mischiefs of resistance . . . taking the whole body together, it is their duty to obey, just as long as it is their interest and no longer.'

Bentham's most important book was the *Principles of Morals and Legislation* published in 1789. Right at the outset he gives a plain statement of the principle of utility (Ex. 78a). The sensations of pain and pleasure govern everything that we do and give us our standard of right and wrong. This is closely akin to the psychology of Hobbes. Bentham seems to be elevating to the status of a binding moral law a natural propensity of each man. As pain and pleasure are individual sensations, Bentham's moral theory would appear to be drawn inevitably towards a subjectivist evaluation of good and evil.

However, if the standard of utility was to be the basis of legislation (and it was Bentham's practical purpose to demonstrate that it could be) and legislators were to act according to the principle of 'the greatest happiness of the greatest number', then it would be necessary to measure objectively the total sum of happiness and unhappiness involved in a legislative enactment. True to his aspiration to be the 'Newton of the Moral Sciences' and convinced, like Helvetius, that moral principles were akin to principles of geometry, Bentham considered that such a measurement was possible and produced his so-called 'felicific calculus'. By this means pleasures and pains may be broken down into measurable dimensions, although it should be stressed that Bentham was not concerned with measurement of the *quality* of pains and pleasures. There could be no differentiation between the pleasure received by an individual from pursuing an intellectually undemanding occupation and the same number of units of pleasure received by another individual engaged in a higher intellectual activity. Furthermore, each person is to count as an equal unit in assessing the greatest happiness. The likes and dislikes of dukes and dustmen are to be on the same level (Ex. 78b).

Bentham's attitude to government was consistent with his moral theory. The government should act to secure the greatest happiness of the greatest number but the problem was how to secure this since members of the government are naturally primarily concerned with their own happiness. Bentham's conclusion was that only under a system of self-government will the interest of government and governed coincide, but as this is impossible in practice, the best solution is to have a fully representative body. Accordingly he advocated universal manhood suffrage (for the literate); annual parliaments, in order to ensure that the representative should keep in close accord with the wishes of his constituents; and voting by secret ballot.

John Stuart Mill (1806-1873)

James Mill, the father of John Stuart, was a contemporary and friend of Bentham and although a convinced philosophic radical (as the utilitarians were now called) contributed little that was new to the Benthamite doctrine. His son, however, was not only the ablest of the nineteenth-century utilitarians but also the most original, modifying the doctrine until it was hardly recognizable.

Although Mill always claimed to be following the philosophical tradition of his father and Bentham, and indeed retained the basic pleasure-pain principle, he was led by his temperamental opposition to the aridity of Benthamism to abandon one detail after another. In his essay *Utilitarianism* (1861), one of the three essays mainly responsible for his reputation as a political philosopher, Mill makes the startling assertion that the quality of pleasures may be differentiated (Ex. 79a). It was essential to the Benthamite position that ethical judgements between the qualities of pleasures and pains could not and should not be made. Scientific legislation had to confine itself to the measurable quantitative facts. Mill's statement therefore tended to destroy the foundations of the 'objective' felicific calculus.

In several other parts of this essay Mill differs substantially from his mentors and in some passages seems to draw nearer to Hume than to Bentham. For example, in discussing moral obligation Mill, like Hume, argues that men possess a natural sentiment of sympathy and love for their fellows. It is this social instinct rather than the external imperatives to action which mainly impels men towards morality.

Liberty

Mill's essay *On Liberty* (1859) is his best known and most characteristic work. Its object is to demonstrate the dangers to individual liberty which democracy brings. Bentham and James Mill had seen in democratic government the solution to the problem of how to ensure that government acted for the good of the whole of society. Mill, while accepting the inevitability of democracy, was also uneasily aware of the fact that democratic rule was synonymous with majority rule, and that majorities may oppress minorities. John Locke had envisaged such a danger and had countered it by his theory of inalienable rights. For the utilitarians, however, such a theory was unacceptable; in Bentham's phrase it was 'nonsense upon stilts'. Mill had therefore to base his theory of individual freedom upon utility alone.

The 'simple principle' which Mill wishes to assert in the essay is that the only rightful deprivation of a person's freedom of action stems from a desire to prevent harm to others (Ex. 79b). When an individual's action concerns only himself then society has no grounds for interfering with him. It might be objected that in most modern societies very little that a person does falls into this category of 'self-regarding' actions, but it is in different directions that Mill qualifies his extremely individualist proposition. Liberty is to apply only to the mature and not to children, persons requiring care, or backward races. Moreover, even in mature societies individuals may be compelled to act for the public welfare when their inaction might cause evil to others.

There are, however, certain liberties which by their very nature must be regarded as absolute and whose presence in a society indicate that society to be a liberal one. They are the 'absolute freedom of opinion and sentiment on all subjects', including freedom to publish opinions; liberty to follow the kind of life we choose, provided we do not harm others in so doing; and finally the freedom to combine with others for a harmless purpose. Mill examines the first of these in the second chapter of the essay and gives a number of reasons why society should not have the right to suppress individual expressions of opinion, however unorthodox (Ex. 79c). If there is one premise that epitomizes liberal democracy and opposes it to that variant of democracy which is indebted to the political theory of Rousseau, it is that there can be no guarantee of infallibility. No government, no community necessarily possesses the whole truth, the right solution to political problems. It must therefore follow that any attempt to suppress unorthodox opinions is unjustified except, perhaps, in terms of a Hobbesian expediency.

In dealing with other liberties, Mill adopts a less individualistic approach. He accepts that a number of activities such as drunkenness and gambling might be anti-social and therefore require control by the state. Similarly the freedom of parents to bring up their children as they wish is to be curtailed by the state provision of compulsory education. Throughout his political writings Mill maintained the qualification that government must always be subject to the principle of utility, yet more and more he found himself in the camp of the radical reformers and even, eventually, admitted a sympathy with socialism (of the utopian rather than the Marxist variety).

T. H. Green and the New Liberalism

John Stuart Mill was the first important liberal philosopher to move away from the earlier utilitarian principle of *laissez-faire*. The trend was reinforced by the Oxford idealist philosopher, T. H. Green (1836-1882) and his followers, Hobhouse and Bosanquet. Green's importance in the history of liberalism is difficult to over estimate. It is at least arguable that he has the greatest single claim to be regarded as the architect of the modern welfare state.

The main stream of liberal ideology up to the second half of the nineteenth century can be traced back through the individualist tradition to Locke and his predecessors. The 'new liberalism' of the second half of the century was heir to a very different intellectual tradition: that of idealist collectivism, originating with Plato and manifested in its modern form by Rousseau and Hegel (see Chapter 21).

The contrast between the 'old' liberalism and the 'new' idealist revision can be best illustrated by Green's discussion of freedom. In the first chapter of his *Lectures on the Principles of Political Obligation* (published posthumously in 1882) Green introduces the notion of 'positive freedom' which he defines as: 'the state in which he shall have realized his ideal of himself, shall be at one with the law which he recognizes as that which he ought to obey, shall have become all that he has it in him to be, and so fulfil the law of his being or "live according to nature".' Clearly this bears a strong resemblance to the kind of freedom conceived of by Rousseau when the individual obeys his 'real will' (Ex. 80a).

The early liberals had argued that human welfare would be maximized when the individual was left alone to choose his course of action. Green, on the other hand, argued that for most people a free choice between alternative actions does not exist because of the economic, cultural and social constraints which bind them. The function of government therefore is to create conditions in which the individual may make a truly free choice, and to this end it follows that the government should provide free and compulsory education, healthy living and working conditions, and relief from the fear of poverty and unemployment.

Green was not, however, in favour of the all-embracing paternalistic state and disagreed with Hegel's sacrifice of the individual to the collective whole. Freedom is a quality of the individual to act morally and he may act morally only when he individually chooses to do so. The state cannot make men good; it can only provide the conditions in which men may make responsible moral decisions.

Green shows the influence of Hegel in his view that true morality is a consequence of historical development, the unfolding of human reason. As the human being is naturally a social and political animal, he can be moral and therefore can will moral decisions only as a member of the wider society. It is in this sense that Green approves of the Rousseauistic notion of the general will, and as the individual recognizes that his nature binds him to society it is his will rather than force which is the basis of the state (Ex. 80b).

Together with Mill, Green's restatement of liberal philosophy was responsible for directing liberalism away from the extreme individualism of *laissez-faire* towards the more humane principle of social welfare. The welfare state with its rejection of both individualist natural rights and totalitarian collectivism is as much the product of idealist liberalism as of Fabian socialism.

FURTHER READING

Texts
D. Hume: *Treatise of Human Nature*
    Of the Original Contract
J. Bentham: *A Fragment on Government*
    Principles of Morals and Legislation

J. S. Mill: *Utilitarianism*
  On Liberty
T. H. Green: *Lectures on the Principles of Political Obligation*
  (Longmans 1941)

Commentaries:
E. Barker: *Political Thought in England, 1848-1914* (Oxford University Press 1947)
C. Brinton: *English Political Thought in the Nineteenth Century* (Harper, N.Y., 1962)
M. Cowling: *Mill and Liberalism* (Cambridge University Press 1963)
W. L. Davidson: *Political Thought in England* (Oxford University Press 1915)
D. Lyons, *In the Interests of the Governed* (Clarendon Press, Oxford 1973)
J. Plamenatz: *The English Utilitarians* (Blackwell 1949)
A. Ryan, *J. S. Mill* (Routledge and Kegan Paul, London, 1974)

77a DAVID HUME: MORALITY DERIVED FROM PLEASURE AND PAIN

Thus the course of the argument leads us to conclude, that since vice and virtue are not discoverable merely by reason, or the comparison of ideas, it must be by means of some impression or sentiment they occasion, that we are able to mark the difference betwixt them. Our decisions concerning moral rectitude and depravity are evidently perceptions; and as all perceptions are either impressions or ideas, the exclusion of the one is a convincing argument for the other. Morality, therefore, is more properly felt than judg'd of; tho' this feeling or sentiment is commonly so soft and gentle, that we are apt to confound it with an idea, according to our common custom of taking all things for the same, which have any near resemblance to each other.

The next question is, Of what nature are these impressions, and after what manner do they operate upon us? Here we cannot remain long in suspense, but must pronounce the impression arising from virtue, to be agreeable, and that proceeding from vice to be uneasy. Every moment's experience must convince us of this. There is no spectacle so fair and beautiful as a noble and generous action; nor any which gives us more abhorrence than one that is cruel and treacherous. No enjoyment equals the satisfaction we receive from the company of those we love and esteem; as the greatest of all punishments is to be oblig'd to pass our lives with those we hate or contemn. A very play or romance may afford us instances of this pleasure, which virtue conveys to us; and pain, which arises from vice.

Now since the distinguishing impressions, by which moral good or evil is known, are nothing but *particular* pains or pleasures; it follows, that in all enquiries concerning these moral distinctions, it will be sufficient to shew the principles, which make us feel a satisfaction or uneasiness from the survey of any character, in order to satisfy us why the character is laudable or blameable. An action, or sentiment, or character is virtuous or vicious; why? because its view causes a pleasure or uneasiness of a particular kind. In giving a reason, therefore, for the pleasure or uneasiness, we sufficiently explain the vice or virtue. To have the sense of virtue is nothing but to *feel* a satisfaction of a particular kind from the contemplation of a character. The very *feeling* constitutes our praise or admiration. We go no farther; nor do we enquire into the cause of the satisfaction. We do not infer a character to be virtuous. The case is the same as in our judgments concerning all kinds of beauty, and tastes, and sensations. Our approbation is imply'd in the immediate pleasure they convey to us.

(David Hume, *Treatise of Human Nature*, Bk 3, sect. 2, in David Hume, *Theory of Politics*, ed. F. Watkins, pp. 522-3, Nelson, London 1951.)

77b DAVID HUME: THE FOUNDATION OF GOVERNMENT

My intention here is not to exclude the consent of the people from being one just foundation of government where it has place. It is surely the best and most sacred of any. I only pretend that it has very seldom had place in any degree, and never almost in its full extent. And that therefore some other foundation of government must also be admitted.

Were all men possessed of so inflexible a regard to justice that, of themselves, they would totally abstain from the properties of others, they had forever remained in a state of absolute liberty, without subjection to any magistrate or political society; but this is a state of perfection of which human nature is justly deemed incapable. Again, were all men possessed of so perfect an understanding as always to know their own interests, no form of government had ever been submitted to, but what was established on consent, and was fully canvassed by every member of the society; but this state of perfection is likewise much superior to human nature. Reason, history, and experience show us that all political societies have had an origin much less accurate and regular; and were one to choose a period of time when the people's consent was the least regarded in public transactions, it would be precisely on the establishment of a new government. In a settled constitution, their inclinations are often consulted; but during the fury of revolutions, conquests, and public convulsions, military force or political craft usually decides the controversy.

When a new government is established, by whatever means, the people are commonly dissatisfied with it, and pay obedience more from fear and necessity, than from any idea of allegiance or of moral obligation. The prince is watchful and jealous, and must carefully guard against every beginning or appearance of insurrection. Time, by degrees, removes all these difficulties, and accustoms the nation to regard as their lawful or native princes that family which, at first, they considered as usurpers or foreign conquerors. In order to found this opinion, they have no recourse to any notion of voluntary consent or promise, which, they know, never was in this case either expected or demanded. The original establishment was formed by violence, and submitted to from necessity. The subsequent administration is also supported by power, and acquiesced in by the people, not as a matter of choice, but of obligation. They imagine not that their consent gives their prince a title; but they willingly consent, because they think that, from long possession, he has acquired a title, independent of their choice or inclination.

Should it be said that by living under the dominion of a prince, which one might leave, every individual has given a *tacit* consent to his authority, and promised him obedience, it may be answered that such an implied consent can only have place where a man imagines that the matter depends on his choice. But where he thinks (as all mankind do who are born under established governments) that by his birth he owes allegiance to a certain prince or certain form of government, it would be absurd to infer a consent or choice which he expressly in this case, renounces and disclaims.

Can we seriously say that a poor peasant or artisan has a free choice to leave his country, when he knows no foreign language or manners, and lives from day to day, by the small wages which he acquires? We may as well assert that a man, by remaining in a vessel, freely consents to the dominion of the master, though he was carried on board while asleep, and must leap into the ocean, and perish, the moment he leaves her.

(David Hume, *Of the Original Contract,* op. cit., pp. 202-3.)

78a   JEREMY BENTHAM: THE PRINCIPLE OF UTILITY

1. Nature has placed mankind under the governance of two sovereign masters, *pain* and *pleasure*. It is for them alone to point out what we ought to do, as well as to determine what we shall do. On the one hand the standard of right and wrong, on the other the chain of causes and effects, are fastened to their throne. They govern us in all we do, in all we say, in all we think: every effort we can make to throw off our subjection, will serve but to demonstrate and confirm it. In words a man may pretend to abjure their empire: but in reality he will remain subject to it all the while. The *principle of utility* recognizes this subjection, and assumes it for the foundation of that system, the object of which is to rear the fabric of felicity by the hands of reason and of law. Systems which attempt to question it, deal in sounds instead of senses, in caprice instead of reason, in darkness instead of light.

But enough of metaphor and declamation: it is not by such means that moral science is to be improved.

2. The principle of utility is the foundation of the present work: it will be proper therefore at the outset to give an explicit and determinate account of what is meant by it. By the principle of utility is meant that principle which approves or disapproves of every action whatsoever, according to the tendency which it appears to have to augment or diminish the happiness of the party whose interest is in question: or, what is the same thing in other words, to promote or to oppose that happiness. I say of every action whatsoever; and there-

fore not only of every action of a private individual, but of every measure of government.

3. By utility is meant that property in any object, whereby it tends to produce benefit, advantage, pleasure, good, or happiness, (all this in the present case comes to the same thing) or (what comes again to the same thing) to prevent the happening of mischief, pain, evil, or unhappiness to the party whose interest is considered: if that party be the community in general, then the happiness of the community: if a particular individual, then the happiness of that individual.

4. The interest of the community is one of the most general expressions that can occur in the phraseology of morals: no wonder that the meaning of it is often lost. When it has a meaning, it is this. The community is a fictitious *body*, composed of the individual persons who are considered as constituting as it were its *members*. The interest of the community then is, what?—the sum of the interests of the several members who compose it.

5. It is in vain to talk of the interest of the community, without understanding what is the interest of the individual. A thing is said to promote the interest, or to be *for* the interest, of an individual, when it tends to add to the sum total of his pleasures: or, what comes to the same thing, to diminish the sum total of his pains.

6. An action then may be said to be conformable to the principle of utility, or, for shortness sake, to utility, (meaning with respect to the community at large) when the tendency it has to augment the happiness of the community is greater than any it has to diminish it.

7. A measure of government (which is but a particular kind of action, performed by a particular person or persons) may be said to be conformable to or dictated by the principle of utility, when in like manner the tendency which it has to augment the happiness of the community is greater than any which it has to diminish it.

8. When an action, or in particular a measure of government, is supposed by a man to be conformable to the principle of utility, it may be convenient, for the purposes of discourse, to imagine a kind of law or dictate, called a law or dictate of utility; and to speak of the action in question, as being conformable to such law or dictate.

9. A man may be said to be a partizan of the principle of utility, when the approbation or disapprobation he annexes to any action, or to any measure, is determined by and proportioned to the tendency which he conceives it to have to augment or to diminish the happiness of the community: or in other words, to its conformity or unconformity to the laws or dictates of utility.

10. Of an action that is conformable to the principle of utility one may always say either that it is one that ought to be done, or at least that it is not one that ought not to be done. One may say also, that it is right it should be done; at least that it is not wrong it should be done: that it is a *right* action; at least that it is not a wrong action. When thus interpreted, the words *ought*, and *right* and *wrong*, and others of that stamp, have a meaning: when otherwise, they have none.

(Jeremy Bentham, *Introduction to the Principles of Morals and Legislation*, ed. W. Harrison, ch. 1, pp. 125-7, Blackwell, Oxford 1948.)

78b   JEREMY BENTHAM: THE FELICIFIC CALCULUS

1. Pleasures then, and the avoidance of pains, are the *ends* which the legislator has in view: it behoves him therefore to understand their *value*. Pleasures and pains are the *instruments* he has to work with: it behoves him therefore to understand their force, which is again, in other words, their value.

2. To a person considered *by himself*, the value of a pleasure or pain considered *by itself*, will be greater or less, according to the four following circumstances:

   1. Its *intensity*.
   2. Its *duration*.
   3. Its *certainty* or *uncertainty*.
   4. Its *propinquity* or *remoteness*.

3. These are the circumstances which are to be considered in estimating a pleasure or a pain considered each of them by itself. But when the value of any pleasure or pain is considered for the purpose of estimating the tendency of any *act* by which it is produced, there are two other circumstances to be taken into account; these are,

   5. Its *fecundity*, or the chance it has of being followed by sensations of the *same* kind: that is, pleasures, if it be a pleasure: pains, it it be a pain.

   6. Its *purity*, or the chance it has of *not* being followed by sensations of the *opposite* kind: that is, pains, if it be a pleasure: pleasures, if it be a pain.

These two last, however, are in strictness scarcely to be deemed properties of the pleasure or the pain itself; they are not, therefore, in strictness to be taken into the account of the value of that pleasure or that pain. They are in strictness to be deemed properties only of the act, or other event, by which such pleasure or pain has been produced; and accordingly are only to be taken into the account of the tendency of such act or such event. . . .

   7. Its *extent*; that is, the number of persons to whom it *extends*; or (in other words) who are affected by it.

(Jeremy Bentham, op. cit., ch. 4, pp. 151-2.)

79a   JOHN STUART MILL: QUALITY OF PLEASURES

It is quite compatible with the principle of utility to recognise the fact, that some *kinds* of pleasure are more desirable and more valuable than others. It would be absurd that while, in estimating all other things, quality is considered as well as quantity, the estimation of pleasures should be supposed to depend on quantity alone.

If I am asked, what I mean by difference of quality in pleasures, or what makes one pleasure more valuable than another, merely as a pleasure, except its being greater in amount, there is but one possible answer. Of two pleasures, if there be one to which all or almost all who have experience of both give a decided preference, irrespective of any feeling of moral obligation to prefer it, that is the more desirable pleasure. If one of the two is, by those who are competently acquainted with both, placed so far above the other that they prefer it, even though knowing it to be attended with a greater amount of discontent, and would not resign it for any quantity of the other pleasure which their nature is capable of, we are justified in ascribing to the preferred enjoyment a superiority in quality, so far outweighing quantity as to render it, in comparison, of small account.

Now it is an unquestionable fact that those who are equally acquainted with, and equally capable of appreciating and enjoying, both, do give a most marked preference to the manner of existence which employs their higher faculties. Few human creatures would consent to be changed into any of the lower animals, for a promise of the fullest allowance of a beast's pleasures; no intelligent human being would consent to be a fool, no instructed person would be an ignoramus, no person of feeling and conscience would be selfish and base, even though they should be persuaded that the fool, the dunce, or the rascal is better satisfied with his lot than they are with theirs. . . .

It is better to be a human being dissatisfied than a pig satisfied; better to be Socrates dissatisfied than a fool satisfied. And if the fool, or the pig, are of a different opinion, it is because they only know their own side of the question. The other party to the comparison knows both sides.

(J. S. Mill, *Utilitarianism*, in J. S. Mill, *Utilitarianism, Liberty and Representative Government*, pp. 7-9, Everyman Library Edition, Dent, London and E. P. Dutton, New York 1910.)

79b JOHN STUART MILL: LIBERTY

The object of this Essay is to assert one very simple principle, as entitled to govern absolutely the dealings of society with the individual in the way of compulsion and control, whether the means used be physical force in the form of legal penalties, or the moral coercion of public opinion. That principle is, that the sole end for which mankind are warranted, individually or collectively, in interfering with the liberty of action of any of their number, is self-protection. That the only purpose for which power can be rightfully exercised over any member of a civilised community, against his will, is to prevent harm to others. His own good, either physical or moral, is not a sufficient warrant. He cannot rightfully be compelled to do or forbear because it will be better for him to do so, because it will make him happier, because, in the opinions of others, to do so would be wise, or even right. These are good reasons for remonstrating with him, or reasoning with him, or persuading him, or entreating him, but not for compelling him, or visiting him with any evil in case he do otherwise. To justify that, the conduct from which it is desired to deter him must be calculated to produce evil to some one else. The only part of the conduct of any one, for which he is amenable to society, is that which concerns others. In the part which merely concerns himself, his independence is, of right, absolute. Over himself, over his own body and mind, the individual is sovereign.

It is, perhaps, hardly necessary to say that this doctrine is meant to apply to human beings in the maturity of their faculties. We are not speaking of children, or of young persons below the age which the law may fix as that of manhood or womanhood. Those who are still in a state to require being taken care of by others, must be protected against their own actions as well as against external injury. For the same reason, we may leave out of consideration those backward states of society in which the race itself may be considered as in its nonage. The early difficulties in the way of spontaneous progress are so great, that there is seldom any choice of means for overcoming them; and a ruler full of the spirit of improvement is warranted in the use of any expedients that will attain an end, perhaps otherwise unattainable. Despotism is a legitimate mode of government in dealing with barbarians, provided the end be their improvement, and the means justified by actually effecting that end. Liberty, as a principle, has no application to any state of things anterior to the time when mankind have become capable of being improved by free and equal discussion. Until then, there is nothing for them but implicit obedience to an Akbar or a Charlemagne, if they are so fortunate as to find one. But as soon as mankind have attained the capacity of being guided to their own improvement by conviction or persuasion (a period long since reached in all nations with whom we need here concern ourselves), compulsion, either in the direct form or in that of pains and penalties for non-compliance, is no longer admissible as a means to their own good, and justifiable only for the security of others.

It is proper to state that I forego any advantage which could be derived to my argument from the idea of abstract right, as a thing independent of utility. I regard utility as the ultimate appeal on all ethical questions; but it must be utility in the largest sense, grounded on the permanent interests of a man as a progressive being. Those interests, I contend, authorise the subjection of individual spontaneity to external control, only in respect to those actions of each, which concern the interest of other people. If any one does an act hurtful to others, there is a *prima facie* case for punishing him, by law, or, where legal penalties are not safely applicable, by general disapprobation. There are also many positive acts for the benefit of others, which he may rightfully be compelled to perform; such as to give evidence in a court of justice; to bear his fair share in the common defence, or in any other joint work necessary to the interest of the society of which he enjoys the protection; and to perform certain acts of individual beneficence, such as saving a fellow-creature's life, or interposing to protect the defenceless against ill-usage, things which whenever it is obviously a man's duty to do, he may rightfully be made responsible to society for not doing. A person may cause evil to others not only by his actions but by his inaction, and in either case he is justly accountable to them for the injury. The latter case, it is true, requires a much more cautious exercise of compulsion than the former. To make any one answerable for doing evil to others is the rule; to make him answerable for not preventing evil is, comparatively speaking, the exception. Yet there are many cases clear enough and grave enough to justify that exception. In all things which regard the external relations of the individual, he is *de jure* amenable to those whose interests are concerned, and, if need be, to society as their protector. There are often good reasons for not holding him to the responsibility; but these reasons must arise from the special expediencies of the case: either because it is a kind of case in which he is on the whole likely to act better, when left to his own discretion, than when controlled in any way in which society have it in their power to control him; or because the attempt to exercise control would produce other evils, greater than those which it would prevent. When such reasons as these preclude the enforcement of responsibility, the conscience of the agent himself should step into the vacant judgment seat, and protect those interests of others which have no external protection; judging himself all the more rigidly, because the case does not admit of his being made accountable to the judgment of his fellow-creatures.

But there is a sphere of action in which society, as distinguished from the individual, has, if any, only an indirect interest; comprehending all that portion of a person's life and conduct which affects only himself, or if it also affects others, only with their free, voluntary, and undeceived consent and participation. When I say only himself, I mean directly, and in the first instance; for whatever affects himself, may affect others through himself; and the objection which may be grounded on this contingency, will receive consideration in the sequel. This, then, is the appropriate region of human liberty. It comprises, first, the inward domain of consciousness; demanding liberty of conscience in the most comprehensive sense; liberty of thought and feeling; absolute freedom of opinion and sentiment on all subjects, practical or speculative, scientific, moral, or theological. The liberty of expressing and publishing opinions may seem to fall under a different principle, since it belongs to that part of the conduct of an individual which concerns other people; but, being almost of as much importance as the liberty of thought itself, and resting in great part on the same reasons, is practically inseparable from it. Secondly, the principle requires liberty of tastes and pursuits; of framing the plan of our life to suit our own character; of doing as we like, subject to such consequences as may follow: without impediment from our fellow-creatures, so long as what we do does not harm them, even though they should think our conduct foolish, perverse, or wrong. Thirdly, from this liberty of each individual, follows the liberty, within the same limits, of combination among individuals; freedom to unite, for any purpose not involving harm to others: the persons combining being supposed to be of full age, and not forced or deceived.

No society in which these liberties are not, on the whole, respected, is free, whatever may be its form of government; and none is completely free in which they do not exist absolute and unqualified. The only freedom which deserves the name, is that of pursuing our own good in our own way, so long as we do not attempt to deprive others of theirs, or impede their efforts to obtain it. Each is the proper guardian of his own health, whether bodily, or mental and spiritual. Mankind are greater gainers by suffering each other to live as seems good to themselves, than by compelling each to live as seems good to the rest.

Though this doctrine is anything but new, and, to some persons, may have the air of a truism, there is no doctrine which stands more directly opposed to the general tendency of existing opinion and practice. Society has expended fully as much effort in the attempt (according to its lights) to compel people to conform to its notions of personal as of social excellence. The ancient commonwealths thought themselves entitled to practise, and the ancient philosophers countenanced, the regulation of every part of private conduct by public authority, on the ground that the State had a deep interest in the whole bodily and mental discipline of every one of its citizens; a mode of thinking which may have been admissible in small republics surrounded by powerful enemies, in constant peril of being subverted by foreign attack or internal commotion, and to which even a short interval of relaxed energy and self-command might so easily be fatal that they could not afford to wait for the salutary permanent effects of freedom. In the modern world, the greater size of political communities, and, above all, the separation between spiritual and temporal authority (which placed the direction of men's consciences in other hands than those which controlled their worldly affairs), prevented so great an interference by law in the details of private life; but the engines of moral repression have been wielded more strenuously against divergence from the reigning opinion in self-regarding, than even in social matters; religion, the most powerful of the elements which have entered into the formation of moral feeling, having almost always been governed either by the ambition of a hierarchy, seeking control over every department of human conduct, or by the spirit of Puritanism. And some of those modern reformers who have placed themselves in strongest opposition to the religions of the past, have been noway behind either churches or sects in their assertion of the right of spiritual domination: M. Comte, in particular, whose social system, as unfolded in his *Système de Politique Positive*, aims at establishing (though by moral more than by legal appliances) a despotism of society over the individual, surpassing anything contemplated in the political ideal of the most rigid disciplinarian among the ancient philosophers.

Apart from the peculiar tenets of individual thinkers, there is also in the world at large an increasing inclination to stretch unduly the powers of society over the individual, both by the force of opinion and even by that of legislation; and as the tendency of all the changes taking place in the world is to strengthen society, and diminish the power of the individual, this encroachment is not one of the evils which tend spontaneously to disappear, but, on the contrary, to grow more and more formidable. The disposition of mankind, whether as rulers or as fellow-citizens, to impose their own opinions and inclinations as a rule of conduct on others, is so energetically supported by some of the best and by some of the worst feelings incident to human nature, that it is hardly ever kept under restraint by anything but want of power; and as the power is not declining, but growing, unless a strong barrier of moral conviction can be raised against the mischief, we must expect, in the present circumstances of the world, to see it increase.

(J. S. Mill, *On Liberty*, op. cit., Introduction, pp. 72-7.)

79c JOHN STUART MILL: FREEDOM OF EXPRESSION

We have now recognised the necessity to the mental well-being of mankind (on which all their other well-being depends) of freedom of opinion, and freedom of the expression of opinion, on four distinct grounds; which we will now briefly recapitulate.

First, if any opinion is compelled to silence, that opinion may, for aught we can certainly know, be true. To deny this is to assume our own infallibility.

Secondly, though the silenced opinion be an error, it may, and very commonly does, contain a portion of truth; and since the general or prevailing opinion on any subject is rarely or never the whole truth, it is only by the collision of adverse opinions that the remainder of the truth has any chance of being supplied.

Thirdly, even if the received opinion be not only true, but the whole truth; unless it is suffered to be, and actually is, vigorously and earnestly contested, it will, by most of those who receive it, be held in the manner of a prejudice, with little comprehension or feeling of its rational grounds. And not only this, but, fourthly, the meaning of the doctrine itself will be in danger of being lost, or enfeebled, and deprived of its vital effect on the character and conduct: the dogma becoming a mere formal profession, inefficacious for good, but cumbering the ground, and preventing the growth of any real and heartfelt conviction, from reason or personal experience.

(J. S. Mill, *On Liberty*, op. cit., ch. 2, pp. 111-12.)

80a   THOMAS HILL GREEN: POSITIVE FREEDOM

1. Since in all willing a man is his own object, the will is always free. Or, more properly, a man in willing is necessarily free, since willing constitutes freedom, and 'free will' is the pleonasm 'free freedom'. But while it is important to insist upon this, it is also to be remembered that the nature of the freedom really differs—the freedom means quite different things—according to the nature of the object which the man makes his own, or with which he identifies himself. It is one thing when the object in which self-satisfaction is sought is such as to prevent that self-satisfaction being found, because interfering with the realisation of the seeker's possibilities or his progress towards perfection: it is another thing when it contributes to this end. In the former case the man is a free agent in the act, because through his identification of himself with a certain desired object—through his adoption of it as his good—he makes the motive which determines the act, and is accordingly conscious of himself as its author. But in another sense he is not free, because the objects to which his actions are directed are objects in which, according to the law of his being, satisfaction of himself is not to be found. His will to arrive at self-satisfaction not being adjusted to the law which determines where this self-satisfaction is to be found, he may be considered in the condition of a bondsman who is carrying out the will of another, not his own. From this bondage he emerges into real freedom, not by overcoming the law of his being, not by getting the better of its necessity,—every fancied effort to do so is but a new exhibition of its necessity,—but by making its fulfilment the object of his will; by seeking the satisfaction of himself in objects in which he believes it *should be* found, and seeking it in them *because* he believes it should be found in them. For the objects so sought, however various otherwise, have the common characteristic that, because they are sought in such a spirit, in them self-satisfaction is to be found; not the satisfaction of this or that desire, or of each particular desire,

but that satisfaction, otherwise called peace or blessedness, which consists in the whole man having found his object; which indeed we never experience in its fulness, which we only approach to fall away from it again, but of which we know enough to be sure that we only fail to attain it because we fail to seek it in the fulfilment of the law of our being, because we have not brought ourselves to 'gladly do and suffer what we must.' . . .

Hegel holds that freedom, as the condition in which the will is determined by an object adequate to itself, or by an object which itself as reason constitutes, is realised in the state. He thinks of the state in a way not familiar to Englishmen, a way not unlike that in which Greek philosophers thought of the πόλις, as a society governed by laws and institutions and established customs which secure the common good of the members of the society—enable them to make the best of themselves—and are recognised as doing so. Such a state is 'objective freedom'; freedom is realised in it because in it the reason, the self-determining principle operating in man as his will, has found a perfect expression for itself (as an artist may be considered to express himself in a perfect work of art); and the man who is determined by the objects which the well-ordered state presents to him is determined by that which is the perfect expression of his reason, and is thus free.

5. There is, no doubt, truth in this view. I have already tried to show how the self-distinguishing and self-seeking consciousness of man, acting in and upon those human wants and ties and affections which in their proper human character have as little reality apart from it as it apart from them, gives rise to a system of social relations, with laws, customs, and institutions corresponding; and how in this system the individual's consciousness of the absolutely desirable, of something that should be, of an ideal to be realised in his life, finds a content or object which has been constituted or brought into being by that consciousness itself as working through generations of men; how interests are thus supplied to the man of a more concrete kind than the interest in fulfilment of a universally binding law because universally binding, but which yet are the product of reason, and in satisfying which he is conscious of attaining a true good, a good contributory to the perfection of himself and his kind. There is thus something in all forms of society that tends to the freedom at least of some favoured individuals, because it tends to actualise in them the possibility of that determination by objects conceived as desirable in distinction from objects momentarily desired, which is determination by reason. To put it otherwise, the effect of his social relations on a man thus favoured is that, whereas in all willing the individual seeks to satisfy himself, this man seeks to satisfy himself, not as one who feels this or that desire, but as one who conceives, whose nature demands, a permanent good. So far as it is thus in respect of his rational nature that he makes himself an object to himself, his will is autonomous. . . .

6. On the other hand, it would seem that we cannot significantly speak of freedom except with reference to individual persons; that only in them can freedom be realised; that therefore the realisation of freedom in the state can only mean the attainment of freedom by individuals through influences which the state (in the wide sense spoken of) supplies,—'freedom' here, as before, meaning not the mere self-determination which renders us responsible, but

determination by reason, 'autonomy of the will'; and that under the best conditions of any society that has ever been such realisation of freedom is most imperfect. To an Athenian slave, who might be used to gratify a master's lust, it would have been a mockery to speak of the state as a realisation of freedom; and perhaps it would not be much less so to speak of it as such to an untaught and under-fed denizen of a London yard with gin-shops on the right hand and on the left. What Hegel says of the state in this respect seems as hard to square with facts as what St. Paul says of the Christian whom the manifestation of Christ has transferred from bondage into 'the glorious liberty of the sons of God.' In both cases the difference between the ideal and the actual seems to be ignored, and tendencies seem to be spoken of as if they were accomplished facts. It is noticeable that by uncritical readers of St. Paul the account of himself as under the law (in *Romans* vii.), with the 'law of sin in his members warring against the law of his reason,' is taken as applicable to the regenerate Christian, though evidently St. Paul meant it as a description of the state from which the Gospel, the 'manifestation of the Son of God in the likeness of sinful flesh,' set him free. They are driven to this interpretation because, though they can understand St. Paul's account of his deliverance as an account of a deliverance achieved for them but not in them, or as an assurance of what is to be, they cannot adjust it to the actual experience of the Christian life. In the same way Hegel's account of freedom as realised in the state does not seem to correspond to the facts of society as it is, or even as, under the unalterable conditions of human nature, it ever could be; though undoubtedly there is a work of moral liberation, which society, through its various agencies, is constantly carrying on for the individual.

(T. H. Green, *Lectures on the Principles of Political Obligation*, pp. 2, 3, 6-9, Longman, London 1941.)

80b THOMAS HILL GREEN: WILL IS THE BASIS OF THE STATE

114. To ask why I am to submit to the power of the state, is to ask why I am to allow my life to be regulated by that complex of institutions without which I literally should not have a life to call my own, nor should be able to ask for a justification of what I am called on to do. For that I may have a life which I can call my own, I must not only be conscious of myself and of ends which I present to myself as mine; I must be able to reckon on a certain freedom of action and acquisition for the attainment of those ends, and this can only be secured through common recognition of this freedom on the part of each other by members of a society, as being for a common good. Without this, the very consciousness of having ends of his own and a life which he can direct in a certain way, a life of which he can make something, would remain dormant in a man. . . .

116. The doctrine that the rights of government are founded on the consent of the governed is a confused way of stating the truth, that the institutions by which man is moralised, by which he comes to do what he sees that he must, as distinct from what he would like, express a conception of a common good;

that through them that conception takes form and reality; and that it is in turn through its presence in the individual that they have a constraining power over him, a power which is not that of mere fear, still less a physical compulsion, but which leads him to do what he is not inclined to because there is a law that he should.

Rousseau, it will be remembered, speaks of the 'social pact' not merely as the foundation of sovereignty or civil government, but as the foundation of morality. Through it man becomes a moral agent; for the slavery to appetite he substitutes the freedom of subjection to a self-imposed law. If he had seen at the same time that rights do not begin till duties begin, and that if there was no morality prior to the pact there could not be rights, he might have been saved from the error which the notion of there being natural rights introduces into his theory. But though he does not seem himself to have been aware of the full bearing of his own conception, the conception itself is essentially true. Setting aside the fictitious representation of an original covenant as having given birth to that common 'ego' or general will, without which no such covenant would have been possible, and of obligations arising out of it, as out of a bargain made between one man and another, it remains true that only through a recognition by certain men of a common interest, and through the expression of that recognition in certain regulations of their dealings with each other, could morality originate, or any meaning be gained for such terms as 'ought' and 'right' and their equivalents.

117. Morality, in the first instance, is the observance of such regulations, and though a higher morality, the morality of the character governed by 'disinterested motives,' i.e. by interest in some form of human perfection, comes to differentiate itself from this primitive morality consisting in the observance of rules established for a common good, yet this outward morality is the presupposition of the higher morality. Morality and political subjection thus have a common source, 'political subjection' being distinguished from that of a slave, as a subjection which secures rights to the subject. That common source is the rational recognition by certain human beings—it may be merely by children of the same parent—of a common well-being which is their well-being, and which they conceive as their well-being whether at any moment any one of them is inclined to it or no, and the embodiment of that recognition in rules by which the inclinations of the individuals are restrained, and a corresponding freedom of action for the attainment of well-being on the whole is secured.

(T. H. Green, op. cit., pp. 122-5.)

CHAPTER 21

Communism

Karl Marx, as everybody knows, was the founder of modern communism. But Marxism, in common with all modern collectivist political philosophies, owes a great deal to the German idealist philosopher G. W. F. Hegel (1770-1831); in particular to Hegel's theory of history and his so-called 'dialectic triad'.

Hegel can be grouped with Rousseau and Burke in that all three were opposed to the predominant rationalism of the eighteenth century, that is, to the view which can be traced as far back as Plato, that complete truth may be discovered by the process of unaided reason. Against this contemporary optimism, Hegel argued that rational truth cannot be understood by man until historical development has reached its fulfilment. The history of the world operates according to a pattern predetermined by God. The pattern, called by Hegel the 'Idea' (*Weltgeist*), is purposeful and rational in the truest sense, but cannot be fully understood until it has been completely realized. At any particular stage of historical development, concepts of religion, law, morality, etc., possess only a relative truth and reality. Absolute truth will be manifested in human institutions only when the final stage of historical evolution has been reached and man is able to comprehend the divine reality of the Idea.

The vehicle by which the Idea is carried forward is the state: the process by which history develops is the dialectic. The concept of the state as the divinely ordained institution to carry forward God's universal plan had important implications for the development of right-wing political ideas in the nineteenth and twentieth centuries, as we shall show in the next chapter. It was Hegel's dialectical theory that was to provide the basis of Marxist philosophy. The word 'dialectic' recalls the Platonic method of achieving knowledge through the interaction of ideas presented in discussion. In the Hegelian sense of the dialectic, the Idea is represented by a stage of civilization, the 'thesis', which, being an incomplete manifestation of human destiny, contains within itself the seeds of change. Forces are set in motion which stimulate the rise of a contradictory thesis, the 'antithesis'. These two opposing manifestations of the *Weltgeist* come into conflict from which a higher and more real 'synthesis' emerges, produced by a fusion of the more valid elements of the original 'thesis' and 'antithesis'.

Karl Marx (1818-1883) and Friedrich Engels (1820-1895)

The two founders of modern communism, Marx and Engels, must be treated together since it is almost impossible (and also rather pointless) to differentiate between their contributions to the theory of 'scientific socialism'. Marx was born into a bourgeois Jewish family at Trier in south-western Germany. In 1836 he began his studies at the University of Berlin where he came under the influence of Hegelian philosophy. On leaving university he became a journalist and began his career as a revolutionary, although at first he confined himself to attacking social conditions in Germany. In 1843, thinking it advisable to leave Germany, he went to Paris where he came into contact with revolutionary and utopian socialists of many different persuasions. Most importantly, it was in Paris at this period that he met Engels, who was to become his life-long partner and friend. Engels was the son of a German textile manufacturer and part-owner of a Manchester cotton mill—an unlikely background for a disciple of Karl Marx.

In 1845 Marx and Engels left Paris for Brussels, where they lived for the next three years. It was there that in 1848 they jointly wrote the *Communist Manifesto* as a statement of principles of the international Communist League. After his involvement in the revolutions of the same year in France and Germany, Marx was forced to go into exile and in 1849 took up residence in London. Here he remained for the rest of his life engaging in polemical writing, particularly on behalf of the International Working Men's Association, and composing his painstakingly researched indictment of the capitalist system, *Capital*. For much of this period he was financially supported by Engels who eventually settled an annuity on him enabling him and his family to live comfortably without paid employment.

The synthesis which we know as Marxism is made up of various important elements not only from politics and philosophy but also from the fields of economics and sociology. According to Lenin, Marxism 'is the legitimate successor to the best that man produced in the nineteenth century, as represented by German philosophy, English political economy, and French socialism.'

The Materialist Conception of History

The dialectic method of Hegel which we have glanced at above was retained by Marx as the core of his philosophy. Unlike the Hegelian idealist version, however, Marx interpreted the dialectic triad in a materialistic sense (Ex. 81a). In other words, the dialectical process which Hegel applied to the development of ideas, or rather the Idea, was applied by Marx to the development of the objective material world, and in particular to the development of economic and social forces. It should perhaps be stressed that Marx's materialism was quite unlike that of earlier materialist philosophers such as Hobbes, who had sought to demonstrate that the universe was a mere mechanical contrivance. Marx, on the contrary, had to show that development was not only possible but inevitable.

Marx considered that human society develops in a particular way not because men are influenced by theories about politics and religion, but because economic factors change in accordance with the laws of the dialectic. The basic principle which underlies man's relation to his fellows is the acquisition and exchange of the material necessities of life. This relationship, which alters in accordance with changes in the methods of production, is called by Marx the 'economic structure of society'. Its importance lies in the fact that upon it rests the 'legal and political superstructure' of society, that is, the systems of law, politics, religion, philosophy and art. In short, the whole intellectual apparatus of society is determined by the economic interrelationships of men (Ex. 81b).

In turn, these economic relationships reflect the ownership of the means of production and hence the economic class structure of society. That class which owns the productive forces is inevitably responsible for determining the ideological superstructure of society since economic power is the foundation of all other kinds of power. Marx distinguishes three broad historical epochs characterized by differences in the economic sub-structure: 'ancient', based upon the relationship of slave owners to slaves; 'feudal', characterized by the relationship of feudal lord to serf; 'bourgeois', resting upon the relation of capital owners (capitalists) to workers possessing nothing but their labour power (proletariat). In *The Poverty of Philosophy* Marx summarizes the principle that the class structure depends upon the methods of production as follows: 'The hand-mill gives you society with the feudal lord; the steam-mill society with the industrial capitalist.'

The Class Struggle

The opening words of the first section of the *Communist Manifesto* explain that history is a constant struggle between economic classes (Ex. 81c). As each class rises to predominance by its ownership of the means of production, contradictions and antagonisms develop which will eventually bring about a struggle for supremacy. For instance, under conditions of feudalism where the means of production, land, was entirely owned by the aristocratic ruling class, the emergent merchants and craftsmen were, in time, able to challenge the land-owners for predominance. In terms of the Hegelian dialectic triad: the thesis (aristocracy) was faced with its contradiction or antithesis (the rising middle class). From the struggle between the two (the 'negation of the negation') was derived the synthesis (capitalism), the bourgeois society in which all values are determined by the owners of capital.

Capitalism, like feudalism before it, contains the seeds of its own destruction. The bourgeoisie can only exist as a ruling power if there exists concurrently a proletariat. One is meaningless without the other. The proletarians, who possess little or no property other than their own labour power which they sell in order to live, are exploited by their bourgeois masters, who steal from them part of the fruits of their labour. This part, called by Marx 'surplus value', is the value produced by the labourer above what he is paid and which goes as profit to the capitalist.

Because he is cheated in this way, because his employment is insecure, being at the mercy of financial and economic crises, and because he is reduced to 'an appendage of the machine', the proletarian can have no common interest with the bourgeoisie. In fact his interest is so opposed to that of his employer that ultimately the proletarians will unite to overthrow the whole capitalist system. Violent revolution is almost inevitable; because no ruling class will voluntarily abandon its power, its power must be forcibly eliminated and its values forcibly destroyed.

The result of the proletarian revolution will be the establishment for a time of a 'dictatorship of the proletariat' in which the state apparatus will be used by the new proletarian ruling class to establish a new superstructure reflecting the interests of the majority rather than the bourgeois minority. As the bourgeois counter-revolutionary elements are purged away by the proletarian dictatorship, the state, which is the expression of class interests, becomes redundant since society is no longer divided into classes. In the words of Engels in *Anti-Duhring* the state 'withers away'. The final stage of social evolution is realized when a truly communist classless society replaces the oppressive state, although little information is given to us about this utopian society other than the statement that the principle will be, 'from each according to his ability, to each according to his needs.'

Vladimir Ilyich Lenin (1870-1924)

Lenin was the third great contributor to the communist philosophical synthesis. In Stalin's well known definition: 'Leninism is Marxism of the era of imperialism and the proletarian revolution.' In other words, Lenin applied the Marxist analysis to the contemporary world and, in particular, used the ideas of Marx and Engels to make practical points about revolutionary strategy. Of the voluminous works of Lenin, *The State and Revolution* is perhaps the best known and of greatest general interest and therefore will be taken as representative.

This book, written but unfinished just before the Russian revolution of October 1917, is very largely an exegesis of the teaching of Marx and Engels on the state and particularly of their references to the 'dictatorship of the proletariat' and the 'withering away' of the state. In his *Critique of the Gotha Programme* (1875), Marx had stated that after the proletarian revolution a period of transition would be inevitable before the realization of a truly communist society. Lenin points out that during the period of proletarian dictatorship the state as a coercive power will be maintained in order to suppress the oppressors (Ex.82). The state in any form is incompatible with democracy and freedom for every citizen. Under capitalism, democracy and freedom exist for a small minority only; most men are prevented by various means from participating in the democratic process. Under the dictatorship of the proletariat, democracy is made a possibility for the vast majority but for the capitalist exploiters there can be no democracy, no freedom.

Sooner or later the former exploiters will be crushed; when that happens the class society will have disappeared, for classes exist only as reflections of exploiters and exploited. As the classless society becomes more and more a reality so the state begins to 'wither away' since its function is no longer necessary. In a passage which recalls Plato's *Republic*, Lenin argues that the mass of the people will eventually obey voluntarily the fundamental rules of social life without the compulsion of the state apparatus, since anti-social behaviour is nearly always the result of economic exploitation. In cases of individual aberration, the people themselves will suppress such behaviour. Only at this final stage of social evolution when the state has disappeared is it possible to speak of true democracy and true freedom.

The Marxist-Leninist concept of freedom is fundamentally similar to that of Rousseau. In both, freedom is regarded as activity in accordance with one's real will; in neither is it concerned with guarantees of individual 'rights'. Such a conception of freedom is in the 'positive' anti-liberal tradition because it implies that the community knows infallibly what is right for itself as an organic whole.

FURTHER READING

Texts
Marx and Engels: *Selected Works* (Lawrence and Wishart 1968)
Marx and Engels: *Basic Writings on Politics and Philosophy*, ed. L. S.
    Fluer (Collins-Fontana 1969)
Lenin: *The State and Revolution*

Commentaries
H. B. Acton: *The Illusion of the Epoch* (Cohen and West 1955)
R. N. Berki, *Socialism* (Dent, London 1975)

R. S. Carew-Hunt: *The Theory and Practice of Communism* (Penguin 1963)

A. Gray: *The Socialist Tradition* (Longmans 1954)

J. Lewis: *The Marxism of Marx* (Lawrence and Wishart 1972)

J. Plamenatz: *German Marxism and Russian Communism* (Longmans 1954)

R. Plant, *Hegel* (Unwin University Books, Allen and Unwin, London 1973)

K. Popper: *The Open Society and its Enemies* vol. II (Routledge and Kegan Paul 1966)

81a KARL MARX: THE DIALECTIC METHOD

My dialectic method is not only different from the Hegelian, but is its direct opposite. To Hegel the life process of the human brain, i.e., the process of thinking, which, under the name of 'the Idea,' he even transforms into an independent subject, is the demiurgos of the real world, and the real world is only the external, phenomenal form of 'the Idea.' With me, on the contrary, the ideal is nothing else than the material world reflected by the human mind and translated into forms of thought. . . .

The mystification which dialectic suffers in Hegel's hands by no means prevents him from being the first to prescribe its general form of working in a comprehensive and conscious manner. With him it is standing on its head. It must be turned right side up again if you would discover the rational kernel within the mystical shell.

In its mystified form dialectic became the fashion in Germany because it seemed to transfigure and to glorify the existing state of things. In its rational form it is a scandal and abomination to bourgeoisdom and its doctrinaire professors because it includes in its comprehension and affirmative recognition of the existing state of things, at the same time also, the recognition of the negation of that state, of its inevitable breaking up; because it regards every historically developed social form as in fluid movement, and therefore takes into account its transient nature not less than its momentary existence; because it lets nothing impose upon it, and is in its essence critical and revolutionary.

(Karl Marx, *Capital*, Preface to second edition, 1873, in *Marx and Engels: Basic Writings on Politics and Philosophy*, ed. L. S. Feuer, pp. 186-7, Collins-Fontana, London 1969.)

81b KARL MARX: HISTORICAL MATERIALISM

In the social production of their life, men enter into definite relations that are indispensable and independent of their will, relations of production which correspond to a definite stage of development of their material productive forces. The sum total of these relations of production constitutes the economic structure of society, the real foundation, on which rises a legal and political superstructure and to which correspond definite forms of social consciousness. The mode of production of material life conditions the social, political and intellectual life process in general. It is not the consciousness of men that determines their being, but, on the contrary, their social being that determines their consciousness. At a certain stage of their development, the material productive forces of society come in conflict with the existing relations of production, or—what is but a legal expression for the same thing—with the property relations within which they have been at work hitherto. From forms of development of the productive forces these relations turn into their fetters. Then begins an epoch of social revolution. With the change of the economic foundation the entire immense superstructure is more or less rapidly transformed. In considering such transformations a distinction should always be made between the material transformation of the economic conditions of production, which can be determined with the precision of natural science, and the legal, political, religious, aesthetic or philosophic—in short, ideological forms in which men become conscious of this conflict and fight it out. Just as our opinion of an individual is not based on what he thinks of himself, so can we not judge of such a period of transformation by its own consciousness; on the contrary, this consciousness must be explained rather from the contradictions of material life, from the existing conflict between the social productive forces and the relations of production. No social order ever perishes before all the productive forces for which there is room in it have developed; and new, higher relations of production never appear before the material conditions of their existence have matured in the womb of the old society itself. Therefore mankind always sets itself only such tasks as it can solve; since, looking at the matter more closely, it will always be found that the task itself arises only when the material conditions for its solution already exist or are at least in the process of formation. In broad outlines Asiatic, ancient, feudal, and modern bourgeois modes of production can be designated as progressive epochs in the economic formation of society. The bourgeois relations of production are the last antagonistic form of the social process of production—antagonistic not in the sense of individual antagonism, but of one arising from the social conditions of life of the individuals; at the same time the productive forces developing in the womb of bourgeois society create the material conditions for the solution of that antagonism. This social formation brings, therefore, the prehistory of human society to a close.

(Karl Marx, *A Contribution to the Critique of Political Economy*, Preface, in *Marx and Engels: Selected Works*, pp. 181-2, Lawrence and Wishart, London 1968.)

81c KARL MARX AND FRIEDRICH ENGELS: THE CLASS STRUGGLE

The history of all hitherto existing society is the history of class struggles.

Freeman and slave, patrician and plebeian, lord and serf, guildmaster and journeyman, in a word, oppressor and oppressed, stood in constant opposition to one another, carried on an uninterrupted, now hidden, now open fight, a fight that each time ended, either in a revolutionary reconstitution of society at large, or in the common ruin of the contending classes.

In the earlier epochs of history, we find almost everywhere a complicated arrangement of society into various orders, a manifold gradation of social rank. In ancient Rome we have patricians, knights, plebeians, slaves; in the Middle Ages, feudal lords, vassals, guild-masters, journeymen, apprentices, serfs; in almost all of these classes, again, subordinate gradations.

The modern bourgeois society that has sprouted from the ruins of feudal society has not done away with class antagonisms. It has but established new classes, new conditions of oppression, new forms of struggle in place of the old ones.

Our epoch, the epoch of the bourgeoisie, possesses, however, this distinctive feature: it has simplified the class antagonisms. Society as a whole is more and more splitting up into two great hostile camps, into two great classes directly facing each other: Bourgeoisie and Proletariat.

From the serfs of the Middle Ages sprang the chartered burghers of the earliest towns. From these burgesses the first elements of the bourgeoisie were developed. . . .

Each step in the development of the bourgeoisie was accompanied by a corresponding political advance of that class. An oppressed class under the sway of the feudal nobility, an armed and self-governing association in the mediaeval commune; here independent urban republic (as in Italy and Germany), there taxable 'third estate' of the monarchy (as in France), afterwards, in the period of manufacture proper, serving either the semi-feudal or the absolute monarchy as a counterpoise against the nobility, and, in fact, corner-stone of the great monarchies in general, the bourgeoisie has at last, since the establishment of Modern Industry and of the world-market, conquered for itself, in the modern representative State, exclusive political sway. The executive of the modern State is but a committee for managing the common affairs of the whole bourgeoisie.

The bourgeoisie, historically, has played a most revolutionary part.

The bourgeoisie, wherever it has got the upper hand, has put an end to all feudal, patriarchal, idyllic relations. It has pitilessly torn asunder the motley feudal ties that bound man to his 'natural superiors,' and has left remaining no other nexus between man and man than naked self-interest, than callous 'cash payment.' It has drowned the most heavenly ecstasies of religious fervour, of chivalrous enthusiasm, of philistine sentimentalism, in the icy water of egotistical calculation. It has resolved personal worth into exchange value, and in place of the numberless indefeasible chartered freedoms, has set up that single, unconscionable freedom—Free Trade. In one word, for exploitation, veiled by religious and political illusions, it has substituted naked, shameless, direct, brutal exploitation.

The bourgeoisie has stripped of its halo every occupation hitherto honoured and looked up to with reverent awe. It has converted the physician, the lawyer, the priest, the poet, the man of science, into its paid wage-labourers.

The bourgeoisie has torn away from the family its sentimental veil, and has reduced the family relation to a mere money relation. . . .

The bourgeoisie, during its rule of scarce one hundred years, has created more massive and more colossal productive forces than have all preceding generations together. Subjection of Nature's forces to man, machinery, application of chemistry to industry and agriculture, steam-navigation, railways, electric telegraphs, clearing of whole continents for cultivation, canalisation of rivers, whole populations conjured out of the ground—what earlier century had even a presentiment that such productive forces slumbered in the lap of social labour?

We see then: the means of production and of exchange, on whose foundation the bourgeoisie built itself up, were generated in feudal society. At a certain stage in the development of these means of production and of exchange, the conditions under which feudal society produced and exchanged, the feudal organisation of agriculture and manufacturing industry, in one word, the feudal relations of property became no longer compatible with the already developed productive forces; they became so many fetters. They had to be burst asunder; they were burst asunder.

Into their place stepped free competition, accompanied by a social and political constitution adapted to it, and by the economical and political sway of the bourgeois class.

A similar movement is going on before our own eyes. Modern bourgeois society with its relations of production, of exchange and of property, a society that has conjured up such gigantic means of production and of exchange, is like the sorcerer, who is no longer able to control the powers of the nether world whom he has called up by his spells. For many a decade past the history of industry and commerce is but the history of the revolt of modern productive forces against modern conditions of production, against the property relations that are the conditions for the existence of the bourgeoisie and of its rule. It is enough to mention the commercial crises that by their periodical return put on its trial, each time more threateningly, the existence of the entire bourgeois society. In these crises a great part not only of the existing products, but also of the previously created productive forces, are periodically destroyed. In these crises there breaks out an epidemic that, in all earlier epochs, would have seemed an absurdity—the epidemic of over-production. Society suddenly finds itself put back into a state of momentary barbarism; it appears as if a famine, a universal war of devastation had cut off the supply of every means of subsistence; industry and commerce seem to be destroyed; and why? Because there is too much civilisation, too much means of subsistence, too much industry, too much commerce. The productive forces at the disposal of society no longer tend to further the development of the conditions of bourgeois property; on the contrary, they have become too powerful for these conditions, by which they are fettered, and so soon as they overcome these fetters, they bring disorder into the whole of bourgeois society, endanger the existence of bourgeois property. The conditions of bourgeois society are too narrow to comprise the wealth created by them. And how does the bourgeoisie get over these crises? On the one hand by enforced destruction of a mass of productive forces; on the other, by the conquest of new markets, and by the more thorough exploitation of the old ones. That is to say, by paving the way for more extensive and more destructive crises, and by diminishing the means whereby crises are prevented.

The weapons with which the bourgeoisie felled feudalism to the ground are now turned against the bourgeoisie itself.

But not only has the bourgeoisie forged the weapons that bring death to itself; it has also called into existence the men who are to wield those weapons—the modern working class—the proletarians.

In proportion as the bourgeoisie, *i.e.*, capital, is developed, in the same proportion is the proletariat, the modern working class, developed—a class of labourers, who live only so long as they find work, and who find work only so long as their labour increases capital. These labourers, who must sell themselves piecemeal, are a commodity, like every other article of commerce, and are consequently exposed to all the vicissitudes of competition, to all the fluctuations of the market.

Owing to the extensive use of machinery and to division of labour, the work of the proletarians has lost all individual character, and, consequently, all charm for the workman. He becomes an appendage of the machine, and it is only the most simple, most monotonous, and most easily acquired knack, that is required of him. Hence, the cost of production of a workman is restricted, almost entirely, to the means of subsistence that he requires for his maintenance, and for the propagation of his race. But the price of a commodity, and therefore also of labour, is equal to its cost of production. In proportion, therefore, as the repulsiveness of the work increases, the wage decreases. Nay more, in proportion as the use of machinery and division of labour increases, in the same proportion the burden of toil also increases, whether by prolongation of the working hours, by increase of the work exacted in a given time or by increased speed of the machinery, etc.

Modern industry has converted the little workshop of the patriarchal master into the great factory of the industrial capitalist. Masses of labourers, crowded into the factory, are organised like soldiers. As privates of the industrial army they are placed under the command of a perfect hierarchy of officers and sergeants. Not only are they slaves of the bourgeois class, and of the bourgeois State; they are daily and hourly enslaved by the machine, by the overlooker, and, above all, by the individual bourgeois manufacturer himself. The more openly this despotism proclaims gain to be its end and aim, the more petty, the more hateful and the more embittering it is. . . .

The proletariat goes through various stages of development. With its birth begins its struggle with the bourgeoisie. At first the contest is carried on by individual labourers, then by the workpeople of a factory, then by the operatives of one trade, in one locality, against the individual bourgeois who directly exploits them. They direct their attacks not against the bourgeois conditions of production, but against the instruments of production themselves; they destroy imported wares that compete with their labour, they smash to pieces machinery, they set factories ablaze, they seek to restore by force the vanished status of the workman of the Middle Ages.

At this stage the labourers still form an incoherent mass scattered over the whole country, and broken up by their mutual competition. If anywhere they unite to form more compact bodies, this is not yet the consequence of their own active union, but of the union of the bourgeoisie, which class, in order to attain its own political ends, is compelled to set the whole proletariat in motion, and is moreover yet, for a time, able to do so. At this stage, therefore, the proletarians do not fight their enemies, but the enemies of their enemies, the remnants of absolute monarchy, the landowners, the non-industrial bourgeois, the petty bourgeoisie. Thus the whole historical movement is concentrated in the hands of the bourgeoisie, every victory so obtained is a victory for the bourgeoisie.

But with the development of industry the proletariat not only increases in number; it becomes concentrated in greater masses, its strength grows, and it feels that strength more. The various interests and conditions of life within the ranks of the proletariat are more and more equalised, in proportion as machinery obliterates all distinctions of labour, and nearly everywhere reduces wages to the same low level. The growing competition among the bourgeois, and the resulting commercial crises, make the wages of the workers ever more fluctuating. The unceasing improvement of machinery, ever more rapidly developing, makes their livelihood more and more precarious; the collisions between individual workmen and individual bourgeois take more and more the character of collisions between two classes. Thereupon the workers begin to form combinations (Trades' Unions) against the bourgeois; they club together in order to keep up the rate of wages; they found permanent associations in order to make provision beforehand for these occasional revolts. Here and there the contest breaks out into riots. . . .

Altogether collisions between the classes of the old society further, in many ways, the course of development of the proletariat. The bourgeoisie finds itself involved in a constant battle. At first with the aristocracy; later on, with those portions of the bourgeoisie itself, whose interests have become antagonistic to the progress of industry; at all times, with the bourgeoisie of foreign countries. In all these battles it sees itself compelled to appeal to the proletariat, to ask for its help, and thus, to drag it into the political arena. The bourgeoisie itself, therefore, supplies the proletariat with its own elements of political and general education, in other words, it furnishes the proletariat with weapons for fighting the bourgeoisie.

Further, as we have already seen, entire sections of the ruling classes are, by the advance of industry, precipitated into the proletariat, or are at least threatened in their conditions of existence. These also supply the proletariat with fresh elements of enlightenment and progress.

Finally, in times when the class struggle nears the decisive hour, the process of dissolution going on within the ruling class, in fact within the whole range of old society, assumes such a violent, glaring character, that a small section of the ruling class cuts itself adrift, and joins the revolutionary class, the class that holds the future in its hands. Just as, therefore, at an earlier period, a section of the nobility went over to the bourgeoisie, so now a portion of the bourgeoisie goes over to the proletariat, and in particular, a portion of the bourgeois ideologists, who have raised themselves to the level of comprehending theoretically the historical movement as a whole.

Of all the classes that stand face to face with the bourgeoisie today, the proletariat alone is a really revolutionary class. The other classes decay and finally disappear in the face of Modern Industry; the proletariat is its special and essential product.

The lower middle class, the small manufacturer, the shopkeeper, the artisan, the peasant, all these fight against the bourgeoisie, to save from extinction their existence as fractions of the middle class. They are therefore not revolutionary, but conservative. Nay more, they are reactionary, for they try to roll back the wheel of history. If by chance they are revolutionary, they are so only in view of their impending transfer into the proletariat, they thus defend not their present, but their future interests, they desert their own stand-point to place themselves at that of the proletariat.

The 'dangerous class,' the social scum, that passively rotting mass thrown off by the lowest layers of old society, may, here and there, be swept into the movement by a proletarian revolution, its conditions of life, however, prepare it far more for the part of a bribed tool of reactionary intrigue.

In the conditions of the proletariat, those of old society at large are already virtually swamped. The proletarian is without property; his relation to his wife and children has no longer anything in common with the bourgeois family-relations; modern, industrial labour, modern subjection to capital, the same in England as in France, in America as in Germany, has stripped him of every trace of national character. Law, morality, religion, are to him so many bourgeois prejudices, behind which lurk in ambush just as many bourgeois interests.

All the preceding classes that got the upper hand, sought to fortify their already acquired status by subjecting society at large to their conditions of appropriation. The proletarians cannot become masters of the productive forces of society, except by abolishing their own previous mode of appropriation, and thereby also every other previous mode of appropriation. They have nothing of their own to secure and to fortify; their mission is to des-troy all previous securities for, and insurances of, individual property.

All previous historical movements were movements of minorities, or in the interests of minorities. The proletarian movement is the self-conscious, in-dependent movement of the immense majority, in the interests of the immense majority. The proletariat, the lowest stratum of our present society, cannot stir, cannot raise itself up, without the whole superincumbent strata of official society being sprung into the air.

(Karl Marx and Friedrich Engels, *The Communist Manifesto*, in *Marx and Engels: Selected Works*, pp. 35-8, 40-5, Lawrence and Wishart, London 1968.)

82   VLADIMIR ILYICH LENIN: THE TRANSITION FROM CAPITALISM TO COMMUNISM

Marx continued:

'Between capitalist and communist society lies the period of the revolutionary transformation of the one into the other. Corresponding to this is also a political transition period in which the state can be nothing but *the revolutionary dictatorship of the proletariat.*'

Marx bases this conclusion on an analysis of the role played by the proletariat in modern capitalist society, on the data concerning the development of this society, and on the irreconcilability of the antagonistic interests of the proletariat and the bourgeoisie.

Previously the question was put as follows: to achieve its emancipation, the proletariat must overthrow the bourgeoisie, win political power and establish its revolutionary dictatorship.

Now the question is put somewhat differently: the transition from capitalist society—which is developing towards communism—to communist society is impossible without a 'political transition period', and the state in this period can only be the revolutionary dictatorship of the proletariat.

What, then, is the relation of this dictatorship to democracy?

We have seen that the *Communist Manifesto* simply places side by side the two concepts: 'to raise the proletariat to the position of the ruling class' and 'to win the battle of democracy'. On the basis of all that has been said above, it is possible to determine more precisely how democracy changes in the transition from capitalism to communism.

In capitalist society, providing it develops under the most favourable conditions, we have a more or less complete democracy in the democratic republic. But this democracy is always hemmed in by the narrow limits set by capitalist exploitation, and consequently always remains, in effect, a democracy for the minority, only for the propertied classes, only for the rich. Freedom in capitalist society always remains about the same as it was in the ancient Greek republics: freedom for the slave-owners. Owing to the conditions of capitalist exploitation, the modern wage slaves are so crushed by want and poverty that 'they cannot be bothered with democracy', 'cannot be bothered with politics'; in the ordinary, peaceful course of events, the majority of the population is debarred from participation in public and political life. . . .

Democracy for an insignificant minority, democracy for the rich—that is the democracy of capitalist society. If we look more closely into the machinery of capitalist democracy, we see everywhere, in the 'petty'—supposedly petty—details of the suffrage (residential qualification, exclusion of women, etc.), in the technique of the representative institutions, in the actual obstacles to the right of assembly (public buildings are not for 'paupers'!), in the purely capitalist organisation of the daily press, etc., etc.—we see restriction after restriction upon democracy. These restrictions, exceptions, exclusions, obstacles for the poor seem slight, especially in the eyes of one who has never known want himself and has never been in close contact with the oppressed classes in their mass life (and nine out of ten, if not ninety-nine out of a hundred, bourgeois publicists and politicians come under this category); but in their sum total these restrictions exclude and squeeze out the poor from politics, from active participation in democracy.

Marx grasped this *essence* of capitalist democracy splendidly when, in analysing the experience of the Commune, he said that the oppressed are allowed once every few years to decide which particular representatives of the oppressing class shall represent and repress them in parliament!

But from this capitalist democracy—that is inevitably narrow and stealthily pushes aside the poor, and is therefore hypocritical and false through and through—forward development does not proceed simply, directly and smoothly, towards 'greater and greater democracy', as the liberal professors and petty-bourgeois opportunists would have us believe. No, forward development, i.e., development towards communism, proceeds through the dictatorship of the proletariat, and cannot do otherwise, for the *resistance* of the capitalist exploiters cannot be *broken* by anyone else or in any other way.

And the dictatorship of the proletariat, i.e., the organisation of the vanguard of the oppressed as the ruling class for the purpose of suppressing the oppressors, cannot result merely in an expansion of democracy. *Simultaneously* with an immense expansion of democracy, which *for the first time* becomes democracy for the poor, democracy for the people, and not democracy for the money-bags, the dictatorship of the proletariat imposes a series of restrictions on the freedom of the oppressors, the exploiters, the capitalists. We must suppress them in order to free humanity from wage slavery, their resistance must be crushed by force; it is clear that there is no freedom and no democracy where there is suppression and where there is violence.

Engels expressed this splendidly in his letter to Bebel when he said, as the reader will remember, that 'the proletariat needs the state, not in the interests of freedom but in order to hold down its adversaries, and as soon as it becomes possible to speak of freedom the state as such ceases to exist.'

Democracy for the vast majority of the people, and suppression by force, i.e., exclusion from democracy, of the exploiters and oppressors of the people—this is the change democracy undergoes during the *transition* from capitalism to communism.

Only in communist society, when the resistance of the capitalists has been completely crushed, when the capitalists have disappeared, when there are no classes (i.e., when there is no distinction between the members of society as regards their relation to the social means of production), *only* then 'the state . . . ceases to exist', and '*it becomes possible to speak of freedom*'. Only then will a truly complete democracy become possible and be realised, a democracy without any exceptions whatever. And only then will democracy begin to *wither away*, owing to the simple fact that, freed from capitalist slavery, from the untold horrors, savagery, absurdities and infamies of capitalist exploitation, people will gradually *become accustomed* to observing the elementary rules of social intercourse that have been known for centuries and repeated for thousands of years in all copy-book maxims. They will become accustomed to observing them without force, without coercion, without subordination, *without the special apparatus* for coercion called the state.

The expression 'the state *withers away*' is very well chosen, for it indicates both the gradual and the spontaneous nature of the process. Only habit can, and undoubtedly will, have such an effect; for we see around us on millions of occasions how readily people become accustomed to observing the necessary rules of social intercourse when there is no exploitation, when there is nothing that arouses indignation, evokes protest and revolt, and creates the need for *suppression*.

And so in capitalist society we have a democracy that is curtailed, wretched, false, a democracy only for the rich, for the minority. The dictatorship of the proletariat, the period of transition to communism, will for the first time create democracy for the people, for the majority, along with the necessary suppression of the exploiters, of the minority. Communism alone is capable of providing really complete democracy, and the more complete it is, the sooner it will become unnecessary and wither away of its own accord.

In other words, under capitalism we have the state in the proper sense of the word, that is, a special machine for the suppression of one class by another, and, what is more, of the majority by the minority. Naturally, to be successful, such an undertaking as the systematic suppression of the exploited majority by the exploiting minority calls for the utmost ferocity and savagery in the matter of suppressing, it calls for seas of blood, through which mankind is actually wading its way in slavery, serfdom and wage labour. . . .

Furthermore, during the *transition* from capitalism to communism suppression is *still* necessary; but it is now the suppression of the exploiting minority by the exploited majority. A special apparatus, a special machine for suppression, the 'state,' is *still* necessary, but this is now a transitional state; it is no longer a state in the proper sense of the word; for the suppression of the minority of exploiters by the majority of the wage slaves of *yesterday* is comparatively so easy, simple and natural a task that it will entail far less bloodshed than the suppression of the risings of slaves, serfs or wage labourers, and it will cost mankind far less. And it is compatible with the extension of democracy to such an overwhelming majority of the population that the need for a *special machine* of suppression will begin to disappear. The exploiters are naturally unable to suppress the people without a highly complex machine for performing this task: but *the people* can suppress the exploiters even with a very simple 'machine,' almost without a 'machine,' without a special apparatus, by the simpler *organization of the armed masses* (such as the Soviets of Workers' and Soldiers' Deputies, let us remark, anticipating somewhat).

Lastly, only communism makes the state absolutely unnecessary, for there is *nobody* to be suppressed—'nobody' in the sense of a *class*, in the sense of a systematic struggle against a definite section of the population. We are not utopians, and do not in the least deny the possibility and inevitability of excesses on the part of *individual persons*, or the need to suppress *such* excesses. But, in the first place, no special machine, no special apparatus of suppression is needed for this; this will be done by the armed people itself, as simply and as readily as any crowd of civilized people, even in modern society, interferes to put a stop to a scuffle or to prevent a woman from being assaulted. And, secondly, we know that the fundamental social cause of excesses, which consist in the violation of the rules of social intercourse, is the exploitation of the masses, their want and their poverty. With the removal of this chief cause, excesses will inevitably begin to 'wither away.' We do not know how quickly and in what succession, but we know that they will wither away. With their withering away the state will also *wither away*.

(V. I. Lenin, *The State and Revolution*, pp. 137-45, Progress Publishers, Moscow.)

CHAPTER 22

Fascism and National Socialism

Fascism and national socialism can conveniently be examined together as the main manifestations of extreme right-wing ideology in the twentieth century. Neither can be said to possess a coherent philosophy although both movements have made such claims. Both were political organizations which came into existence in response to political circumstances rather than to political theory, although it is possible to trace their intellectual antecedents at least as far back as the French Revolution. This is not to propose the absurd thesis that the propounders of conservative or élitist political theories in the nineteenth century were themselves embryonic fascists; rather it is to suggest that the various elements, some quite incongruous, which came together in modern fascism can be separately identified in earlier philosophies.

Nationalism

The collectivist and nationalist elements in fascism can be traced back to the German idealist philosophers such as Johann Fichte (1762-1814) and G. W. Hegel (see Chapter 21). Both stressed the importance of the national state as an organic unity and the comparative unimportance of the individual. Both believed that each nation has its special cultural contribution to make to history, although Hegel went further and argued that the state, 'the march of God in the world', was the vehicle which carried forward the 'world spirit'. Moreover, Hegel considered that dialectical historical progress was largely brought about by war which was therefore a desirable activity, particularly as it tended towards increased state power. Peace, on the other hand, he saw as the 'blank pages' of history.

The nationalist element in idealist philosophy was reinforced by the Prussian historians Savigny and Treitschke. Heinrich von Treitschke (1834-1896), the most famous of nineteenth-century German historians, sounds somewhat reminiscent of Machiavelli. He insisted that all things were justified in order to make the state strong and the people unified and secure. He believed in the necessity for war and the cultural domination of others by Germany. The Jews he regarded as an alien force engaged in the destruction of the true Germanic virtues.

Irrationalism

A further tradition which was incorporated into modern fascism, particularly in the German national socialist variety, was that of romantic irrationalism. Here, once more, Rousseau is the starting point. His emphasis upon 'will' rather than 'reason' was the first shot in the battle against eighteenth-century rationalism which culminated in the German romantic movement. In the arts, the writings and music dramas of Richard Wagner (1813-1883) epitomize the zenith of European romanticism. His glorification of the *Volk* and of the hero who expresses the spirit of the *Volk*, prepared the cultural soil of Germany for the racist seeds of Houston Chamberlain and Adolf Hitler.

Philosophically, irrationalism was taught by Arthur Schopenhauer (1788-1860) and Friedrich Nietzsche (1844-1900). Both saw as irrational the natural world in which human life has no apparent logical meaning. Nietzsche's philosophy is that of the struggle for power. The basic force in the world is not reason but will. Those who possess the strongest will to power will succeed; the mass of men who are inferior, conventional and philistine will be crushed into servility and the 'superman', the 'big blond beast', will rule. It follows that the conventional virtues—equality, democracy, humility, happiness—are elements of a slave morality. True morality is concerned with the superiority of the strong, pride in success and the heroic life.

It is tempting to see Nietzschean philosophy as the most direct source of modern fascism. Certainly his moral teachings found a ready echo in the cynical dismissal of many of the conventional virtues by fascists and national socialists. His conception of the superman and his contempt for the masses could be seen by Hitler and Mussolini as reflecting their own positions. On the other hand, Nietzsche was never a German nationalist, nor did he regard the Jews and Slavs as inferior races.

Racialism

The racialist element in national socialism (it was to be much less significant in Italian fascism) was built upon the theories of Arthur de Gobineau (1816-1882) and Houston Stewart Chamberlain (1855-1926). Gobineau was responsible for first formulating the myth of Aryan superiority. Of the three distinct races of the world, Negro, Chinese and European, the latter alone possesses the qualities of high rationality, energy and creativity. But among the European race there are important differences. The Jews are inferior to the others because they possess Negro as well as European blood. The Aryans are the superior group because their blood is purest; they are to be found mainly in Germany and England.

Chamberlain, an Englishman who adopted German nationality (and married one of Wagner's daughters), was important as the popularizer of Gobineau's racial theories in Germany. Passages from his book *The Foundations of the Nineteenth Century* are almost indistinguishable from those in *The Myth of the Twentieth Century* written by Alfred Rosenberg, his aptest pupil.

Italian Fascism

Fascism in Italy is associated pre-eminently with its founder and leader Benito Mussolini (1883-1945) who seized power in 1922. The fascist success was in large part a consequence of the success in Russia of communism which the middle classes feared would extend to Italy and dispossess them. Democratic institutions were thought by many to be incapable of protecting them against potential anarchy and, moreover, such institutions seemed to be doing little to end the post-war economic depression.

The success of Mussolini's fascists could not be regarded as the triumph of an ideology; it was a response to events supported by a bourgeois anti-Marxism. The ideology came later when Mussolini decided that a philosophy of fascism was needed.

Without doubt, fascist philosophy was most clearly expressed by Mussolini himself in his article written in 1932 for the *Enciclopedia Italiana* entitled *La dottrina del fascismo* (*The Doctrine of Fascism*) (Ex. 83). All the various elements alluded to above are here. The Hegelian dialectic of history and the supremacy of the organic state over lesser associations; the general will; the attack on ballot-box democracy; the anti-pacificism; the opposing of 'holiness and heroism' to Marxist materialism as the motivation of human conduct; the irrational emphasis upon the 'will to power' as the vital force of the fascist state. Mussolini's debt to Georges Sorel (1857-1922) is illustrated by his view that the mythical content of a philosophy is more important than the rational content. The nationalist element in Italian fascism is essentially based upon myth, particularly the myth that fascist Italy is the heir to the Roman imperial tradition.

Mussolini was, of course, not a philosopher, and it is likely that his article was prepared, at least in part, by the man who has most claim to be regarded as the philosopher of fascism, Giovanni Gentile (1875-1944). Gentile, who professed a Hegelian philosophy, was associated with Mussolini from the latter's earliest fascist years and was Minister of Education in the fascist government. In response to Mussolini's demand for a non-Marxian collectivist theory of the state, Gentile's talents were pressed into service and his theory—a rather confusing mixture of the rational (Hegel) and the irrational (Nietzsche)—apparently met with Mussolini's approval.

Gentile's book, *The Genesis and Structure of Society*, written in 1943, is a semi-Hegelian analysis of the state, society and the individual which amplifies a number of the points in Mussolini's article. The extracts quoted are concerned with the relationship of the individual to the state. In the first (Ex. 84a), Gentile attempts to argue, in highly metaphysical language, that the truly free individual is created by the 'spiritual community' which exists in the corporate fascist state. The second passage (Ex. 84b), develops this relationship. It is absurd to talk of a 'private' sphere of actions in contrast to the 'public' sphere since every individual, as has been shown, implies the existence and all-embracing nature of the state. Attempts, therefore, to exclude the state from the so-called private sphere are never legitimate. In a Rousseauistic passage, Gentile argues that liberty and democracy in their true sense are preserved in the 'totalitarian' state which expresses the real will of each individual.

German National Socialism

In the German version of fascism little or nothing is left of the rational elements of Hegel and his successors. What remains is a compound of German nationalism, Nietzschean irrationalism, and the doctrine of Aryan supremacy. The two most significant writers on the theory of national socialism are Adolf Hitler and Alfred Rosenberg. Hitler (1889-1945) founded his National Socialist German Workers' Party in 1919 in the period of gloom following Germany's defeat in the war. Although, at first, it was merely one of a host of extremist parties it soon acquired a distinct success under Hitler's leadership and spurred by this he made his ill-fated *Putsch* at Munich in 1923. It was during his imprisonment following the *Putsch* that Hitler wrote *Mein Kampf (My Struggle)*, which was published in 1925. This is not a work of political philosophy in the traditional sense; rather it is an autobiography in which the development of national socialism is described.

Hitler's anti-semitic ravings are illustrated in the first extract from *Mein Kampf* (Ex. 85a). The later policy of the Nazi government of exterminating all Jews in their 'final solution' is foreshadowed in these pages of hate-filled denunciation. Hitler sees the Jew as the sub-human tyrant who, by cynically invoking the Marxist theory of the dictatorship of the proletariat, overthrows everything that is decent and ends by enslaving the people for his own interests.

An equally important element in the collection of prejudices known as Hitlerism was the theory of the supremacy of the Aryan master race. In this Hitler differs substantially from Mussolini. Whereas the latter, influenced by Hegel, considered the state to be the all-important organic association, Hitler, influenced by the social Darwinism of Gobineau and Chamberlain, regarded the race as the bearer of human culture. Because the Aryan *Volk* is superior to other races, its purity must be maintained against those, Marxists and Jews, who are attempting to destroy it (Ex. 85b).

The closest Nazi parallel to the fascist philosopher Gentile, was Alfred Rosenberg, the foremost national socialist ideologist whose book *Der Mythus des 20 Jahrhunderts* (*The Myth of the Twentieth Century*) appeared in 1930 and contained the nearest thing to a philosophy of race since Chamberlain's work. In his use of the term 'myth' and his reliance upon irrationalism, Rosenberg showed as much of a debt to Georges Sorel as to Houston Chamberlain. The extract quoted (Ex. 86), well illustrates Rosenberg's racial theory which attempts to interpret history as a struggle between the Aryan races and the 'subhumans'. Only the former are capable of providing a valuable culture. The non-Aryans and, in particular the Jews, are capable only of cultural destruction.

In his use of words such as 'myth', 'will', 'blood', 'soul', Rosenberg is seen to be firmly in the irrationalist tradition. Although some commentators have affected to see important similarities between the totalitarian systems of the left and the right, the fascist doctrine is intellectually at the opposite pole from Marxist communism. The liberal observer of totalitarian political systems can draw comfort from the observation that the doctrine which, like liberalism itself, claims to be 'scientific' and 'rational' seems destined to advance, whereas the fascist doctrine of blood and soil has led to nothing but sterility and its own destruction.

FURTHER READING

Texts

B. Mussolini: *The Doctrine of Fascism*

M. Oakeshott: *The Social and Political Doctrines of Contemporary Europe* (Cambridge University Press 1939)

G. Gentile: *Genesis and Structure of Society*, tr. H. S. Harris (University of Illinois Press, Urbana 1960)

A. Hitler: *Mein Kampf*, tr. R. Manheim (Hutchinson 1949)

A. Rosenberg: *Selected Writings*, ed. R. Pois (Cape 1970)

Commentaries

E. Barker: *Reflections on Government* (Oxford University Press 1942)

P. Hayes, *Fascism* (Allen and Unwin, London 1973)

W. Maser: *Hitler's Mein Kampf: An Analysis*, tr. R. H. Barry (Faber and Faber 1970)

E. Nolte: *Three Faces of Fascism* (Mentor, N.Y. 1969)

E. Weber: *Varieties of Fascism* (Van Nostrand Reinhold Co., N.Y. 1964)

J. Weiss: *The Fascist Tradition* (Harper & Row, N.Y. 1967)

83 BENITO MUSSOLINI: FASCISM

Fascism is a religious conception in which man is seen in his immanent relationship with a superior law and with an objective Will that transcends the particular individual and raises him to conscious membership of a spiritual society. Whoever has seen in the religious politics of the Fascist regime nothing but mere opportunism has not understood that Fascism besides being a system of government is also, and above all, a system of thought.

Fascism is an historical conception, in which man is what he is only in so far as he works with the spiritual process in which he finds himself, in the family or social group, in the nation and in the history in which all nations collaborate. From this follows the great value of tradition, in memories, in language, in customs, in the standards of social life. Outside history man is nothing. Consequently Fascism is opposed to all the individualistic abstractions of a materialistic nature like those of the eighteenth century; and it is opposed to all Jacobin utopias and innovations. It does not consider that 'happiness' is possible upon earth, as it appeared to be in the desire of the economic literature of the eighteenth century, and hence it rejects all teleological theories according to which mankind would reach a definitive stabilized condition at a certain period in history. This implies putting oneself outside history and life, which is a continual change and coming to be. Politically, Fascism wishes to be a realistic doctrine; practically, it aspires to solve only the problems which arise historically of themselves and that of themselves find or suggest their own solution. To act among men, as to act in the natural world, it is necessary to enter into the process of reality and to master the already operating forces.

Against individualism, the Fascist conception is for the State; and it is for the individual in so far as he coincides with the State, which is the conscience and universal will of man in his historical existence. It is opposed to classical Liberalism, which arose from the necessity of reacting against absolutism, and which brought its historical purpose to an end when the State was transformed into the conscience and will of the people. Liberalism denied the State in the interests of the particular individual; Fascism reaffirms the State as the true reality of the individual. And if liberty is to be the attribute of the real man, and not of that abstract puppet envisaged by individualistic Liberalism, Fascism is for liberty. And for the only liberty which can be a real thing, the liberty of the State and of the individual within the State. Therefore, for the Fascist, everything is in the State, and nothing human or spiritual exists, much less has value, outside the State. In this sense Fascism is totalitarian, and the Fascist State, the synthesis and unity of all values, interprets, develops and gives strength to the whole life of the people.

Outside the State there can be neither individuals nor groups (political parties, associations, syndicates, classes). Therefore Fascism is opposed to Socialism, which confines the movement of history within the class struggle and ignores the unity of classes established in one economic and moral reality in the State; and analogously it is opposed to class syndicalism. Fascism recognizes the real exigencies for which the socialist and syndicalist movement arose, but while recognizing them wishes to bring them under the control of the State and give them a purpose within the corporative system of interests reconciled within the unity of the State.

Individuals form classes according to the similarity of their interests, they form syndicates according to differentiated economic activities within these interests; but they form first, and above all, the State, which is not to be thought of numerically as the sum-total of individuals forming the majority of a nation. And consequently Fascism is opposed to Democracy, which equates the nation to the majority, lowering it to the level of that majority; nevertheless it is the purest form of democracy if the nation is conceived as it should be, qualitatively and not quantitatively, as the most powerful idea (most powerful because most moral, most coherent, most true) which acts within the nation as the conscience and the will of a few, even of One, which ideal tends to become active within the conscience and the will of all—that is to say, of all those who rightly constitute a nation by reason of nature, history or race, and have set out upon the same line of development and spiritual formation as one conscience and one sole will. Not a race, nor a geographically determined region, but as a community historically perpetuating itself, a multitude unified by a single idea, which is the will to existence and to power: consciousness of itself, personality.

This higher personality is truly the nation in so far as it is the State. It is not the nation that generates the State, as according to the old naturalistic concept which served as the basis of the political theories of the national States of the nineteenth century. Rather the nation is created by the State, which gives to the people, conscious of its own moral unity, a will and therefore an effective existence. . . .

Fascism, in so far as it considers and observes the future and the development of humanity quite apart from the political considerations of the moment, believes neither in the possibility nor in the utility of perpetual peace. It thus repudiates the doctrine of Pacifism—born of a renunciation of the struggle and an act of cowardice in the face of sacrifice. War alone brings up to their highest tension all human energies and puts the stamp of nobility upon the peoples who have the courage to meet it. . . .

Such a conception of life makes Fascism the precise negation of that doctrine which formed the basis of the so-called Scientific or Marxian Socialism: the doctrine of historical Materialism, according to which the history of human civilizations can be explained only as the struggle of interest between the different social groups and as arising out of change in the means and instruments of production. That economic improvements—discoveries of raw materials, new methods of work, scientific inventions—should have an importance of their own, no one denies, but that they should suffice to explain human history to the exclusion of all other factors is absurd: Fascism believes, now and always, in holiness and in heroism, that is in acts in which no economic motive—remote or immediate—plays a part. With this negation of historical materialism, according to which men would be only by-products of history, who appear and disappear on the surface of the waves while in the depths the real directive forces are at work, there is also denied the immutable and irreparable 'class struggle' which is the natural product of this economic conception of history, and above all it is denied that the class struggle can be the primary agent of social changes. Socialism, being thus wounded in these two primary tenets of its doctrine, nothing of it is left save the sentimental aspiration—old as humanity—towards a social order in which the sufferings and the pains of the humblest folk could be alleviated. But here Fascism rejects the concept of an economic 'happiness' which would be realized socialistically and almost automatically at a given moment of economic evolution by assuring to all a maximum prosperity. Fascism denies the possibility of the materialistic conception of 'happiness' and leaves it to the economists of the first half of the eighteenth century; it denies, that is, the equation of prosperity with happiness, which would transform men into animals with one sole preoccupation: that of being well-fed and fat, degraded in consequence to a merely physical existence.

After Socialism, Fascism attacks the whole complex of democratic ideologies and rejects them both in their theoretical premises and in their applications or practical manifestations. Fascism denies that the majority, through the mere fact of being a majority, can rule human societies; it denies that this majority can govern by means of a periodical consultation; it affirms the irremediable, fruitful and beneficent inequality of men, who cannot be levelled by such a mechanical and extrinsic fact as universal suffrage. By democratic regimes we mean those in which from time to time the people is given the illusion of being sovereign, while true effective sovereignty lies in other, perhaps irresponsible and secret, forces. Democracy is a regime without a king, but with very many kings, perhaps more exclusive, tyrannical and violent than one king even though a tyrant. . . .

But the Fascist repudiations of Socialism, Democracy, Liberalism must not make one think that Fascism wishes to make the world return to what it was before 1789, the year which has been indicated as the year of the beginning of the liberal-democratic age. One does not go backwards. The Fascist doctrine has not chosen De Maistre as its prophet. Monarchical absolutism is a thing of the past and so also is every theocracy. So also feudal privileges and division into impenetrable and isolated castes have had their day. The theory of Fascist authority has nothing to do with the police State. A party that governs a nation in a totalitarian way is a new fact in history. References and comparisons are not possible. Fascism takes over from the ruins of Liberal Socialistic democratic doctrines those elements which still have a living value. It preserves those that can be called the established facts of history, it rejects all the rest, that is to say the idea of a doctrine which holds good for all times and all peoples. If it is admitted that the nineteenth century has been the century of Socialism, Liberalism and Democracy, it does not follow that the twentieth must also be the century of Liberalism, Socialism and Democracy. Political doctrines pass; peoples remain. It is to be expected that this century may be that of authority, a century of the 'Right', a Fascist century. If the nineteenth was the century of the individual (Liberalism means individualism) it may be expected that this one may be the century of 'collectivism' and therefore the century of the State. That a new doctrine should use the still vital elements of other doctrines is perfectly logical. No doctrine is born quite new, shining, never before seen. No doctrine can boast of an absolute 'originality'. It is bound, even if only historically, to other doctrines that have been, and to develop into other doctrines that will be. Thus the scientific socialism of Marx is bound to the Utopian Socialism of the Fouriers, the Owens and the Saint-Simons; thus the Liberalism of the nineteenth century is connected with the whole 'Enlightenment' of the eighteenth century. Thus the doctrines of democracy are bound to the *Encyclopédie*. Every doctrine tends to direct the activity of men towards a determined objective; but the activity of man reacts upon the doctrine, transforms it, adapts it to new necessities or transcends it. The doctrine itself, therefore must be, not words, but an act of life. Hence, the pragmatic veins in Fascism, its will to power, its will to be, its attitude in the face of the fact of 'violence' and of its own courage. . . .

The Fascist State is a will to power and to government. In it the tradition of Rome is an idea that has force. In the doctrine of Fascism Empire is not only a territorial, military or mercantile expression, but spiritual or moral. One can think of an empire, that is to say a nation that directly or indirectly leads other nations, without needing to conquer a single square kilometre of territory. For Fascism the tendency to Empire, that is to say, to the expansion of nations, is a manifestation of vitality; its opposite, staying at home, is a sign of decadence: peoples who rise or re-rise are imperialist, peoples who die are renunciatory. Fascism is the doctrine that is most fitted to represent the aims, the states of mind, of a people, like the Italian people, rising again after many centuries of abandonment or slavery to foreigners. But Empire calls for discipline, co-ordination of forces, duty and sacrifice; this explains many aspects of the practical working of the regime and the direction of many of the forces of the State and the necessary severity shown to those who would wish to oppose this spontaneous and destined impulse of the Italy of the twentieth century, to oppose it in the name of the superseded ideologies of the nineteenth, repudiated wherever great experiments of political and social transformation have been courageously attempted: especially where, as now, peoples thirst for authority, for leadership, for order. If every age has its own doctrine, it is apparent from a thousand signs that the doctrine of the present age is Fascism. That it is a doctrine of life is shown by the fact that it has resuscitated a faith. That this faith has conquered minds is proved by the fact that Fascism has had its dead and its martyrs.

Fascism henceforward has in the world the universality of all those doctrines which, by fulfilling themselves, have significance in the history of the human spirit.

(B. Mussolini, *The Doctrine of Fascism*, in M. Oakeshott, *The Social and Political Doctrines of Contemporary Europe*, pp. 165-7, 170-2, 175, 178-9, Cambridge University Press 1939.)

84a GIOVANNI GENTILE: THE INDIVIDUAL AND THE STATE (i)

The concrete reality of the individual

The concrete reality of the individual is not to be found in his existence in space and time as a natural phenomenon, an object of sense, but rather in his spiritual existence as a self-conscious being. He exists as a particular person, but not as one among others; his existence is unique and therefore infinite and universal. So the real individual is not opposed to the universal—he *is* the universal; and the concrete universal is just the individual himself as an actual, self-conscious, determinate, unique being.

If one wishes to grasp the essence of this spiritual individuality, it is vital not to slip back into conceiving the individual as one physical object among others in experience. That is just the old Aristotelian, realistic conception, an illusion from which we have to free ourselves. The individual qua self-consciousness is not a natural entity in space and time; he contains space, time and nature, all within himself. Only in this way can he have the unconditioned freedom that is his.

It should also be noted that when once the individual is thought of in this way, the relation that we generally imagine to exist between the individual and the community is overthrown. Instead of the community containing the individual, it is the individual who contains—or rather establishes—the community, within his own act of self-consciousness. And here again we must not think of that natural physical community that the imagination suggests to us, but of the spiritual community which is its soul and essence. For example, the language or the law that establishes brotherhood and equality—nay more than equality, even identity—between individuals who are naturally diverse; the bond of feeling which they recognize as creating a unique reciprocal relation between them, the essence of which is not divided among them but exists whole and perfect in each one. Not the imaginary community that we think of as resulting from the accidental meeting of a number of individuals, but the community that is the constitutive principle of society and makes life in common possible. The community that is universality—for universality could not be the end toward which the individual strives if it were not first of all the fount from which individuality arises.

(G. Gentile, *Genesis and Structure of Society*, tr. H. S. Harris, p. 86, University of Illinois Press, Urbana 1960.)

84b GIOVANNI GENTILE: THE INDIVIDUAL AND THE STATE
(ii)

'Private' and 'public'

. . . An action is either 'public' or 'private', depending on whether we think of it concretely or in the abstract. And the truth is that within the State everything that is abstractly 'private' becomes 'public' in a concrete situation; relations between particular separate individuals need to be regulated by what is called 'private' law to distinguish it from 'public' law which regulates relations between the State and its citizens—but the very existence of 'private' law proves that the State has an interest to protect, by intervening in 'private' relations, and by granting them its seal of approval.

In any case, the distinction can no longer be maintained when the empirical character of all distinctions between 'individual' and 'society' or 'individual' and 'State' is recognized; for, as we have seen, the State exists already in the private individual, and every empirical State is only a development of a new form of this original transcendental State. What is vital is that we should attribute to the transcendental State the absolute infinite universality that belongs to it from the beginning; then the imagination will not compel us to break open this infinity and conceive a wider State, which can never be anything but an empty fancy. For at any given time the only State that really exists is the one that expresses our own perpetually infinite and absolutely universal will.

The theory of the limits of the State

In reality, every time that this distinction of 'private' and 'public' is appealed to, the attempt to employ it is motivated by the desire to limit the activity of the State in practice, so as to secure and guarantee for the individual a sphere of interests outside the State's competence. *That the State's competence is limited* has been one of the classic tenets of the individualistic philosophy that liberal theory always tends to fall back on. Catholics in every country have used it as a weapon in their struggle to take the education of the young at least partially out of the hands of the State, by requiring its agreement to a 'private' school system parallel with and independent of the 'public' system. . . .

The tendency to limit the power of the State is surely nothing but a way of opposing a potential State will to the actual positive will of the State. It is a sort of revolutionary action establishing a new State of one's own that is to be the negation of the existing State. Obviously someone who is entirely satisfied with the way the State acts does not seek permission to act on his own account within the sphere of State action; so that in practice the request for permission always implies dissatisfaction and criticism of the State. The criticism may be legitimate but this can never mean that there is an abstract right to limit the action of the State; it represents a concrete effort toward a State that is or could be really ours, and the consequent virtual negation of the State actually in power which does not properly act for us. This negation in its turn would not make sense if it did not implicitly contain at least the virtual affirmation of a State that is really ours, a State which, as far as we are concerned, is the only genuine and effective State there is—the possibility of any other divergent yet still legitimate State being thereby excluded.

The authoritarian State and democracy

There is nothing really private then; and there are no limits to State action. This doctrine has two aspects: if we examine only one of them it becomes disfigured and essentially altered. It appears to make the State swallow the individual, and to absorb into authority completely the liberty that should be set against every authority that limits it. The regime corresponding to such a doctrine is called 'totalitarian' and 'authoritarian' and is set off against 'democracy,' the system of liberty. But one might say just the opposite: for in this conception the State is the will of the individual himself in its universal and absolute aspect, and thus the individual swallows the State; and since legitimate authority cannot extend beyond the actual will of the individual, authority is resolved completely into liberty. Lo and behold, absolutism is overturned and appears to have changed into its opposite; and the true absolute democracy is not that which seeks a limited State, but that which sets no limits to the State that develops in the inmost heart of the individual, conferring on his will the absolutely universal force of law.

(G. Gentile, op. cit., pp. 177-9.)

85a ADOLF HITLER: THE JEWISH PERIL

Slowly fear of the Marxist weapon of Jewry descends like a nightmare on the mind and soul of decent people.

They begin to tremble before the terrible enemy and thus have become his final victim.

The Jew's domination in the state seems so assured that now not only can he call himself a Jew again, but he ruthlessly admits his ultimate national and political designs. A section of his race openly owns itself to be a foreign people, yet even here they lie. For while the Zionists try to make the rest of the world believe that the national consciousness of the Jew finds its satisfaction in the creation of a Palestinian state, the Jews again slyly dupe the dumb *Goyim*. It doesn't even enter their heads to build up a Jewish state in Palestine for the purpose of living there; all they want is a central organisation for their international world swindle, endowed with its own sovereign rights and removed from the intervention of other states: a haven for convicted scoundrels and a university for budding crooks.

It is a sign of their rising confidence and sense of security that at a time when one section is still playing the German, Frenchman, or Englishman, the other with open effrontery comes out as the Jewish race.

How close they see approaching victory can be seen by the hideous aspect which their relations with the members of other peoples takes on.

With satanic joy in his face, the black-haired Jewish youth lurks in wait for the unsuspecting girl whom he defiles with his blood, thus stealing her from her people. With every means he tries to destroy the racial foundations of the people he has set out to subjugate. Just as he himself systematically ruins women and girls, he does not shrink back from pulling down the blood barriers for others, even on a large scale. It was and it is Jews who bring the Negroes into the Rhineland, always with the same secret thought and clear aim of ruining the hated white race by the necessarily resulting bastardisation, throwing it down from its cultural and political height, and himself rising to be its master.

For a racially pure people which is conscious of its blood can never be enslaved by the Jew. In this world he will forever be master over bastards and bastards alone.

And so he tries systematically to lower the racial level by a continuous poisoning of individuals.

And in politics he begins to replace the idea of democracy by the dictatorship of the proletariat.

In the organised mass of Marxism he has found the weapon which lets him dispense with democracy and in its stead allows him to subjugate and govern the peoples with a dictatorial and brutal fist.

He works systematically for revolutionisation in a twofold sense: economic and political.

Around peoples who offer too violent a resistance to attack from within he weaves a net of enemies, thanks to his international influence, incites them to war, and finally, if necessary, plants the flag of revolution on the very battle-fields.

In economics he undermines the states until the social enterprises which have become unprofitable are taken from the state and subjected to his financial control.

In the political field he refuses the state the means for its self-preservation, destroys the foundations of all national self-maintenance and defence, destroys faith in the leadership, scoffs at its history and past, and drags everything that is truly great into the gutter.

Culturally he contaminates art, literature, the theatre, makes a mockery of natural feeling, overthrows all concepts of beauty and sublimity, of the noble and the good, and instead drags men down into the sphere of his own base nature.

Religion is ridiculed, ethics and morality represented as outmoded, until the last props of a nation in its struggle for existence in this world have fallen.

Now begins the great last revolution. In gaining political power the Jew casts off the few cloaks that he still wears. The democratic people's Jew becomes the blood-Jew and tyrant over peoples. In a few years he tries to exterminate the national intelligentsia and by robbing the peoples of their natural intellectual leadership makes them ripe for the slave's lot of permanent subjugation.

The most frightful example of this kind is offered by Russia, where he killed or starved about thirty million people with positively fanatical savagery, in part amid inhuman tortures, in order to give a gang of Jewish journalists and stock exchange bandits domination over a great people.

The end is not only the end of the freedom of the peoples oppressed by the Jew, but also the end of this parasite upon the nations. After the death of his victim, the vampire sooner or later dies too.

(A. Hitler, *Mein Kampf*, tr. R. Manheim, vol. 1, ch. 11, pp. 294-6, Hutchinson, London 1969.)

85b ADOLF HITLER: THE MASTER RACE

In opposition to [Marxism] the folkish philosophy finds the importance of mankind in its basic racial elements. In the state it sees on principle only a means to an end and construes its end as the preservation of the racial existence of man. Thus, it by no means believes in an equality of the races, but along with their difference it recognises their higher or lesser value and feels itself obligated, through this knowledge, to promote the victory of the better and stronger, and demand the subordination of the inferior and weaker in accordance with the eternal will that dominates this universe. Thus, in principle, it serves the basic aristocratic idea of Nature and believes in the validity of this law down to the last individual. It sees not only the different value of the races, but also the different value of individuals. From the mass it extracts the importance of the individual personality, and thus, in contrast to disorganising Marxism, it has an organising effect. It believes in the necessity of an idealisation of humanity, in which alone it sees the premise for the existence of humanity. But it cannot grant the right to existence even to an ethical idea if this idea represents a danger for the racial life of the bearers of a higher ethics; for in a bastardised and niggerised world all the concepts of the humanly beautiful and sublime, as well as all ideas of an idealised future of our humanity, would be lost forever.

Human culture and civilisation on this continent are inseparably bound up with the presence of the Aryan. If he dies out or declines, the dark veils of an age without culture will again descend on this globe.

The undermining of the existence of human culture by the destruction of its bearer seems in the eyes of a folkish philosophy the most execrable crime. Anyone who dares to lay hands on the highest image of the Lord commits sacrilege against the benevolent creator of this miracle and contributes to the expulsion from paradise.

And so the folkish philosophy of life corresponds to the innermost will of Nature, since it restores that free play of forces which must lead to a continuous mutual higher breeding, until at last the best of humanity, having achieved possession of this earth, will have a free path for activity in domains which will lie partly above it and partly outside it.

We all sense that in the distant future humanity must be faced by problems which only a highest race, become master people and supported by the means and possibilities of an entire globe, will be equipped to overcome.

It is self-evident that so general a statement of the meaningful content of a folkish philosophy can be interpreted in thousands of ways. And actually we find hardly a one of our newer political formations which does not base itself in one way or another on this world view. And, by its very existence in the face of the many others, it shows the difference of its conceptions. And so the Marxist world view, led by a unified top organisation, is opposed by a hodgepodge of views which even as ideas are not very impressive in face of the solid, hostile front. Victories are not gained by such feeble weapons! Not until the international world view—politically led by organised Marxism—is confronted by a folkish world view, organised and led with equal unity, will success, supposing the fighting energy to be equal on both sides, fall to the side of eternal truth.

A philosophy can only be organisationally comprehended on the basis of a definite formulation of that philosophy, and what dogmas represent for religious faith, party principles are for a political party in the making.

Hence an instrument must be created for the folkish world view which enables it to fight, just as the Marxist party organisation creates a free path for internationalism.

This is the goal pursued by the National Socialist German Workers' Party.

(A. Hitler, op. cit., vol. 2, ch. 1, pp. 348-9.)

86　ALFRED ROSENBERG: ARYAN CULTURE

Today, a new belief is arising: the *Mythus* of the blood; the belief that the godly essence of man itself is to be defended through the blood; that belief which embodies the clearest knowledge that the Nordic race represents that *Mysterium* which has overthrown and replaced the old sacraments.

Spanning history from the present, the many-faceted character of Nordic creative strength lies stretched out before us. Aryan India bequeathed to the world a metaphysic whose depths have yet to be plumbed, even today. The Aryan Persian composed for us the *religious* myths from which we still draw sustenance. Doric Hellas dreamed of a *beauty*, which, as we see it in completed form before us, will never be further developed. Italian Rome illustrates for us an example of formal *state loyalty*; how a threatened human community must organize and defend itself. And German Europe bequeathed to the world the radiant ideal of humanity, as exemplified in its teaching that *character value* must be the foundation of all morality, and in its paean to the highest value of the Nordic being—to the idea of freedom of conscience and of *honour*. All military and scholarly struggles revolve around this ideal and if, in the great struggle to come, this idea is not victorious, all the West and its blood will perish, as India and Hellas once did, vanishing into eternity in chaos.

In recognizing that Europe and all its creative products result from character, we have uncovered the underlying theme of European religion, German scholarship and even Nordic art. To become inwardly conscious of this fact, to experience it with the full beat of an heroic heart, is to prepare the way for rebirth. This recognition is the foundation for a new *Weltanschauung*, a new-yet-old theory of state, the *Mythus* of that new life-feeling which, alone, will give us the strength to overthrow the presumptuous domination of sub-humans and to create a unique civilization which will penetrate into all areas of life.

. . . Each race has its soul, each soul its race—its own unique inner and outer architectonic shape, its characteristic form of appearance and characteristic expression of life style, and unique relationships between the strengths of will and reason. Each race cultivates, as its fixed goal, only *one* high ideal. If this should be transformed or overthrown by another system of allegiance or by an overpowering intrusion of foreign blood and foreign ideas, the external consequence of this inner metamorphosis is chaos, designated as epochs of catastrophe. . . .

(A Rosenberg, *The Myth of the Twentieth Century*, in R. Pois, ed., *Selected Writings*, pp. 82-4, Jonathan Cape, London 1970.)

Index

386

INDEX

Middle Ages: and natural law, 94; development of Christianity in, 116
Middle classes (Aristotle), 49, 56-8, 259
Middle Stoa (Roman), 72-5
Might is right, 17
Milan, Archbishop of, 136
Milan, Edict of, 103, 108-9
Milesian school of cosmology, 13
Mill, James, 332
Mill, John Stuart, 332-3, 340-5
Milton, John, 257-8, 267-9, 278
Minorities (J. S. Mill), 333
Mithraism, 102
Mixed constitution (Cicero), 74, 84
Mob rule (Polybius), 73, 84
Monarchy: (Aristotle) 49, 56; (Bodin) 240; (Cicero) 84, 85; (Dante) 179-81, 195-6, 241; Germanic, 120; in Greece, 3; growing importance of in the middle ages, 176; (Harrington) 258; limitation of power of, 254; (Panaetius) 81; (Polybius) 73, 82-3; (Rousseau) 311; see also Anti-monarchy; Divine right of kings; Kings; Priesthood and kingship; Regnum and Sacerdotium; Sovereignty
Money: (Diggers) 257; (Locke) 296, 303; see also Property; Wealth
Monophysites, 119
Montesquieu, Baron de, 309-10, 317-18
Moral concepts (Hobbes), 274
Moral direction (Aquinas), 164
Moral duties (Cicero), see De Officiis
Morality: (Bentham) 332, 338-9; (Callicles) 17, 22-4; (Green) 335, 347-8; (Hegel) 335, 349; (Hume) 330, 336-7; (Nietzsche) 365; (Rousseau) 311-12; see also Good; Justice; Pleasure; Utility; Virtue
Moral sciences, Bentham as the Newton of, 332
More, Sir Thomas, 257
Mosaic law, 95
Moses, 139; and kingship (Honorius), 151-2
Music (Plato), 30
Mussolini, Benito, 365, 366-7, 369-72
Mycenae, King of, 2
Myth, and Italian fascism, 366; and national socialism, 368, 378
Myth of the Twentieth Century, The (Rosenberg), 366, 368, 378
Myths (Plato), 30

National socialism, 364-6, 367-8, 375-78: Aryan culture (Rosenberg), 378; German national socialism, 367-8; Hitler, Adolf, 365, 367, 375-7; irrationalism, 365; Jewish peril, the (Hitler), 375-6; master race, the (Hitler), 376-7; Mein Kampf (Hitler), 367, 375-7; Myth of the Twentieth Century, The (Rosenberg), 366, 368, 378; nationalism, 364-5; racialism, 365-6; Rosenberg, Alfred, 366, 367, 368, 378
Natural law: (Aquinas) 164, 165-6, 167, 170-1, 172-3; (Augustine) 106; (Bodin) 240, 246; (Cicero) 74-5, 86-7; (Dante) 181, 200; (Diggers) 257; (Dubois) 179; (Grotius) 272, 279; (Hobbes) 275, 283-4, 284-5; (Hooker) 293, 299-300; (Locke) 295, 296, 297, 301, 302, 304; (Marsilius) 181, 182; (Montesquieu) 310; (New Testament) 94, 97;

(Nicholas of Cusa) 184, 208; (Pufendorf) 278, 290; (Roman) 77-8; (Stoics) 63, 68, 70, 165; (Spinoza) 277, 288-90; see also Natural rights
Natural rights: (American Declaration of Independence) 326-7; (Burke) 316, 328-9; in the city state, 5; (Declaration of the Rights of Man and of Citizens, French) 315, 325-6; (Hobbes) 275, 283-4; (Levellers) 256, 263; and liberalism, 330; (Locke) 293, 295, 296-7, 298, 301, 302; (Rousseau) 312, 313, 315, 319-20; (Spinoza) 277, 288-90; see also Natural law
Nature, laws of, see Natural law
Nature, state of: (Bossuet) 242; (Hobbes) 274-5, 276, 282-3; (Locke) 295, 296, 300-3, 304, 305; (Mariana) 225; (Pufendorf) 278, 290-1; (Rousseau) 311-12, 319; (Spinoza) 277; see also Social contract
Nazism, see National socialism
Neoplatonism, 104, 118
New Testament, 94-101: Acts of the Apostles, 96, 100-1; Corinthians, Epistle to, 98; Ephesians, Epistle to, 96, 99-100; Equality, 94; James, Epistle of, 96-7, 100-1; Luke, St, 100-1; Matthew, St, 98; natural law, 94; obedience, 94-6, 98-9; organic community (St Paul), 97-8; Paul, St, 97-101; Peter, Epistle of, 98-9; Philemon, Epistle to, 96, 99-100; Property, 96-7, 100-1; Romans, Epistle to, 94, 97, 98-9; slavery, 96, 99-100
Newton, Isaac, 309
Nicaea, Council of, 103
Nicene Creed, 103
Nicholas I, Pope, 122, 134
Nicholas II, Pope, 135, 143
Nicholas of Cusa, 183-4, 208
Nicomachean Ethics (Aristotle), 47, 163
Nietzsche, Friedrich, 365, 366
Noah, descent from (Filmer), 243, 252
Noah pre-figures Christ (Honorius), 151-2
Nominalists, 162
Nomos (Greek law), 13-17
Nurseries, state (Plato), 31

Obedience: (Aquinas) 166-7, 173; (Barclay) 241; (Calvin) 222, 230; (Gregory I) 120-1, 129-30; (Honorius) 140; (James I) 249; (John of Paris) 178; (Luther) 221, 228; (New Testament) 94-6, 98-9; oath of in coronation ceremony, 138; (Rousseau) 313, 321; (Spinoza) 277; see also Passive disobedience; Rebellion
Oceana (Harrington), 258-9, 269-71
Ochlocracy (Polybius), 73
Of Judicature (Bacon), 254, 260
Of Secular Authority (Luther), 220, 226-8
Of Seditions and Troubles (Bacon), 254, 260-1
Of the Original Contract (Hume), 331, 337-8
Oligarchy: (Aristotle) 49; (Polybius) 73, 83
Onesimus (a slave), 96
On Laws and God the Law-giver (Suarez), 225-6, 237-8
On Liberty (J. S. Mill), 333, 341-4
On Truth (Antiphon), 16
Ordination of Clement, 123-4
Organic commonwealth (John of Salisbury), 140, 153-4
Organic community (St Paul), 97-8